# BIBLICAL PROTOLOGY
*Commentary on
Genesis 1-11*

James E. Smith, Ph.D.

Copyright © 2007 by James E. Smith
All Rights Reserved


Unless otherwise indicated
Scripture translation is
that of the author.


Dedicated to
Sunday Evening
Bible Study Fellowship
First Christian Church
Winter Park, Florida
Whose Penetrating Questions
Provoked the Author to
Reflection and Research
on Genesis 1-11


ISBN 978-1-4303-2727-1

# PREFACE

*Eschatology* is one theological term with which many laymen are familiar. The term refers to the study of final things—life beyond death, the second coming, "rapture," resurrection, Antichrist and similar matters. Scriptures relating to eschatology are found throughout the Bible; but the Book of Revelation is a special focus of eschatological studies.

Less familiar to the layman is the term *protology*. The term comes from the combination of two elements of Greek origin. *Proto* refers to what is *first, foremost, or foundational*. *Ology* has virtually become an English word by usage. It refers to any science or branch of knowledge, as in *biology*, *geology*, and *theology*. If eschatology deals with the question, how will it all end, protology addresses the question, how did it all begin? So protology focuses on earth's earliest ages. More particularly, *protology* is that branch of theological studies that focuses on the revelation of God in the earliest periods of biblical revelation. Although there are vv throughout the Bible that shed light on this subject matter, the primarily scriptural text for the discipline is Gn 1-11.

Two kinds of error are observable in commentaries on Genesis. First, there is a tendency to see something in the biblical text that is not there. Second, there is another tendency to miss something in the biblical text that is there. Only by exposing oneself to differing points of view can blind spots be removed and hobbyhorses tethered.

The literature relating to Gn 1-11 is vast. No student of Gn can possibly digest all that has been written. The ground has been plowed and re-plowed over the centuries. Yet, like so much of Scripture, the more one reads these chs, the more one can learn from them. Each scholar builds on the insights of predecessors. Views must be tested and re-tested. New interpretations must be examined from different points of view and by specialists in various fields.

There is an old rabbinic adage "Turn it, turn it, everything is in it" (*M. 'Abot* 2:22). By bringing the conclusions of countless researchers to the table and by subjecting this ancient and revered text to a re-examination some new insight

3

may be forthcoming. As one approaches these chs it will serve well to take under advisement the dictum of another Jewish sage: "He who hesitates to ask questions does not learn." Isaac Newton is reputed to have said: "If I have seen further [than others], it is by standing upon the shoulders of Giants." It is in this humble spirit that these reflections on biblical protology are offered.

This is not a textbook on apologetics. It is written by a believer for believers. It addresses questions I have asked myself, and questions that have been asked of me. I have not attempted to be innovative. Much of my reflection mirrors traditional views of Gn 1-11. On a few points I defend minority interpretations.

I do not believe that there will ever be a time when believers will agree on every point at issue in these chapters. My own views have changed on some points over the years. I am hardly in a position to exclude from Christian fellowship those who currently hold those views, or who reach contrary conclusions.

Gn 1-11 is the foundation for the whole of divine revelation. Four foundational teachings of these chs are set forth, which if not true invalidate, trivialize or render irrelevant all other teachings of the Scripture. First, the world was created out of nothing by an eternal Being. This teaching guarantees the absoluteness of God and his perfect control of the entire material world. Second, Gn 1-11 stresses the importance of man. He is not one among many animals. He is *sui generis*. Man has dominion over the earth, subordinate only to God himself. Third, Gn 1-11 teaches the unity of the human race. All men are descended from Adam. All share Adam's propensity for sin. All in fact have become subject to sin (Rom 5:12ff; 1 Cor 15:22f, 45f). Fourth, Gn 1-11 teaches that all stand in need of redemption. The monotonous and emphatic repetition of the formula *and he died* points to the penalty for sin. A caption for Gn might well be, *salvation is essential*.

The Christian does not have the option of dismissing the protological teaching of Gn 1-11 as irrelevant or inconsequential, or tangential to NT theology. The Christian must ascertain what it is that Gn 1-11 is teaching. Then he must incorporate that teaching into his belief system. The Master himself once declared: "If you believed Moses, you would believe me, for he wrote about me. But since you do not believe what he wrote, how are you going to believe what I say?" (Jn 5:46f NIV).

The Bible may be likened to Solomon's temple with its dual chambers where holy services were performed. The OT is the outer chamber—the holy place. Here the daily rituals of the Mosaic dispensation were conducted. The NT is the inner chamber—the holy of holies. Only on the Day of Atonement did the high priest enter this chamber. The NT focuses on the final Day of Atonement when Christ died on the cross for the world's sins.

In this analogy Gn 1-11 may be likened to the *porch* (*'ûlām*) of the temple. This area was dominated by two huge pillars of bronze that appear to symbolize the power and eternity of God. Like the edifice itself, the porch was carefully crafted and beautiful. So it is with Gn 1-11, the vestibule to the holy temple of God's word. These chs are no awkward appendage to the Bible, no clumsy and primitive attempt to explain origins. They are an indispensable, irreplaceable and non-negotiable part of God's inerrant word. Here massive pillars of biblical truth are prominently displayed. Every paragraph has been designed carefully to facilitate entry into the holy areas beyond. Only in recent years have scholars appreciated the master craftsmanship of the writer of this material.

The following chs are adaptations of the author's notes from a class taught over thirty years entitled *Seminar in Genesis*. Variations of this material have also been presented in local church settings. The audience targeted in these pages is the student who wants something more than an overview. Questions addressed are those frequently asked in actual class settings. An effort has been made to digest scholarly research on Gn 1-11 and present the best of it in a format that serious students of the Bible can understand and utilize. Extensive bibliography has been provided in order to enable a student to pursue specific topics in more depth.

The translation of the OT text throughout is that of the author unless otherwise indicated. It is a translation that tries to convey as much as possible the flavor of the original Hebrew, except in cases where paraphrase is necessary to make any sense of the passage in English.

Although copious documentation of sources has been provided, inevitably materials over the years found their way into class notes where the documentation was incomplete or inadvertently omitted.

James E. Smith
Florida Christian College

# CONTENTS

Preface ... 3

## Introduction

1. Introduction to Genesis 1-11 ... 13
2. Hermeneutics and Genesis 1-11 ... 25

### Part One: Revelation in Creation

3. Introduction to Genesis 1 ... 37
4. In the Beginning (Gn 1:1) ... 49
5. Unformed and Unfilled (Gn 1:2) ... 69
6. Six Creative Days ... 83
7. Forming of the Earth (Gn 1:3-13) ... 107
8. Filling the Earth (Gn 1:14-25) ... 133
9. Crown of Creation (Gn 1:26-2:4a) ... 153

### Part Two: Revelation in the Edenic Period

10. Provision and Probation (Gn 2:4b-17) ... 179
11. The Garden Marriage (Gn 2:18-25) ... 207
12. Tempter and Temptation (Gn 3:1-8) ... 223
13. Punishment and Promise (Gn 3:9-24) ... 239

### Part Three: Revelation in the Antediluvian Period

14. Rapid "Progress" of Sin (Gn 4:1-16) ... 263
15. Beginnings of Civilization (Gn 4:17-26) ... 287
16. Adam's Successors (Gn 5:1-32) ... 307
17. Corruption of the Race (Gn 6:1-8) ... 337

### Part Four: Revelation in the Noachian Period

18. Deluge Announcement (Gn 6:9-22) ... 357
19. The Waters Prevailed (Gn 7:1-24) ... 375
20. Extent of the Flood ... 395
21. Re-creation after Judgment (Gn 8:1-22) ... 413

## Part Five: Revelation in the Postdiluvian Period

| | |
|---|---|
| 22. Post-Flood World (Gn 9:1-17) | 433 |
| 23. Sin and Prophecy (Gn 9:18-10:1a) | 451 |
| 24 Descendants of Noah (Gn 10:1b-32) | 469 |
| 25. Dispersion at Babel (Gn 11:1-9) | 497 |
| 26. Shemite Genealogy (Gn 11:10-26) | 513 |

Bibliography　　　　　　　　　　　　　　　521

## Charts and Diagrams

| | | |
|---|---|---|
| 1. | Structure of Genesis | 15 |
| 2. | Ancient Sources in Genesis | 24 |
| 3. | "Real History" vs. Gn 1-11 | 28 |
| 4. | Sin and Punishment Theme | 29 |
| 5. | Sin and Grace Theme | 30 |
| 6. | Western History vs. Biblical History | 34 |
| 7. | Implications of Two Translations of Gn 1:1 | 52 |
| 8. | Parallelism in the Creative Days | 93 |
| 9. | Heaven/Earth Pattern in Gn Days | 96 |
| 10. | Overview of Day Three | 123 |
| 11. | The Expanse in Gn 1 | 145 |
| 12. | Animals Mentioned on Day Six | 166 |
| 13. | Dual Names for God in Gn 2 | 181 |
| 14. | Cainite/Sethite Alleged Parallel Names | 288 |
| 15. | Textual Variations in Gn 5 Genealogy | 311 |
| 16. | Gn 5 Interpreted as Family Genealogy | 327 |
| 17. | Flood Chronology | 426 |
| 18. | Table of Japhethites | 471 |
| 19. | Table of Hamites | 475 |
| 20. | Table of Shemites | 486 |
| 21. | Parallelism in the Babel Narrative | 508 |
| 22. | Textual Variations in Gn 11 Genealogy | 514 |
| 23. | Gn 11 Interpreted as Family Genealogy | 518 |

# Abbreviations

| | |
|---|---|
| *AB* | E.A. Speiser, *Genesis: Introduction, Translation, and Notes.* Anchor Bible. Garden City, N.Y.: Doubleday, 1964. |
| *ANET* | James Pritchard, ed., *Ancient Near Eastern Texts.* 3$^{rd}$ ed. Princeton, NJ: Princeton University, 1969. |
| *ASV* | American Standard Version (1901) |
| *AUSS* | *Andrews University Seminary Studies* |
| *BA* | *Biblical Archaeologist* |
| *BAR* | *Biblical Archaeological Review* |
| *BASOR* | *Bulletin of the American Schools of Oriental Research* |
| *BDB* | Francis Brown, S.R. Driver and Charles Briggs, *The New Brown—Driver—Briggs—Gesenius Hebrew and English Lexicon.* Peabody, Mass.: Hendrickson, 1979. |
| *BETS* | *Bulletin of the Evangelical Theological Society* |
| *BGIC* | R. Youngblood, *The Book of Genesis: An Introductory Commentary.* Grand Rapids: Baker, 1992. |
| *BSac* | *Bibliotheca Sacra* |
| *BSC* | Aalders, G. Ch. *Genesis* in *Bible Student's Commentary.* Grand Rapids: Zondervan, 1981. |
| *BT* | *The Bible Translator* |
| *CBG* | U. Cassuto, *A Commentary on the Book of Genesis* 2 vols. Jerusalem: Magnes, 1961, 1964. |
| *CBQ* | *Catholic Biblical Quarterly* |
| *CBT* | R Clifford and J. Collins, eds. *Creation in the Biblical Tradition.* Washington: Catholic Biblical Association, 1992. |
| *CEN* | *Creation Ex Nihilo* |
| *CENTJ* | *Creation Ex Nihilo Technical Journal* |
| *CRSQ* | *Creation Research Society Quarterly* |
| *CT* | *Christianity Today* |
| *CVSS* | Bernard Ramm, *The Christian View of Science and Scripture* (pb; Grand Rapids: Eerdmans, 1976). |

| | |
|---|---|
| *EBC* | J. Sailhamer, "Genesis," *Expositor's Bible Commentary* |
| *EQ* | *Evangelical Quarterly* |
| *FAT* | *Faith and Thought* |
| *GAC* | Bruce Waltke and Cathi Fredericks. *Genesis: A Commentary.* Grand Rapids: Zondervan, 2001. |
| *GK* | E. Kautzsch, ed. *Gesenius' Hebrew Grammar.* 2$^{nd}$ English Ed. revised by A.E. Cowley. Oxford: Clarendon, 1963. |
| *HTR* | *Harvard Theological Review* |
| *HUCA* | *Hebrew Union College Annual* |
| *ICC* | J. Skinner, *A Critical and Exegetical Commentary on Genesis* in *International Critical Commentary*. 2$^{nd}$ ed.; Edinburgh: T. & T. Clark, 1930. |
| *ISIBF* | R. Hess and D.T. Tsumura, eds. "I Studied Inscriptions from before the Flood." Winnoa Lake, IN: Eisenbrauns, 1994. |
| *ITC* | *International Theological Commentary* |
| *IOT* | *Introduction to the OT* |
| *JASA* | *Journal American Scientific Affiliation* |
| *JATS* | *Journal American Theology Society* |
| *JB* | *Jerusalem Bible.* |
| *JBQ* | *Jewish Biblical Quarterly* |
| *JETS* | *Journal of the Evangelical Theological Society* |
| *JNES* | *Journal of Near Eastern Studies* |
| *JSOT* | *Journal for the Study of the OT* |
| *JTS* | *Journal of Theological Studies* |
| *KJV* | *King James Version (1611; 1711)* |
| *MT* | *Masoretic (standard) Hebrew Text* |
| *NAB* | *New American Bible (1999)* |
| *NAC* | K.A. Mathews, *Genesis 1-11:26*, New American Commentary. Broadman & Holman, 1996. |
| *NASB* | *New American Standard Bible* (1960) |
| *NEB* | *New English Bible (1981)* |
| *NICOT* | V. Hamilton, *The Book of Genesis: Chapters 1-17* in *New International Commentary on the OT* (Grand Rapids: Eerdmans, 1990). |

| | |
|---|---|
| NIDOTTE | *New International Dictionary of OT Theology & Exegesis.* Ed. Willem VanGemeren. Grand Rapids: Zondervan, 1997. |
| NIV | *New International Version* (1973) |
| NJB | *New Jerusalem Bible* (1985) |
| NJPS | *Tanakh: The Holy Scriptures* (Jewish Publishing Society, 1985) |
| NKJV | *New King James Bible* (1982) |
| NRSV | *New Revised Standard Version* (1989) |
| OTL | *Old Testament Library* |
| PSCF | *Perspectives on Science and Christian Faith* |
| SBLMS | *Society of Biblical Literature Monograph Series* |
| SOTI | Gleason Archer, *A Survey of OT Introduction.* Chicago: Moody, 1964. |
| STPG | Patrick O'Connell, *Science of Today and the Problems of Genesis.* Two books in one. 2$^{nd}$ ed. Hawthorne, CA: Christian Book Club, 1969. |
| TOTC | D. Kidner, *Genesis: An Introduction and Commentary.* Tyndale OT Commentaries. London: Tyndale, 1967. |
| TB | *Tyndale Bulletin* |
| VT | *Vetus Testamentum* |
| WBC | G. Wenham, "Genesis 1-15," *Word Biblical Commentary* (Waco: Word, 1987). |
| WTJ | *Westminster Theological Journal* |
| ZAW | *Zeitschrift für die altestamentliche Wissenschaft* |

# 1
# INTRODUCTION TO GN 1-11

For the student of Scripture the first eleven chs of Gn constitute a problem on several levels. First, there is the *content problem*. These chs deal with difficult subjects. Creation, the Fall, and the Flood raise controversial issues. Even those committed to the authority of Scripture are divided on many points. The meaning of certain vv in these chs has been debated for centuries.

Second, there is the *chronological problem*. There is an obvious gap between the time of the author of these chs, and the events that he narrates. The traditional view of the church is that Gn was written by Moses who lived, at the most conservative date, at about 1400 BC. Clearly creation occurred centuries before 1400 BC. How did Moses come to have the information narrated in these chs?

Third, there is the *critical problem*. Biblical critics alleged that the first eleven chs of Gn consist of contradictory accounts of the same events. For example, they argue that there are two creation accounts that come from different sources and reflect contradictory details. Such theories clutter up the exegetical landscape and make interpretation of these chs more difficult.

Fourth, Gn 1-11 contains a *cultural problem*. For several of the narratives in these chs there are similar narratives in the literature of the ancient Near East. How does one explain, for example, the similarities (and differences) between pagan and biblical accounts of creation and the Flood. Did the Hebrews "borrow" from their pagan neighbors? Or is it the intention of the biblical writer theologically to sanitize the common notions of the period? Or is there some other way of explaining the relationship between similar accounts?

By way of introduction to Gen 1-11 certain contextual and authorial considerations must be addressed.

# CONTEXTUAL CONSIDERATIONS

To try to understand the first eleven chs of Gn apart from their context is a mistake. One must consider the immediate context of these chs, and their larger context as well.

### A. Immediate Context

*1. Name.* The immediate context of Gen 1-11 is the Book of Genesis. In Jewish tradition this book is named after the first word *Bereshith, in the beginning.* In the Latin Vulgate the book was called *LIBER GENESIS.* This name goes back in turn to the Greek version of the OT.

*Genesis* means *beginning.* This is most fitting because of the position of the book in the sacred canon. Gn has been called "the stately portal to the magnificent edifice of Scripture" (*Butler's Bible Work*). The name is also fitting because the book deals with beginnings—the beginning of the created world, sin, God's program of redemption, marriage, messianic prophecy, government, and much more. One could also argue that the title is appropriate because of the antiquity of the book. Gn is certainly not the oldest book known to man; but if it was written by Moses at about 1400 BC it certainly is among the oldest.

*2. Purpose.* The immediate purpose of Gn is to give a history of God's dealings with man from the beginning of time to the coming of the Hebrews into Egypt—the so-called *eisodus*. The ultimate purpose of the book is to

Introduction to Gn 1-11

give man an account of his origin, his fall into sin and the beginning of the redemptive program.

*3. Structure.* Two major divisions of the Book of Gn are generally recognized. Gn 1-11 deals with the beginnings of the created world; the remainder of the book focuses on the chosen people. The first division centers around four pivotal events: Creation, the Fall, the Flood and the Dispersion of mankind. The second division focuses on four major characters: Abraham, Isaac, Jacob and Joseph. In the first division man lost Paradise; in the second the chosen family is given a Promised Land. In the first division all forms of human community are disrupted by sin and judgment; in the second God begins to form a community of faith. If the first division focuses on broken relationship and wrath, the second focuses on blessing and a new covenant. The structure of Gn is depicted in Chart 1.

| Chart 1 Parallel Structure of Genesis ||
|---|---|
| **Genesis 1-11** | **Genesis 12-50** |
| Beginnings of the Created World | Beginnings of the Chosen People |
| **Focus on Events** Creation Fall Flood Dispersion | **Focus on Characters** Abraham Isaac Jacob Joseph |
| Paradise Lost | Promised Land Bestowed (Cf. Dt 8:7-10) |
| Human Community Becomes Impossible | Faith Community Emerges |
| Wrath | Blessing |
| Broken Relationship | New Covenant |

*4. Chronology.* A vexing problem for students of Gn is that of chronology. Event-wise it can be said that Gn begins with *creation* and ends with a *coffin*—that of

15

Joseph (Gn 50:26). Using internal biblical data Gn 12-50 can be dated approximately. The account of Joseph's death in the last ch of Gn can be dated ca. 1806 BC. Working backward from that point places the date for the call of Abraham (Gn 12) in ca. 2092 BC. Thus the second, and larger, division of Gn covers 286 years.

What about Gn 1-11? How much time elapsed between creation and the call of Abraham? While some try to add up the numbers in the genealogies of Gn 5 and 11 to establish a precise chronology for these chs, most conservative biblical scholars are content to leave the question unanswered. Suffice it to say at this point that nowhere has Scripture given an explicit reference to the number of years between creation and Abraham's call, as it does for other periods of biblical history (cf. 1 Kgs 6:1). Thus the chronology of Gn 1-11 is uncertain. For that reason the amount of time covered in the entire Book of Genesis is also uncertain. The date of creation cannot be computed on the basis of biblical material.

## B. Larger Context

*1. Pentateuch.* If Gn 1-11 cannot be studied in isolation from the Book of Gn, neither can the Book of Gn be isolated from the remainder of the canon. The student of protology will do well to remind himself that Gn is also a part of a five-book collection known as the Books of Law, or Pentateuch (*Five Scrolls*). The focus of these five books is on the covenant Yahweh made with Israel at Mount Sinai. The covenant itself unfolds in Ex 19:3-Nm 10:10. All that precedes Ex 19:3 is part of the historical prologue to the Sinai covenant.

Written treaties were key instruments in the international politics of the ancient Near East. Superior kings expected vassal states to abide by the stipulations of such covenants. Similarities between these secular treaties and the Sinai covenant between Yahweh and Israel have been identified. For the purpose of this study, the historical prologues preceding the earlier treaties are what are significant. A typical covenant prologue consisted of a survey of past relations between the two covenanting parties. The aim of such a prologue was to engender gratitude, respect and trust on the part of the vassal. Such appears to be the purpose of Gn 1:1-Ex 19:2 as well.

*2. Old Testament.* A still larger circle of context is the OT as a whole. The Pentateuch is part of a library of thirty-nine books (English) or twenty-four books (Hebrew). This sacred collection, called Scriptures in the NT, was viewed as authoritative by Christ and the early church. Jesus testifies to the authority of the Scriptures as a whole, and of Gn in particular. He once quoted from the commentary of the Gn narrator in 2:24 and declared it to be a declaration of God (Mt 19:5). To Jesus, what Scripture says, God says.

*3. Bible.* The largest circle of context is the entire Bible, containing the NT as well as the Old. Whatever conclusions one reaches concerning the meaning of the vv in Gn 1-11 must be shaped by unwavering conviction that these chs are part of God's word. Furthermore, inspired writers of later books of the Bible cite vv from Gn 1-11 in ways that reveal their interpretation of the text. Those committed to the inspiration of Scripture approach Gn 1-11 with a willingness to listen to inspired authors when they shed light on the earlier texts.

# AUTHORIAL CONSIDERATIONS

### A. Traditional View

There are no direct claims of authorship in Gn. Throughout history, however, Gn has been considered part of a five-volume work attributed to Moses. The Pentateuch teems with claims that the material found therein goes back to Moses (e.g., Ex 17:14; Nm 33:2). The remaining books of the OT reflect the view that the Law can be traced back to Moses (e.g., Josh 1:7; 23:6). Likewise one finds numerous citations in the NT attributing portions of the Pentateuch to Moses (e.g., Mk 12:19, 26; Jn 8:5; Acts 15:21). Thus the ancient and conservative view is that Moses wrote the Pentateuch, and thus the first eleven chs of Gn.

No convincing reason has been put forward that overturns the traditional view that Moses penned Gn. Written records and even everyday correspondence antedate Moses by over a thousand years. Physical evidence establishes the existence of alphabetic language similar to Hebrew at ca. 1400 BC, the time of Moses. As the adopted son of Pharaoh's daughter Moses no doubt received the best education of his day. This prince of Egypt was probably literate in several languages.

**B. Critical View**

Modern scholars all but unanimously reject the Mosaic authorship of Gn. They have proposed a complex multiple authorship theory for this book. In the simple version of the theory the first book of the Bible is viewed as a composite work consisting of three parallel but contradictory accounts written at widely different points in time.

Parts of Gn are traced back to a source designated J (for *Jehovistic* or *Judah*). According to the theory this is the oldest material in Gn. It was written down in Judah about 950 BC, roughly the days of Solomon. Supposedly this source preferred the name Jehovah (Yahweh) for God.

The second source for Gn was designated by the critics E (for *Elohistic* or *Ephraim*). This source supposedly was written down in the Northern Kingdom of Ephraim about 750 BC, toward the end of the Divided Monarchy period. The name *Elohim* is the preferred name for God in this source.

The third and latest material found in Gn is derived from the P (for *priestly*) source. This source supposedly was written down about 450 BC. The priestly writers and editors wove together the materials of J and E with their own contributions, thus fashioning the Book of Gn as a patchwork of conflicting opinions.

## C. Unity of Genesis

Various writers have challenged the basic assumptions of the critical view of Gn. Yehuda Radday[1] defended the singular authorship of Gn in a five-year computer analysis of the vocabulary and style. K.A. Kitchen defended Mosaic authorship by showing that the same features used by critics to divide up the Pentateuch were present in the pagan rock monuments with no prehistory.[2] U. Cassuto defended unitary authorship by critical reappraisal of the criteria from the text itself. (E.g., how the divine names are used outside the Pentateuch. He found in Ps 19 that *Elohim* = *creator* and *Yahweh* = *lawgiver*).[3]

Kikawada and Quinn have shown that Gn 1-11 is a literary masterpiece, not a hodgepodge of conflicting sources. Their conclusion is worth citing: "The evidence commonly used to show that Gen 1-11 is a literary patchwork ... supports the view that Gen 1-11 is a liter-

---

[1] Yehuda Radday, *Genesis: An Authorship Study* (Rome: Biblical Institute Press, 1985).
[2] I.M. Kikawada, and A. Quinn, *Before Abraham Was: The Unity of Genesis 1-11* (Nashville: Abingdon, 1985), 83.
[3] U. Cassuto, *A Commentary on the Book of Genesis*. Trans. I. Abrahams (Jerusalem: Magnes, 1961), 1:86-88. These authors also defend Mosaic authorship: O.T. Allis, *The Five Books of Moses* (Philadelphia: Presbyterian and Reformed, 1949); Gleason Archer, Jr. *A Survey of OT Introduction* (Chicago: Moody, 1964). W.H. Green, *The Unity of the Book of Genesis* (1895; Grand Rapids: Baker, 1979); E.J. Young, *An Introduction to the OT* (Grand Rapids: Eerdmans, 1964).

ary masterpiece by an author of extraordinary skill and subtlety."[4]

In 1964 Speiser stated that the documentary interpretation of the Noah account was established beyond doubt. Now the wheel has come full circle. Again citing Kikawada and Quinn:

> Objections to a unitary reading of Noah have, one after another, been explained, and objections to a documentary reading — apparently unanswerable objections—have been, one after another, raised.[5]

### D. Time-lapse Problem

The unity of Gn 1-11 is defensible, and the Mosaic authorship of these chs is plausible. Even so, there is a problem that must be addressed. Moses was born about 1527 BC. The last event in Gn can be dated about 1806 BC. Therefore, the *last* event in Gn occurred about 280 years *before* the birth of Moses. The question then arises, where did Moses get the information he related in Gn? Three possible sources of information for the early chs of Gn can be named.

*1. Revelation.* Some of the information in Gn 1-11 must have been received by direct revelation from God. Information about creation, for example, had to have been revealed to someone. Perhaps that someone was Adam, or perhaps it was Moses.

*2. Oral tradition.* Oral tradition may have played a role. Harrison points out that the Joseph story (Gn 37-50) reflects a strong Egyptian background. He believes that this story "was still in oral form when Moses was alive."[6] Oral tradition, however, seems to be a less suit-

---

[4]Kikawada and Quinn, *Before Abraham Was,* 83.
[5]Ibid, 84.
[6]R.K. Harrison, *Introduction to the OT* (Grand Rapids: Eerdmans, 1969), 552.

Introduction to Gn 1-11

able explanation for the earliest chs in Gn. Two objections can be raised to the theory of a long transmission of the earliest material in Gn. First, there is the subtlety of the overall structure of the text. The superlative literary quality of Gn 1, for example, makes the theory of long transmission improbable. Second, one wonders how much information could survive thousands of years of oral transmission, especially since in the time between Adam and Moses life was often very precarious.

In fairness an argument in favor of oral transmission can be made. If the genealogies in Gn 5 and 11 are taken to be *consecutive*, the links in the chain of tradition between Adam and Abraham would be only three men. (The chronology of Gn 1-11 is a thorny topic that will be addressed later.) Abraham's day was a time of intense literary activity. It may have been in his day that the creation tradition was written down (if not before). Without doubt the godly men who perpetuated this tradition employed extreme care to preserve it correctly in all its parts. Through the centuries the culture of the Near East tended to favor memory over written records. The memory of people in such a culture tends to be unusually retentive. Regardless of the length of time that it may represent, one should not assume that oral tradition is faulty.

*3. Tablets.* Some have raised the possibility that Moses had access to written records when he penned Gn. Of this there may be a hint. In Gn 5:1 and the Greek version of Gn 2:4 the word *book* [*sepher*] appears. If Moses had access to written tablets dating back to the earliest days of the human race the time lapse problem disappears.

With Moses the original revelation became Scripture under the guidance of the Holy Spirit. Wherever he got the basic information, the Holy Spirit guided Moses to include all that God wished to be included, and to elimi-

21

nate anything erroneous or unnecessary. The result is a beautiful and satisfying explanation of origins.

### E. Wiseman's Theory[7]

*1. Use of tôl$^e$dōth.* The author of Gn had an overall plan. The key to the organization of the book is the word *tôl dōth* which appears 10x. Some observations about the use of the term *tôl$^e$dōth* (generations) are appropriate.

First, the phrase does not introduce all the prominent people in Gn, for it is not used of Abraham. Therefore, it is hard to see how the *tôl$^e$dōth* formula could have been intended as an outlining device. Second, the phrase does not always belong to a genealogical list for in some instances no list follows. In only two instances does a genealogical list follow the formula without intervening material. Third, following the phrase *these are the generations of X* nothing about X is related except his age at his death. The main history of that person appears *before* the phrase. Fourth, the word appears in Mt 1:1, followed by a list of the ancestors of Christ. Thus the word *generations* points backward rather than forward to what follows.

*2. Colophon markers.* P.J. Wiseman proposed that *tôl$^e$dōth* is the key to the authorship of Gn. The word comes from the root *yld,* to *bear, begat.* In the Hiphil form the word refers to what is begotten. The term is translated various ways in English versions: "These are the generations of" (KJV); "these are the descendants of" (NRSV); and "this is the account of" (NIV; NASB).

---

[7]P.J. Wiseman, *Ancient Records and the Structure of Genesis* (Nashville: Nelson, 1985); Harrison, *IOT,* 543-551; Henry Morris, *The Genesis Record* (Grand Rapids: Baker, 1976); Curt Sewell, "The Tablet Theory of Genesis Authorship," *Bible and Spade,* 7(Winter 1994); C. Taylor, *The Oldest Science Book in the World* (Assembly Press, 1984).

Generally commentators take the *tôlᵉdōth* phrase to signal the beginning of a new section of the book. Wiseman, however, suggested that these phrases are colophons marking the ends of a series of ancient tablets known to and used by Moses. Wiseman proposed that there were eight or ten of these tablets. The name attached to each use of *tôlᵉdōth* he took to indicate the writer or owner of the preceding tablet. Chart 2 displays the ancient sources used by Moses in composing Gn according to Wiseman.

J.E. Shelley accepts Wiseman's theory and goes beyond. He thinks the OT *tᵉrāphîm* (ASV) are the tablets utilized by Moses. In standard English versions this term is translated "images" (KJV); "household gods" (NIV; NRSV); and "household idols" (NASB; NJPS; NKJV) Rachel stole the *tᵉrāphîm*, obviously items of great value (Gn 31:19). Laban called them "my gods," suggesting that he venerated them (Gn 31:30). The *tᵉrāphîm* seem to be distinguished from images in Judg 17:5; 18:14, 18, 20.[8]

*3. Opposition.* Wiseman's theory is opposed by most commentators. They see the *tôlᵉdōth* passages as superscriptions rather than subscriptions. The following comment from W.H. Green is typical: "It can be shown beyond question that it [*tôlᵉdōth*] is the heading of the section that follows."[9]

The main Scriptural argument against Wiseman's theory is Ruth 4:18, "these are the generations of Perez." This statement is followed by a genealogy beginning with Perez and continuing through nine generations. The *tôlᵉdōth* phrase certainly has the appearance of a superscription here. Nonetheless, there is another Perez who

---

[8] J.E. Shelley, "Teraphim," *Bible League Quarterly* (Sept 1939). Reprinted in *Religious Digest*.

[9] W.H. Green, *Unity*, 9. For criticism of Wiseman's theory see D. Kidner, *Genesis: An Introduction and Commentary* (1967); 23f; G. von Rad *Genesis, a Commentary* (Philadelphia: Westminster, 1972), 68 and Gordon in *CT*, 4(1959): 133.

was contemporary with David and father of one of his commanders. See 1 Chr 27:3. He may have been the author or owner of the histories recorded in the Book of Ruth. In theory, at least, Ruth 4:18 could be a subscription to a historical document with an appended genealogy bringing the record down to the time of the author.

| Chart 2 ANCIENT SOURCES IN GENESIS (According to Wiseman) ||||
|---|---|---|---|
| Owner/Writer | Extent | Colophon | Content |
| (Heavens & Earth) | 1:1-2:4a | 2:4a | Creation |
| Adam | 2:4b-5:2 | 5:1 | Fall/Cainites |
| Noah | 5:3-6:10 | 6:9 | Sethites/Sin |
| Sons of Noah | 6:11-10:1 | 10:1 | Flood |
| Shem | 10:2-11:11 | 11:10 | Dispersion |
| Terah | 11:12-32 | 11:27 | Shem's Line |
| (Ishmael)* | (12:1-25:12) | (25:12) | Abraham |
| Isaac | 25:13-19a | 25:19a | Ishmael |
| (Esau)* | (Ch. 36) | 36:1,9 | Esau |
| Jacob | 25:19a-37:2a | 37:2a | Isaac/Jacob |

*Isaac may have been the owner/writer of a larger tablet (12:1-25:19a) into which he incorporated the record of Ishmael. The same may be true of the Esau tablet (ch. 36) which was probably incorporated into the larger Jacob tablet.

# CONCLUSION

Whataever his sources of information the Holy Spirit guaranteed that Moses did not incorporate anything misleading or unworthy in Gn. The believer can be assured that what is contained in Gn 1-11 is there because God intended for it to be there. These chs communicate as much as God intended for mankind to know about earth's earliest ages.

# 2
# HERMENEUTICS AND GN 1-11[10]

Hermeneutics is the science of interpretation. In the voluminous literature on Gn 1-11 one can find a variety of hermeneutical approaches. Each approach has distinct presuppositions. Each has its own focus. Each makes its own contribution to the study of these chs. It is the purpose of this ch to define the more prominent approaches to Gn 1-11, and to set forth the principles that undergird the present study.

## VARIOUS APPROACHES

### A. Scientific Approaches[11]

Two opposite scientific approaches to protology are represented in the literature. These approaches are concordism and creationism.

*1. Concordism.* Concordism is the attempt to interpret Gn 1-11 in the light of the theories of modern science. In this approach the interpreter looks for coherence. The concordist argues that all facts arise from God. Truth is truth wherever it may be found. Scientific facts are as much a part of God's truth as biblical truth. In his Book of Nature God has left a record of his protological activities. For the concordist, scientists are the God-appointed interpreters of the Book of Nature, or general revelation. Whatever conclusions one reaches

---

[10] For the structure of this ch the author is indebted to G. Van Groningen, *JETS* 13 (Fall, 1970): 199-217.

[11] R.T. Wright identifies four models for dealing with science/Bible issues: 1) concordism—the Bible supplies some information that can be harmonized with science; 2) substitutionism—the Bible is given priority over science; 3) compartmentalism—Bible and science reflect totally different realms of knowledge; and 4) complementarism—the Bible and science are complementary ways of viewing the universe. *Biology through the Eyes of Faith* (San Francisco: Harper, 1989), 84-92.

about the Gn accounts of creation or the Flood, therefore, must be harmonized with scientific fact.

There are problems in the approach of concordism. First, there is the danger of reading too much into the text of Gn. This sometimes results in making the real meaning of the text obscure. Second, concordism makes scientific knowledge prior to and essential to an understanding of the biblical message. Third, it is extremely dangerous to anchor biblical exegesis to current scientific opinions. What is presented as fact to one generation is repudiated by the scientists of the next generation. Fourth, concordism seems to demean special revelation (the Bible) by making it subservient to an external authority (science). Treated in this manner the biblical account becomes nothing more than the musings of uninformed religious zealots.

*2. Creationism.* At the opposite end of the spectrum of the scientific approach to Gn 1-11 is the approach called *creationism*. The proponents of this approach generally have respectable credentials in the various scientific disciplines. Their approach to Scripture, however, is quite different from that of the concordist. The creationist takes a very literalistic approach to Gn 1-11. He levels a strong protest against the elevation of science to the status of a religion. Creationism offers alternative explanations for scientific opinions that are deemed to be at variance with a literal reading of the Gn text. Creationists generally debunk the alleged objectivity of those who work in the sciences. Scientists are fallen men with clouded minds forced into certain stances because they are in rebellion against the Creator. Creationists regard current scientific accounts of origins as nothing but "conjectural science."

There are problems in the Creationist approach. First, Creation Science has not presented an alternative comprehensive explanation of origins that commands respect either within the scientific community or in larger circles. Second, Creation Science seems to have undervalued the agreement of thousands of researchers who reach their conclusions neither by chance nor by conspiracy. Third, Creation Science advocates sometimes attribute to Gn a meaning that biblical scholars do not find.

*3. Fideism.* A middle-of-the-road approach to the issue of science and the Bible is fideism. This is total reliance on faith rather than reason. Fideism keeps science and Scripture in separate compartments. One who follows this approach can wear two hats. He can wear his scientist hat five days a week at work then don his faith hat when he associates with God's people on the weekend. He can accept the naturalistic pre-suppositions of a scientific discipline, and yet cling to his faith in Christ and the Bible.

Those who follow this approach display the following tendencies. First, fideism tends to make a rigid distinction between the realms of faith and scientific research. Second, fideism denies the basic premise both of concordism and creationism, viz. that revealed truth has implications for various areas of scientific research. Third, fideism recognizes that the text of Gn is often forced when it is used to engage contemporary scientists.

The problem in fideism can be stated this way. Because the Bible is not a handbook of science does not mean that it will have nothing to teach modern man when it touches on scientific disciplines.

## B. Mythological Approach

In respect to the hermeneutical approach to Gn 1-11 no person has been more influential than Hermann Gunkel. As early as 1895 he began to make the distinction between history and legend. He came to the conclusion that Gn 1-11 did not measure up to the standards of real history that he had identified. Chart 3 summarizes the comparison.

In 1901 Gunkel introduced his famous Gn commentary with these words: "Are the narratives of Genesis history or legend? For the modern historian this is no longer an open question...."[12]

| Chart 3 Real History vs. Genesis 1-11 (Gunkel) ||
|---|---|
| **Real History** | **Genesis 1-11** |
| Based on written documents. | Based on oral tradition. |
| Deals with great events of public interest. | Deals with personal & family stories. |
| Can be traced back to first-hand evidence. | Depends on the imagination of later raconteurs. |
| Records the possible. | Narrates the impossible. |
| In prose form & is designed to inform. | In poetic form & is designed to inspire. |
| Identical in form & style to 1 Samuel 9-20. | Differs from classical Hebrew historiography. |

Gunkel's approach to Gn 1-11 calls forth criticism along several lines. First, this approach assumes that only by looking to ancient primitive man can one find an explanation for the content of the early chs of Gn. Second, this approach assumes that mythological accounts were reliably recorded. Third, there is an assumption that mythological accounts have certain basic elements that are true and that can serve as criteria for biblical truths. Fourth, in this approach to Gn 1-11 there is a cavalier treatment of biblical authority. Gunkel and his

---

[12] The introductory essays of Gunkel's commentary have been reproduced in English translation by Schocken Books under the title, *The Legends of Genesis* (1964).

disciples dismissed the fact that Jesus and the apostles considered the early accounts of Gn to be factual. They regarded the Lord as merely a man of his times who articulated the generally accepted views of his peers. He had no more authority than any other rabbi of that day.

## C. Literary Approach

Clearly Gn 1-11 is a distinct unit within the structure of Gn. The beginning point is the creation narrative. The concluding point is a brief introduction to Abraham, who is the focus of the next unit.

The literary approach to Gn 1-11 emphasizes the theme of these chs. These scholars look for parallelism between narrative blocks, and structural balance in the way the writer has presented his material. Scholars looking at the text from this perspective present a counterbalance to the atomistic dissection of these chapters into J, E, P and other sources supposedly identified by the critical scholars of a previous generation. The emphasis in this school is upon the unity of Gn 1-11.

| | **Chart 4** | | | |
|---|---|---|---|---|
| | **Sin and Punishment Theme** | | | |
| **Narratives** | **A** **Sin** | **B** **Speech** | **C** **Mitigation** | **D** **Punishment** |
| 1. Fall | 3:6 | 3:14-19 | 3:21 | 3:22-24 |
| 2. Cain | 4:8 | 4:11-12 | 4:15 | 4:16 |
| 3. Sons of God | 6:2 | 6:3 | ?6:8, 18ff. | ?7:6-24 |
| 4. Flood | 6:5, 11f. | 6:7, 13-21 | 6:8, 18ff. | 7:6-24 |
| 5. Babel | 11:4 | 11:6f. | ?10:1-32 | 11:8 |

As for the theme of Gn 1-11, three main proposals have been put forward. The first is the theme of sin followed by punishment. To be more specific, the sin of an individual or group is followed by a divine speech, some mitigation of the disaster, and finally punishment. Chart 4 displays this pattern in detail.

A second proposal for the theme of Gn 1-11 is the sin/grace theme. Four episodes of the spread of sin followed by ever-increasing judgment, followed by ever-increasing grace are found in Gn 1-11. This pattern is displayed in Chart 5.

| Chart 5 Sin and Grace Theme |||
|---|---|---|
| **Increasing Sin** | **Increasing Judgment** | **Increasing Grace** |
| 1. Disobedience of Adam & Eve | Expulsion from the Garden | Clothes Adam & Eve & gives a promise |
| 2. Murder of Cain | Expulsion from tillable land | Gives Cain a solemn promise of protection |
| 3. Total corruption & violence of Flood generation | Near annihilation of mankind | Preserves Noah; solemn commitment of preservation |
| 4. Pride & defiance of post-Flood population | Dissolution of mankind's unity | Formation of a covenant people |

A third proposal for a theme in Gn 1-11 identifies a pattern of creation, uncreation and re-creation. The moral and spiritual corruption of human kind reaches a climax in the judgment of the Flood. The Flood, however, is presented, not just as a punishment for sin, but as a reversal of creation (uncreation). After the Flood reached its maximum, again God separated the water and the land (8:3, 7, 13) just as he did in Gn 1 at the original creation. After the Flood the original creation mandates were renewed (8:17; 9:1-7). Soon after the Flood, however, the trend toward disunity (uncreation) began almost immediately with the sin of Noah's son Ham.

There is obvious overlap in these proposals. Each offers helpful insights. The danger in this approach, however, is that of forcing a meaning on an individual narrative in order to make it fit a pre-determined theme.

### D. Revelational Approach

Those who use the revelational approach to Gn 1-11 regard the Book of Gn as a part of God's self-revelation. The supernatural and divine aspects of these chs are stressed as the starting point. God took the initiative, not man, in producing Gn. The focus in this approach is not on the people for whom Gn was written—their conditions, history, language, opinions, myths; nor is it on the writer—his literary techniques, personal abilities, and characteristics. Rather the focus in this approach is on what God has chosen to reveal about earth's origins and early history.

Among those who generally follow the revelational approach to Gn 1-11 there are differences. On the left side of the spectrum are the members of the American Scientific Affliction. These folks sometimes permit the natural sciences to exert undue influence upon the interpretation of Scripture. The human element in Scripture is allowed too much importance. In the literature produced by ASA members non-scriptural principles, approaches or tools are sometimes employed as equal to or above the Scriptures. At the opposite end of the spectrum is the Creation Research Society. Members of this organization defend the historical nature of Gn 1-11. Sometimes even among these scholars, however, there is a danger of tying Scripture to the ever-changing conclusions of science.

# HISTORICITY OF GENESIS 1-11

The nature of Gn 1-11, whether sober history or religious epic, is the key issue facing the student of biblical protology. Some camouflage their true opinion of the nature of these chs with clever terminological distinctions. They distinguish in their minds between holy history (*heilsgeschichte*) and real history (*geschichte*). They say that Gn 1-11 is historical in the former sense, but not the latter.

## A. Historical Difficulties in Gn 1-11

Some allege that Gn 1-11 cannot be regarded as true history because the text is full of legend, fable and chronological impossibilities. One example[13] often cited is the reference to iron in Gn 4:22 well in advance of the Iron Age that is usually dated about 1200 BC. Knowledge of the working of iron, however, is clearly earlier than 1200 BC. The very word for *iron* seems to go back to a Sumerian word. Working iron is attested as early as 6500-5800 BC at Catal Huyuk in Turkey.[14] These data suggest that arts and crafts were mastered and then lost only to reappear again in another age. Thus one should be hesitant to label as "impossible" the mention of iron in Gn 4:22.

## B. Indications of Historical Intention

Was it the intention of the original writer of Gn 1-11 that his work be viewed as sober history? This question can be answered in the affirmative. The text of Gn 1-11 indicates that the writer had historical intention as he wrote.

---

[13]Other alleged historical problems will be treated in subsequent chs.
[14]See W. Kaiser, "The Literary Form of Genesis 1-11," in *New Perspectives on the OT*, ed. J. Barton Payne (Waco: Word, 1970), 55.

*1. Prose narrative.* A writer who intends to produce serious history generally chooses to write in prose. Gn 1-11 is mainly prose, rather than poetry. This is indicated by use of the *vav* consecutive (usually translated *and*) with the verb to describe sequential acts. Such usage is characteristic of Hebrew historical narrative, but not of Hebrew poetry. Another indication of prose intention is the frequent use of the sign of the definite direct object, which cannot be translated into English. A third indication of prose narrative is the frequent use of the particle of relation *ʾăšer* (usually *which*).[15] A fourth indication that Gn 1-11 is prose is the way in which the writer spreads out events in sequential order. Within Gn 1-11 poetic units do appear (e.g., 4:23-24). Comparing the overall text to the poetic units within these chs makes clear the contrast between prose and poetry.

*2. Tôlĕdōth structure.* The use of the *tôlĕdōth* formula in Gn 1-11 was noted earlier. The same phrase is used in Gn 12-50 as well. Archeology continues to discover confirmation of the accuracy of Gn 12-50. By using the *tôlĕdōth* formula in both parts of his book the author signals his readers that the entire book was cast in the same literary form. The writer's choice of structuring Gn 1-11 around this formula argues for considering these chs as historical.

*3. Clues within narrative.* Details within the narrative point in the same direction. There are sixty-four geographical terms in these chs. There are eighty-eight personal names, and forty-eight generic names. There are twenty-one identifiable cultural items (e.g., gold, bdellium, onyx, and harp). The interest in chronology, life spans, and birth dates in Gn 1-11 is not characteristic of myths and folktales. Interest in numbers of years be-

---

[15]In Gn 1-11 *ʾăšer* is used sixty-five times, about one time for every 4.5 vv. In Psalms (Hebrew poetry) *ʾăšer* occurs 103 times, about one time for every 23.8 vv.

longs elsewhere to the style of chronicles and historiography.[16]

*4. New Testament usage.* Citations from Gn 1-11 in the NT indicate that Jesus and the apostles regarded these chs as serious history. Allusions to Gn 1-11 are both abundant and compelling. Morris counts 107 allusions to Gn 1-11 in the NT. Each of the eleven chs is cited somewhere in the NT. Each NT writer refers to this section of Gn. Jesus quoted from or referred to something or someone in Gn 1-11 6x. This includes specific references to each of the first seven chs.[17]

| Chart 6 Western History vs. Biblical History ||
|---|---|
| **Western History** | **Biblical History** |
| 1. Human understanding of the past. | 1. Divine understanding of the past. |
| 2. Perspective of man. | 2. Heavenly perspective. |
| 3. Anchored to the historical context of the writer. | 3. Timelessness. |
| 4. Understanding the past so as to validate the present. | 4. Raises serious questions about the past and present. |
| 5. Anchored to a point in time. | 5. Not anchored to a point in time. |

## C. Qualifications

It is clear that the author of Gn 1-11 intended for his work to be interpreted historically. It is equally clear that in the biblical tradition, including the NT, these chs were regarded as sober history. For these reasons conservative commentators argue for the essential accuracy of these chs. Even so certain distinctions between what is recorded in Scripture and "history" as the concept developed in Western Civilization should be acknowledged.

---

[16]Thorkild Jacobsen, "The Eridu Genesis," *JBL* 100(1981): 528.
[17]Following H. Morris, *Record*. See especially appendix four.

Clyde McCone has drawn up the contrast as displayed in Chart 6.[18]

## PRINCIPLES OF INTERPRETATION

While originally applied to Gn 1-2, the following principles serve equally well as a framework for interpreting the first eleven chs.[19] First, recognize these chs are part of the word of God. Because these chs are part of God's word, two interpretive guidelines logically follow. The interpreter must approach these chs reverently and humbly; and he must put forth an earnest effort and have a sincere desire to know the mind of God.

Second, recognize these chs occupy a very important position in God's word. They are foundational to all subsequent theology and history. The numerous references to these chs by Paul[20] underscore that Gn 1-11 is essential to Christian theology.

Third, the events of Gn 1-11 must be interpreted to some extent in the light of the purpose and literary form of these chs. The writer seems to have had a factual purpose. The section is about as factual and literal as any section in the Bible.

Fourth, the interpreter must realize the difference between sources of information and results. While there is a question of where Moses acquired the information reported in Gn 1-11, the solution to that problem is not crucial to a proper assessment of the contents.

Fifth, the interpreter must not read things into the narratives nor assume that the narratives in this section were meant to be complete. Obviously the writer has

---

[18] Clyde McCone, "Origins of Civilization" in *Symposium on Creation* (Grand Rapids: Baker, 1968), 86-87.

[19] Allan MacRae, "The Principles of Interpreting Genesis 1 and 2," *BETS* 2(1959):2.

[20] E.g., Rom 5:14; 1 Cor 15:45; 1 Tim 2:13, 14.

given his readers a selection of materials. The Bible does not purport to give the complete record of everything that transpired prior to Abraham. For example, should interpreters imagine a gap of millions of years between the first two vv of the Bible? Is Gn 1:1 talking about the creation of the entire universe or only of this earth? There are numerous issues in these chs where dogmatism must be avoided.

Sixth, the interpreter must assume that the writer had normal intelligence. Therefore, these chs must be interpreted as harmonious and consistent. One ch should not be pitted against another.

Seventh, Christians should not make it their primary aim to lead people to accept their particular explanation of the creation account, but to bring them to Christ.

## CONCLUSION

The task of the interpreter in respect to Gn 1-11 has been appropriately worded by Blocher: "To study Genesis as God's Word and as human words, in harmony with the whole of Scripture and according to the characteristics of its language."

# 3
# INTRODUCTION TO GN 1

The importance of Gn 1 for the biblical world view cannot be overestimated. The teaching of this ch is foundational to all that the Bible teaches. It would be strange indeed if this marvelous book of God's revelation commenced with anything other than an explanation of the origins of the universe. Gn 1 is a most appropriate introduction to the entire Bible.

Arguably Gn 1 is the most challenging ch in the entire Hebrew Bible.[21] Considered on its own merits, Gn 1 is an amazing composition. Filby calls it "the most amazing composition in all world literature."[22] Blocher praises the ch as "the work of a Master whose thought is profound and expansive."[23]

## LITERARY FORM OF GN 1

There are two general approaches to the first ch of the Bible. Some regard the ch as essentially literal and historical. Others take it to be largely figurative and non-historical.

### A. Literal/Historical View

The Lutheran scholar H.C. Leupold is an able representative of the first approach. Leupold says that the account "goes back beyond the reach of available historical sources and offers not mythological suppositions, not poetical fancies, not vague suggestions, but a positive record of things as they actually transpired and, at the

---

[21]Jaki, *Genesis 1*, 1.
[22]F.A. Filby, *Creation Revealed* (Westwood, NJ: Revell, 1965), 16.
[23]Henri Blocher, *In the Beginning* (Downers Grove, IL: Inter-Varsity, 1984), 33.

same time, of matters of infinite moment for all mankind."[24]

*1. Scriptural support.* Belief in the divine creation of the universe is the unstated presupposition of all Scripture. Other writers of Scripture regarded Gn 1 as a reliable explanation of the origins of the universe. These words come from the pen of Moses:

> In six days the LORD made the heavens and the earth, the sea, and all that is in them, but he rested on the seventh day. Therefore the LORD blessed the Sabbath day and made it holy (Ex 20:11 NIV). Also Ex 17:17.

Jesus clearly accepted the creation chs as literally true.

> "Haven't you read," he replied, "that at the beginning the Creator 'made them male and female,' 5 and said, 'For this reason a man will leave his father and mother and be united to his wife, and the two will become one flesh'? 6 So they are no longer two, but one. Therefore what God has joined together, let man not separate" (Mt 19:4-6 NIV).

The apostolic writings assume the accuracy of the creation narrative.

> But they deliberately forget that long ago by God's word the heavens existed and the earth was formed out of water and by water (2 Pet 3:5 NIV).

> For somewhere he has spoken about the seventh day in these words: "And on the seventh day God rested from all his work." (Heb 4:4 NIV).

*2. Traditional position.* The historic position of the church is that Gn 1 should be regarded as a factual account of origins. The majority of attempts to explain the plain words of this ch in a different manner from that of the traditional church position arose in the last century. Today, however, the climate has changed. Those who hold to the historic position regarding Gn 1 are depicted as enemies of the church. They are branded as "literal-

---

[24]Leupold, *Exposition of Genesis* (Columbus: Wartburg Press, 1942), 25.

ists," "fundamentalists," and "obscurantists." They are regarded as closed-minded, naïve and an obstacle to the effective proclamation of the gospel.

### B. Challenges to Literal View

What has brought about this change in attitude? The traditional interpretation of the first two chs of Gn has fallen upon hard times because of challenges from three directions.

*1. Scientific community.* First, there is the challenge of the scientific community. The theories of the nineteenth century naturalist Charles Darwin have become the foundation of the biological sciences. Most who work in these disciplines see these theories as fundamentally opposed to the biblical doctrine of divine creation. In a world where science is the sacred cow the biblical creation account is brushed aside as inaccurate.

*2. Comparative religions.* Another challenge to the credibility of Gn 1-2 came from the field of comparative religions. Perhaps the key name in this challenge is Hermann Gunkel. Non-Hebrew creation accounts in the ancient Near East were taken as indication that the biblical portrayal was nothing special. Behind the biblical account were outrageous myths that Hebrew priests sanitized in order to promote their monotheistic notions. The comparative religions field challenged the contention that Gn 1-2 presents a divinely inspired account of earth's origins.

*3. Literary criticism.* The third challenge to the general acceptance of the Gn creation account came from the field of literary criticism. The key name here is Julius Wellhausen. He presented the classic defense of the view that the present text of Gn contains within it multiple contradictory accounts of the same event, written at different stages of Israel's history, to further the interests of competing schools within the scribal community. Gn 1 was branded as the P (Priestly) creation account, while Gn 2 was viewed as the J (Jehovistic) account. The P account allegedly emerged a half-millennium after the J account. In making their case the literary critics magnified the differences between Gn 1 and Gn 2 and labeled them as contradictions. The conclusion of this school of thought was that there is no Gn creation account. Rather, there are two contradictory accounts.

*4. Current situation.* Faced with the challenges from the scientific community, comparative religions, and the school of literary criticism the Gn creation account was cast aside. D.F. Payne observes that "by 1900 many people had been educated to believe that the Bible's statements about creation were neither accurate, inspired, nor consistent."[25]

While many of the underlying assumptions of the Gn challengers have been challenged, still there has been no rush to restore Gn 1-2 as the authoritative statement on earth's origins. Many of the arguments put forward in the past century to discredit the biblical account of creation now sound quaint and outdated. Yet most refuse to believe what Gn affirms. Those without a will to believe will not believe. The mere fact that these chs are part of a collection of religious literature disqualifies them in many minds from serious consideration.

## C. Figurative/Non-historical View

The alternative to the traditional view of Gn 1 is to see it as communicating one central truth. The details in the account may be (and probably are) inaccurate. Ultimately the details are unimportant. They serve only as literary trapping to highlight the grand truth that ultimately everything that exists has its origin in God.

---

[25]D.F. Payne, *Genesis One Reconsidered* (London: Tyndale, 1964), 5.

*1. Examples.* Examples of the non-historical approach to Gn 1-2 abound in the literature. A few examples will suffice. Wiley referred to Gn 1 as a "hymn of creation."[26] Sampey called it "a great religious poem."[27] Richardson referred to Gn 1-2 as "parables."[28] Mary Baker Eddy in *Science and Health with Key to the Scriptures* insisted that Gn 1-2 must be interpreted "symbolically."

*2. Emphases.* In this second general approach to Gn 1 there are four points of emphasis. First, the emphasis is on the Creator, not his methods. The purpose of this ch is to lead the reader to a lofty concept of God. How he created the heavens and earth reflects primitive and erroneous ideas that must be surrendered if men are to maintain their intellectual respectability.

Second, there is emphasis on *evolution* not *revelation*. The creation story was not revealed from God, but evolved over the course of time. Gn 1 is the magnificent culmination of centuries of religious debate in the Hebrew community. Monotheism eventually won out, and the victory is reflected in Gn 1-2.

Third, there is emphasis on *polemics* not *dogmatics*. The creation story was written to refute paganism and false cosmologies. It was not designed to set forth Christian doctrine.

Fourth, there is emphasis on *contradiction* not *consistency*. Gn 2 is pitted against Gn 1 in an effort to demonstrate inconsistency. So-called contradictions are then said to indicate that Gn 1-2 cannot and should not be viewed as factual.

---

[26]H. Orton Wiley, *Christian Theology* (Kansas City: Beacon, Hill, 1960), 1:449-54.

[27]John Sampey, *The Heart of the OT* (New York: Harper, 1960), 17.

[28]Alan Richardson, *Genesis I-XI*, 27. Quoted with approval by R. Elliott, *Message*, 15.

*3. Rebuttal.* It is alleged that Gn 1 belongs to a category of poems praising God's creation. Creation poems do exist in other parts of the OT (e.g., Ps 104; Prov 8; Job 38-39). When those poems, however, are read alongside Gn 1 it is clear even to the non-specialist that the Gn material does not have the same literary character.[29]

The arguments in support of the poetic, non-historical approach to Gn 1 are weak. For this reason competent scholars have pronounced against this ch being regarded as poetry. The account is "close to poetry, but its movement towards a solution places it in the order of prose."[30] The whole ch is written in "a solemn tone and in dignified prose."[31] The evidence supports the conclusion of Van der Ploeg: "In spite of everything the text of Gn 1:2-2:4a is sober, not lyrical and certainly no poem."[32]

# CHARACTERISTICS OF GENESIS 1

Four characteristics stand out as one reads Gn 1. Two of these are general in nature, and two more specific.

### A. General Characteristics

A casual reading of Gn 1 produces two impressions.

---

[29] Some seventy-five passages in the Bible speak of the creative work of God. For the most part these passages are poetic re-formulations of the basic Gn creation narrative. See Paul Zimmerman, *Darwin, Evolution and Creation* (St. Louis: Concordia, 1959), 39. A good discussion of the allusions to creation outside Gn is found in Chester K. Lehman, *Biblical Theology of the OT* (Scottsdale, PA: Herald, 1971).

[30] Paul Beauchamp, *Création et séparation* (Paris, 1969) cited by Blocher, *In the Beginning*, 32.

[31] A. Heidel, *The Babylonian Genesis* (Chicago: University of Chicago, 1951), 93 fn.

[32] Cited by N.H. Ridderbos, *Is there a Conflict Between Genesis 1 and Natural Science?* (Grand Rapids: Eerdmans, 1957).

*1. Simplicity.* One is impressed with the simplicity of the text. Only seventy-six root words are used in recounting earth's origins. For the most part there is an absence of technical terms in the ch. The creation account is not written in the language (symbols) of nuclear physics and biochemistry. Desire to communicate is foremost here. For this reason the style had to be one that would appeal to all classes of people in all ages.

*2. Brevity.* Gn 1 is marked by brevity. The ch simply declares what the Creator did. It does not go into great detail about how he orchestrated the various creative actions. Such brevity necessitated omission of details, exceptions, and modifications.

### B. Specific Characteristics

Examining the content of Gn 1 more carefully highlights two more characteristics of the ch.

*1. Popular expressions.* Gn 1 is characterized by popular modes of expression. The ch contains numerous anthropomorphisms. Of necessity when man speaks of divine actions he must speak of them in figures of speech. There are limitations in human language when it comes to God-talk. For this reason the historical purpose of Gn 1-2 is circumscribed to some extent by the limitations of human language.

Gn 1 also contains phenomenal language, i.e., describing things as they appear to be, not as they actually are. The moon, for example, is described as if it were the counterpart of the sun in the night skies. Of course the moon is not actually a nighttime sun, but it appears to give forth light. Phenomenal language is used frequently in everyday speech, even by those who are trained in the sciences. The presence of such language in Gn 1 does not require that the text be regarded as non-historical.

*2. Numerical symmetry.* Gn 1 displays numerical symmetry. Cassuto has pointed out several number patterns in the text. The first example of numerical symmetry is the combination of seven and three. *God said* is used 10x. Of these ten occurrences, three concern mankind (1:26, 28, 29), and seven pertain to the rest of the creatures. The creative fiat *let it be* appears 3x for heavenly objects; seven different verbs express the creation fiats for things on earth. The decalogue (ten) pattern is also used with the verb *to make* and the formula *according to its/their kind*.

The heptad (seven) pattern is used with reference to the accomplishment formula (*and it was so*) and the approval formula (*and God saw that it was good*). The first v of the book contains seven words; the second v contains twice seven. The seventh paragraph contains seven times five words.

The triad pattern is also in evidence. There are three benedictions (blessings) in the creation account. The verbs *made, called,* and *divided* also appear 3x each. The verb *bārā'* (*create*): appears in three places, the third time it is used thrice.[33]

What does this numerical symmetry mean? Cassuto calls it "the golden thread that binds together all parts of the section and serves as convincing proof of its unity."[34] Based on the use of the ten, seven and three patterns in the creation narrative Leupold can make this observation. "Seven is the number of divine works and operations; three, the mark of the divine person; ten, the mark of completeness."[35]

---

[33] If one includes 2:4a, the verb is used altogether 7x.
[34] Cassuto, *CBG*, 1:12, 15.
[35] Leupold, *Exposition*, 53.

# UNIQUENESS OF GENESIS 1

As noted earlier, creation accounts from other civilizations of the Near East have surfaced. The one closest to the Gn account is the Mesopotamian tradition.

### A. Babylonian Creation Account

*1. Discovery.* Between 1848 and 1876 creation tablets were discovered near the ruins of Nineveh by archaeologists Layard, Rassan and Smith. The seven tablets contained about a thousand lines of cuneiform text. These tablets were part of the library collected by the Assyrian King Ashurbanipal (668-626 BC). The text is called *Enuma Elish*, the first two Akkadian words of the tablet. These words mean, *When on high.*

According to Assyriologists the tradition contained in the tablets dates at least to the time of the Babylonian King Hammurabi (1793-1751 BC). Many believe that the creation tradition reflected in the tablets is based upon earlier traditions of the ancient Sumerians.[36]

*2. Outline.* The Babylonian creation tradition unfolds in the following sequence of events. First, the tradition describes the birth of the gods from the union of Apsu (fresh water) and Tiamat (saltwater). Several generations of gods descend from these primeval gods. Apsu becomes annoyed by the noise made by younger gods and plots to destroy them. Second, a conflict arises between Apsu and Ea (earth-water god). Apsu is killed in the conflict. Tiamat then creates monsters with which to fight against Ea and his supporters. Third, Marduk the son of Ea is born and becomes powerful. He is chosen to fight against the raging Tiamat. Fourth, Marduk defeats Tiamat by blowing her up with an evil wind, and ex-

---

[36]M. Unger, *Archaeology and the OT* (Grand Rapids: Zondervan, 1954), 27.

ploding her with an arrow. Fifth, out of the remains of Tiamat Marduk creates the firmament, dry land, and luminaries. Out of the blood of Kingu, leader of Tiamat's forces, he creates man. Sixth, Marduk becomes head of the Babylonian pantheon. Seventh, names of praise are attributed to Marduk. His temple Esagila is dedicated in Babylon.

3. *Comparison.* *Enuma Elish* manifests some similarities with the Gn account. At least nine parallels have been pointed out: 1) earth covered with waters before creation; 2) earth enveloped in primeval darkness; 3) light existing before the luminaries; 4) firmament results from a division of waters; 5) dry land separated from the waters; 6) luminaries serving as time dividers; 7) man created from earth and in the divine image; 8) rest follows creation; and 9) a predilection for the number seven.

The differences between *Enuma Elish* and the Gn account are far more profound than the similarities.[37] For the Babylonians matter always existed. In the beginning there was matter. Gn begins with the eternal God. Creation results from conflict and commotion in *Enuma Elish*. In Gn the creative actions reflect calm and order. The Babylonian tradition speaks most about what transpired in the heavenly realms. Gn, however, focuses on earth. In *Enuma Elish* man is depicted as a slave of the gods; in Gn man is God's viceroy ruling over earth. Clumsy and confused creation characterizes the Babylonian account; but in Gn creation is logical and progressive. Clearly there is a political motivation to *Enuma Elish*; but Gn 1 is apolitical. The Babylonian account is in poetic format; Gn is prose narrative.

---

[37] Cf. Heidel (*Babylonian Genesis*, 139): "In the light of the differences, the resemblances fade away almost like the stars before the sun."

## B. Explanation

How are the similarities and differences between the Babylonian and biblical accounts to be explained? Did Babylonian account borrow from Gn? This does not seem likely. The Babylonian account of creation is older than Gn 1 as it stands today. Did the two accounts arise simultaneously and independently? While this is a logical possibility, it has not found much support in the scholarly world. More popular is the view that Gn borrowed from the Babylonian account. This too, however, is highly unlikely. Blocher writes:

> The idea that the sacred writer might have taken a pagan myth of origins in order to correct it and purify it in line with his monotheistic faith overlooks the perfection of the composition in its finest details; it gives undue weight to a number of resemblances which are incomplete, while neglecting the contrast which is very striking.[38]

In respect to the position that the biblical writer created history out of myth, Currid makes three telling points. First, in the ancient Near Eastern literature simple accounts give rise to elaborate accounts, not vice versa. It is not likely, then, that the simple Gn account is a condensed version of the complex and cumbersome Mesopotamian myth. Second, Gn presents the creation account as sober history. There is no example in the ancient Near East where myth later develops into history. Third, the striking contrasts between the Mesopotamian and biblical accounts cannot be explained by a simplistic theory of Hebrew cleansing.[39]

One can envision a creation tradition going back to the dawn of civilization. That tradition was faithfully transmitted from generation to generation (either orally or in written form) within the circles of those who re-

---

[38] Blocher, *In the Beginning*, 33.
[39] John Currid, *Ancient Egypt and the OT* (Grand Rapids: Baker, 1997), 29.

mained faithful to the Creator. Among those who defied the Creator and began to create gods in man's image the creation tradition became garbled. It was commandeered by zealots for man-made gods and made to serve their theological purposes. Over time creation fact became pagan myth.

The unique aspect of the biblical creation account is the concept of *creation through the divine word.* The Creator has only to speak and his will materializes. His word is almighty, uncompromising, and irresistible. The word of the Babylonian deities was powerful, but not almighty.[40]

## CONCLUSION

The obvious purpose of Gn 1 is to provide an authoritative account of earth's origins. The not-so-obvious purpose is twofold. First, the author intended in Gn 1 to provide a theology for creation, the Sabbath and humanity. Second, he intended to combat idolatry and mythological notions about origins.[41]

As one approaches Gn 1 he should remember the words of Martin Luther: this ch "contains things of the most import, and at the same time the most obscure."[42] The cautions of von Rad must be taken seriously. "Nothing is here by chance; everything must be considered carefully, deliberately, and precisely."[43]

---

[40]C. Westermann, *Genesis 1-11*, 38-41.
[41]See G. Hasel, "The Polemical Nature of the Genesis Cosmology," *EQ* 46 (April-June, 1974): 81-102.
[42]M. Luther, *The Creation: A Commentary on the First Five Chapters of the Book of Genesis*. Trans. Henry Cole, Edinburgh: T. & T. Clark, 1858, p. 23.
[43]G. von Rad, *Genesis*, 45.

# 4
# IN THE BEGINNING
# Gn 1:1

Theologically Gn 1:1 encapsules the basic elements of the Christian doctrine of origins. The *who, when, how* and *what* of creation are summarized in this brief statement. Clearly if this one v is untrue the entire system of biblical theology has no validity, Christianity is a fraud, and the church might as well close her doors.

Gn 1:1 contains seven critical words in the Hebrew, only five of which can be rendered into English. Each of these words has explosive significance. Thus a word-by-word study of this v must be undertaken. Prior to undertaking that study there is a preliminary question that must be addressed.

## PRELIMINARY QUESTION

The literary role of Gn 1:1 in the first ch of Gn is hotly debated. The alternatives can be framed this way: Is Gn 1:1 a title for the first ch, or is it the opening line of an extended creation narrative?

### A. Verse 1 as Summary/Title

Many commentators take Gn 1:1 as an independent clause, but regard it as a summary statement or formal introduction/title for the narrative that follows. Not infrequently Hebrew style makes a summary statement and then amplifies that statement (cf. 1 Kgs 18:30; Gn 18:1). On this understanding, the remainder of Gn 1 gives the details regarding the creation summary of v 1.

There are good reasons not to regard Gn 1:1 as a summary statement or title.[44] First, the structure of the second v of the Bible makes it unlikely that the first v is a summary statement. The second v begins with the connector *vav* rendered *and*. Second, Gn 1:1 is a complete sentence that makes a statement. Titles are not normally formed of complete sentences in the Hebrew Bible.[45] Third, Gn 1 has a summary statement at its conclusion (2:1), making it unlikely it would have another at its beginning. Fourth, the second v speaks of the earth as already in existence; therefore its creation must be recorded in the first v. Fifth, in Gn 1:1 the heavens take precedence over the earth; but in the following vv all things, even sun, moon, and stars seem to be appendages to the earth. Thus if Gn 1:1 were a heading it would not correspond with the narrative.[46]

### B. Verse 1 as Integral to Narrative

Rather than viewing Gn 1:1 as a summary/title for the ch, it is best considered part of the creation narrative. The v has the purpose of identifying the Creator and explaining the origin of the universe.

# FIRST WORD OF THE BIBLE
## *In the beginning*

The first word of the Hebrew Bible ($b^e r\bar{e}\check{s}\hat{i}th$) consists of a noun minus the definite article with an attached preposition. The word is commonly rendered, *in the beginning*. A scholar of a previous generation identified

---

[44]Following Sailhamer.
[45]When verbal clauses serve as summaries, they are generally attached to the end of the narrative (e.g., Gn 2:1; 25:34b; 49:28b). Francis I. Andersen, *The Sentence in Biblical Hebrew* (The Hague: Mouton, 1974), 53.
[46]Anton Pearson, "An Exegetical Study of Genesis 1:1-3," *Bethel Seminary Quarterly* 2(1953): 20-21.

913 different interpretations of $b^e r\bar{e}\check{s}îth$. He stopped at 913 because that is the numerical value of the letters of this word.[47] In truth an entire book could be written on the first word of the Bible. Here only three issues surrounding the initial word of the Bible are discussed.

## A. Translation Issue

Two very different translations of Gn 1:1 are found in English versions. Some variation of *When God began to create* appears in the Jewish NJPS,[48] the Catholic NAB, and NRSV and NEB from the Protestant tradition. Grammatically these translators understand $b^e r\bar{e}\check{s}îth$ to be the first word of a dependent clause. The implications of such a translation are profound. Matter already existed before God took that matter and shaped it into the universe. The contrast between the two approaches to the first word of the Bible is displayed in Chart 7.

*1. Arguments for dependency.* The dependent clause rendering is based upon the following facts: 1) the first word does not have a definite article (*the*) in the Hebrew; 2) elsewhere in the Bible the exact term used here is used dependently;[49] 3) the second creation account begins in Gn 2:4b-6 with a long dependent clause;[50] and 4) the Babylonian creation myth begins with a dependent clause.

---

[47] Reported in the *Jerusalem Post*, Oct 27, 1984, 10.

[48] E.A. Speiser in the influential *Anchor Bible* series also opts for regarding $b^e r\bar{e}\check{s}îth$ as a dependent clause. This approach can be traced back to the Medieval Jewish commentator Ibn Ezra (d. 1167).

[49] Jer 26:1; 27:1; 28:1; 49:34. In these cases, however, $b^e r\bar{e}\check{s}îth$ is followed by an absolute noun (with which it is in construct), not a finite verb as in Gn 1:1.

[50] E.A. Speiser, *Genesis: Introduction, Translation, and Notes*. Anchor Bible (Garden City, NY: Doubleday, 1964), 12; H. Orlinsky, "The New Jewish Version of the Torah. Toward a New Philosophy of Bible Translation," *JBL*, 82 (Sept 1963): 250ff.

Biblical Protology

| Chart 7 | |
|---|---|
| **Implications of Two Translations of Gn 1:1** | |
| **Independent Clause** *In the beginning God created...* | **Dependent Clause** *When God began to create...* |
| 1. Creation *ex nihilo* is explicitly affirmed. | 1. No creation *ex nihilo* is affirmed. |
| 2. God exists before matter. | 2. Matter is already in existence when God begins to create. |
| 3. God creates the heavens, earth, darkness, the deep, and water. | 3. The heavens, earth, darkness, the deep and water already exist at the beginning of God's creative activity. |
| 4. There is an absolute beginning of time for the cosmos. | 4. No absolute beginning is indicated. |

The arguments favoring translating $b^e r\bar{e}š\hat{\imath}th$ *in the beginning of God's creating = when God began to create* are not compelling. First, the absence of the definite article on definite adverbial time designations in the Hebrew Bible is not uncommon.[51] Second, the noun $r\bar{e}š\hat{\imath}th$ (*beginning*) appears some 50x at least two of which are absolute (Isa 46:10; Neh 12:44). Thus taking the word here in the absolute sense is possible. Third, the opening sentence of the second creation account differs from the opening of Gn 1 in structure,[52] verb form and the reversal of the order of the words *heaven* and *earth*. So the parallelism between the two passages breaks down. Fourth, there is no reason to "paganize" the opening vv of the Bible by making them read like the Babylonian creation myth.

---

[51]G. Hasel, "Recent Translations of Genesis 1:1: a Critical Look," *The Bible Translator* 22(Oct 1971): 158-59. Hasel cites studies by König, Heidel, Schmidt, and Procksch.
[52]Westermann, *Genesis 1-11*, 134; 269.

*2. Grammatical arguments.* What is decisive in the translation of the first word of the Bible is the fact that it is followed by a verb in Hebrew, not a noun. The syntax of a construct form followed by a finite verb is without parallel in the Hebrew Bible. Given the fact that the finite verb follows $b^e r \bar{e} \hat{s} îth$ in Gn 1:1, the natural reading of the first word is to make it part of an independent clause: *In the beginning God created.*[53]

The natural rendering of the first word receives support from two directions. First, the accent mark in the Hebrew text (called *tiphchāh*) sets the first word apart from what follows as an absolute form or independent idea. Second, the way v 2 begins (connector *vav* + noun) is the regular Hebrew way of indicating change to a new subject. This supports the idea that v 1 is a self-contained thought.

*3. Precedent.* Abundant precedent exists for the translation *in the beginning God created.* First, the ancient versions without exception translate $b^e r \bar{e} \hat{s} îth$ as an absolute: *in the beginning.* Second, the translation tradition throughout the Christian era overwhelmingly has opted for the rendering *in the beginning.*

*4. Style.* The author's style throughout the first ch supports this understanding of the first word. The author manifests a preference for short, terse statements rather than sentences laden with dependent clauses.

*5. Theological argument.* The theological thrust of the first ch is the transcendence of God over matter. A dependent clause opens the door for viewing God and matter as co-eternal. That idea detracts from the overall theological thrust of the ch.

*6. John 1:1 parallel.* Clearly John is alluding to Gn 1:1 in the opening v of his Gospel when he writes: *en archē* (*in the beginning*). The Greek phrase used by John

---

[53]Cf. Aalders (*BSC*, 51): "Although the alternative interpretation is linguistically possible, it does not reflect common Hebrew usage."

is the exact phrase that appears in the first v of the Bible in the Greek OT (LXX). While the phrase in both Gn and John has no article, it is unmistakably part of an independent clause: "In the beginning was the Word."

### B. Theological Implications

*1. Why highlighted?* Two things in the Hebrew Bible call attention to the first word. First, in most Hebrew Bibles the first letter of the word is enlarged, reflecting the practice of the Hebrew manuscripts. Second, the author himself called attention to the opening of his book by using a catchy, alliterative combination of words: $b^e r\bar{e}\check{s}\hat{\imath}th$ $b\bar{a}r\bar{a}$'. Clearly the author and the copyists through the years wished to call attention to the opening word of Gn.

The theological issue is this: What doctrine does the first word of the Bible convey? The simple answer is, there was a beginning. The first word of the Bible points to the ultimate limits of the past conceivable to human beings.

*2. Which beginning?* Does $b^e r\bar{e}\check{s}\hat{\imath}th$ refer to the beginning of the *material* creation? Or is this the beginning of the *entire* creation—everything except the eternal Creator himself. Probably the author intended the latter. Thus spiritual creatures like angels are included in the scope of the claims of the v.

*3. Period or point?* Does the term $b^e r\bar{e}\check{s}\hat{\imath}th$ indicate a *point* in eternity or a *period* of time. Sometimes in the OT $b^e r\bar{e}\check{s}\hat{\imath}th$ refers to an extended, yet indefinite, period of time, not a specific moment.[54] Thus the creation *could* have occurred over a vast period of time, although this is certainly not required.[55] The fact that the word appears

---

[54] E.g., Job 8:7; Gn 10:10. Scripture frequently refers to *the beginning* of the reign of certain kings by which he refers to the earliest years in the reign of the king.

[55] John Sailhamer, *Genesis Unbound* (Sisters, OR, 1996), 28, 37-45.

without any connection with a noun suggests that the absolute beginning is intended. The author's use of $b^e r\bar{e}\check{s}\hat{\imath}th$ is unique in ancient creation accounts. Reference to an absolute beginning finds no parallel in the literature of the ancient Near East.[56]

*4. Is a beginning necessary?* Most human beings intuitively understand that there must have been an absolute beginning. Some unbelievers object that the concept of an absolute beginning is totally unnecessary. Bertrand Russell commented: "There is no reason to suppose that the world had a beginning at all. The idea that things must have a beginning is really due to the poverty of our imagination."[57]

Russell notwithstanding, the calculations of scientists seem to confirm the intuitive assumption of most people. The universe is not infinitely old, but in fact appears to be running down. Fred Hoyle points out that hydrogen is being steadily converted into helium throughout the universe. This conversion is a one-way process. Hoyle argues: "There would be no hydrogen left if the universe were infinitely old."[58] To avoid the implications of an absolute beginning Hoyle resorts to the concept of "continuous creation." He makes this incredible statement:

> Where does the created material come from? It does not come from anywhere. Material simply appears—it is created. At one time the various atoms composing the material do not exist, and at a later time they do. This may seem a very strange idea and I agree that it is, but in science it does not matter how strange an idea may seem so long as it works, that is to say ...

---

[56]Hermann Gunkel comments: "The cosmogonies of other people contain no word which would come close to the first word of the Bible." *Genesis*, 7th ed. See also Hasel, op. cit.,, 162.
[57]Bertrand Russell, *Why I am not a Christian* (New York: Simon and Schuster, 1957), 7.
[58]Fred Hoyle, *The Nature of the Universe* (New York: Harper, 1960), 113-14.

so long as its consequences are found to be in agreement with observation."[59]

## C. Chronological Issue

When was the beginning? Attempts have been made to date the beginning biblically and scientifically.

*1. Biblical attempts.* Biblical data can be used to establish the date for the birth of Abraham. By assuming that the genealogies in Gn 1-11 were intended to be complete and consecutive, Archbishop James Ussher (1581-1656) computed the date of creation as 4004 BC.[60] Ussher's views were generally accepted by the intellectual community of his day including no less a thinker than Isaac Newton.[61] Four years after the appearance of Ussher's book in 1650 Dr. John Lightfoot, vice chancellor of St. Catherine's College in Cambridge calculated the exact hour and day of creation: 9 a.m. London time, Oct 23, 4004 BC.

Generally today believers do not try to pronounce a date for creation. The majority of those who take the Bible seriously do not believe that the Genesis genealogies were intended to be used for chronological purposes. The interpretation of the genealogies in chs 5 and 11 will be discussed at the proper time.

*2. Scientific attempts.* Some attempt to find clues regarding the date of the beginning by reading God's so-called Book of Nature. The majority of those credentialed in the sciences read the data to point to an extremely ancient universe and earth. Astronomers compute the rate of expansion of the universe, the decrease in star temperature or the distance to stars measured by the time it takes light to reach Earth. Geologists point to

---

[59] Ibid, 112.
[60] Adding up the genealogical numbers found in the Septuagint version suggests the date of 5270 BC.
[61] Colin Renfrew, *Before Civilization* (New York: Knopf, 1973), 21.

the amount of time it would take for seams of coal and oil deposits to form.

Some believers have embraced the conclusions of astronomical and geological sciences regarding the age of the earth. Filby, for example, suggests that the earth is 2,000 or 3,000 million years old.[62] Newman and Eckelmann estimate the universe to be fifteen to twenty billion, the sun five to ten billion, and our solar system five billion years old.[63]

Some read the data from the Book of Nature and come to a different conclusion about the age of the earth. They believe that the scientific data point to a comparatively young earth.[64] These scientists emphasize data from population statistics, helium-4 content of the atmosphere, accumulation of meteorite dust and the imbalance of carbon-14. Using these data Morris estimates that the beginning took place about 10,000 BC.[65]

# SECOND WORD OF THE BIBLE
## *Created*

The second word of the Bible is the verb *bārā'* normally rendered *created*. This verb is used 48x in the OT.[66] It is applied to the creation of a nation, to righteousness, to regeneration, to praise and to joy. Two-thirds of the references, however, refer to physical creation; one-third of those references refer specifically to

---

[62] Floyd Filby, *Creation Revealed*, 52-53.

[63] R. Newman and H. Eckelmann, *Genesis One and the Origin of the Earth* (Downers Grove, IL: Intervarsity, 1977), 30. Davis Young, *Creation and the Flood* (Grand Rapids: Baker, 1977) comes to similar conclusions.

[64] E.g., P.D. Ackerman, *It's a Young World After All* (Grand Raids: Baker, 1991); Harold Slusher, *The Creation Alternative* (Arnold, MO: Shield press, 1970); John Wiester, *The Genesis Connection* (Nashville: Thomas Nelson, 1983).

[65] Henry Morris, *Record*, 45. See also *Scientific Creationism* (San Diego: Creation-Life, 1974).

[66] The r. *br'* occurs in the Qal stem 38x, Niphal 10x.

the creation of mankind. This verb is used 5x in Gn 1—of heavens and earth (v 1); the sea monsters (v 21); and man 3x in v 27. It is also used twice in 2:1-4 for a total of 7x in the first Gn creation account.[67]

### A. Implications of *bārā'*

An examination of the passages where *bārā'* is used indicates four implications in this verb. First, *bārā'* points to newness. The verb never occurs with the object of the material. The primary emphasis is on the novelty of the created object. Something is brought into being that did not exist prior to the action. Second, *bārā'* indicates effortlessness. Third, *bārā'* suggests instantaneous action. Fourth, *bārā'* indicates sovereignty. God is always the subject of this verb wherever it appears in the relevant stems.[68]

### B. Debate about *bārā'*

Does the verb *bārā'* demand creation *ex nihilo*, i.e., creation from nothing?

*1. Biblical context.* Certainly the doctrine of creation *ex nihilo* is taught elsewhere in the Bible. Consider these two passages:

> In the beginning was the Word, and the Word was with God, and the Word was God. He was in the beginning with God. All things came into being by Him, and apart from Him nothing came into being that has come into being (Jn 1:1-3 NASB).

> By faith we understand that the universe was formed at God's command, so that what is seen was not made out of what was visible (Heb 11:3 NIV).

---

[67]Thomas Finley, "Dimensions of the Hebrew Word for 'Create,'" *BSac* 148(Oct-Dec, 1991) 411-12.

[68]BDB takes the Hiphil form to be from a second word spelled *br'*, meaning "to make yourself fat." In the Piel a root *br'* has the connotation of "cut down or cut out." This form is used with men as the subject. Whether this is a special use of the root *br'* or homonym is difficult to say.

*2. Relevant data.* The issue is whether the Hebrew verb *bārā'* alone teaches creation *ex nihilo*. To answer this question the following data must be taken into account. First, no preexisting material is mentioned in conjunction with the creation of the heavens and earth.[69] Second, the verb *bārā'* is used synonymously with other verbs of making in Isaiah 40-66. Because a verb with specific connotations is used poetically parallel to a generic verb of the same domain does not rob the former of its specificity. Third, the expression *in the beginning* presupposes that there was as yet nothing in existence before the act of creation. Fourth, the phrase *heavens and earth* is equivalent to the concept of universe, i.e., all that exists.

*3. Suitability of the word.* The argument that *bārā'* does not inherently mean creation *ex nihilo* is beside the point, because it is doubtful that any word in any language does have that meaning.[70] No more suitable word, however, exists in the Hebrew language for expressing the concept of creation *ex nihilo* if that is what Gn 1:1 intended.[71] Certainly the NT writers cited above assume that the writer intended exactly that.[72] Perhaps the entire issue can be resolved by a formula: *bārā'* + *bᵉrēšîth* + John 1:1 + Hebrews 11:3 = creation *ex nihilo*.

---

[69] The argument is made that *dust* is antecedent to man's creation in Gn 2. Dust, however, is not used in conjunction with the word *bārā'* in that passage. Scripture does not say that God *created* man *from dust*. God *formed* man from dust is clearly metaphorical.

[70] Mark Rooker, "Genesis 1:1-3: Creation or Re-Creation?" *BSac* (1992): 418.

[71] Cf. Thomas McComiskey (*TWOT*, 1:127): "the word lends itself well to the concept of creation *ex nihilo*."

[72] Not all Jews in the first century espoused the doctrine of creation *ex nihilo*. The Wisdom of Solomon, written during the intertestamental period states: *For thy Almighty hand, that made the world of matter without form...* (11:17 KJV).

# THIRD WORD IN THE BIBLE
## *God*

The third word in the Hebrew Bible is *ᵉlōhîm* (hereafter Elohim), usually translated *God*. With this word the Bible lifts the eyes of the reader heavenward. It is Elohim and no other who is responsible for everything that came into being in the beginning. With regard to this noun there are four areas of interest: the form, significance, emphasis and polemics of the term.

**A. Form of the Word**

The form Elohim occurs only in Hebrew and in no other Semitic language, not even in biblical Aramaic.[73] There are three facts to note about the third word in the Bible.

*1. Plural form.* Elohim is a plural. The plural form of the noun appears some 2,570x in the OT. The singular form of this noun (*ᵉlōah*) occurs 58x in the poetic literature, mostly (42x) in Job. In the first creation narrative (Gn 1:1-2:4a) Elohim is used 35x, i.e., five times seven. As noted earlier, the number seven plays an important role in this ch.

*2. No article.* Elohim does not have the article. It is not "the Elohim" who creates. When Elohim is used without the article it either refers to a multiplicity of gods, or is being used as a proper name. Hebrew does not have capital letters, however, so whether or not Elohim here is a common plural noun or a proper name cannot be determined by form alone.

*3. Companion verb.* Elohim in Gn 1:1 is used with a singular verb. This settles the issue of how Elohim is to be understood. Though plural in form, Elohim refers

---

[73] Gustav Oehler, *Theology of the OT* (1883; reprint Grand Rapid: Zondervan, n.d.), 88.

to a singular being. Therefore, in this context Elohim is used as a proper name.

### B. Significance of the Word

In the word Elohim there are two connotations. First, there is the connotation of plurality in the godhead. The plural form is usually interpreted as a plural of majesty. The idea is that the plural form is used of the Creator because he is the God of all gods. A case, however, can be made for understanding Elohim as a "uni-plural," an expression coined by Henry Morris. Taken in this way use of Elohim is one way that God prepared the world for the later revelation of the pluralistic unity of the Godhead. Second, usage throughout the OT suggests that Elohim conceives of God as the one that by his nature and his works rouses man's fear and reverence.[74]

### C. Emphasis on the Word

Without question the spotlight is on Elohim in Gn 1. The use of this name for the Creator stresses his action, satisfaction and power.

*1. Emphasis on action.* In the first creation narrative (1:1-2:4a) Elohim is the subject of a verb 33x, in all but two uses of the word. God is very busy in this ch. He is active in every aspect of the creation. Elohim *created* (3x), *made* (3x), *said* (10x), *saw* (7x) *divided* (2x), *called* (3x), *set* (1x), *completed* (1x), and *blessed* (3x). This, however, is not the complete story. Pronouns referring to Elohim also stress his activity. The verb *called* with a pronoun referring to Elohim appears twice as does the verb *created*.

*2. Emphasis on satisfaction.* Elohim *saw* that what he had created was good (7x), and very good (1x). Twice he *blessed* his creation.

---

[74] H.C. Leupold, *Exposition*, 40. Leupold derives Elohim from a root found in Arabic meaning "to fear or to reverence."

*3. Emphasis on power.* The writer emphasizes Elohim*'s* power by reporting creation events in terms of *fiat* and *fulfillment.* In the account there are seven commands from Elohim, three of them double, making a total of ten altogether. With one exception, the writer has emphasized the compliance with the creation edicts by means of repetitive statements of fulfillment: *Let it be...and there was...and it was so* (cf. Ps 33:6, 9).

### D. Polemics of the Word

The first v of the Bible throws down the gauntlet to a number of competing world views. Contrary to atheism the v clearly affirms that Elohim existed in the beginning. Contrary to the position of pantheism (God is everything, and everything is God) Gn 1:1 affirms that Elohim is a power superior to the material world. The singular verb used with Elohim affirms that only one such all-powerful being existed prior to the beginning. At the same time, the use of the plural form Elohim strikes a blow against Unitarianism. The philosophy of materialism, that holds that matter is eternal, is negated by the whole tenor of the v. Dualism, which rules out any interaction between the spiritual and the material realms, is also challenged in this v. Fatalism is the view that whatever will be will be. That philosophy is challenged by the picture in Gn 1:1 of a God who created and thus is in control of the universe.[75]

# FOURTH & FIFTH WORDS
## *The heavens and the earth*

The fourth and fifth words of the Bible are the words *heavens* and *earth.* These two words will first be inves-

---

[75]See H. Wheeler Robinson, *Inspiration and Revelation in the OT* (Oxford: Clarendon, 1946), 21; Sampey, *Heart,* 14-15.

tigated individually. Then the significance of the combination of the two words will be explored.

### A. Heavens

*1. Usage.* The term *heavens* (*šāmayim*) is a special plural that occurs among words used for things that are extended. In the OT the term is used in a threefold sense. It is used of the heavens where the birds fly (Gn 1:20), the heavens where the sun and planets appear (Ps 8:3; Neh 9:6), and the heavens that constitute the abode of the Creator (Dt 26:15; Lam 3:41).

*2. Angels?* Does the creation of the heavens in Gn 1:1 include the creation of angelic creatures? In answering this question four facts need to be taken into consideration. First, both good and bad angels are referred to in the first three chs of Gn. Their existence would be unexplained by the writer unless he included them in the creation of the heavens.

Second, the term *hosts* in Gn 2:1 could embrace angels as it does in Ps 102:20-21. The term, however, could also refer to the heavenly bodies as in Jer 33:22.

Third, God speaks of the *angels* (lit., "sons of God") celebrating when earth was created (Job 38:7). This requires that angels were created prior to the earth.

Fourth, Paul affirmed the creation of angelic beings by Christ (Col 1:16-17).

These four facts suggest that the term *heavens* in Gn 1:1 does embrace the created beings known collectively as angels.

### B. Earth

*Earth* (*'erets*) has a threefold use in the OT. The term can refer to 1) the whole world (Gn 18:25); 2) the dry land (Gn 1:10); and 3) a country or region, especially the Promised Land (Gn 15:18). Sailhamer opted for this third connotation of *earth* in Gn 1. He argues

Biblical Protology

that this ch has nothing to do with the creation of the sphere known as earth; it refers to the creation of the Promised Land, which later will be given as a gift to Abraham's offspring.[76] Sailhamer's theory has not found wide support.

Earth is said to contain about 267,000 million cubic miles. It has a mass of about 5,000 million million million tons. Yet earth is a pipsqueak planet compared to Saturn, which could take into its body 900 spheres the size of the earth. Jupiter could absorb 1,300 earths.[77]

The earth has a diameter of about 8,000 miles. If the diameter had been the same as that of Saturn or Jupiter, beings like mankind, could not exist. Humans were designed for an atmospheric pressure of approximately 15 lb. p.s.i. at sea level. They would not be able to withstand the tremendous pressure of many *tons* to the square inch such as the atmosphere of these other planets are said to possess.[78]

The position of the earth in respect to both moon and sun was exactly planned by the Creator to make possible life on this planet. A much larger moon, or a moon much closer to earth would cause tides hundreds of miles high, and these would flood the continents twice daily. The sun is about 91 million miles from earth. If it were 120 million miles earth's inhabitants would all freeze; were it only 60 million miles all living things would be incinerated. Compared to other stars, our sun is relatively cool. If this solar system were governed by one of the super-suns, there would be no life on this planet.[79]

---

[76] J. Sailhamer, *Genesis Unbound* (Sisters, OR: Multnomah, 1996), 30.
[77] Beasley, *Architect,* 32.
[78] W.E. Swinton, *The Corridor of Life* (London: Jonathan Cape, 1948), 25
[79] Beasley, *Architect,* 43f.

## C. Combination

The combination *heavens* and *earth* occurs 3x in the first creation account. Some interpreters take *heavens and earth* as a reference to earth and its surrounding heavenly spheres (i.e., the atmosphere and beyond including the solar system). Certainly the terms *heaven* and *earth* used individually in the remaining vv of Gn 1 seems to support this position. In Gn 1:1, however, there is a dyad (*the heavens and the earth*) whereas the rest of the ch uses a triad: *the heavens, the earth,* and *the sea* (see vv 8 and 10).

*The heavens and the earth* is a merism, a figure of speech that combines two words to express a single idea. This merism is the equivalent of the modern word *universe*. So Gn 1:1 declares that Elohim created the entire universe, both visible and invisible. Similar expressions to denote the universe occur in Egyptian, Akkadian, and Ugaritic literature.[80]

## D. Condition of the Universe

Does the combination *heavens and earth* refer to the universe as a finished product? Or is Gn 1:1 referring to the first step in the process of producing the universe as it is known today? E.J. Young, Childs and Waltke argue that the merism *heavens and earth* refers to the well-ordered universe. This in effect makes Gn 1:1 a summary or heading for the rest of the ch.

In response to the view that *heavens and earth* refer to the universe in its completion these points can be made. First, Wenham has demonstrated that the essential meaning of *heavens and earth* is not completion and organization but totality.[81] Second, it is clear from the rest

---

[80] Wenham, *WBC*, 15. Westermann, *Genesis 1-11*, 101; Ross, *Creation and Blessing*, 106; J.H. Sailhamer, *EBC*, 23; H.M Orlinsky, "The Plain Meaning of Genesis 1:1-3," *BA* (1983): 208.
[81] Wenham, *WBC*, 12-13, 15.

of Gn 1 that God intended to create at least the earth in progressive stages. It is not likely that the initial reference to *the heavens and the earth* would have the meaning it does in the vv that follow the completion of the process. Third, if the writer had intended to refer to the universe in its first step of development, how else would he have described it if not by using *the heavens and the earth*?

The conclusion is that *the heavens and the earth* in Gn 1:1 refer to the first step in creation. As Heidel puts it, the expression refers to "heaven and earth as first created out of nothing in a rude state but in their essential basic form."[82]

# VASTNESS OF THE UNIVERSE

### A. Biblical Allusions

Biblical poets emphasize vastness by depicting God "stretching out"[83] or "spreading out" the heavens (Isa 40:22; 48:13). Donald Clark equates this language with the discoveries of Edwin Hubble. Hubble measured the distance of galaxies by luminosity; he measured velocity by red shifts. Hubble found that galaxies are moving away from earth. The further from earth they move, the faster they are moving.[84]

Scientists living about the time of Christ estimated the number of stars at about 3,000, which is about the number that can be observed by the naked eye. Centuries before this, however, Jeremiah declared: "The host of heaven cannot be numbered, neither the sand of the sea measured" (Jer 33:22).

---

[82]Heidel, *Babylonian Genesis*, 91. Aalders (*BSC*, 53) refers to "the substance from which the entire universe was formed."
[83]The metaphor appears at least 10x, six of which are in Isaiah.
[84]Donald Clark, "Stretching out the Heavens," *Bible-Science News*, 33:8 (Nov 1995): 12-13.

The average person finds it difficult to grasp the vastness of the universe that God created. The earth is about 7,900 miles in diameter. It is set in a path about 93 million miles from the sun. Our sun is one star in a galaxy of stars numbering some thousands of millions, extending over an area of space measured in terms of something like 100,000 light years across, a light year is equal to six million million miles. This galaxy is but one of a thousand million such galaxies scattered at distances of a million light years apart.[85]

**B. Modern Illustrations**

Fred Hoyle attempts to illustrate the vastness of space in these words:

> Suppose we make a plan of how the sun and the planets are arranged. In our plan, let us represent the sun as a ball, six inches in diameter, the sort of thing you could easily hold in one hand. This, by the way, is a reduction in a scale of nearly 10,000,000,000. Now, how far away are our planets from our ball? Not a few feet or one or two yards, as many people imagine in their subconscious picture of the solar system, but very much more. Mercury is 7 yards away, Venus about 13 yards, the earth 18 yards, Mars 27 yards, Jupiter 90 yards, Saturn 170 yards, and Pluto 710 yards. On this scale, the earth is represented as a speck of dust, and the nearest stars are about 2,000 miles away.[86]

Since Hoyle wrote a new planet revolving around the sun has been discovered beyond Pluto. The new planet, which is yet to be formally named, is at least as big as Pluto and about three times farther away from the sun. The planet was discovered by the Samuel Oschin Telescope at the Palomar Observatory near San Diego on January 8, 2005.

---

[85]Filby, *Creation Revealed*, 35. See also Beasley, (*Architect*, 30) for similar numbers.
[86]Fred Hoyle, *The Nature of the Universe*, (New York: Harper, 1950), 15.

In order to assist the average person to begin to grasp the size of the universe Willmington[87] offers three illustrations. First, let the thickness of a sheet of paper represent the distance from earth to the sun. To represent the distance to the nearest star (other than the sun) would require a stack 310 miles high. To the edge of the known universe would require a stack of paper 31 million miles high.

Second, if the sun were hollow, 1,300,000 earths could fit inside it. A star named Antares (if hollow) could hold 64,000,000 of our suns. In the constellation of Hercules there is a star that could contain 100,000,000 Antares. The largest known star, Epsilon, could easily swallow up several million stars the size of the one in Hercules!

Third, Earth is traveling around its own axis at 1,000 miles per hour. It moves around the sun at 67,000 miles per hour. It is carried by the sun across our galaxy at a speed of 64,000 miles per hour. It moves in orbit around our galaxy at 481,000 miles per hour. It travels through space at 1,350,000 miles per hour. Every twenty-four hours earth covers 57,360,000 miles. That computes to 20,936,400,000 miles across empty space each year.

## CONCLUSION

Pagan cosmogonies tell how gods were born, how they quarreled, and how the universe was born out of their battles, love affairs, and magic spells. Gn 1:1 breaks with all the mythologies of the ancient Near East. This simple sentence was revolutionary when it was written; it still continues to provoke debate and challenge the dominant explanation of origins in the twenty-first century.

---

[87] Willmington, *Guide*, 13.

# 5
# UNFORMED AND UNFILLED
# Gn 1:2

Gn 1:2 contains fourteen words, twice the number of v 1. The interpretation of Gn 1:2 depends to a certain extent on the interpretation of the first v. Does v 2 describe the state of the heavens and earth in the process of becoming what they are today? Or did the well-ordered heavens and earth of v 1 come to be in the state described in v 2 subsequent to creation? It is the purpose of this ch to evaluate the various interpretations of Gn 1:2.

## View One
## PRECREATION CHAOS VIEW

The first view of Gn 1:2 is that it describes conditions that existed prior to creation. Within the general framework of the precreation chaos approach are three alternatives.

### A. Metaphorical

Some hold that Gn 1:2 is metaphorical of nothingness. Rabast paraphrases: "In the beginning was Nothing, and over this Nothing hovered the Spirit of God."[88] This v is merely a concrete way of saying absolutely nothing whatever existed before creation.[89] The problem with this view is that language similar to this v appears elsewhere in the OT where it cannot be construed as referring to nothingness.

---

[88]K. Rabast, *Die Genesis* (1951), 47. Cited by E.J. Young, *Studies in Genesis One* (Philadelphia: Presbyterian and Reformed, 1964), 15f.
[89]H. Renckens, *Israel's Concept of the Beginning: The Theology of Genesis 1-3* (New York: Herder & Herder, 1964), 51.

## B. Chaos View

The term *chaos* is used of the void and formless infinite, the confused, unorganized state of primordial matter before the creation of distinct and orderly forms. According to this approach chaos indicates "the contrary of creation" (E. Jacob), what is antithetical to the nature of the Creator in whom there is no darkness.

Given this understanding of the term *chaos*, is it the appropriate term to use in describing what is depicted in v 2? Is this v the Hebrew equivalent of a struggle between the gods and hostile forces as alleged by Gunkel? Hardly! Elohim is in total control in Gn 1:2. The earth is in exactly the shape that he intended for it to be at that stage of the creative process. Pagan mythological ideas should not be read back into this v.

## C. Preexisting Matter

Some think that Gn 1:2 is describing the raw material out of which God formed the heavens and earth in v 1. Recently this view has been defended by Blocher[90] and Waltke.[91] Regarding Gn 1:2 as a reference to preexisting matter would not necessarily deny that God created this raw material prior to the beginning of Gn 1:1.

This approach requires a beginning before the beginning. In spite of protestations to the contrary, this view undercuts the doctrine of creation *ex nihilo*. It is also an unnecessary reading of Gn 1:1-2, one that complicates what seems intended to be a straight forward statement about how all things began.

---

[90] Blocher, *In the Beginning*, 65f.
[91] Bruce Waltke, *Creation and Chaos* (Portland, OR: Western Conservative Baptist Seminary, 1974). Arguments against this view are put forward by Mark Rooker, "Genesis 1:1-3: Creation or Re-Creation?" *BSac* (1992): 316-323; 411-427.

# View Two
# POST CREATION CATASTROPHE

Popularly known as the gap theory, this view holds that the world was created orderly. Then after an enormous period of time, the orderly universe created in Gn 1:1 came to be in the condition described in v 2. The six days that follow in the ch are understood as days of restoration, not days of original creation. Those who hold this view harmonize Gn with the so-called geological ages by suggesting that those eons of time can be placed in the gap between Gn 1:1 and Gn 1:2.

### A. Variations in the View

While the gap theory advocates hold to the general tenets outlined above, they differ among themselves about the cause of the catastrophe. There are two major permutations of the theory.

*1. Restitution gap.* The more popular of the two schools of thought views the catastrophe that resulted in the conditions described in Gn 1:2 as due to an act of divine judgment. Supposedly Satan (prior to his fall) presided over the worship of God in the pre-catastrophe Eden. At some point Satan rebelled. His rebellion brought total destruction to earth. The pre-Adamite "human" population lost their bodies in the judgment. Their spirits became the demons that surface in the Gospels. The fossil bones of pre-historic "men" are viewed as the physical remains of the pre-Adamites.

*2. Cataclysmic gap.* Those who hold to this variation of the gap theory assign the shaping of the present earth to the millions of years they postulate between Gn 1:1 and Gn 1:2. Supposedly during that vast period of time God used natural processes like floods, volcanoes and violent storms to form the features of the planet. The last of this series of natural cataclysms brought about the chaotic conditions depicted in Gn 1:2 and set the stage for the creation of the present order in the remainder of the first ch of Gn.

## B. Exegetical Battlefield

The foundational argument offered in support of the gap theory is that the first verb in Gn 1:2 (*hāyāh*) should be translated "became" not "was." The well-ordered earth "became waste and void at some point in the distant past. Some writers, in responding to the gap theory, have vigorously denied that the verb in Gn 1:2 can be translated "became."[92] An equal number of competent Hebrew scholars concede that *hāyāh* can in fact legitimately be translated "became."[93]

Vigorous protests notwithstanding, it can hardly be questioned that *hāyāh* can be translated "became."[94] This verb is not static like the verb "to be" in English, but dynamic. Thus the verb implies more the idea of "becoming" than that of simply "being." Reading implications of some massive judgment into the verb, however, is a different matter. Certainly there is nothing in the verb or the language that follows it that requires a judgmental act of devastation. Properly understood Gn

---

[92]For example, see the strong denials in B. Ramm, *The Christian View of Science and Scripture* (1954; Grand Rapids: Eerdmans, 1976), 139; J. Whitcomb, *Creation Research Society Quarterly* 4 (1967): 71; J. Skinner, *Genesis* in *International Critical Commentary*, 14fn; F. Filby, *Creation Revealed*, 57-58; J. Barr, *The Semantics of Biblical Language* (Philadelphia: Trinity, 1991).

[93]For example, see G. Archer, *SOTI*, 174, n. 3; E.B. Pusey, *Daniel the Prophet* (1865; Oxford: James Parker, 1978), pp. xii-xiv; A. Dillmann, *Genesis* 1:57; S.R. Driver, *Westminster Commentary on Genesis* (1904; London: Methuen, 1948), 22; Alfred Edersheim; Snaith; T. Boman, *Hebrew Thought Compared with Greek* (Philadelphia: Westminster, 1960).

[94]Ancient versions witness to the possibility of rendering *hāyāh* as *became*. After they got past Gn 1:2, the Septuagint (ca. 250 BC) had no trouble rendering *hāyāh* by the Greek *ginomai* (to *become*) 21x in the first ch of Gn. After he got past Gn 1:2, Jerome in his Latin Vulgate (ca. AD 390) rendered *hāyāh* with the Latin for *become* 13x.

1:2 says, in effect: "Now this is how the earth was when it first came into being."

## C. Supporting Arguments

Understanding Gn 1:2 to teach that the well-ordered earth was devastated by some cataclysmic judgment is possible linguistically. Gap theory advocates produce a number of other arguments to contend that this is the *only* possible meaning of the v.

*1. Waste and void.* The combination of the two terms *tōhû* (*unformed*) and *bōhû* (*unfilled*) appears in two other passages, Isa 34:11 and Jer 4:23-26. In both passages the phrase indicates a destruction that is the result of divine judgment. This may mean nothing more then that in judgment God causes a nation to cease to function in a well-ordered manner.

*2. Isaiah 45:18.* Isaiah stated that God did not create the earth a *tōhû*. If this is the case, then Gn 1:2 could not be describing the earth as it appeared just after the original creative act. There are various renderings of this v: "did not create it a waste place" (NASB); "did not create it to be empty" (NIV); "created it not a waste" (ASV); "did not create it a chaos" (NRSV). The v could be rendered: "did not create it in vain," making *tōhû* an adverbial accusative (cf. NASB mar). The purpose of creation is in view. God created the earth not for the purpose of making it *tōhû*, but to be inhabited. Taken in this way there is nothing in *tōhû* that precludes the word being used to describe earth in its earliest form. The rest of Gn 1 indicates that it was not God's intention to leave earth in the condition of *tōhû*. That is the very point Isaiah was making.

*3. Ezekiel 28:11f.* Ezekiel 28:11f is alleged to refer to Satan walking about in a paradise of an earlier earth. Actually this passage contains hyperbolic language describing the downfall of the prince of Tyre. Furthermore, some statements made in the oracle clearly refer to the Tyrian prince, not Satan. The one who strutted about in his garden (Tyre) is told "through your widespread trade you were filled with violence and you sinned" (Ezek 28:16 NIV). The passage speaks of the prince's "dishonest trade" (v 18). Clearly these vv allude to the far-flung trading ventures of the Tyrians. In v 17 Yahweh claims: "I made a spectacle of you before kings," again suggesting a point in history, not pre-history. Although Ezekiel is difficult on any interpretation, still the text clearly affirms that the language applies to the prince of Tyre (Ezek 28:12).

*4. Isaiah 14:12.* Isaiah 14:12 likewise must be wrenched out of context to have it refer to Satan's fall in a pre-Adamic world. The rendering of KJV has misled many: "How art thou fallen from heaven, O Lucifer, son of the morning!" Fortunately Lucifer has disappeared from modern renderings of the v, and for good reason. The Hebrew term translated *Lucifer* means "morning star" (NIV). It is a figurative name for the king of Babylon (cf. 14:4).

Isaiah 14 describes five grandiose aspirations of the king of Babylon. First, he aspired to ascend into the heavens, figurative of the political domain. Second, the tyrant planned to set his throne above the stars of God, i.e., other luminaries that had been placed in position by God and who served at his pleasure.[95]

Third, having achieved mastery over the other luminaries (kings), he intended to sit in the mount of meeting with the gods, i.e., he aspired to deity.[96] Fourth, the tyrant intended to ascend above the high places of the

---

[95] Another possibility is that the *stars* in Isa 14 are the people of God as in Dan 8:10; 12:3.

[96] Obviously the king is speaking as a heathen. Pagan mythology postulated a mountain far to the north where a council of deities met to decide the fate of earth.

clouds, i.e., exalt himself above God.[97] Finally, the tyrant aspired to be compared to the Most High, i.e., Yahweh.

So a careful exegesis of Isa 14 yields no information about Satan's fall from a position of prominence prior to the creation of Adam.

5. *Job 38:4-7*. The morning stars or angels sang for joy when the earth was created. If, however, the creation was at first formless and empty what would be the cause of rejoicing? The problems with this argument are multiple. It assumes that the condition described in Gn 1:2 would be viewed as negative by the angels. The poetic text does not make clear whether the angels sang continuously, intermittently or climatically, i.e., at the conclusion of the entire creation process. Far too little is known about the creation singing of the angels to base any conclusion about the meaning of Gn 1:2.

6. *Verb make (ʿāsāh)*. Gap theorists have argued that the verb *ʿāsāh* (*made*) means "to shape out of existing material; to appoint; to give a new role to something already in existence." This verb is used 7x in Gn 1. Thus the six days were days of re-shaping, re-designing, and re-organizing the ruins of the original creation described in v 1 and destroyed in v 2.

The facts do not seem to support this argument. The term *ʿāsāh* is used in Gn 1 for the sky (v 7), the great luminaries (v 16), and indeed everything (v 31). This verb seems to have the colorless meaning *make* in all of its Gn 1 usage. In 5:1 the author uses *ʿāsāh* in parallel with the verb *create* (*bārāʾ*), implying that in the creation context they are virtually synonymous.

---

[97]This he does by attempting to thwart the plan of God for Israel. When human plans displace God's plan, arrogance has mounted above the clouds.

## D. Objections to the Gap Theory

The arguments supporting the gap theory are paper thin. That in itself is reason enough to reject the theory. In addition, however, a number of arguments can be marshaled against the gap theory. These arguments may be grouped under four heads.[98]

*1. General arguments.* The general impression created by Gn 1 is that it is outlining the process by which the present world (not some pre-Adamic world) came into being. Furthermore, the brevity of Gn 1:1 weighs against the gap theory. Why devote one v to original creation, and thirty-two vv to the reconstruction? The gap theory exploits biblical silence.

*2. Theological arguments.* Among the theological arguments against the gap theory are these: First, there is total silence in the Bible regarding any primeval catastrophe. The Gn judgmental interventions of God (e.g., Flood, Sodom) are mentioned in warnings in the OT prophets and NT epistles. There is, however, no clear reference to any judgmental disaster befalling pre-Adamic earth anywhere in the Bible.

Second, the gap theory is not easily harmonized with the teaching that sin and death entered the world through Adam (1 Cor 15:21; Rom 5:12; 8:20-22). The gap theory postulates wide-spread death prior to the creation of Adam. (See, however, comments on 3:19).

Third, Ex 20:11 and Gn 2:1-3 seem to require that the present world was created in or resulted from what was created in the six days of Gn 1. This excludes any creation prior to the six days.

Fourth, if fossil men are regarded as evidence of a pre-Adamic race, how could Adam be the first man?

*3. Logical argument.* The gap theory proponents have difficulty explaining how a fall of Satan in heaven

---

[98]See Weston Fields, *Unformed and Unfilled; A Critique of the Gap Theory of Genesis 1:1, 2* (Winona Lake, IN: Light and Life, 1973).

could have any connection with a judgment on pre-Adamites (pre-historic men) on earth. Furthermore, following gap theory exegesis one would have to believe that sun and moon were destroyed in the catastrophe reported in Gn 1:2, and then were re-created on day four.

*4. Scientific argument.* According to the gap theory there was a total destruction of the earth about seven thousand years ago. Where, however, is the evidence of a worldwide cataclysm in very recent geologic time? The gap theory pushes five billion years of evolution back into a pre-Genesis world. Would God, however, use evolution in the pre-world and then switch to direct creation in the six days? Those who think the gap theory removes any friction between the scientific disciplines and biblical theology had better take another look into both areas.

## View Three
## INITIAL STAGE OF CREATION

Gn 1:2 is best viewed as describing the first stage in the preparation of the earth for the habitation of man. The earth in this v is just like God intended for it to be at this stage. The only problem in this view is that the phrase *heavens and earth* elsewhere always refers to the well-organized universe. If, however, it was God's intention to create the earth by an unfolding process (as clearly it was) the earth could hardly be well-organized until God organized it. Thus context argues that in Gn 1:1 the dyad *heavens and earth* of necessity has a different connotation then it carries elsewhere in the OT.

**A. Condition of the Earth** (1:2a-e)

*1. Subject (1:2a): **Now as for the earth**.* Gn 1:2 begins with a conjunctive *vav* attached to the subject of the v. This syntax generally introduces a shift of focus in a

## Biblical Protology

narrative. Like a camera zooming in on an object of interest, the writer narrows the focus from the entire universe to the earth. A geocentric emphasis characterizes the remainder of the account. For the most part all but the earth is excluded from the creation narrative.

*2. Verb (1:2b):* ***it came into being.*** The second word in 1:2 is the verb *hāyāh* discussed at length above. This verb is usually understood simply to introduce a description of a state of existence in past time.[99] Thus the common rendering is "and the earth was" such and such (cf. KJV; NIV; NRSV; NASB). It is best, however, to give the opening words of 1:2 the full weight of a verbal clause. The remainder of the v describes the condition of the earth before Elohim began the process of shaping it.[100] Four nouns, rather than adjectives, are used to strengthen the description. In English, however, it is somewhat awkward to translate these words as nouns.

*3. Descriptive noun pair (1:2c):* ***as formlessness and emptiness.*** The verb in Gn 1:2 is followed by two similar sounding nouns joined by a connective *vav*. They indicate the manner in which the earth came into being. The earth was *tōhû vābōhû*.

*Tōhû* occurs 20x in the OT, eleven of which are in Isaiah. In English versions it is rendered "without form" (NKJV), "unformed" (NJPS); "formless" (NIV; NASB; NRSV), and "waste" (ASV). The term is used of a trackless waste or desert (Dt 32:10; Job 6:18) and emptiness (Job 26:7). It is used metaphorically of what is baseless and futile (1 Sam 12:21; Isa 29:21). In Isa 45:18 this term is placed in contrast to a term meaning to "be inhabited." Thus the earth was uninhabitable.

---

[99] GK §141 i. The statement "might also appear in the form of a pure noun-clause."

[100] David Tsumura, *The Earth and the Waters in Genesis 1 and 2: A Linguistic Investigation*. JSOT Supplement Series 83 (Sheffield: JSOT, 1989).

The term *bōhû* always appears in combination with *tōhû*. It has essentially the same meaning. In the common English versions it is rendered "void" (ASV; NJPS; NASB; NKJV); and "empty" (NIV).

The combination of the two terms *tōhû vābōhû* is a rhythmic and eye-catching phrase. The NRSV prefers to combine the two words into the phrase "formless void." It is best, however, to render them by two separate words, *formlessness* and *emptiness* or *unformed and unfilled*. The two words together point to a situation in which the earth is not producing life.[101]

From a literary point of view *unformed and unfilled* point in the two directions in which the earth will undergo change in the rest of the ch. In the first three creative days the earth is shaped or formed, i.e., made productive; in the last three days the earth is filled.

*4. Third descriptive noun (1:2d):* **and darkness...** The third noun used to depict the condition of the earth when it came into being is taken by most English versions as the subject of a verbless clause in which the verb *was* must be supplied: "darkness was upon the face of the deep" (KJV). *Darkness* (*chōšeck*) stands first in the noun clause for emphasis. It is equally possible, however, that *darkness* is to be connected with the previous verb, so that the sentence reads: "Now as for the earth, it came into being (as) formlessness and emptiness and darkness over the face of the deep."[102]

Ancient man feared the darkness. Darkness, however, is not represented in the Bible as some power hostile to God. Isaiah declared that darkness was created by God (Isa 45:7). Often the Bible uses darkness as a metaphor for evil. This does not mean, however, that every time darkness is mentioned in the Bible the term has some evil or sinister connotation. In Gn 1 darkness is

---

[101] Tsumura, *Earth*, 42-43.
[102] For arguments favoring this rendering see Aalders, *BSC*, 54.

viewed positively. God named it *night* (v 5), thus asserting his authority over darkness. Furthermore, at the end of day one God pronounced both light and darkness to be good, i.e., part of God's design for the world.

    5. *Fourth descriptive noun (1:2e):* **[darkness] over the face of the deep** (*'al p$^e$nê t$^e$hôm*). In Scripture the term *deep* may indicate simply depth (Ps 71:20), or subterranean waters (Gn 7:11; 8:2) or the seas. *The deep* is defined here by the term *waters* in the subsequent clause. The *deep* terrified ancient man, perhaps partially because the Babylonians deified it and worshipped it as a mythological dragon of the watery chaos. The *deep*, however, is no more to be feared than the darkness. Both were created by a loving God.[103]

    Some try to make a connection between *t$^e$hôm* and Tiamat, the salt water god of the Babylonian creation account. Whatever the linguist background of *t$^e$hôm*, the term in Gn 1:2 clearly does not refer to any goddess. When Moses used this word he used it in such a way that it was free of mythological connotations that it might have had elsewhere in the ancient world. Whether Moses was consciously demythologizing the Babylonian concept of creation is hard to say. He may simply have chosen the one word in the Hebrew language that best expressed his thought without regard to whether that word might have had different connotation for other peoples.[104]

    The main point so far is this: man could not have lived on the earth because it was dark and covered with water.

## B. Action of God (1:2f-g)

    *1. God's Spirit (1:2f):* **But the Spirit of God**. The last clause of the v begins with the connector *vav* indi-

---

[103] Youngblood, *BGIC*, 24.
[104] E.J. Young, *Genesis One*, 29.

cating a condition parallel to the previous statement regarding the darkness. While darkness was over the face of the deep, something else was there too. The connector here probably has the adversative sense, hence the translation *but*. The construct phrase *Spirit of God* has the emphatic position in the clause. Even before the process of forming and filling the earth began God was actively involved with this planet.

There is some ambiguity in the word translated *Spirit* (*rûach*) because it is also the Hebrew word for *wind*. For this reason some see in 1:2 a mighty wind sweeping over the primeval earth. That *Spirit of God* is the proper rendering of the Hebrew phrase is indicated by the following considerations.[105] First, the phrase *rûach ᵉlōhîm* always refers to the Spirit of God, never to a "mighty wind" or "wind from God" (NEB; NAB; NRSV; NJPS). Second, the participle describing the action of the *rûach ᵉlōhîm* is appropriate for God's Spirit, but not for storm actions.

*2. God's movement (1:2g):* **was hovering over the face of the waters.** The action of God's Spirit prior to day one is described by the participle *mᵉrachephet*, rendered "hovering" (NKJV; NIV); "moving/moved" (NASB; ASV); "sweeping/swept" (NJPS; NRSV). In Dt 32:11 Moses used the same verb to compare the leadership of Yahweh in Israel to an eagle hovering over its nest of young. The use of the similar image of God both at the beginning of the Pentateuch and at the end suggests that it is the picture of the Spirit of God that is intended here.[106] Similar ornithologic imagery is used at the inauguration of the new creation when the Holy Spirit descended on Jesus in bodily form like a dove (Lk 3:22).

The text does not indicate the purpose for the hovering of God's Spirit over the waters. Two OT usages of

---

[105] Hamilton, *NICOT*, 111-14.
[106] Sailhamer, *EBC*, loc.

**81**

the concept of God's Spirit might be relevant. First, God's Spirit is connected with displays of God's power. The thought in this case is that the Creator is very much in control of the situation. Second, God's Spirit has life-giving power (e.g. Ps 104:30). The Spirit may have been preparing the earth to support life.[107]

God's Spirit was hovering *over* (or *above*) *the face* (surface) *of the waters*. This phrase is parallel to *over the face of the deep* earlier in the v.

## CONCLUSION

Analysis of Gn 1:2 from the theological perspective yields four truths that are taught or implied. First, God existed before he spoke in v 3. Second, in the Spirit God drew near to the universe, yet remained distinct from it. Third, the Spirit and Word alongside God in the creation suggest a monotheism that is more complex than is generally recognized. Fourth, God was in control at every step of the creation process. The Hebrews rejected the pagan notion that creation resulted from battles between various gods.

---

[107]Cf. Aalders (*BSC*, 56): The Spirit "preserves this created material and prepares it for the further creative activity of God." For another intriguing suggestion regarding the hovering of the Spirit see M.G. Kline, "Creation in the Image of the Glory Spirit," *WTJ* 39(1976-77): 250-272.

# 6
# SIX CREATIVE DAYS
# Gn 1:3-31

So far Moses has declared that God created everything in the beginning (1:1). He has described how the earth appeared immediately after that initial creative act (1:2). The rest of the creation account unfolds in six carefully crafted paragraphs.

## PHENOMENOLOGY OF THE DAYS

### A. Pattern

The day paragraphs follow a similar pattern. First, there is divine speech (*God said*) in the form of a fiat (*let there be*). Second, there is a statement of fulfillment (*and there was*). Third, there is a divine appraisal (*and it was good*). Finally, there is a concluding formula (*there was evening and there was morning day x*).

### B. Progression

There is an orderly progression in the six paragraphs. The description of the days grows progressively longer. The first two days are described in thirty-one and thirty-eight words respectively. Days three and four contain sixty-nine words each. There is a slight drop off to fifty-seven words in the fifth paragraph. The sixth paragraph (day) contains more than twice the number of words of any of the previous days. The writer thus conveys the notion of ever-increasing variety, complexity and importance. This progression reaches its climax in man as divinely appointed ruler over earth and the Creator enjoying the rest of satisfaction and accomplishment.

Obviously the account is arranged linearly (i.e., sequentially by days). A secondary parallel arrangement, however, is also discernable between the first and second triads of days. The parallelism is intended to convey the notion of orderliness. The Creator proceeded in a very methodical and systematic way. In both the linear and the parallel arrangements the seventh-day (Sabbath) is highlighted.

## C. Uniqueness

The allocation of creative acts to separate days is a unique contribution of the Hebrew creation account. Neither the Babylonian nor Egyptian mythology regarding creation knows anything about a division of creative work into days. The 6 + 1 formula, as it is called, does appear in Akkadian and Ugaritic literature regarding other projects. This usage indicates that seven consecutive days were considered a perfect period in which to develop some important work—the action reaching its climax on the seventh day.[108]

## D. Purpose

The use of the six days + a climatic seventh serves several purposes. First, it underscores that the Creator works in methodical, logical and progressive ways. Second, this pattern is a protest against an exclusively anthropocentric view of the world. The Creator "is not totally preoccupied with human creatures. God has his own relations with the rest of creation."[109] Third, the 6 + 1 pattern serves to underscore the value of all parts of God's creation. The Creator evaluates each facet of creation as *good*. This serves to enhance man's sense of stewardship of all that God made. Fourth, the pattern tends to reveal hierarchies in the created order. Fifth, ascribing creation to six days climaxing in a seventh organizes

---

[108]Cassuto, *CBG*, 1:13.
[109]W. Brueggemann, *Genesis* in "Interpretation: A Bible Commentary for Teaching and Preaching" (Atlanta: John Knox, 1982), 30f.

ganizes time and highlights the function of the Sabbath as a day of rest and remembrance.

The nature of the six days of creation in Gn 1 has been hotly debated over the centuries. Were these ordinary days, long ages, or are they merely a literary device that has nothing to do with the actual sequence in the creative actions of God? The pros and cons of these approaches will now be examined.

## View One
## DAY-AGE THEORY[110]

The day-age or concordistic theory can be traced back to early Christian times. Augustine (5th century) wrote: "It is more than probable that the seven days of Genesis were entirely different in their duration from those which now mark the succession of time.... The seventh day had no evening; it means there a period of time, the other six are likewise."[111] As a response to the scientific revolution this view gained popularity in the eighteenth and nineteenth centuries. Today it may well be the most popular view among Evangelicals.

### A. Supporting Arguments

The arguments put forth in support of the concordistic theory can be grouped under eight headings.

*1. Linguistic argument.* The word *day* (*yôm*) is sometimes used figuratively of a period of time of in-

---

[110] Some supporters of this approach are: F. Harder, "Literary Structure of Genesis 1:1-2:3: An Overview," in *Creation Reconsidered*; L. Herr, "Genesis One in Historical-Critical Perspective," *Spectrum* 13(Dec 1982): 51-62; C. Hyers, *The Meaning of Creation: Genesis and Modern Science* (1984); G. Schroeder, *Genesis and the Big Bang: The Discovery of Harmony Between Modern Science and the Bible* (New York: Bantam, 1990); D. Young, *Creation and the Flood: An Alternative to Flood Geology and Theistic Evolution* (1974).

[111] Cited by C.F.H. Henry, *The Protestant Dilemma*, 66.

definite duration. Examples of this usage are references to the "day of Yahweh" (Amos 5:18-20) or "day of salvation" (2 Cor 6:2). Clearly the term *yôm* can be used figuratively to refer to longer periods than ordinary days.

The writer of the creation account knew of this usage of *yôm*, and actually employed it. Where *yôm*, however, points to a period longer than an ordinary day there is usually something in the context that points in the direction of a figurative usage. In Gn 2:4, for example, one is compelled to understand *yôm* in a figurative sense because the previous vv made it clear that the creation of the heavens and earth took place over a period longer than a single day. The question that must be answered, then, is there anything in the context of Gn 1 that compels the interpreter to give to *yôm* a figurative meaning? The possibility that *yôm* can be used figuratively does not demand that the word be so interpreted in the context of Gn 1.

Another argument in this category is the absence of the definite article from the enumeration of the days. The text says *day one* etc. rather than "the first day." Some think that this points to an indefinite period of time.[112]

*2. Time declarations.* At least two passages teach that with God a day is like a thousand years (Ps 90:4; 2 Pet 3:8). Thus the Creator, from whom the details of creation were ultimately derived, does not measure time as man measures time.

Two things about these time declarations should be noted. First, neither passage has a creation context. Second, in both passages the noun has a comparative particle attached, thus indicating an analogy. The text does not say that with God a day *equals* a thousand years, but that a day is *like* a thousand years.

---

[112]John Davis, *Genesis and Semitic Tradition* (1894; Grand Rapids: Baker, 1980), 18.

*3. Seventh-day argument.* The day-age school argues that the omission of the formula *evening and morning* at the end of the seventh day was deliberate. This was Moses' way of saying that the seventh day is eternal. If the seventh day is of indefinite duration, the first six days must be likewise.

Two NT passages are cited in support of the indefinite duration of the Sabbath. Hebrews 4:3-5 is difficult and inconclusive regarding the issue of the length of the Gn creation Sabbath. In Jn 5:17 Jesus defended his healing on the Sabbath by arguing, "My Father works even until now." The argument of Jesus is taken to be: I may work on the Sabbath because my Father continues to work even though he declared a Sabbath after his creative works. Taken in this way the Gn Sabbath lasts throughout history. Thus Jesus himself did not see the seventh day as a literal day.

The Jn 5:17 argument is invalid for two reasons. First, if "my Father works even until now" means that God has never rested from his works at any time since the end of day six, then the argument denies what Gn explicitly affirms. God did rest on the seventh day in some sense (Gn 2:2). If God "rested" and God "works until now" are both true, then the working must have commenced after the resting concluded. If that is the case, then Jn 5:17 says nothing to indicate the length of the seventh day in Gn.

Second, it was not Jesus' intention to make a statement, even by implication, about the length of the Gn days. Rather it was his intention to defend his Sabbath healing by pointing out that throughout history God providentially has been at work sustaining and maintaining the world without regard to days of the week. His point was that God does not take every seventh day off.

*4. Fourth-day argument.* On day four of creation week God made the two great luminaries, the sun and the moon (Gn 1:16). Ordinary days could not have occurred before the creation of the sun. Therefore, one would have to concede that at least the first three days were not ordinary days.

The fourth day argument is easily refuted. For each of the six creative days the text explicitly states *there was evening and there was morning*, hence an alternation of light and darkness. What happened on day four must not be construed in a way that offsets this explicit evidence. Furthermore, light was created on day one. All that is needed for the evening/morning cycle is a light source and a rotating earth. Therefore the fact that the luminaries were made on day four does not prove that the first three days could not have been ordinary days.

*5. Rain argument.* What appears to be a casual remark in Gn 2:5 has become a pivotal textual argument in support of the long age theory. The passage in its context reads as follows:

> When the LORD God made the earth and the heavens, no shrub of the field had yet appeared on the earth and no plant of the field had yet sprung up; the LORD God had not sent rain on the earth and there was no man to work the ground, but streams came up from the earth and watered the whole surface of the ground (Gn 2:4b-6 NIV).

The report about the lack of rain prior to the creation of man has been taken to indicate that God used natural means (i.e., rain) for the development of the earth during the creation week. This calls for long ages.[113] Dry land and vegetation appeared on the third day of creation week; why would the author note on Friday that it had not rained? That Moses included this statement in 2:5 is proof that he never intended the days of ch 1 to be taken as ordinary days.

---

[113]The argument is developed by M.G. Kline, "Because it had not Rained," *WTJ* 20(1957-58): 146-157.

The rain argument may be answered this way. If it had not rained prior to the creation of man, and if the preceding days were all eons of time, then one would have to believe that rain had nothing to do with the shaping of the early earth. Under no cosmogony yet proposed has any hypothesis been advanced that explains the present earth without the shaping effects of rain. See further the comments on 2:5.

6. *Tôl$^e$dōth argument.* The use of the term *tôl$^e$dōth* ("generations" KJV; "account" NIV) is thought by some to point to a long span for the creation week.[114] As noted earlier, the term is used to identify tablets used by Moses in writing Gn. In each case the tablet embraces a long span of time. Use of the term for a single ordinary week is disanalogous. The time referent in the term *tôl$^e$dōth*, however, is determined by its context. The term itself has no implications of time.

7. *Day-three argument.* Vegetation not only was created, but also grew to maturity on day three. Thus the third day must have lasted longer than twenty-four hours.[115] The response to this argument is that the plants may have been created in various stages of growth. Before assuming that mature vegetation mandates a long period for development one should not overlook the plant in Jonah 4 that grew up overnight.

8. *Non-textual arguments.* For some the pressure to adopt the day = long age view comes, not from the text, but from factors outside the text. Long-age creation days seem to harmonize better with the conclusions of geology.[116] Other writers are influenced by the Babylonian tradition. This tradition depicts various stages in the de-

---

[114] Hugh Ross, *Creation and Time* (Colorado Springs: Navpress, 1994), 52.

[115] Norman Geisler, *Baker Encyclopedia of Christian Apologetics* (Grand Rapids: Baker, 1999), 272.

[116] W.J. Beasley, *Creation's Amazing Architect* (London: Marshall, Morgan & Scott, 1955).

velopment of the ordered universe that appear to represent long periods of unspecified duration. Should Christians, however, allow pagan tradition to be the guide to Gn 1?

**B. Problems in the Day-Age View**

Those who endorse the day-age view of the Gn days must respond to five areas of difficulty.

*1. Scientific problems.* Outlandish expansions of time are necessary to transform the Gn days into eons of sufficient length to produce the results required by evolution. Even so the correspondence between the order of creation (Gn 1) and historical geology is superficial.[117] A few examples of the conflict will suffice to illustrate the problem.

Evolution has plants and trees created after marine life; Gn 1 has plants created on day three and marine life on day five. Evolution has birds evolving from reptiles long after fish and probably even after mammals; Gn 1 has birds appearing on day five, reptiles and mammals on day six. Evolution has creeping things among the earliest creatures on earth; Gn 1 has creeping things created on day six after birds and at the same time as mammals. Evolution assumes the existence of the sun before vegetation; Gn 1 has vegetation appearing on day three, the sun on day four. These examples of conflict with evolutionary theory indicate that accommodation cannot be reached between biblical cosmogony and current scientific theory simply by adopting the day-age view.

*2. Theological problems.* The day-age advocates face some difficulties in the theological realm. For example, how does this view relate to the biblical teaching that death and suffering resulted from man's sin? (See, however, comments on 3:19). Second, Ex 20:9-11 seems

---

[117]Henry Morris, *The Bible and Modern Science* (Chicago: Moody, 1968), 34. *Bible-Science Newsletter*, Feb 1971.

to teach that the world was created in six ordinary days. Third, if God can create by fiat and *ex nihilo* then he can create instantaneously. He takes no more time for any operation than his purpose in that action requires. Since God could have created the entire world in an instant, he must have had a purpose in prolonging creation for even a week. It was God's purpose in this account to provide a basis for the Sabbath. What possible motive, however, would the Creator have for expanding the creative activity over eons of time?

*3. Logical problems.* Here are some logical problems with the day-age view. First, even if the days in Gn were not ordinary days, it would not follow that they represent eons of time. Second, even if the seventh day could be shown to have lasted thousands of years, it would not follow that the previous six days were eons of millions of years. Third, even if a day with the Lord is as a thousand years (2 Pet 3:8), it does not follow that a day of creation was several million years long.

*4. Contextual problems.* The phrase *evening and morning* does not receive a satisfactory explanation from advocates of the day-age view. Clearly the word *day* (*yôm*) is used of literal days in Gn 1:5 and 1:14-19. This suggests that the word has the same sense throughout the ch.

*5. Communication problem.* If the writer wanted to express the idea of long ages he had a perfectly good Hebrew word (*'ôlām*) that he could have used. What more could the writer have done to indicate that he intended the Gn days to be viewed as ordinary days?

## View Two
## FRAMEWORK HYPOTHESIS[118]

The framework theory about the days in Gn 1 also has been called the ideal interpretation, the topical view, the double symmetry view, the aristico-historical view and the literary interpretation view. Essentially this theory says that God's creative works are placed in a figurative framework of days. The "days" are only a literary device—an anthropomorphic figure. Both the duration and the sequence of the days are figurative. In other words, the creation material is arranged in a topical (or logical) rather than a chronological sequence. God did not intend to communicate anything about the order of creation. His sole purpose for organizing the material in the framework of "days" was to present a theology for the Sabbath. So Gn 1 does not give any information about how long it took God to create the earth, or the order in which he created the various components of the earth.

---

[118]Early advocates: James Dana of Yale (1858). First edition of *Davis Dictionary of the Bible* s.v. "Creation" (1898). J.P. Lange and Hermann Strack. F. Filby, *Creation Revealed* (Westwood, NJ: Revell, 1965); C. Hauret, *Beginnings: Genesis and Modern Science* (Dubuque, IA: Priory, 1955); C. Hyers, *The Meaning of Creation* (Atlanta: John Knox, 1984); L. Irons, "Douglas Kelly on the Framework Interpretation of Genesis One," *PSCF* 50(1998): 272-4; L. Irons, with Meredith Kline, "The Framework View" in *The Genesis Debate: Three Views on the Days of Creation*, ed. David Hagopian (2001): 217-256; J. Jordan, *Creation in Six Days* (1999); M.G. Kline, *New Bible Commentary Revised* (1970); A. Kulikousky, "A Critique of the Literary Framework View of the Days of Creation," *CRSQ* 37(Mar 2001): 237-44; D.F. Payne, *Genesis One Reconsidered* (1964); N.H. Ridderbos, *Is there a Conflict Between Genesis One and Natural Science?* (1957); M. Ross, "The Framework Hypothesis: An Interpretation of Genesis 1:1-2:3," in *Did God Create in Six Days?* ed Joseph Pipa, Jr., and David Hall (1999); J. Starnbaugh, "The Days of Creation—a Semantic Approach," *CENTJ* 6(1991). Also Lagrange, Noordtzij, Ramm, J.A. Thompson, Youngblood.

Six Creative Days

**A. Supporting Evidence**

Those who embrace the framework theory accept the arguments advanced by the day-age advocates that the days in Gn are figurative, not literal. They have no problem with the long eons of time involved in the creation of earth postulated by the scientific disciplines. This school of thought avoids the difficulty of harmonizing the sequence of the biblical days with the sequence proposed by evolutionary geology and biology. The point of Gn 1 is to underscore that God is the Creator of everything. It is not the purpose of Gn 1 to teach how God did the creating. Six main arguments are used to buttress the framework theory regarding the sequence.

*1. Topical accounts.* Much information in the Bible is presented topically, not chronologically. Even material that appears to be chronological in some cases can be shown to be topical. Matthew and Luke contain reports of Christ's wilderness temptations. Both accounts appear to be chronological, but they disagree as to sequence. Therefore, one or the other (probably Luke) is arranged topically.

While it is true that much material in the Bible is presented topically that does not prove that Gn 1 has been arranged topically.

| Chart 8 ||
| Parallelism in the Creative Days ||
| Days 1-3 | Days 4-6 |
| --- | --- |
| 1. Works of Division | 1. Works of Embellishment |
| 2. Preparation | 2. Accomplishments |
| 3. Spaces/spheres Created | 3. Spaces Peopled |
| 4. Motionless Objects | 4. Moving Objects |
| 5. Domains | 5. Rulers of Domains |

*2. Parallelism argument.* Correspondence between the first three and the last three creative days suggests that the writer has arranged the material topically. Chart

8 displays some of the ways the parallels between the ch triads have been described.

*3. Recapitulation argument.* Repetition in the narrative suggests topical rather than chronological development. For example, all functions ascribed to the sun on day four already have been described earlier. In 1:4 the text declares that God separated light from darkness; in 1:18 the writer relates how God accomplished that separation.

*4. Beginning/end argument.* At the beginning of the creation account the writer signals the two directions that his topical development will take. In 1:2 the earth is *tōhû (unformed)* and *bōhû (unfilled)*. Days 1-3 describe the forming of the earth; days 4-6 describe the filling. The writer concludes the creation account in 2:1 with these words: *Thus the heavens and earth were finished* (days 1-3), *and all the host of them* (days 4-6).

*5. Syntactical argument.* Sterchi has advanced an argument based on the use of the definite article in connection with the seven days. In the light of the use of the article on the number *one (ʼechād)* in 2:11 Sterchi thinks its absence on the noun *day (yôm)* and on the number *(ʼechād)* in 1:5 may indicate that the author intended day one to be taken indefinitely—"one day" not "the first day." Days two through five in the Hebrew are indefinite with no article present. The article is present on the number in day six, and present on the number and noun in day seven. Sterchi concludes that this pattern of the absence of the article on days one through five, and its presence on the sixth and seventh days is the author's way of signaling that he is providing a list of days without implying that there is a chronological connection between them.[119]

---

[119]David Sterchi, "Does Genesis 1 Provide a Chronological Sequence?" *JETS* 39(Dec 1996): 529-536.

*6. Sabbath argument.* Ex 20:8-11 teaches that the Sabbath was to serve as a weekly reminder of the fact that God created the universe. The Sabbath is an actual day of twenty-four hours. The six phases of creation were also referred to as "days" in order to strengthen the connection between the Sabbath and the creation of the universe.

## B. Variations

Variations in the Framework Theory have surfaced. The search for literary patterns in the days of creation week continues apace. In place of the 3//3+1 day pattern of days described above, Jaki offers a 1+2//2+1+1 pattern. Jaki thinks the Hebrews considered the universe as a huge tent (based on Isa 40:22). The main *parts* of the tent (ceiling = heavens; floor = earth) were created on days two and three. The particulars of the heavens and the earth were assigned to days four and five. The climax of the week comes on days six and seven. The point is that the statement of totality in 1:1 is emphasized by means of particulars in the six days. This pattern was depicted in order to portray God as the worker, setting a pattern for mankind.[120]

In Jaki's theory day one seems awkward. Furthermore, he offers no explanation of the significance for the animals being created on day six along with man. One would think that on the tent model the land animals would have been included on day five.

Another pattern to the Gn days is diagrammed in Chart 9. The "discovery" of alternative patterns in Gn 1 calls into question the validity of this approach to the Gn days. Those who suggest patterns within patterns impose a complexity on the simple narrative of creation that would probably shock the writer of this biblical ch.

---

[120]Stanley Jaki, *Genesis 1 Through the Ages* (London: Thomas More Press, 1992), 290-96.

Biblical Protology

|  | Chart 9 Heaven/Earth Pattern in the Gn Days |  |  |  |  |
|---|---|---|---|---|---|
| Day 1 Heaven | Day 2 Heaven |  | Day 4 Heaven |  |  |
|  |  | Day 3 Earth |  | Day 5 Earth | Day 6 Earth |

## C. Criticism

In evaluating the framework hypothesis the first question that must be addressed is this: Is the observable symmetry between the first and second triads of days intended? The answer is probably "yes." The second question then is this: Does pattern destroy chronological sequence?[121] In the narrative of the ten plagues a pattern of two announced plagues followed by one unannounced plague is discernable. Yet most expositors do not question the sequence of the plagues. Therefore, a discernable pattern in the two triads of days in Gn 1 does not prove that the narrative should be interpreted topically rather than chronologically.

In Ex 20:11 the creative activity of God is given as a pattern for the workweek of man. The analogy between man's workweek and creation week is weakened if the creative acts have been artificially arranged in a six-day pattern.

If one holds language to mean anything at all the typical day one/day four; day two/day five; day three/ day six parallelisms must indicate at least a three-stage chronology.

---

[121] Weeks, "The Hermeneutical Problem of Genesis 1-11," *Themelios* 4(Sept 1978): 12-19.

Six Creative Days

The 6 + 1 scheme is found in ancient Near Eastern literature (e.g., Gilgamesh Epic, *Enuma Elish*, and Ugaritic texts). The scheme is always chronological.[122] There is, however, this modification. The extra-biblical poems tell their stories in terms of three sets of two days followed by a seventh climactic day. On the other hand, Gn 1 uses two sets of three days, each set having its own preliminary climax. The whole narrative then concludes with a majestic climactic paragraph describing the seventh day.[123]

There are indicators of sequence in the paragraphs describing the days, which should not be there if the author intended his work to be interpreted topically. First, the text has the grammatical mark of sequential narrative. The so-called *vav-consecutive* is used some 55x in Gn 1. Second, the use of *day* with the ordinal number demands a sequential reading. There is not one example of *day* (*yôm*) with an ordinal number used non-sequentially. To these observations it may be added that biblical accounts elsewhere (e.g., Ps 104) parallel the sequence of Gn 1.

The conclusion then is that the Master Artist, God, created artistically, building symmetry into the very structure of the creation week.

## Third View
## REVELATORY DAYS

The revelatory day view is that God revealed to Moses in six days upon Mount Sinai the fact that he had created the heavens and the earth. On six successive days Moses was given a series of visions revealing various facets of creation. Thus the forming of the heaven

---

[122] E.J. Young., *Genesis One*, 79-81. E.g., see ANET, 94, 134, 144, 150.
[123] Youngblood, *BGIC*, 31.

and the earth may have actually taken place over eons of time. Furthermore, one cannot assume that the works of creation took place in the same order that they were revealed on the six days of revelation to Moses.[124]

Bernard Ramm espoused this view:

> We believe ... that creation was *revealed* in six days, not performed in six days. We believe that the six days are *pictorial-revelatory* days, not literal days nor age-days. The days are means of communicating to man the great fact that *God is Creator*, and that *He is Creator of all* (italics his).[125]

A variation of this view says that God revealed the creation days not by means of visions, but rather by means of a historical narrative written on seven tablets. P.J. Wiseman points out that the custom in Babylonia was to write the story of creation on a series of tablets.[126]

### D. Supporting Evidence

Those who feel compelled to remove all conflict between the Gn creation account and current dogma from the scientific disciplines think that the revelatory day view is a panacea. The arguments supporting the revelatory view, however, are few and weak. First, this view avoids the problem of harmonizing the twenty-four hour creative days with geological records, while maintaining the natural interpretation of the word *day* (*yôm*) in Gn 1.

---

[124] Advocates: F. Bettex, *The Six Days of Creation in the Light of Modern Science* (Burlington, IA: Lutheran Literary Board, 1924); G. Brantley, "Six Days of Creation or Revelation? Reason and Revelation 14(6): 45. D. Garrett, *Rethinking Genesis: The Sources and Authority of the First Book of the Pentateuch* (1991); J.M. Gibson, *The Ages Before Moses* (1879; Edinburgh: Oliphant, Anderson & Ferrier, 1978; H. Miller, *The Testimony of the Rock* (1957); P.J. Wiseman, *Creation Revealed in Six Days* (1948).
[125] Bernard Ramm, *CVSS*, 151.
[126] P.J. Wiseman, *Clues to Creation in Genesis* (London: Marshall, Morgan & Scott, 1977), 110.

Second, in some contexts the verb *'āsāh* normally translated *made*, is rendered "showed" 43x in the KJV. So Ex 20:11 could be understood to say that in six days God "showed" or "revealed" to Moses the creation of the heavens, the earth, the sea and all that is in them.

Third, certain ancient Near Eastern myths refer to pagan gods instructing rulers in the arts, crafts, agriculture, etc., for six days. This raises the possibility that Gn 1 also chronicles six tutorial classes delivered by God to man.

Fourth, to further bolster this theory, P.J. Wiseman suggested the following translation of Gn 2:3-4:

> And God blessed the seventh day and set it apart, for in it he ceased from all his business which God did creatively in reference to making these histories of the heavens and the earth, in their being created in the day when the Lord God made the earth and the heavens.[127]

This translation draws a subtle distinction between the creation of the earth and heavens, and the activity from which God ceased on the seventh day, i.e., revealing the histories of the heavens and earth.

### E. Criticism

Though visionary views nicely avoid all the problems of attempting to ascertain whether the days of Gn were literal or symbolic, they do have weaknesses. First, the visionary views do not result from a natural reading of the text. The language of Gn is that of historical narration, not of dramatic vision. There is nothing in the context to suggest that the days were revelatory days rather than creative days of whatever length. The revelatory day explanation is driven by external data, especially the theories of modern science.

---

[127] P.J. Wiseman, *Clues* 201f.

Second, Wiseman's translation of Gn 2:3-4 is inconsistent with the structure of the Hebrew text. The Masoretic scribes indicated a paragraph division at the end of v 4. Wiseman ignored this ancient textual notation, and forced the two vv into one cumbersome and ambiguous sentence. Wiseman's translation is a forced, unnatural reading of the text.

Third, Ex 20:11 seems to oppose the idea of revelatory days by stating that God made the heavens and the earth in six days. Efforts to argue that the verb *'āsāh* really means "show" have been refuted by F.F. Bruce.[128] There is no Hebrew dictionary that supports "show" as a translation of *'āsāh*. The KJV renders *'āsāh* as "show" when the reference is to the display of a positive emotional quality. In no case, however, does KJV take the term *'āsāh* to refer to the revelation of truth or communication of knowledge. Furthermore, in the two vv preceding Ex 20:11 the verb *'āsāh* is used twice in its regular sense of *do* or *make*. It is not likely that the verb would take on a different meaning in 20:11.

Fourth, the use of visions to record the past is not the usual way in which the Bible speaks.

Fifth, the fact that God told people to rest upon the seventh day because he rested after six days of work assumes some chronological sequence of creation.

## View Four
## NATURAL DAYS

The literal day interpretation was advocated by almost all the church Fathers, medieval schoolmen and older Protestant theologians. Nineteenth century advocates included Pember, Keil, and Baumgarten. The view

---

[128] F.F. Bruce, *EQ*, 20(Oct, 1948):302.

has also been defended by a number of more recent writers.[129]

## A. Supporting Argument

Some interpreters cling to the ordinary day view because that is what they were taught in their youth, or because they think ordinary days magnify the Creator more than long ages or revelatory days. Beyond those considerations, four major arguments have been advanced in support of the literal interpretation of the days.

*1. Word meaning (yôm).* Standard Hebrew lexicons agree that the primary meaning of *yôm* is that of a natural day. The Septuagint rendered *yôm* by the Greek *hermera* (not *aion* or *ainos*), which refers to the natural day (sunrise to sunset) or to the civil day of twenty-four hours. The word *yôm* is used in the singular 1,150x. Clearly in 1,048 places it has the primary meaning. When used with a numeral in the OT (359x outside Gn 1) the word *yôm* always means an ordinary day.[130] The context in 1:5 defines *yôm* as the light period in the suc-

---

[129] W. Booth, "Days of Genesis 1: Literal or Non-Literal?" *JATS* 14 (Spring 2003): 101-120; J.L. Duncan III, and D. Hall. "The 24-Hour View," in *The Genesis Debate: Three Views on the Days of Genesis*, 21-66; T. Fretheim, "Were the Days of Creation Twenty-Four Hours Long? YES," in *The Genesis Debate*, ed. Ronald Youngblood (1990); R. Grigg, "How Long were the Days of Genesis 1? *CEN*, 19(Dec 1996): 23-25; _____. "Naming the Animals: All in a Day's Work for Adam," *CEN* 18(1996): 46-9; G. Hasel, "The 'Days' of Creation in Genesis 1: Literal 'Days' or Figurative 'Periods/Epochs' of Time?" *Origins* 21 (1994): 5-38; J.W. Kloz, *Genes, Genesis and Evolution* (Menlo Park, CA: W.A. Benjamin, 1972); R. McCabe, "A Defense of Literal Days in the Creation Week," *Detroit Baptist Seminary Journal* 5 (2000): 97-123; J. Pipa, Jr., "From Chaos to Cosmos: A Critique of the Non-Literal Day Interpretation," in *Did God Create in Six Days?* ed. Joseph Pipa and David Hall (Taylors, SC: Southern Presbyterian Press, 1999), 153-198; P. Zimmerman, *Darwin, Evolution and Creation* (St. Louis: Concordia, 1959).

[130] See the remarkable parallel in wording in Nm 7:12-88. Possible exceptions to *yôm* + numeral = ordinary day are Zech 3:9; 14:7; Hos 6:2. Arthur Williams, *Creation Research Annual*, (Creation Research Society, 1965), 10.

cessive periods of light and darkness. Gn 1:14 states that God created the lights to divide the day from the night, and that they were to be for signs, for seasons, for days and for years. If the days were ages, then what were the years? If a day is an age, then what is a night? Marcus Dods commented: "If the word *day* in this chapter does not mean a period of 24 hours, the interpretation of Scripture is hopeless."[131]

*2. Evening/morning formula.* The division of the days into *evening* and *morning* is proof of ordinary days.[132] The terms are used together elsewhere in the OT 31x. In addition one or the other of the terms is used in conjunction with the word *day* 38x other than in the creation account. All references point clearly to a literal solar day. In no way can the phrase *evening and morning* legitimately be applied to anything corresponding to a geological period.[133]

*3. Exodus 20:11.* Moses himself wrote a commentary on the days in Gn 1. He wrote: "In six days Yahweh made the heavens and the earth, the sea, and all that is in them." The plural *days* (*yāmîm*) is used over 700x in the OT always in reference to natural days. According to Ex 20:11 the Hebrew pattern for the week was to prevail *on account of* (*'al kēn*) that was the divine pattern originally.

*4. Manner of creation.* The acts of creation are represented in the text as being instantaneous. God speaks and things come into being. There is, therefore, no need for more than one day for any stage of the creation.

---

[131]"Genesis," *Expositor's Bible*, ed. Roger Nicoll (Grand Rapids: Eerdmans, 1948), 4-5.
[132]See Dan 8:14, 26 for similar language.
[133]Morris, *Record*, 55f.

## B. Relevant Considerations

The Christian church has nowhere dogmatized the present measurement of time (twenty-four hours) for the creation days. While it is true that most writers who have a high regard for Scripture embrace the literal day view, this is not inevitably true. Some staunchly conservative commentators who hold to the inerrancy of Scripture opt for the framework or long-age view. On the other hand, some very liberal commentators champion the literal day view only to discredit the entire narrative. The following citation from *Interpreter's Bible* is illustrative of the latter approach:

> There can be no question but that by 'day' the author means just what we mean—the time required for one revolution of the earth on its axis. Had he meant an eon he would certainly, in view of his fondness for numbers, have stated the number of millenniums each period embraces.[134]

## C. Harmony with External Data

Those who hold that the Gn 1 days were ordinary days generally argue that the earth is much younger than most scholars in the scientific disciplines propose. Creation happened miraculously and suddenly only a few thousand years ago. How do those who hold to the ordinary day view explain the fossils, the seams of coal and oil deposits that orthodox science claims were formed over millions of years? The ordinary day people generally employ one or more of the following arguments to bridge the time gap.

*1. Apparent age.* The essence of this theory is that the earth was created with fossils and strata. Every object of creation has two times: real time—the actual age at creation; and ideal time—the age that it appears to be. Creation necessitated that God make things look older

---

[134]C.A. Simpson, *Interpreter's Bible* ed. G. Buttrick (New York: Abingdon, 1962), 1:471.

than they actually were. One minute after he was created, Adam looked like a fully mature man. In real time he was one minute old. If God created animals and plants fully mature they too would appear much older than they actually were. To suggest, however, that God put fossils in the rocks comes close to suggesting that God was being deliberately deceptive.

*2. Flood geology.* To explain the phenomena that appear to require an earth of enormous age some writers have developed an alternative geological paradigm.[135] The basic idea of Flood geology is this: the various rock strata, which give appearance of great age to the earth, were actually created by the enormous pressure of the Great Flood in relatively recent years. God flooded the earth through direct or indirect means (e.g., an approaching astronomical body). Huge waves rushing at a thousand miles an hour swept over the earth. When the waves lost their velocity they deposited the mud, dirt, and animals as huge strata. Under pressure of water and other strata laid down on top, the mud strata hardened into rock. The various strata reveal the distribution of plants and animals before the Flood. Man had fled to the high hills and is thus found in the highest strata.

Not all Bible believers have embraced the tenets of Flood Geology.[136] The basic question raised by critics of the theory is this: Could a single flood lasting but a few weeks or months have produced all the deposits that have been discovered? For example, at Yellowstone

---

[135]George McCrudy Price, *The New Geology* (1923); Byron Nelson, *The Deluge Story in Stone* (1968); Alfred Rehwinkel, *The Flood* (1957); Harold Clark, *The New Diluvialism* (1946); John Whitcomb and Henry Morris, *The Genesis Flood* (1961).

[136]E.g., see Davis Young, *Creation and the Flood* (1977). Others opposed to Flood geology: J. Lawrence Kulp, "Deluge Geology," *JASA* 2(Jan 1950): 1-15. R.M. Allen, "The Evaluation of Radioactive Evidence on the Age of the Earth," *JASA* 4(1952): 11-20. F.E. Zeuner, *Dating the Past: An Introduction to Geochronology* (3rd ed. 1952).

there are two thousand feet of exposed strata representing some eighteen successive forests wiped out by lava. Why are fossilized human remains never found among the fossilized plants and animals? Does this not suggest that these strata were produced before human life appeared?

*3. Gap theory.* As noted in an earlier ch, some students postulate a huge gap between the first two vv of the Bible. Geological history is placed in that gap. The six days of creation are regarded as days of re-creation in relatively recent times.

*4. Interspersed gaps.* Some writers have proposed that the days in Gn 1 were ordinary days, as the text seems to imply. Between the creative days, however, were periods of unspecified duration. The six days represent six great creative interjections into earth history. This view is sometimes called the transcendent-activity or progressive creationism view.[137] Carl Henry comments on this view as follows:

> This view supplies a novel bridge between the day and age theories. It does not deny the vast antiquity of origins, nor the slow providential development of new forms, yet it finds in the Genesis account the divine fiat acts which punctuated this process at dramatic intervals.[138]

## View Five
## LOCAL CREATION

The local creation view holds that in Gn the six days are not describing the creation of the entire planet, but only the Mediterranean world or the Promised Land. This view was originally put forward by John Pye Smith. During the six days God reorganized the Medi-

---
[137]See Newman and Eckelmann, *Genesis One*, 64-65.
[138]Carl F.H. Henry, *Contemporary Evangelical Thought*, 277.

terranean world after the total destruction of the original creation in Gn 1:2. Geology tells of the history of the earth; Gn tells of a special creation by God only a few thousand years ago. Since Gn and geology are speaking about different creations there is no conflict between the two.

A recent variation of the local creation view was put forward by John Sailhamer.[139] The land in Gn 1:2ff is the same as the Garden of Eden in Gn 2. Furthermore, the Garden of Eden is the same as the Promised Land. Gn 1:1 describes the creation of the universe billions of years ago. The rest of Gn 1-2 describes how God created a special land for his people.

The theory of local creation cheapens Gn 1 and flies in the face of what appears to be the obvious intention of the text. Furthermore, geologic research in the Mediterranean world shows no evidence of recent renovation.

# CONCLUSION

Whatever one's conclusion about the nature of the Gn 1 days, there are some important truths conveyed by the seven-day framework. First, Gn 1 teaches that God creates time as well as matter. Second, God creates *with* time, not in an instant. Third, God creates *in* time. He enters into his work. Fourth, God completed his creation in a time-span.

---

[139] John Sailhamer, *Genesis Unbound*, 1996.

# 7
# FORMING THE EARTH
# Gn 1:3-13

In Gn 1:2 the text indicates that the earth was *tōhû*, *unformed*. During the first three days of the creation week the Creator removed that condition step by step. He formed the earth. The verbs *separate* and *gather* characterize the first three days. These are verbs that speak of formation.

## PRELIMINARY CONSIDERATIONS

### A. Beginning of Day One

At what point in Gn 1 does the first creative day begin? Leupold holds that the first day begins in 1:1. In support of this view is the mention in 2:1 of *the heavens* in the summary statement of the work of the six days. Allusion to the heavens in such a summary statement presupposes that 1:1 is part of the first creative day (Morris). If one regards 1:1 as a summary statement (as many do) then the first day of creation may have begun in 1:2. More likely, however, is the view that day one begins in 1:3 with the words *and God said*.

If day one begins in 1:3, then a second question becomes relevant. How long before creation week was the universe (*the heavens and the earth*) created (1:1)? The text does not answer this question. See previous discussion of the date of the beginning. Perhaps an analogy will illustrate what Gn 1 seems to be saying. A potter first gathers his materials, and then later begins shaping the pot on the potter's wheel. So God, the Master Potter, first created the "raw materials" for the earth (1:2), and then at the appropriate creative moment, began to form and fill the earth in six literal days.

The idea that God *formed* the earth from previously created materials finds support from two directions. First, The emphasis in 1:3ff is on God's creating by differentiation or separation involving previous created materials. Second, Gn 2 supports the concept that God create new things from previously created raw materials. He created man from the dust/clay, and woman from the rib of man.

### B. Focus of the First Triad

As noted earlier, Gn 1:2 signaled the transition from concern about the origin of the universe as a whole to this planet. In the first triad of days earth is described from the perspective of the three-fold habitat of this planet, viz. *heavens, earth* and *sea*. It is this threefold habitat that is the object of God's creative power during the entire six days. During the first three of the days the threefold habitat is shaped and made suitable for life. Likewise, Ex 20:11 indicates that in six days God create the heavens and earth and the sea—the threefold habitat of this planet, not the galactic universe. Gn 1:1 speaks of the creation of the universe; the rest of Gn 1 focuses on the development of planet earth.

# FIRST DAY OF FORMING
# Gn 1:3-5

The first words of God on the first day of formation shatter the silence, penetrate the darkness and signal the beginning of something new.

### A. Declaration (1:3a)

*1. Nature of divine speech:* **And God said.** The language is anthropomorphic. God does not speak in physical sounds or in anything analogous to a particular human language. Nonetheless, he does speak; he does communicate. The Creator is also a Communicator! It pleased him, in order to create, to break the silence.

In three successive vv Gn sets forth three foundational theological concepts. In 1:1 the omnipotent power of God is in view. In 1:2 it is his providential presence, and in 1:3 the point stressed is God's desire to communicate.

Biblical writers use anthropomorphic language probably because man was created in the image of God. Yet the OT never equates the reality of God with any human analogy (Isa 40:25; Hos 11:9). Without question the fundamental truth about God is that he is the *living* God (Jer 10:10). Because God lives, men can speak of him as they would speak of a living person. The converse is also true. By attributing to God the attributes of a living person, men are reminded that he is the *living* God.

God speaks 9x in Gn 1. By speaking God accomplishes several things. First, he reveals his "heart," his desire and his will. Second, in communication God demonstrates his intelligence. Third, the divine speech in Gn 1 demonstrates God's authority and underscores his power. Fourth, by speaking during creation week God establishes the expectation that he can and will communicate with mankind.

*2. Divine fiat (1:3b).* **Let there be light!** The initial divine speech takes the form of a fiat. In the Hebrew this fiat consists of only two powerful words, $y^e h\hat{\imath}$ '$\hat{o}r$. God has only to speak in order to make profound changes in this planet. "God spoke and it was" (Ps 33:9). For nonmaterial things Elohim's mandate is unaddressed. Nonetheless, the order is carried out instantly. There is total silence regarding the nature of the matter upon which the divine word acted (if there was any). This is not a word of magic, but the expression of the omnipotent, sovereign and unchallengeable will of the transcendent God.

The Apostle Paul quotes this first fiat in 2 Cor 4:6 as an illustration of the power in which spiritual light illumines the hearts of believers in Christ.

### B. Implementation (1:3c)

*And there was light.* In the case of the first day the writer uses the simple two-word fulfillment formula *vay$^e$hî 'ôr*, which could also be translated "and light came into being." Probably God's presence was the source of light on the first day of creation. First, the text hints that this is the case. In 1:4 God himself *separated the light from the darkness*, while in Gn 1:18 it is the luminaries that are to *separate the light from the darkness*. Initally God himself performed the function that he delegated to the sun and moon on day four.

Second, Ps 104:2, which parallels the first day of creation, furnishes another clue. The Psalmist depicts God as "covering himself with light as with a garment."

Third, any thought that God cannot be the light source and at the same time divide the light from the darkness is removed by Ex 14:19-20. In that passage the angel of God and the pillar of cloud moved between the armies of Israel and Egypt. "Throughout the night the cloud brought darkness to the one side and light to the other."

Fourth, Gn 1 is theocentric (God-centered). Viewing God as the source of light for days 1-3 fulfills the theocentric purposes of the writer.

### C. Significance

What is the purpose of the teaching that a light source for earth existed before sun, moon or stars? There are both scientific and polemic ramifications.

*1. Scientific ramifications.* Some critics have accused Moses of error in affirming the creation of light prior to the creation of luminaries on day four. Certain popular cosmological theories (e.g., the Nebular Hypothesis) also teach that light existed prior to the sun. Only anti-biblical prejudice can charge Moses with error while at the same time touting a scientific theory that says the same thing. How could Moses have known that it was possible to have light apart from the sun? Either Moses was as learned in the sciences as modern astronomers or he was inspired by the Creator.

Aviezer links the command to bring forth light to the Big Bang that astronomers think created the universe. At that moment there appeared out of nothing an enormous source of energy called the primeval fireball. The amount of energy in that fireball was so enormous that it became the source of all matter that now exists in the entire universe. Matter existed in the form of "plasma" that trapped the light. When this "plasma" was suddenly transformed into atoms and molecules the light began to "shine" visibly. This corresponds to God separating the light from the darkness. Aviezer documents that scientists refer to this event in terms formally found only in theology books, viz. "creation from nothing."[140]

Linking the Big Bang to day one seems to contradict v 1. That is where the universe was created out of nothing. Gn 1:2 zooms in on the earth. The light in 1:3 refers to light that illuminated the primeval earth until that function was assumed by the sun and moon on day four. Therefore the light in v 3 has nothing to do with the theoretical Big Bang.

*2. Polemic ramifications.* The revelation that light existed before the sun and moon undercuts the theological tenets of sun and moon worship. For the writer of Gn

---

[140]Nathan Aviezer, *In the Beginning; Biblical Creation and Science* (Hoboken, NJ: KTAV, 1990), 9-15.

1 sun and moon were but created objects to which certain functions were assigned. For him light can and did exist independently of these bodies. The teaching of Gn 1:3 that God functioned as the original light source served to deter worship of heavenly luminaries.

Sailhamer has put forward a curious interpretation of the first creative day. He argues that *let there be light* is simply a figurative way of describing sunrise on the first day. He points to other passages using *light* to describe sunrise (Ex 10:23; Neh 8:3; Gn 44:3). Sailhamer does not believe that this v describes the first of all sunrises. Rather he believes this particular sunrise is mentioned because it initiated the week in which God prepared a special land (the garden) for the man and the woman. If Sailhamer is right, however, then what did God accomplish on the first day? Absolutely nothing!

### D. Evaluation (1:4a)

***And Elohim saw that the light was good.*** The verb *saw* (r. *r'h*) is used 7x of God in Gn 1. Clearly the writer wished to stress this point. Unlike the idols that have eyes and cannot see (Dan 5:23), the Creator sees all. Throughout the Book of Gn and the Pentateuch the activity of "seeing" is continually put at the center of the author's concept of God. Hagar gave him the name El Roi, the God who sees (Gn 16:13). In the crucial ch 22 Abraham called God *Yahweh Yir'eh*, lit., "Yahweh will see" (Gn 22:14).[141]

In Gn 1 the term *good* probably has a narrow sense. What is *good* is what is regarded as beneficial to man. So the emphasis throughout the ch is not only that God knows what is good for man, he has provided all that is good for him. This emphasis forms the backdrop to the account in ch 3 when man foolishly regarded what God

---

[141] Sailhamer, *EBC*, loc.

had forbidden him to be as *good* (3:6). The divine evaluation of the light depicts God as Judge, as well as Landlord.[142]

Only here and in 1:31 is the object of God's delight specifically named. The formula means that light was adequate for the purpose that God intended. The statement invites the question, How is light a blessing from God? Light illuminates. It makes possible the beauty of color. Light is essential for the processes of photosynthesis, photography and photocells. Infra-red and ultraviolet light therapy is treatment for certain maladies. Because of the property of illumination light sometimes symbolizes God.[143]

### E. Explanation (1:4b)

*And Elohim separated the light from the darkness.* The separations of the first days serve the cause of order. The v teaches that the Creator is not a God of disorder (1 Cor 14:33). Separations remove confusion. They are foundational to classification by categories. All created things have their proper place. The Creator is the great Organizer.

The theme of God as the Creator of order is found throughout Scripture. God imposed a limit on the sea (Job 38:10f; Ps 104:9; Prov 8:29). He specified the distinction between clean and unclean animals (Lv 20:24-26). Non-biblical religion fosters a fascination with intermixture—a longing for dissolution of all differences.[144] God's law, however, prohibited the mixing of kinds (Lv 10:19; Dt 22:9-11).

The light source in 1:3 did not envelop the earth; it shone upon the earth from one angle. All of the darkness

---

[142] Kenneth Mathews, *Genesis 1-11:26*, The New American Commentary (Broadman & Holman, 2001), 146.
[143] Ps 27:1; Mic 7:8; Mt 4:16; Jn 1:5; 8:12; 9:5; 1 Jn 1:5.
[144] See excellent discussion of this point in Blocher, *In the Beginning*, 72.

of 1:2 was not removed by the appearance of light in 1:3. Light now penetrated that darkness; the two existed alongside each other.

The verb *separated* (*bādal* in the Hiphil) appears 31x in the OT. It means to set apart from each other things that properly function independently, things which if mingled contaminate or render dysfunctional. The verb is used of separating the holy from the unholy or the more holy from the less holy (Lv 10:10), the people of Yahweh from the people of the world (Lv 20:24), and Levites from Israelites (Nm 8:14). Light and darkness do not belong together. Separate, however, both are vital in the function of God's earth.

The separation of light and darkness should not be viewed as a separate act following the creation of light, but as a commentary on the consequences of the creation of the light. The light was focused on half of the planet, thus automatically creating the separation from the darkness. A parallel occurred on the second day when the creation of the expanse resulted in a separation of the waters.

### F. Designation (1:5a)

***And Elohim called the light day and the darkness he called night.*** By naming the light and the darkness God was asserting sovereignty over both. Perfect order requires hierarchy as well as rigid separations. This hierarchy is expressed in Gn 1 in four ways: mandates, benedictions, evaluations, and namings. Since both light and darkness are named, both must be good. Since the light, however, is specifically named as *good*, light has the priority over darkness.

There was yet another function of the naming process. Other examples of God's bestowing of names indicate that names are predictive of outcomes. God made people to experience or become what the given name implied (e.g., Gn 17:15). By naming the light *day* God made the light to become day. Similarly the naming of the darkness *night* made the darkness to become night.

### G. Conclusion of Day One (1:5b)

*And it became evening and it became morning, one day.* A remnant of the primal darkness (v 2) is retained for the benefit of man. Each *evening* (followed by darkness) serves to illustrate something of what the world was like before God spoke the word that launched the shaping of earth.

*1. Temporal formula.* With the creation of light the first morning began; then it *became* (r. *hāyāh*) evening. Finally when it had once again become morning, one day was complete. There is in this formula, as Leupold puts it, "the conclusion of a progression."[145] With evening the creative work ceased. Evening merges into night. From here on out God's creative activity will be in the light, not in the night.

*2. Implications.* The temporal formula has four implications. First, as noted earlier, this formula suggests that the writer intended his readers to attribute to the word *day* its normal meaning. Second, the language suggests that in earth's earliest ages the days were regarded as beginning and ending with sunrise. The Mosaic Law later will change the beginning of a new day to evening. Third, the formula implies the rotation of the earth. Fourth, in the act of creating the earth, Elohim also created time. He initiated the fundamental rhythm of the life of mankind.

*3. Definition.* The Hebrew has a cardinal number (*one*) not the ordinal (*first*). Neither the number nor the noun *day* has the definite article. It is true that a cardinal number can function as an ordinal when it is used for the

---

[145]Leupold, *Exposition,* 57.

first day of a specific month or the first year of a king's reign, but only then when the accompanying noun is definite. The usual translation *the first day* (NRSV; NIV; NKJV; NJB) is derived solely from the context. Much to be preferred is the translation of NJPS "a first day" or even better "one day" (NASB). The primary emphasis in the wording is not enumeration but definition.[146] Night terminates with morning. When morning was reached one day concluded and a second day began.

*4. Significance.* In a widely distributed essay entitled "Seven Reasons Why a Scientist Believes in God,"[147] A. Cressy Morrison pointed out the significance of the precise timing of earth's rotation. If the earth rotated at one tenth of its present rate our days and nights would be increased tenfold. During the long days the sun would burn up all vegetation; if any survived, it would freeze during the long night.

# SECOND DAY OF FORMING
# Gn 1:6-8

Based on what transpired on the second creative day one must conclude that prior to this day waters in the oceans and in the clouds were together on the surface of the earth. Perhaps the idea is that all the water was in the form of vapor that hung like a blanket over the earth.

## A. Declaration (1:6)

The second creative word consists of two clauses. The first clause is a mandate, the second sets forth the purpose for the mandate.

*1. Fiat (1:6a):* **Then Elohim said, Let there be an expanse in the midst of the waters.** This fiat orders a

---
[146]A.E. Steinmann, "*'echād* as an Ordinal Number and the Meaning of Genesis 1:5," *JETS*, 45(Dec 2002): 577-84.
[147]Published in *Readers Digest*. Currently available on multiple websites.

second stage of separation or organization. The *waters* mentioned here are the same as the *waters* mention in 1:2.

The term *expanse* (*rāqîaʻ*) is much discussed. The Septuagint translated the word by *stereoma*, a word that connotes something that is solid or firm. This led to the rendering "firmament" in KJV and ASV. For this reason some insist that *rāqîaʻ* refers to a solid dome over the earth. The term is taken to indicate that the Hebrews embraced the erroneous view that the universe is three storied.

Pagans of Moses' world believed that the earth was covered with a solid dome with holes in it through which rains came upon the earth. The earth itself was flat held up by pillars. Beneath the earth was a geographical place called Sheol where the dead reside.[148] It is difficult to believe, however, that Moses would have used such an erroneous heathen concept.

The idea that the Hebrews accepted pagan notions of a three-storied universe has been refuted effectively by R. Laird Harris.[149] He makes the following points. First, nowhere does the Bible state or imply that the *rāqîaʻ* is solid. This idea comes from the LXX and Vulgate, but not the Hebrew. Second, the heavens are clearly said to be like a curtain or a scroll that can be rolled up (Isa 34:4; 40:22). Third, the word *windows* (*ᵃrubbāh*) is a special Hebrew word, not the more common word (*challôn*). In the OT barley (2 Kgs 7:2), trouble (Isa 24:18) and blessing (Mal 3:10) are said to come through the heavenly windows. So it is not just sunshine and rain that are said to come through the holes in the dome.

---

[148] Paul H. Seely, "The Three-Storied Universe," *JASA* (Mar 1969): 18-22.

[149] A series of three articles in *BETS* 4(1961): 129-35; 5(1962):11-17; 11(1968): 177-9. Diagrams supposedly displaying the Hebrew concept the world appear in Elliott, *Message*, 26; and B. Vawter, *A Path through Genesis* (New York: Sheed & Ward, 1956), 40.

Surely, then, the heavenly windows are metaphorical. Fourth, the waters under the earth might refer to waters below the shoreline where the fish dwell (Dt 4:18). Fifth, Sheol often refers simply to the afterlife without implications of geographical location. Since burial was connected with the dead, sometimes poetically Sheol is depicted as beneath the earth. Sixth, while some poetic passages describe the "foundations" of the earth as resting on "pillars," Harris notes that both of these words are used metaphorically. The Scriptures also speak of the earth as resting on nothing (Job 26:7).

*2. Purpose (1:6b):* **And let it separate the waters from the waters.** The injection of an expanse (space) in the midst of the vapor surrounding the earth produced a separation of the waters. This resulted in upper waters (clouds) and lower or surface waters. This organization of waters continued into the third day when the water was gathered into seas and the dry land appeared.

**B. Explanation** (1:7)

The simple fulfillment formula of day one is replaced by a complex sentence consisting of two clauses. The first clause describes the divine action. The second clause sets forth the result of the divine action. This twofold statement of divine action corresponds to the twofold mandate of the previous v. This could be taken to mean that Elohim fulfilled his own mandate. It also could suggest that the mandate should be regarded more as an expression of sovereign will.

Joining divine action to creative mandate accomplishes two things. First, it underscores the supernatural origin of the expanse. Second, the coupling of word and work indicates the greater complexity of the creative work of day two.

*1. What God did (1:7a):* **So Elohim made the expanse.** The verb *made* (*'āsāh*) is used for the first time.

Often this verb means to "set right or to make suitable." According to Sailhamer, God did not create from nothing the expanse on the second day. Rather he arranged for the clouds over the land (garden) so as to provide rain for vegetation that would appear on day three. In the context of creation, however, the verb *make* and the verb *create* are used interchangeably (cf. Gn 5:1).

The *expanse* (*rāqîaʻ*) comes from a root that means "to beat out or stamp out." If gold or silver is stamped out it becomes very thin. Thus *rāqîaʻ* acquired the idea of thinness. In the creation narrative *rāqîaʻ* clearly refers to something very thin that separates the clouds from the oceans. The term *rāqîaʻ* must be a reference to the visible atmosphere or sky.[150] One of the best comments on the term is found in the Douai Version: "the whole space between the earth and the highest stars, the lower part of which divides the waters that are upon the earth from those that are above the clouds."

2. *What God accomplished (1:7b):* **And [Elohim] separated the waters that were below in respect to the expanse from the waters that were above in respect to the expanse.** When God made the *rāqîaʻ* he simultaneously organized the waters into two divisions, upper and lower. The Hebrew does not necessarily imply that some water was above the expanse itself. It only implies that part of the water was at a lower level and part at a higher level.[151] Perhaps this separation was achieved by causing some water to ascend to become the clouds. Whether the powerful light that came into being on day one had anything to do with this massive and rapid evaporation of water cannot be determined. In any case, the clouds

---

[150]The verb root is used in the sense of *stretch out, spread out* or *beat thin* in 2 Sam 22:43; Isa 42:5; 44:24; and Ex 39:3.

[151]Aalders (*BSC*, 60) cites 2 Chr 26:19 as evidence that the construction *mēʻal* can mean *by* or *at* rather than *above*.

are positioned over the earth so as eventually to provide rain.

### C. Implementation (1:7c)

*And it was so* or *and it came to be*. In the Hebrew this is a two-word fulfillment formula: $v^ay^eh\hat{\imath}$ $k\bar{e}n$. This formula underscores that again on day two the will and work of the Creator were unobstructed in any way. The sequence of the assertions is bold (in the light of pagan cosmogonies) and clear. God willed it; God did it; and that is the way it happened. There is in this short formula a stubborn, uncompromising insistence. Biblical theology will not compromise with naturalism or paganism.

### D. Designation (1:8a)

*And Elohim called the expanse heaven*. As on the first day, naming serves several purposes. First, naming is an assertion of sovereignty. Second, naming indicates an ability and desire to communicate. Third, naming prepares for the later creation of humankind, for among earth creatures only man possesses vocabulary. Fourth, naming parts of creation suggests that language is as much the product of divine creation as material objects.

The act of naming on day two also implies affirmation and approval. Much has been made of the absence of the evaluation formula on day two. The suggestion has been made that God did not declare the expanse (air; atmosphere) *good* because that was the domain of Satan (Job 15:15; 25:5; Eph 6:12; 2:2).

Others have offered a narrative explanation for the absence of the appraisal formula. They argue that the entire creation account is oriented toward God's creation of humankind on the sixth day. What is *good* in Gn 1 is what will benefit the man and the woman. Since man was not designed for flight through the clouds or life in the water there was nothing on day two that directly benefited mankind.[152]

In response to the allegations that what emerged on day two was not *good* in the Gn 1 sense of that term two points can be made. First, alleging that the *expanse* did not directly benefit mankind defines the term too narrowly. If the *expanse* also includes what fills it, viz. air or atmosphere, then clearly it was essential to the existence of mankind. Second, at the conclusion of the creative days there is an all-inclusive statement that God saw everything that he had made and judged it to be *good*. This surely includes the expanse. Therefore, the absence of the evaluation formula on day two has no theological or narrative significance.

God named the expanse *heaven* (*shāmyim*). The term is used in various senses in the Bible. In Gn 1:20 the reference is to the atmospheric heaven where the birds fly. In Gn 1:14 the reference is to the sidereal heaven where the stars are located. The dwelling place of God is also designated *heaven*. Paul designates the abode of God as the third heaven (2 Cor 12:2). Presumably heavens one and two are the heavens mentioned in Gn 1:14 and 1:20.

Clearly the expanse is a blessing to mankind. It provides essential gases (oxygen and carbon dioxide); it provides a shield about the planet from the rays of the sun and bombardment of meteorites; it acts as a carrier for water vapor, seed, and pollen; it provides a warm blanket without which earth would experience a perpetual ice age; it is responsible for aesthetically pleasing twilight and sunrise skies; it enables birds and insects to fly; it permits sound to travel. All of the functions of the expanse are of direct or indirect benefit to mankind.

---

[152]Cf. Sailhamer, *EBC*, loc.

## E. Conclusion of Day Two (1:8b)

*And it became evening, and it became morning, a second day.* The second day concludes with the formula that concluded day one with one exception. The number here is clearly an ordinal and is properly rendered *second*. The lack of the definite article on each of the first five days has been taken to indicate that the days do not necessarily reveal a chronological order of creation.[153] Clearly ordinals with the definite article indicate sequence (cf. Nm 7:12-78). Ordinals without the article appear about 71x in the OT. A survey of these uses indicates that sequence is also implied when the article is not used, except when the ordinal is being used to express a fraction. Therefore, the absence of the definite article on each of the first five days has no implications regarding sequentiality.

Aviezer thinks that day two describes the creation of the solar system. He points out that outer space contains vast quantities of water in the form of frozen ice. It has been estimated that were all the comets of outer space to melt they would supply enough water to fill all the ocean basins on earth more than a thousand times. In addition, there are layers of ice hundreds of miles thick covering some of the outer planets and moons. According to Aviezer, the solar system is the expanse in the midst of the waters.[154]

It is not likely that the expanse created on the second day was the solar system. The focus on the second day is still the earth. The natural explanation is that the expanse refers to earth's atmosphere as explained above.

---

[153]M. Throntveit, in *Genesis Debate*, 53. See also D.A. Sterchi, "Does Genesis 1 Provide a Chronological Sequence?" *JETS* 39 (1996): 529-36.
[154]Aviezer, *In the Beginning*, 21-25.

# THIRD DAY OF FORMING
## Phase One
## Gn 1:9-10

The first triad of days—days of formation—reaches a climax on the third day. This is indicated by the fact that Elohim speaks twice and performs two creative acts. In effect, two days of creative work took place in one day. The description of the third day unfolds in two phases that parallel one another as displayed in Chart 10.

**A. Declaration** (1:9a, b)

*1. Fiat (1:9a):* ***Then Elohim said, Let the waters below the heavens be gathered into one place.*** Day three begins with a two-clause fiat of forming. The first expresses the will of God regarding how the surface of the earth should be reconfigured. This is a vivid way of describing the location of the "seas" that surround the dry ground on all sides and into which the rivers flow.

| Chart 10 <br> Overview of the Third Day ||
|---|---|
| **Phase One** <br> 1:9-10 | **Phase One** <br> 1:11-12 |
| Fiat of Forming | Fiat of Furnishing |
| Simple Fulfillment Formula | Simple Fulfillment Formula |
| Double Act of Naming | Verification Statement |
| Evaluation Formula | Evaluation Formula |
| Temporal Formula <br> 1:13 ||

*2. Purpose (1:9b):* ***And let the dry land appear.*** The second clause sets forth the divine intent of the reconfiguration. This v seems to have been on the mind of the Psalmist when he wrote: The earth was "founded … upon the seas" (Ps 24:2). Peter must have been thinking of this v when he declared that the earth was "formed out of water" (2 Pet 3:5).

The point of the third act of separation/organization is that the waters have a place upon this planet. The seas are not to cross the boundaries God set for them on the third day of creation (cf. Ps 104:7-9; Jer 5:22).

### B. Implementation (1:9c)

*And it was so* or *and it came to be*. The precise two-word fulfillment formula (*vay$^e$hî kēn*) that was used on day two documents that the sovereign and creative will of Elohim was instantly carried out. By spoken word alone Elohim effected this major transformation of the earth's surface. The mighty oceans obeyed his powerful word.

### C. Designation (1:10)

In the first phase of day three a double naming serves the purpose of amplifying and verifying the simple fulfillment formula. Previously Elohim has named the light and the darkness *day* and *night* respectively (1:5); and he has named the expanse *heaven* (1:8). On the third day two more aspects of the created order are named by Elohim, viz., the dry land and the gathering of waters.

*1. Dry land (1:10a):* **And Elohim called the dry land earth.** The term *dry land* (*yabbāšāh*) suggests that the divine word caused the ground to appear in a dry condition. *Earth* (*'erets*) is used for the third time in the narrative, and in yet a different sense. In 1:1 the earth was part of a merism depicting the entire universe. In 1:2 the earth refers to the entire planet. Now the same term is applied to the antithesis of the gathering of waters (i.e., the seas). Later in Gn 1 this will be the realm inhabited by beast and man. This earth and all that inhabits it belongs to Yahweh (Ps 24:1-2).

Moses need not be interpreted to mean that all the present dry land became free from water on the third creative day. It is clear from the geological record that mountain building took place in stages. The geological record is supported by eyewitness accounts of the formation of the island of Surtsey in the North Atlantic in 1963.[155]

The birth of Surtsey has such far reaching implications that a citation from a close observer is appropriate. He published this account within a year of the event.

> When the news of a volcanic eruption in the sea off the Vestmann Islands reached the ears of Icelandic geologists in the early morning of November 14th, 1963, some of them had to have it repeated to them, and received it with a pinch of salt all the same. And when they now wander about the island which was being born then, they find it hard to believe that this is an island whose age is still measured in months, not years. An Icelander who has studied geology and geomorphology at foreign universities is later taught by experience in his own homeland that the time scale he had been trained to attach to geological developments is misleading when assessments are made of the forces—constructive and destructive—which have moulded (*sic*) and are still moulding (*sic*) the face of Iceland. What elsewhere may take thousands of years may be accomplished here in one century. All the same he is amazed whenever he comes to Surtsey, because the same development may take a few weeks or even a few days here. ... On Surtsey only a few months have sufficed for a landscape to be created which is so varied and mature that it is almost beyond belief.[156]

Likewise, Moses need not be made to say that all the land mass was configured in exactly the same way that it appears today. The waters were to be gathered into *one*

---

[155] The amazing story of the birth of Surtsey was reported in *National Geographic*, May 1965; *Life* April 3, 1964; Dec 13, 1963; *Popular Science* Oct 1965; *Saturday Review* June 3, 1965.

[156] Eyjan Nyja, *I Atlantschafi*. Almenna Bokafelagid, 1964.

*place* (1:9), not many places. This suggests that in the beginning there was one land mass surrounded by water.

The idea of continental drift is credited to a German scientist named Alfred Lothar Wegener (1880-1930). Wegener was intrigued by the apparent fit of the coastlines of Africa and South America. In 1912 he suggested that the continents had once been a single land mass, which he called *Pangaea* (*All Earth*) encircled by ocean. At some point the supercontinent splintered and the fragments plowed through the sea floor to their present, still-changing positions. Initially the theory had few supporters, because it did not explain how the land masses maneuvered through the rocky bottom of the ocean.

In the last half of the twentieth century many geologists embraced the theory called plate tectonics. This theory, that the continents are in motion, has demanded the reinterpretation of almost every bit of geologic data gathered during the preceding two centuries of research. The modern version of continental drift holds that the land masses are riding along with parts of the ocean floor aboard mobile plates.[157]

The theory that the land mass on earth was once part of a supercontinent has serious implications for several of the thorny problems of biblical protology, including such issues as the extent of the Flood, and the distribution of animal and human population before and after the Flood.

 *2. Gathering of waters (1:10b):* **And the gathering of the waters he [Elohim] called seas**. The account is cheapened if, following Sailhamer, *the seas* are restricted to those in and around the Promised Land. The natural interpretation is to take *the seas* to refer to the world's oceans.

---

[157]Dava Sobel, "Notes on the Plate Tectonics Revolution," *Harvard Magazine* (Sept 1976): 24-27.

The world's oceans are vast. There are 335 million cubic miles of water in the seas—about 71% of earth's surface. The ratio of water to land results in evaporation that is sufficient in volume to produce the annual rainfall. The average depth of the ocean is 14,000 feet or 2.5 miles; but there are chasms in the oceans up to seven miles. There are 1,400,000,000,000,000 tons of water held in their proper bounds by the regular rotation of the moon. The oceans are an important source of man's food. Minerals (e.g., iodine, magnesium, etc.) are found there in abundance. A river called the Gulf Stream flows through the ocean. When it leaves the Gulf of Mexico it has a temperature of 86 degrees. Its heat makes possible the temperate climate of North America and Northern Europe.

## THIRD DAY OF FORMING
### Phase Two
### Gn 1:11-13

The earth is not considered fully formed until vegetation appears on it. Vegetation is separated from other living things in the creation week for three reasons. First, by placing it in the second phase of day three, vegetation is highlighted as the climax of the first triad of days. Second, vegetation is stationary and for that reason unlike the living creatures brought into being on days five and six. Third, land vegetation is essential in the food chain for earth's creatures.

**A. Declaration** (1:11a, b)

*1. Verb (1:11a):* **Then Elohim said, Let the earth vegetate vegetation.** The filling or furnishing of the earth begins with a detailed fiat that orders vegetation to appear on the newly formed dry land. This is the fourth of the creative words in Gn 1. *Vegetate vegetation* attempts to reproduce the paronomasia of the original. The earth is commanded to *vegetate*, i.e., "sprout" or "produce" (NIV). Although ultimately a divine act, creation sometimes took place through secondary means. Because vegetation is such an important part of the food chain, there is logic in having plants cover the earth prior to the creation of the animals.

2. *Vegetation (1:11b):* **grasses, plants yielding seed, and fruit trees bearing fruit after their kind, with seed in them upon the earth.** Three broad types of vegetation are named in the fiat. They are not intended to be all inclusive, but representative of all vegetation. The order in which the vegetation is mentioned happens to correspond to the sequence of appearance proposed by evolutionary botanists.

First named are the *grasses* (*deše'*), the type of vegetation that serves as ground cover. This includes the mosses.[158]

Second, the earth is to bring forth *plants yielding seed* (*'ēsebh mazrî'a zera'*), i.e., seed bearing vegetation. The grasses in the first category also produce seed. In this second broad category are those plants where the seed is more visible and prominent, i.e., plants that produce seed-bearing pods.

Third, the earth is to bring forth *fruit trees bearing fruit* (*'ēts p$^e$rî 'ōseh p$^e$rî*). Two characteristics of this third broad category of vegetation are mentioned. *With seed in them* means the seed is inside the fruit. The phrase *upon the earth* is too far removed from the verb to be governed by it. This phrase further describes the third broad category. In this case the phrase means "above ground," even "over the ground." The picture is of the limbs of fruit trees loaded with fruit some distance above the ground.

---

[158] Some commentators take *deše'* in this v to be the general term for all vegetation which is then broken down into two broad categories.

Some have questioned whether vegetation can exist without sunlight. There was, however, a light source before the sun began to function. If there is a problem with vegetation appearing before sunlight, it is a greater problem for the day-age proponents. Vegetation could surely survive part of one ordinary day without the sun; but could it survive a long eon without sunlight?

**B. Limitation** (1:11c)

The vegetation is to reproduce *after their kind* (*lᵉmînô*). As God established proper boundaries for the sea, so here he establishes proper boundaries for living things. The suffix is singular, but it is probably a collective referring to all vegetation.

This is the first of ten uses of the noun *kind* (*mîn*) in Gn 1. In the entire OT the term is used 31x, all but once in the Pentateuch. Etymologically the word means "split" or "division." For a noun that appears this number of times there is an amazing consistency in usage. The word *mîn* is always governed by the preposition *lamedh*, meaning "to or in respect to." It is always singular in respect to the life it describes. It is always followed by a possessive suffix.

The use of the term *mîn* (*kind*) ties the plants to the animals created on days five and six. The plants yield seed according to their own kind, much as the birds, fish and land animals bring forth offspring according to their kind. So the writer recognizes vegetation as possessing life, but life of a lower order than that of the creatures that both reproduce and move about.

To what does *mîn* (*kind*) refer? Moving from commonality to less commonality, modern authorities classify organisms into species, genus, family, order, class, sub-phylum, and phylum. The Hebrew *mîn* is not equivalent in meaning to the English word *species*. New spe-

species of plants and animals do come into existence from time to time.

After careful study of the term Payne argued that Hebrew *mîn* is equivalent to the modern classification of *family*.[159] Whatever the exact equivalent of *mîn* in the modern classification system, this divine mandate puts limits on the reproductive capability of living things. While the limitation formula allows for variation within the circle of the *mîn* (*kind*), it rules out evolution from one-cell creature to man.[160]

Plants and later animals are to reproduce *after their kind*. No such language is used of man. Human beings do not come in different kinds. Ethnic, racial, and language differences among humans do not detract from the commonality of the entire human order of being.

### C. Implementation (1:11d)

***And it was so*** or ***and it came to be***. For the second time in this paragraph the narrator employs the simple two-word fulfillment formula (*vay$^e$hî kēn*) to declare that the expressed will of Elohim was executed. This simple statement is amplified and verified by the detailed explanation that follows.

### D. Explanation (1:12a)

***And the earth brought forth vegetation, plants yielding seed after their kind and trees bearing fruit, with seed in them after their kind***. This statement corresponds to the fiat with the following exceptions. First, a new verb is used. *Vegetate* (r. *dš'*) in the fiat becomes *brought forth* (r. *yts'* in Hiphil) in the explanation. There does not appear to be any particular significance in the change of verbs. Second, the limitation formula is stated

---

[159] J. Barton Payne, "The Concept of 'Kinds' in Scripture," *JASA* 10 (June 1958): 18.
[160] Surburg, *Darwin, Evolution and Creation*, 67.

twice making clear that herbs as well as trees reproduced according to *kind*. Third, *of fruit* has disappeared after the word *trees*, since this idea is included in the phrase *bearing fruit*.

Thus the verification statement is close enough to the fiat to communicate precise compliance. It does not, however, mechanically and redundantly reproduce verbatim the language of the fiat. It is worth noting that the plants were created full-grown, able to produce seed and fruit.

Aviezer thinks that day three describes what is called the Permian period of geologic history about 250 million years ago. This was the age of the supercontinent Pangaea, the great Permian ice age, and the proliferation of plant life. The Permian period, however, ended with the mass extinction of perhaps as many as ninety per cent of all animal species.[161] For those trying to force Gn 1 to conform to the geologic ages, here is the rub. No animal life has yet been mentioned as coming into existence on day three.

### E. Evaluation (1:12b)

*And Elohim saw that it was good*. The exact formula from v 10 is repeated.

### F. Conclusion of Day Three (1:13)

*And it became evening, and it became morning, a third day*. The third day concludes with the temporal formula in the same pattern as on day two.

## CONCLUSION

There is a sense in which the creation of the vegetation is transitional in the creative week. Vegetation

---

[161] Aviezer, *In the Beginning*, 31-38.

completes the shaping of the environment in which higher forms of life will reside. Calling forth vegetation upon the earth anticipates what is to follow in two ways. First, though vegetation is an element of the immobile environment, it is at the same time the first inhabitant of the earth. Second, the power of reproduction relates vegetation to the animals and thus anticipates the second triad of days. Clearly the writer did not think of the first triad as a closed or independent unit. For him vegetation has no value in and of itself.

# 8
# FILLING OF THE EARTH
# Gn 1:14-25

The second triad of days focuses on the filling of the earth, the removal of the condition of *bōhû* in 1:2. The theme of reproduction is picked up from day three to become a major theme in the second triad of days. The theme of movement is introduced on day four. Together these two themes are developed on days five and six. The climax of the double theme—movement and reproduction—is reached in Gn 1:28 in the command to *be fruitful and multiply and fill the earth.*

## Day Four
## FIRST DAY OF FILLING
## Gn 1:14-19

The fourth day has a kind of centrality in the creative week. First, in a span of seven days the fourth day is central. The themes employed by the writer for the fourth day are Janus-like. *Light* and *heavens* point back to days one and two. *Signs for seasons* or *festivals* points forward to seventh day with its Sabbath emphasis.

If one is thinking only of the six-day work week, the fourth day also is central. The creative word of the fourth day is the fifth word out of ten. By word count the fourth day completes half the creation account: The total number of words in Days 1-4 is 206 and for days 5-6 it is 205. Word-wise the first half of the creation work ended with the appointment of the heavenly "rulers." The second half of the work week will conclude with the appointment of man to rule over the earth.

## A. Declaration (1:14-15)

The fourth day fiat mandates three functions for the heavenly bodies in respect to earth.

*1. Separating function (1:14a):* **Let lights in the expanse of the heavens separate between day and night.** The language of the fifth creative fiat is more complex than any of the preceding fiats.[162] Literally the Hebrew reads, "Let there be lights...for separating," i.e., let lights separate.[163] The emphasis is not on the initial creation of the lights, but their function. The command assumes that the lights were already in the expanse. Three points stand out in the first clause of the fiat.

First, the word *lights* (*mᵉ'ōrōth*) points to the sun and moon in particular, and to the stars in a more general way. The *light* (singular) of 1:3 now becomes *lights* (plural). It is not clear whether the writer is saying that the luminaries replaced the light of day one, supplemented it, or whether the day one light was now concentrated in the heavenly bodies. It is also possible that the light of the luminaries was the light of 1:3, the sources of which now become discernable on the earth. Thinning of a thick cloud cover may have revealed the sun as a light-bearing object. Some modifications in the intensity of solar heat may have been necessary before the sun could assume its routine functions without harming the life that God was about to create.

Second, the *expanse* is stipulated as the location for the luminaries. The term *expanse* (*rāqîaʽ*) ties the work of day four to that of day two (1:6-7). Some writers assume that the *expanse* in both cases is the same space.

---

[162]The first fiat consisted of one clause, two words (v 3); the second, two clauses, nine words (v 6); the third, two clauses, nine words (v 9); the fourth, one clause, sixteen words (v 11); and the fifth, three clauses, twenty-one words (vv 14-15).

[163]Sailhamer, *EBC*, loc. In v 6 *hāyāh* is used alone, indicating bringing the expanse into existence. Here, however, the syntax is *hāyāh* + *l* + infinitive; cf. GKC, 114h.

The *expanse* of day two, however, is said to be *in the midst of the waters*. That clearly refers to the air or atmosphere separating surface waters from cloud waters. Day four speaks about *the expanse of the heavens*, space beyond the atmosphere, or outer space. If the atmosphere in 1:8 is called *heavens*, now it becomes clear that there are heavens beyond that heavens. In Jewish tradition this was called the second heaven.

The writer makes clear that the luminaries were to function *in the expanse* of the heavens, not merely "in the heavens." Had he said merely, "in the heavens," people of ancient times might have regarded this as an affirmation that Elohim created the astral deities that inhabitant the celestial realms.

Third, the fiat stipulates that luminaries function *to divide the day from the night*. The three pairs of evenings and mornings that preceded the fourth day were made possible by the rotation of earth in respect to an unspecified light source. Now the function of that initial light is delegated to (or concentrated in) the heavenly bodies. The alternation of day and night is the fundamental rhythm of the planet. Life on earth is adapted to this rhythm.

2. *Measuring functions (1:14b)*: **And let them become for signs and for seasons, and for days and years.** The second clause of the fifth mandate sets forth the time functions of the luminaries. The luminaries, though not to be worshiped, are useful to the inhabitants of earth, especially as chronometers. At least three measuring functions of the luminaries are spelled out.

First, heavenly bodies serve as *signs* in several legitimate ways in Scripture: miraculous signs (Josh 10:12-14; 2 Chr 32:24), predictive signs (Mt 2; Lk 21:25, 26), evidential signs (Pss 8; 19), weather signs (Mt 16:2, 3), and navigational signs (Acts 27:20). Later

Scripture makes clear that it is a misuse of the heavenly bodies to study them for astrological signs (Jer 10:2).

Second, the heavenly bodies are associated with the *seasons*. The term may refer to agricultural seasons (Hos 2:9, 11; 9:5); seasons for seafaring men (Acts 27:12); and seasons for birds and beasts (Jer 8:7).

Third, the luminaries are useful in measuring time. *Days and years* are linked by sharing a common preposition. Days are the shortest and years the longest periods of time fixed by movements of the heavenly bodies. The entire phrase, however, appears to be the Hebrew way of referring to an extended period of time (cf. Isa 32:10). So the heavenly bodies are to serve for chronological purposes.

Early in human history men used the phases of the moon to define the beginning of months, and the accumulation of months to define years. As early as 3000 BC Sumerian astronomers charted the heavens every day. Patterns in the positions of the stars over time were noted. The length of years was computed. Solar, lunar, and stellar calendars (or combinations of the three) are attested in various civilizations.[164]

Modern man measures time by the stars. The whole celestial system runs on a mighty schedule that varies only by split seconds. This is the basis of correct time. The staff of astronomers at the Naval Observatory checks to see when a fixed point on earth's surface passes under a certain star each night. Four photographs of the star are taken. Some eighty different stars are used over the course of a year. The interval between any two

---

[164]For a very readable account of how sun, moon, and stars were employed by ancient man in calendar-making see Jack Finegan, *Handbook of Biblical Chronology* (1964), 7-25. One example: by observing the movements of the star Sirus the ancient Egyptians determined that a year lasted 365.25 days.

times when a given star is passed is always the same within a tiny fraction of a second.

Probably it is because of the superstitions of the heathen regarding the sun and moon that the writer goes into such detail regarding their functions. Though the details of this purpose statement for the luminaries are debated by the commentaries, the main point is that all functions of the sun and moon have been stipulated by the Creator. These luminaries do not function independently of his will. Sun and moon are but servants carrying out the task assigned by the Almighty.

*3. Illuminating function (1:15a):* **And let them become for lights in the expanse of the heavens to give light on the earth.** The last clause of the fifth creation mandate may simply be a repetition for emphasis. Yet carefully considered this v adds some additional thoughts to the preceding. First, the luminaries are to be *for lights*, that and nothing more. They are not gods to be worshiped or feared. Second, they are *in the expanse of the heavens*. That is their sphere. Beyond the light that they display, they are far removed from the everyday affairs of earth's inhabitants. There is no need, then, to plot one's daily activity according to the position of the luminaries. Third, they exist *to give light on the earth*. While ancient man viewed the sun as deity, and modern man thinks of earth as the stepchild of the sun, the Bible portrays the sun as the servant of the earth. Although physically the solar system is heliocentric, in terms of God's purposes it is geocentric.

**B. Implementation** (1:15b)

*And it was so* or *and it came to be*. This expression marks the end of the author's "report" about what transpired on day four. On day one this simple fulfillment formula followed the fiat (1:3). On day two the explanation is followed by the simple fulfillment formula (1:7).

Biblical Protology

On day three the simple fulfillment formula is used twice, the second time followed by a lengthy explanation (1:9, 11-12). On day four the simple fulfillment formula is followed by an even longer explanation (1:16-18).

## C. Explanation: Making (1:16)

The explanation has two distinct parts, focusing on the God's action of making (v 16), and placing (vv 17-18). The action of making is one sentence in the Hebrew, not three parallel clauses. There are four objects of the verb *made* as indicated by the untranslatable Hebrew particle *'et*.

*1. Two great lights (1:16a):* ***And Elohim made the two great lights.*** Both sun and moon are *great lights* because the apparent sizes of the sun and moon are exactly the same. Although the diameter of the sun is four hundred times larger than the moon, the sun is also four hundred times farther away from earth. This equality of apparent size is most obvious when the disk of the moon completely covers the disk of the sun during a total eclipse.[165]

Some interpret this v to mean that the luminaries were formed on day four. This notion is then taken to prove that the creation account is unscientific, or at least is not sequential. Even if the v is teaching that the sun was formed after the earth, that in itself would not necessarily indicate that the concepts of the writer were naïve or uninformed. C. Payne-Gaposchkin of Harvard wrote: "The sun (as we know it) may indeed be younger than the earth, not older."[166] A.G.W. Cameron, Goddard Institute Lecturer and professor at Yeshiva University commented: "The creation of the solar system might

---

[165] Aviezer, *In the Beginning*, 47.
[166] C. Payne-Gaposchkin, *Stars in the Making* (New York: Pocket Books, 1959), 107.

have occurred so rapidly that the earth and some of the planets could have formed shortly before the sun did."[167]

Moses' comment in 1:16, however, probably is not a reference to the initial creation of the two great lights. The view that best fits the language of the text is that the luminaries began to function on day four in the ways stipulated in the text. Sun, moon and stars were created *in the beginning* (1:1) in their *tōhû* (*unformed*) state; on day four they were *made* (*'āsāh*) into their fully functional state. This means either they were completed on day four (Rashi, Calvin, Keil), or that they could not be seen from earth until day four (Scofield, Hugh Ross).

Moses avoids using the terms *sun* and *moon* in this paragraph for two polemical reasons. First, these heavenly bodies were worshiped under the names *sun* and *moon*. Moses did not want to dignify such practice by even mentioning the names. Second, *lights* indicates the proper perspective one should have of these heavenly bodies. They are not fundamentally different from hundreds of other light-emitting objects visible to the naked eye in the expanse of the heavens. They are called *the great lights* because from earth perspective they are larger and give forth more light. Nonetheless, for earth sun and moon are *lights* to be appreciated, not deities to be worshiped.

2. Greater light (1:16b): **the greater light to govern the day.** The sun is the *greater* light because it is of greater consequence to the earth. This object phrase explains the sense in which the verb *made* (*'āsāh*) is used in 1:16. In this v God is shaping, adapting, moderating the sun to fulfill the role that it was designated to play for the earth. The sun governs or rules the day in that the day begins with sunrise, and ends with sunset. The light from other heavenly bodies is dwarfed to invisible when

---

[167]Reported in *Science Digest*, Oct 1972.

the sun has fully risen. The domain of the day was brought into being and named on day one. Now here on day four the ruler of that kingdom is named.

The sun is truly an amazing creation. According to astronomer Fred Hoyle, the sun is 93,000,000 miles from earth. It is 864,000 miles in diameter. It would take 1,300,000 earths to equal its size. It is estimated that the sun will continue to give out heat at the present rate for ten thousand million years. The center of the sun is twenty million degrees; the outer surface is 10,000 degrees. The outer blanket of the sun keeps earth from being vaporized.

3. *Lesser light (1:16c)*: **the lesser light to govern the night.** This phrase is the third object of the verb *made*. The sense is that the night sky is dominated by the moon. Moses is using phenomenal language, i.e., he is describing things as they appear to be. The moon appears to give light, and does in fact reflect the light of the sun in the night sky. Modern man knows that the moon produces no light of its own. Still men talk and sing about the light of the moon. It seems disingenuous to accuse Moses of error while those credentialed in science continue to speak of moonlight.

4. *Stars (1:16d)*: **together with the stars.** The rendering: God "made the stars" (KJV; NIV; NASB) is not as close to the original as the NRSV: "God made the two great lights--the greater light to rule the day and the lesser light to rule the night--and the stars." The NJPS is similar. The former translation is weak because it gives the impression that on day four God created the stars. The latter translation is weak in that it implies that no function was assigned to the stars.

The point is not that God created the stars on day four. He did that in 1:1. Rather the sense is that God made the arrangements for the stars to assist the moon in governing the night skies[168] (cf. Ps 136:9).

The casual reference to the stars is significant because the ancients were superstitious about the stars, even worshiped some planets-called-stars (e.g., Saturn). Gn stresses that the stars are only created objects. The God of the Bible is superior to them all.

### D. Explanation: Placing (1:17-18)

The action of God on day four is also described by a verb of placement. For emphasis the commands of vv 14-15 are fulfilled in reverse order in vv 17-18.

*1. Action of placing (1:17a):* **And Elohim placed them in the expanse of the heavens...** The verb in Hebrew does not imply that God fashioned the sun and moon elsewhere and then relocated them to the expanse of the heavens. The original idea in the verb *nātan* is "to give." This verb also is used with the connotation of "appointment." Since the luminaries are so vital to man's life on the planet, certainly the verb may reflect more of its original meaning of "give." God gave the luminaries to man just as surely as he later will give the vegetation to him (1:29). Thus the verb *made* in the previous v is explained. God "gave" or "appointed" to earth (and ultimately to man) lights in the expanse of the heavens.

*2. Functions reiterated (1:17b-18a):* **to give light upon the earth, to rule over the day and over the night, and to separate the light from the darkness.** Three functions of the luminaries are reiterated, viz. giving light (cf. 1:15), governing day and night (cf. 1:16), and separating light and darkness (cf. 1:14). The juxtaposition of the second and third purposes suggests that one

---

[168]For discussion of this v see especially Collin House, *AUSS* 25 (1987): 241-48.

way the luminaries govern is by separating light from darkness.

The statement in 1:17-18 serves several purposes. First, it summarizes what has previously been stated. Second, it clarifies the use of the verb *made* in the previous v. Third, it circumscribes the functions of the two great lights.

Scientists theorize that in the earliest days of the earth the number of hours in a day was far fewer than twenty-four, and the number of days in a year was far greater than 365. At that time the seasons did not correspond to the pattern of spring, summer, fall and winter as known today because the orbit of the earth was not configured as it has been for the past several thousand years. "This configuration is responsible for our day of 24 hours, our year of 365 days, and the mild seasons found in most areas of our planet."[169] Perhaps this information sheds light on what transpired on day four. The Creator fixed the pattern for the days and years. Time as man has known it throughout his history was as much the creation of Elohim as the material world.

The importance of the moon along with the sun in conjunction with the establishment of days, years and seasons has been recognized by scientists only in recent decades. It is now accepted as well-established fact that the moon's gravitational attraction is responsible for the present-day mild climate that has enabled mankind to flourish on this planet.[170] The moon, then, is far more than a night-time sky ornament.

### E. Evaluation (1:18b)

*And Elohim saw that it was good*. The fourth day repeats the appraisal formula from day three. The fixing of the seasons, days and years by the present-day rela-

---

[169]Aviezer, *In the Beginning*, 47.
[170]Ibid, 47, 49.

tive positions of the sun, the moon and the earth was essential to man's well-being. This was the focus on the fourth day's work. For unbelievers the lights in the sky may be sources of terror (Jer 10:2); but for God's people they are viewed as serving a beneficial purpose.

### F.  Conclusion of Day Four (1:19)
*And it became evening and it became morning, a fourth day.* The formula is unchanged from the second and third days.

## Fifth Day
## SECOND DAY OF FILLING
## Gn 1:20-23

Moses devotes two days to the creation of living creatures. On the fifth day God created the creatures of the sea and the sky. On the sixth day (vv 24-28), God created the land creatures, including man.

### A.  Declaration (1:20)
On the fifth creative day Elohim ordered the twofold furnishing of the waters and the expanse, two spheres of earth's environment created on day two.

*1. Waters furnished (1:20a):* **Let the waters swarm with swarms of living creatures.** Here there are four things to note. First, the language of God's command is not parallel to the command of the third day where the earth was told to bring forth vegetation. Here the waters do not bring forth. The next v explains that the swarms of aquatic creatures were created directly by God.

Second, the verb (r. *šrts*) and its cognate accusative (*šerets*) rendered *swarm with swarms* is quite colorful. The paronomasia parallels the fiat on day three. This is a description of creatures that habitually travel in shoals (schools) that are constantly agitating, intertwining and intermingling. When the waters *swarm with swarms* the condition of *bōhû* (unfilled) depicted in 1:2 is partially removed. The verb makes clear that God did not create a single pair of the different kinds of aquatic creatures; he brought them into being *en masse*.

Third, the phrase *living creatures* (*nepheš chayyāh*) is used for the first time. Plants are not viewed biblically as having life in the sense implied in this expression. The term *nepheš,* sometimes translated "soul," refers to the passionate appetites and desires of all living beings, e.g., desire for food and mating. Craving for God distinguishes human *nepheš* from animal *nepheš* (e.g., Ps 42:1-2; 63:1).[171] Primarily *living creatures* are those that require breathing for survival. A threshold is crossed in the creation account with the appearance of creatures that breathe and have volitional movement. The following v makes clear that the Creator's intervention was necessary before living creatures could make their appearance.

Fourth, the wording of this fiat is polemically significant. In pagan mythology waters were the primal generative force. Here the waters are responsive to the will of God.

Appearance of aquatic creatures before land animals agrees with the sequence of the appearance of sentient life as envisioned by historic geology.

*2. Expanse furnished (1:20b):* **and let flying creatures fly about over the earth in the face of the expanse of the heavens.**[172] In this half of the divine fiat there are four things to note. First, as in the previous sentence the writer uses catchy paronomasia (*'ôph yᵉôphēph*), rendered here *flying creatures fly about*. The verb root connotes movement similar to the *swarming* ordered in the

---

[171]Waltke, *GAC*, 63.
[172]At the end of 1:20 the LXX adds the phrase "and it came into being." The Greek translators have the tendency to force uniformity on the text.

first half of the fiat. The verb should not be rendered merely *fly* as it is usually translated, but *fly about* (Polel form). The picture is of winged creatures darting about hither and yon.

Second, the emergence of birds after aquatic life differs from the sequence of the appearance of life postulated by historic geology in which real birds appear after mammals. Those committed to harmonizing Gn and geology take the word *'ôph* (*flying creatures*) to refer to winged insects (as in Lv 11:20).

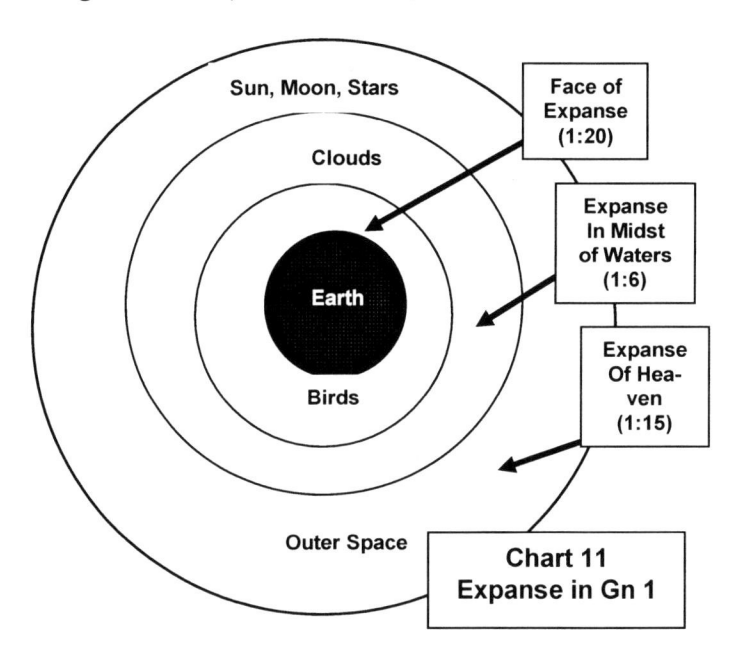

**Chart 11
Expanse in Gn 1**

Concentric circles (from center outward): Earth; Birds; Clouds; Sun, Moon, Stars; Outer Space.
- Face of Expanse (1:20) → points to Birds region
- Expanse In Midst of Waters (1:6) → points to Clouds region
- Expanse Of Heaven (1:15) → points to Sun, Moon, Stars region

Third, the location of the flying creatures is designated by two phrases. The flying creatures fly about *above* (*'al*) *the earth*. Thus these creatures are tied to earth. Their sphere of flight is also designated as (literally) *the face of the expanse of the heavens*. On day two the *expanse in the midst of the waters* is mentioned (1:6), a clear reference to the atmosphere. On the fourth day *the expanse of the heavens* is mentioned as the location of the luminaries (1:14). Here in v 20 the new terminology refers to that part of the greater *expanse of the heavens* (space) that is closest to earth and most recognizable to mankind. Metaphorically, space is viewed, as Leupold noted, "facing the earth." The term *face of* first was used in 1:2 where it referred to the surface of the waters. So here *the face of the expanse of the heavens* is the surface, so to speak, of all space.

Fourth, the winged creatures were created in a mature state, able to fly from the outset.

### B. Explanation (1:21)

The writer explains how the divine intentions expressed in the previous v were carried out. God took action to fulfill his own fiat. For the second time in Gn 1 the text says that *Elohim created* (*bārā'*). Each new stage of creation—the universe (1:1); the living creatures (1:20-21); and humanity (1:26-27)—is introduced by the term *bārā'*. On the significance of this term see on 1:1. The verb *created* (*bārā'*) in this v has three objects.

*1. Sea monsters (1:21a):* **Elohim created the great sea monsters** (*hattannînîm hagg$^e$dōlîm*). The term seems to refer to long creatures of the sea. The great sea monsters are not mentioned elsewhere in the Bible.[173] While the language is appropriate to use of whales, it could also refer to large creatures such as sharks, crocodiles and even the water-bound dinosaurs—perhaps the sea dragons of pagan mythology.[174]

For good reason special mention is made of the fact that the sea monsters were *created* (*bārā'*) by Elohim.

---

[173] The word *tannin* minus the adjective is used in Ex 7:9-12 in reference to what Moses' staff became when he threw it down. In the Ex passage the term is taken to be a snake by most English versions. This is based on the use of the term *serpent* (*nāchāš*) in the authorization passage (Ex 4:3).

[174] The fossil records as currently interpreted reveal the earliest animals to be large aquatic creatures called technically the Ediacaran fauna.

The ancients feared these creatures, and associated them with evil. The writer aims to reassure his readers that their God created these creatures and is sovereign over them.

*2. Swarming creatures (1:21b):* **[Elohim created] every living creature that moves, with which the waters swarmed after its kind.** The first expression (*every living creature*) stresses that each distinct type of the swarming creatures owed it existence to the creative work of God. The participle (*hārōmeseth*) translated *moves* (lit., "the moving ones") seems to introduce another class of the swarmers mentioned in the previous v. The verb root means "to move lightly, creep or move about" whether on land or sea. The word "glide" is a good equivalent. The terminology is appropriate for describing amphibians that creep on land and glide through the waters. The verb *swarmed* (*šārats*) used in the previous v generally is used of small animals. From the standpoint of the Creator, however, all creatures are small. So 1:21 indicates that various size creatures were included. On day five, as on day four, the Creator distinguishes between the greater and the smaller.

*3. Flying creatures (1:21c):* **[Elohim created] ... every winged flying creature after its kind.** What appears to be redundant terminology is intended to stress that God created every type of being that has wings, not merely those that we call birds. The term *'ôph* is broad enough to include anything that flies, including insects (Dt 14:19-20). No further differentiation is given to the winged creatures.

*4. Limitation formula.* Twice in 1:21 the limitation formula *after its/their kind* appears, once regarding water creatures, and once regarding the flying creatures. In the first instance the suffix on *min* is masculine plural recognizing two distinct categories embracing both *the sea monsters* (mas.) and the *gliders* or *swarmers* (fem.).

In the second instance the suffix on *min* is masculine singular, lumping all the flying creatures into one category. For the meaning of the phrase *after their kind*, see on 1:11.

### C. Evaluation (1:21c)

*And Elohim saw that it was good.* Creative activity of the fifth day concluded with the evaluation formula as it was found in the report of days one, three (twice) and four. Even the sea monsters, so feared by ancient man, are included in this declaration. They too fulfilled the purposes of the Creator.

### D. Benediction (1:22)

The seventh creative word takes the form of a blessing, the first of the creation week. A blessing from the Creator indicates that the newly created life forms were more important than the vegetation created on day three. The blessing has two components embracing both major categories of creatures created on day five.

*1. Blessing on water creatures (1:22a):* ***And Elohim blessed them saying, Be fruitful and multiply, and fill the waters in the seas.*** Reproductive fruitfulness is a common part of blessings pronounced throughout the OT. In Gn 1 fruitful multiplication is associated with dominion (cf. 1:28). The implication is that water creatures have dominion over the seas. Although swarms of creatures came into being on the fifth day still God wanted the waters filled. Some of that filling is due to natural reproduction. The Creator is glorified when the spheres created on days one through three are filled. The amazing fecundity of fish is here attributed to the blessing of the Creator.

The omission of reference to fresh waters is explained by the abbreviated nature of the account, and by the obvious aim of the writer to parallel the events of

## Filling the Earth

day two. So in this v the writer has picked up on the use of the word *seas* and *earth* that came into being on day two.

2. *Blessing on flying creatures (1:22b):* **Let the flying creatures multiply on the earth.** The winged creatures are not blessed with the same fertility as the water creatures, since the term *multiply* is used rather than the term *swarm*. That the flying creatures multiply *on the earth* makes clear that they are earth-bound creatures. On the earth they make their nests and hatch their young.

Great disparity exists in the number of species within the various classes of animals. Biologists have identified about four thousand species of mammals, nine thousand of birds, six thousand of reptiles, but nearly one million different species of insects have been identified.[175]

3. *Implications.* Further implications of God's fifth-day blessing should be noted. First, no mention of sexuality among the creatures is made by the writer, but it is implied. God has made it possible for all living creatures to reproduce. He has placed within them a drive to perpetuate their species. The ability to reproduce is here regarded as a divine blessing. Second, the blessing/command to reproduce anticipates the creation of the higher forms of life on day six, for fifth-day creatures will become a significant part of the food chain required by the land animals and man. Third, the dictum *be fruitful and multiply* "provides these creatures with the security of a continued existence."[176]

---

[175]Aviezer, *In the Beginning*, 83.
[176]Mathews, *NAC*, 158f.

## E. Conclusion of Fifth Day (1:23)

*And it became evening and it became morning, a fifth day.* The fifth day concludes with the standard temporal formula of days two, three and four.

# SIXTH DAY
# Phase One: Animals
# Gn 1:24-25

As the third day was the climax of the first triad of days, so day six is the climax of the second triad. As such there are two phases to the creative work of this day, just as there was on day three. God speaks twice, and God acts twice on day six. The second phase of the sixth-day creative work is discussed in the following ch.

## A. Declaration (1:24)

*1. General fiat (1:24a):* **Then Elohim said, Let the earth bring forth living creatures after their kind.** The eighth creative word is a fiat regarding the land creatures paralleling the fiat on day three. These words suggest that the animals were created out of materials that were present in the earth.[177] The focus here is on *living creatures (nepheš chayyāh)* of the land, paralleling the *living creatures* of the waters in 1:20.

*2. Specifications (1:24b):* **cattle, and creeper and beast of the earth after its kind.** The sixth day fiat specifies three categories of land animals. Why these three? Some think the key is movement (cf. 1:28). The cattle walk on top of the earth, the creepers glide along the earth, and the wild beasts dig through it.[178] More likely the three are named in order of proximity to man.

---

[177]Aalders, *BSC*, 68.
[178]Kikawada and Quinn, *Before Abraham*, 79. Cf. W.M. Clark, "The Animal Series in the Primeval History," *VT* 18(1968):433-49.

Filling the Earth

The *cattle* (*bᵉhēmāh*) are the domesticated animals. The *creeper* or *glider* (*remes*) refers to animals that move close to the ground. The *beast of the earth* (*chayᵉtô 'erets*) are the *wild animals* (NIV), especially the carnivores, that are the most distant from man. *After its kind* appears twice in the fiat, a total of 5x in the paragraph. For an explanation of this phrase, see on 1:11.

### B. Implementation (1:24c)

*And it was so* or *and it came to be*. What God ordered was implemented. This repeats what has been said four previous times in this ch (1:4, 7, 9, and 15).

### C. Explanation (1:25a)

*And Elohim made the beast of the earth after its kind, and the cattle after its kind, and every creeper of the ground after its kind*. The work of the Creator in fulfilling his own design for day six is described in this statement. While the fiat of day five parallels the fiat of day three, the accompanying explanation is dissimilar. After the fiat regarding vegetation (*let the earth bring forth*) the comment is *and the earth brought forth* (1:12). Here it is *Elohim made* the living creatures. The writer stresses the different origins of the two forms of life. Animals possess life in a sense that plants do not. Sentient life springs from God.

In this explanatory word the land creatures are named in reverse order of their mention in the fiat.

The connection with the concluding words of the previous v is this: "it happened thus" because God "made" it happen thus.

### D. Evaluation (1:25b)

*And Elohim saw that it was good*. This initial phase of sixth-day work concludes with the evaluation formula that has appeared 5x previously in Gn 1. The major question debated regarding this evaluation formula is whether or not it puts the stamp of divine approval on the actions of predatory animals. Two positions have been taken.

Some believe that all the animals created on day six were herbivores before the Flood. After the Flood, God genetically reprogrammed some animals.[179] Others argue that God foresaw that man would spend only a short time in the garden. He therefore, created the animals in the state they are found today.[180] Theologically the issue is whether all death entered the world because of Adam's sin, or only human death. Probably the Creator made the carnivores as well as the herbivores in the day six creative work.

The absence of a blessing upon the land animals is consistent with the use of blessing in this ch. Blessing in Gn 1 implies reproduction as a means of dominion. Since man shares the land with animals and is given the dominion (1:28), there is no divine blessing upon the animals. Fish and birds, however, dominate their respective realms without challenge to the dominion of humankind. So both birds and fish are blessed (1:22).

## CONCLUSION

The earth has now been formed (days 1-2) and filled (days 3-6). All is ready for the creation of the first humans. The remainder of day six was devoted to the creation of that one being that reflects the image of the Creator.

---

[179] E.g., David J. Taylor, "Herbivores, Carnivores, and the Created Order," *Creation Matters* 1(May-June, 1996): 1-2.
[180] P.V. Vorpahl, "Predators and Paradise, One More Time," *CRSQ* 34:2(Sept 1997): 84-85.

# 9
# CROWN OF CREATION
# Gn 1:26-2:4a

The most important day of the creation week was the sixth. In phase one of the activities of the sixth day God created the animals to fill the earth. In phase two humankind came into being.

## CREATION OF MAN
## Gn 1:26-27

Structurally the report of phase two of day six replicates the structure of the report of phase one. Both sixth-day creative phases begin with a divine word and then amplify that word with a description of God's work.

**A. Declaration** (1:26)

*1. Contemplation (1:26a):* **Then Elohim said, Let us make man.** The ninth creative word suggests divine contemplation concerning the nature of the final object of God's creative powers. The impersonal *let there be* (and equivalents) that has been used to describe the previous seven creative acts is replaced by the personal *let us make*.

In four passages the plural *us* is used in reference to God (cf. 3:22; 11:7; Isa 6:8). To whom does the pronoun *us* refer in this contemplation?[181] Totally objectionable is the idea that the *us* is the remnant of a myth attributing creation to a pantheon of gods. Gn 1 has taken every opportunity, directly and indirectly, to challenge the basic tenets of ancient Near Eastern mythology.

---

[181] Gerhard Hasel, "The Meaning of 'Let Us' in Gen 1:26," *AUSS* 13(1975): 58-66.

Some suggest the reference is to angels. There are three reasons why the referent cannot be angels. First, in 1:27 the singular *his image* is used. Second, in 5:1 the text affirms that man was created in *the likeness of Elohim*, who throughout this text is the Creator. Humanity is said to be in *God's image*, not that of angels. Third, Nehemiah 9:6 affirms that angels are objects of creation, not participants in the process.

Another view that must be rejected is that God is addressing creation itself as if the Creator and what he has previously created are partners in the creation of mankind. Gn 1 carefully distinguishes between Creator and creation. Never does the writer personify creation so as to make it appropriate to use a first person plural pronoun in reference to it. Creation has no independent intelligence, no volition. There is no Mother Nature or Mother Earth in the Gn scheme of things.

Others have proposed that the writer uses a majestic plural such as kings often use when referring to themselves. The phrase *let us* occurs 147 times in the OT in addition to the use twice in God-speech in Gn (1:26; 11:7). In every case a plurality of persons is evident in the context. The custom of western kings speaking with a plural of majesty is not documented in the royal speech of the biblical records.[182]

Another view is that the plural is an expression of deliberation on God's part as he sets out to create man. Where the writer, however, refers to unequivocal delib-

---

[182]Cf. Aalders (*BSC*, 70): "Hebrew does not have such a use of the plural." Cassuto (*CBG*, 1:55) cites 2 Sam 24:14 as an example of a plural of exhortation spoken by King David: "Let us fall now into the hand of Yahweh." The context, however, is a response to a threat of pestilence against *the land*. When speaking of a threatened punishment against himself David says in the same v: "Let me not fall into the hand of man." Waltke (*GAC*, 64) contends that grammatically Hebrew pronouns are always countable plurals.

eration it is not the plural that is used but rather the singular (18:17).

Clines comes closer to the true meaning when he suggests that when God said *let us* he was conversing with his Spirit. Clines argues that "this is the only one with whom he could converse, so far as the context is concerned."[183] Why, however, restrict the conversation to Elohim and his Spirit? It is difficult to read *let us* in God-speech without taking into account the totality of biblical revelation. "In the beginning was the Word, and the Word was with God and the Word was God" (Jn 1:1).

Since alternative explanations cannot be sustained, and in the light of total biblical revelation, the best view of *let us* in Gn 1:26 is that it refers to contemplation within the godhead (Father, Son and Holy Spirit). The writer speaks of *man* (singular) as a duality (*male and female*) in the next v (cf. 5:1-2a). So here the one God created man through an expression of his plurality. Plurality within the godhead anticipates the human duality of the man and woman.

*2. Focus of contemplation.* The focus of contemplation within the godhead is *man*. *Man* is singular minus the definite article. This might be taken to refer to a single man (i.e., Adam); the verb in the second half of the v, however, is plural. This suggests that the singular *man* is a collective or refers to the class of mankind just as the singulars refer to classes of animals in 1:24.[184]

The land creatures were made each *according to its own kind*. Each animal displays a likeness to other animals of its own kind or category. Man's likeness, however, is not shared merely with all other human beings; rather man shares the likeness of God. This harmonizes

---

[183]Clines, "The Image of God in Man," *TB* 19(1968): 68f.

[184]That *man* on the sixth day refers to *mankind* already was recognized by Sforno (Rabbi Ovadiah ben Jacob of Italy) in the sixteenth century.

with ch 2 that describes in more detail the process of creating that man.

*3. Goal of contemplation (1:26b):* **as our image, according to our likeness.** The goal of contemplation is to create a being that in very special ways resembles the Creator. The prepositions are important. The human person is not merely compared with the image of God; a human being *is* the image of God.

The term *image* (*tselem*) is used 5x of man as a created being. It can refer to any type of similarity in form. It is most frequently used of idols, which are visible representations of invisible deities. Representation is the most central concept involved in the term *image*.[185] Gn 1 takes issue with the common notion in the ancient Near East that only the king was the image of deity.

*Likeness* (*dᵉmût*) is used 25x in the OT. The term indicates simple comparison, whether of sound (Isa 13:4), sight (Ezek 23:15), or shape (2 Kgs 16:10). In Gn 1 *dᵉmût* specifies the nature of the image. The term does not erase the profound difference between the infinite Creator and the finite human creature. In this passage the emphasis falls on the similarity rather than the difference in order to establish the high position of the human person.

The concepts of *image* and *likeness* in the ancient Near East have been illustrated in an inscription discussed by Gropp and Lewis. A statue of the king of Guzan was placed in the territory of Sikan across the river. The accompanying inscription indicates that the statue not only resembled the king in form, it functioned as a representation of the rule of the king in the territory of Sikan. Both of the terms (*image/likeness*) that are used in Gn are used in this inscription. In Gn heaven's King is not represented by statue, but by a living being that

---

[185]Clines, op. cit., 70-101.

that resembles the Creator in crucial respects and that rules in his stead.[186]

*4. Dominion (1:26b):* ***And let them rule over the fish of the sea and over the birds of the sky and over the cattle and over all the earth, and over every creeping thing that creeps on the earth.*** A second area of contemplation concerns the relationship of man to what previously has been created and pronounced *good* by the Creator. In the ancient world the common idea was that images shared in the powers of the beings they represented.[187] Because man is to be the created being most like God, man is to rule (r. *rdh*) over other creatures. It is striking that the wild animals are omitted from the list.[188]

Blaming biblical tradition for the abuse of nature is popular today.[189] Brueggemann, however, presents the biblical view when he writes: "The image of God...is a mandate of power and responsibility. But it is power exercised as God exercises power."[190] The passion and concern that the Creator manifests for the created order in Gn 1 must forever guide man in the exercise of his delegated dominion.

### B. Explanation: Image (1:27)

***And Elohim created man in his image, in the image of Elohim he created him.*** The report of the divine work on day six focuses on two aspects of man's creation—image and sexuality.

---

[186] D.M. Gropp and T.J. Lewis, "Notes on Some Problems in the Aramaic Text of the Hadad-Yith'I Bilingual," *BASOR* 259 (1985): 45-61.
[187] Blocher, *In the Beginning*, 87.
[188] The wild animals are mentioned in the Syriac version, but this can hardly be the original reading.
[189] See, for example, L. White, "The Historical Roots of our Ecological Crisis," *Science* 155:1203-7.
[190] Brueggemann, *Genesis*, 32.

*1. Importance of image.* The writer has employed chiasmus to emphasize a fundamental tenet of his theology. The second half of the line repeats in reverse order the first half of the line. The writer will use the same technique in 9:6. Such chiasmus makes the line memorable. Double use of the verb *created* (*bārā'*) stresses the divine origin of man.

*2. Involvements.* What is involved in the concept of divine image (*imago Dei*)? Four views have been advanced. The *Lutheran view* is that the image of God refers to man's moral status before God. Man was created morally perfect. The *relational view* emphasizes *us* and *the male and female* in the context. The image of God is man's capacity for interpersonal relationships mirroring the interpersonal relationships within the godhead. This view was advanced by K. Barth. Some define image in *functional* terms. Man is made in the image of God because his exercise of dominion over the earth reflects God's ultimate Lordship. Certainly there is a connection between dominion and the image of God. Is dominion, however, the definition of image, or the assignment of man because he is created in God's image? The *substantive view* holds that the image is the rational soul. It includes memory, understanding, will, love, and human personality. This view, formulated by Augustine, Aquinas, and Calvin, is the most widely held view.

Perhaps the best explanation is that the terms *image* and *likeness* have slightly different nuances. *Image* points to all that man is; *likeness* points to what man does—rule as the representative of the Creator.

*3. Implications.* Three points regarding the image concept seem secure. First, image has nothing to do with the physical body. God is an incorporeal Spirit (Jn 1:18; 1 Tim 6:16). Yet the human body must have been carefully planned by God as the most appropriate tabernacle for man's spirit. Second, the image of God in man refers to man's spiritual nature. It is all that makes a being human—reason, capacity for worship, emotion, communication, et al. Third, since man is made in God's image, every human being is worthy of honor and respect. See Gn 9:6; 1 Cor 11:7; Jam 3:9.

### C. Explanation: Sexuality (1:27b):
*Male and female he created them.* Up to this point the writer has not considered gender an important feature to stress. This statement regarding the creation of sexuality has impact in four areas.

*1. Polemical impact.* The cosmos does not exist because of sex (as in the Babylonian tradition). God is sovereign over sex. He created it. The statement also refutes the pagan myth and Jewish speculation that the first man was androgynous—half man and half woman.

*2. Ethical impact.* Among the creatures, only the sexuality of man is specifically mentioned in Gn 1. His sexuality is unique. It is qualitatively different from that of the animals. This statement regarding human sexuality undercuts the extremes of sexploitation and prudery. The writer intends his words to prepare for the revelation concerning marriage in ch 2. Mathews offers this trenchant comment: "There is no place in God's good order for unisexuality or for any diminishing or confusion of sexual identity."[191]

*3. Theological impact.* God is not a sexual being. In this respect man is not made in God's image. Brueggemann puts it this way: "Sexuality, sexual identity, and sexual function belong not to God's person but to God's will for creation."[192] Yet human sexuality is the work of God as much as the creation of the divine image in man. Sex is not incompatible with the privilege of the *image*.

---

[191]Mathews, *NAC*, 173.
[192]Brueggemann, *Genesis*, 33.

*4. Anthropological impact.* There are three anthropological implications of the Gn 1 statement regarding human sexuality. First, man and woman have equal standing and worth. No place does the text directly assert that women posses the image of God. The language of 1:27, however, makes it clear that man was created a duality. Whatever attributes are attributed to man in vv 26-27 must therefore be shared by the female counterpart of the duality. Being immediately associated with the revelation that man was made in God's image, this clause is intended to teach that both man and woman share equally in that privilege. If men and women share equally in the divine image, then fundamentally they are equal in nature.

Second, sexuality is the only differentiation made in humankind. No other distinction—whether racial, ethnic or social—belongs to the essence of what it means to be man. The phrase *after its kind* appears 10x in reference to plants and animals; but it does not appear in this paragraph. Mankind does not divide into different species and sub-species like the birds and the beasts.

Third, the implication of the statement regarding the creation of human sexuality is that humankind was a community from the beginning. The details of the original community of man and wife will be spelled out in Gn 2.

As in day two, there is no specific statement regarding day six that God found what he had created good. Concerning the absence of the evaluation formula the rabbis observed: man's good is in his own hand. He can choose good or evil.

### D. Benediction (1:28)

*1. General blessing (1:28a):* **And Elohim blessed them**. The words God addressed to the man and the woman after their creation in 1:28-30 are often referred to as the creation mandate. The five imperatives of 1:28 are not to be understood as commands (as some rabbis understood them), for the opening words identify them as a *blessing*. These words should be viewed more as invitation, permission, and implied promise rather than obligation. They may be likened to a parental "go ahead" to activity that is proper, enjoyable, fulfilling and beneficial.[193]

Blessing is a major theme in Gn and the Pentateuch. The living creatures already have been blessed on the fifth day (1:22); thus the writer views the blessing as extending beyond humanity to all of God's living creatures.

*2. Reproduction blessing (1:28b):* **and Elohim said to them, Be fruitful and multiply.** In the creation account God speaks directly only to human creatures. The rabbis observed: the fish were blessed first (1:22); but fish did not qualify for a special address. God can only communicate with those who reflect his image. Indeed, that is one of the very implications of the image of God in man. Man is capable of understanding the words of the Creator.

The first blessing was pronounced on swarms of aquatic creatures; the second, however, is pronounced on a single pair. The similarity in the language suggests that God is telling man to be as fruitful as the fish of the seas. The words of this v are a slap at the pagan creation tradition. In Mesopotamian tradition overpopulation was an evil to be controlled by the gods by means of plagues and flood; in Gn population growth is viewed as a divine blessing.

*3. Implications.* Since the proliferation of the race can only be accomplished through sexuality, one must

---

[193] From *be fruitful and multiply* the rabbis deduced that every man had a duty to marry and have children. This responsibility was incurred at age eighteen, while all other commandments were obligatory at age thirteen.

conclude that human sexuality fulfills God's purposes for the earth.

In procreation there is a reflection of creation. Man and woman are the image of God separately. They are also the image of God together, procreating as he created. In Gn 5:1-3 the begetting of Seth, who is the image and likeness of his father, follows immediately on the reminder of creation in the divine likeness, male and female. As the heavenly Father created man and woman in his image, they together procreate offspring in their own image. So the image of God is passed on from parents to children throughout the generations. Eve was amazed at this mystery (4:1).

*4. Occupational blessing (1:28c):* **and fill the earth, and subdue it.** The sea creatures were to *fill the water in the seas*; mankind is to *fill the earth*. Gn 11 indicates that the Creator will not permit his purpose of filling the earth to be thwarted.

Not only is man to *fill* the earth, he is to *subdue* (r. *kbš*) it. The linkage of the two verbs *fill/subdue* suggests that man subdues the earth by filling it. Into whatever area of the earth man spread, he soon dominated the other creatures in that area and used them for his own well being.

*5. Dominion blessing (1:28b):* **And rule over the fish of the sea and over the birds of the heavens, and over every beast that creeps on the earth.** Dominion is man's destiny. Man is commissioned to rule over those creatures that dominate air, water and dry land. God values the animal world. For this reason he decrees that man shall be the caretaker of the lower creatures. *Cattle*, mentioned in v 26, are here omitted for it is understood by definition that domesticated animals are subject to man's rule. It is not clear whether *beast that creeps on the earth* is the same as the *creeper* in v 24 and the *creeper of the ground* in v 25.

Man's dominion over the creatures has its limitations. In no way does God's creation mandate authorize tyranny. Blocher astutely observes: "The reign of the created image could only be that of a deputy. Mankind is a vassal prince who will follow the directives of the Sovereign and will give an account to him."[194] In theory the ancient kings were seen as mediators of blessings to their subjects. So should mankind be a blessing to the other creatures of the earth. Man should rule the creatures like a shepherd, with a view to their own welfare as well as to his own.

### E. Provisioning (1:29-30)

In the Mesopotamian tradition man is created to provide food for the gods. In Gn, however, God is depicted as a beneficent Provider. He provides food for man and beast alike.

*1. Gracious gift (1:29a):* **Then Elohim said, Behold.** God's direct address to the couple continues in this v. The statement was made to man in the context of his commission to rule over the *earth* (*'erets*). In the light of ch 2 the statement was made to man in the geographical context of the garden after the creation of the woman, as indicated by two plural pronominal suffixes (*to you*) in the v. The first couple is invited by *behold* to observe all of their surroundings.

*2. Bountiful gift (1:29b):* **I have given you every plant yielding seed ... and every tree that has fruit yielding seed; it shall be food for you.** God's bountiful provision to the couple is indicated by the verb *I have given* (r. *ntn*). Two of the three categories of vegetation mentioned in 1:11 are offered to him. The provision was gracious beyond anything that man might expect, as indicated by the twice-used adjective *every*. The implica-

---

[194]Blocher, *In the Beginning*, 90.

tion of the provision in 1:29 is that all plants growing in the garden were eatable.

*3. Limited gift (1:29c):* **that is on the face of all the land.** The term *land* (*'erets*) can refer to the entire planet, or it can refer to a more limited area of the planet— a land. Context determines the proper understanding of the term. The *face of* something in the OT is that part which is visible to a speaker or viewer—the part with which the viewer is familiar. The expression *face of the waters* was used in 1:2 in reference to the Spirit of God. In 1:29 the expression *face of the land/earth* is used for the first of 28x in the OT. The reference is to the garden environment—that part of the planet with which man was familiar. The words of 1:29 were spoken in the garden and about the garden.

*4. Various views.* There are four views as to the import of 1:29. First, some see these instructions as the Creator's way of drawing attention to the bountiful provisions of the garden so as to put the prohibition of 2:17 in proper perspective. In essence these words say the same thing as 2:16.

Second, some see these instructions as simply a way of teaching that directly or indirectly all life depends on vegetation that is provided by God's hand. The point is to indicate a limitation of the dominion of man over the earth. Man is ruler of creation, yet he must draw the means of his subsistence from the creation he rules.

Third, others see these instructions as a complete guide to man's diet. Cf. 9:3. According to this view man was a vegetarian before the Flood. These instructions, however, do not specifically exclude animals or animal products. If man is prohibited by these instructions from using animals or their products as food it is difficult to see in what meaningful way man has dominion over them.

Fourth, still others regard Gn 1:29 as further definition of the dominion of man. He not only rules over the creatures of earth, sea and air, he also has dominion over vegetation.

*5. Provisions for beasts (1:30a):* **And to every beast of the earth and to every bird of the sky and to every creeper on the earth that has life, [I have given] every greenness of plant for food.** If man is being addressed in the garden and about the garden in the previous v, then this v also must be interpreted in the light of the garden context. *Beast of the earth,* as in v 25, refers to wild animals. *Plant* (*'ēsebh*) is the same word used in the food provision of man in the previous v, except for the restrictive modifier preceding (*yereq* = *greenness*).

Those who hold that a stipulated provision excludes any other possibilities logically must hold that the garden animals were restricted to one type of vegetation, viz. the second of the three categories named in 1:11. This in turn necessitates the conclusion that the garden animals were totally unlike their counterparts today, or that the eating habits of the animals were radically changed at some point. These layers of speculation can be removed if the original premise is denied. A stipulated provision does not in fact exclude other possibilities. The animals in the garden no doubt ate grasses and fruit as well as the category of *greenness of plants*.

By mentioning the one category of food provision for the garden animals the narrator accomplishes three things. First, he highlights the abundance of the provision for man in the previous v. Second, he nonetheless makes the point that the Creator graciously provides for the needs of the lower creatures as well as for man. Third, he intimates that all the animals in the garden were herbivores.

It is surprising that *cattle* are not mentioned in this list. The animal lists on the sixth day clearly are not intended to be complete, but only selective and general.

| Chart 12 | | | |
|---|---|---|---|
| Animals Mentioned on Day Six | | | |
| **1:24** **Fiat** | **1:25** **Fulfillment** | **1:28** **Mandate** | **1:30** **Provision** |
| Cattle | Beast of the earth | Fish of the sea | Beast of the earth |
| Creeper | Cattle | Bird of the heavens | Bird of the heavens |
| Beast of the earth | Creeper of the ground | Beast that creeps on the earth | Creeper upon the earth |

### F. Implementation (1:30b)

*And it was so* or *and it came to be*. The report of the sixth day concludes with the simple fulfillment formula. There is no reason to limit the fulfillment formula just to the provision of vegetation as food for man and beast. Most likely the formula applies to the entirety of God's sixth day word and work.

### G. Evaluation (1:31a)

*Elohim saw all that he had made, and it was very good.* Coming as it does at the end of the creation work week, this formula probably applies to the entire creative work of God, not just that of the sixth day. This is not an aesthetic judgment. The garden was beautiful, but not necessarily everything outside that garden. The appraisal formula here, as indeed on each of the previous five days (excepting the second), is a practical judgment in terms of God's purpose. Everything was functioning toward the desired end of reproducing on earth God's image in the form of man.

In this declaration of the basic goodness of all that God created the biblical view is set apart from all other ancient cosmogonies.[195] Plaut comments: "being is better than nothingness, order superior to chaos, and man's existence—with all its difficulties—a blessing." Plaut goes on to observe that whereas creation is said to be *very good*, it is not said to be perfect.[196]

### H. Conclusion of Sixth Day (1:31b)

*And it became evening, and it became morning, the sixth day.* The sixth day concludes with the temporal formula used with each of the preceding days (1:31b). There is one modification. Here the definite article is used—*the sixth day*—for the first time in the narrative. The exact significance of this change is unclear. Perhaps it emphasizes the importance of the sixth day. The importance of this day is also indicated by its position as the last of the creative days, and by the fact that it is the only day on which the evaluation formula was *very good*.

## FOUNDATIONAL TEACHING

### A. Value of Human Life

Mankind was the crown of God's creation. The narrator stresses this truth in several ways. First, human life stands atop an ascending hierarchy of entities as the pinnacle of creation. Second, the creation of man was the only creative act preceded by contemplation (v 26). Third, impersonal language (*let there be, let the earth*) is replaced by personal divine involvement in man's creation (*let us make*). Fourth, only man was created in God's image. Fifth, man was given dominion over all other creatures. Sixth, more words are devoted to the sixth day than any previous creative day. Seventh, the

---

[195] Jaki, *Genesis 1*, 8.
[196] Gunther Plaut, *Genesis, The Torah, A Modern Commentary* (New York: Union of American Hebrew Congregations, 1974), 11.

## Biblical Protology

narrator has used the device of chiasmus to emphasize the concept of image in v 27. Eighth, man receives a blessing from God, but the other land creatures do not. Ninth, the narrator stresses that man was a direct creation of God.

### B. Unity of Mankind

Non-believers generally hold to the theory of the polygenetic origin of man. R.R. Gates, for example, accepts "independent evolution" on the different continents from different ancestral stock.[197] Some Christian writers have tried to accommodate the Gn 1 account with the naturalistic explanation. E.L. Mascall, a Catholic writer, comments:

> Common descent from one ancestor is not the only way of explaining and understanding the relationship of all men to the Fall; it is perfectly conceivable that God might have made a number of independent human races with such a common metaphysical and moral unity that the sin of one would involve all in that mysterious predicament which we describe as original sin.[198]

Christian theology must be based on revelation, not imagination, what happened, not what is conceivable. The doctrine of the unity of the human race is "one of the most important matters in Christian theology."[199] The common ancestry of the entire human race is a clear teaching of Scripture. Although this doctrine needs no external support, it can be deduced from several facts in the physical realm. Anatomically, the human body is the same from pygmies to the giant Wattusies, from the fairest Scandinavians to the darkest Africans. Physio-

---

[197]R.R. Gates, *Human Ancestry* (Cambridge: Harvard, 1948), 3-12, 144, 236.

[198]E.L. Mascall, *Christian Theology and Natural Science* (London: Longmans, Green, 1956), 33.

[199]Ramm, *CVSS*, 214. See Rom 5:12-17; 1 Cor 15:21-58.

logically, throughout the human race the pulse rate, breathing, etc. are the same. Psychologically, all men have powers of perception. They show similar patterns of reaction. The central nervous system of representatives of all racial groups is similar. Above all, there is racial interfertility.[200]

P.A. Moody has summarized the argument against the polygenetic origin of modern man in a fine way:

> If one race arose from one group of lower primates and another race arose from another group of them, how could the descendants possibly become so intricately alike in generic constitution and in all aspects of physiology as to develop the interfertility observable today?[201]

More recent research by geneticists has put to rest theories of polygenetic origin for the human race. In 1988 news reports were widely published that "scientists claim to have found our common ancestor—a woman who lived 200,000 years ago and left resilient genes that are carried by all of mankind."[202] One team of scientists traces this genetic Eve to the heart of Africa; another team traces her origins to southwest Asia. Obviously not all of the conclusions of the geneticists are acceptable to Bible believers. The discovery, however, that the human race is a biological brotherhood is consistent with the biblical teaching that humankind began with the creation of a single couple.

## C. Significance of Man

The account of the creation of man is foundational to the biblical view. Non-Christian religions sometimes

---

[200] F. Weidenreich, *Apes, Giants, and Man* (Chicago: University Press, 1946), 2.
[201] P.A. Moody, *Introduction to Evolution* (New York: Harper, 1953), 227.
[202] "The Search for Adam and Eve," *Newsweek*, (Jan 11, 1988). An Associated Press dispatch (Nov 25, 1995) reported a similar genetic confirmation of an original male progenitor of the human race.

idealize man as angel, as basically good. Some deify man, or at least see men as gods in the making. Materialism contends that man is nothing but beast. In popular thought man is seen as an angel/beast hybrid. The biblical view is that man is not god, angel, beast or hybrid. Man is unique. He is made in God's image. From this basic assertion two implications can be deduced.

First, the concept of image requires that man subordinate himself to the Creator. Man is image, not a replica. The concept excludes any notion that man is god, or a little piece of God, or that he is evolving into a god. In a multitude of ways the text has emphasized man's creaturely weakness. His kinship with the animals is indicated by the fact that both were created on the same day. Food for both animals and man was appointed at the same time. Both man and beast were fashioned from the ground (2:7, 19). The name *Adam*, given by God (5:2), is related to the Hebrew word *ªdhāmāh*, "ground." Man is the earthling. He is of the clay (2:7). Even the modern word *human* traces its origin back to *humus*, earth!

Second, the only legitimate image of God in the world is man. In part this is the rationale for the Second Commandment, which forbids the making of idols. In a sense we pay homage to God when we render service to our fellowmen who are made in God's image.

## TRANSITIONAL VERSE
### Gn 2:1

***Thus the heavens and the earth were completed, and all their hosts***. This v serves as a transition from the workweek to the day of rest. The first half of the v points to the forming of the earth on days 1-3; the second half seems to refer to the filling of the heavens and earth on days 4-6. Thus the writer has completed the outline of events as initially set forth in 1:2. The *tōhû* (*unformed*) and *bōhû* (*unfilled*) character of the earth have been addressed.

The dyad *heavens and earth* is the ancient way of referring to the universe. See on 1:1. The whole process of creating the universe was finished at the end of the creation week. The Gn 1 creation week is the "finishing touch" of the creative work of God. This fact again points to the unique place of this planet in the plan of God.

In all of its usages *host* or *army* designates a diverse totality that is properly arranged, organized and differentiated. Creation *host* is not, however, an army that fights, but one that parades in honor to the Creator.[203] The term *host* is frequently used of the celestial creation, including angels (e.g., 1 Kgs 22:19) and stars (e.g., Dt 4:19). The concept of *host of the earth*, however, is found only in Gn 2:1. The implication is that in the original creation earth's living creatures followed as perfect an order as the luminaries of the heavens.

## SEVENTH DAY REST
## Gn 2:2-4a

Three vv are devoted to the Sabbath day. It seems strange that these vv were assigned to ch 2. The six creative days reach their climax in the Sabbath. One would think that the account of the Sabbath would be placed at the end of ch 1. The division of chs in early Jewish editions did assign these vv to ch 1. The Latin Vulgate, however, assigned them to ch 2 for some inexplicable reason. Thereafter this became the standard format for Gn in Christian circles. It since has been adopted by most Hebrew texts as well.

---

[203]Beauchamp, *Création*, 377. Cited by Blocher, *In the Beginning*, 71.

## A. Declaration (2:2a)

***And God declared finished on the seventh day his work that he had made.*** The seventh day declaration is more subtle than the divine declarations on the previous days. Traditionally this is rendered "and on the seventh day God ended his work which he had made" (KJV). Certainly no one can quibble with the accuracy of such a translation. The Greek translators, however, thought that this rendering implied that some work took place on the seventh day. They took the liberty of changing the text to read, "God finished on the sixth day." Newer versions have tried to avoid the problem by rendering "and by the seventh day God had completed" (NASB) or "finished" (NIV) his work. This is a possible solution.

The Hebrew text, however, offers another explanation. The verb form is Piel, which often has a declarative force. So on the seventh day God *declared* his work to be finished (r. *klh*). Each of the previous six days began with a divine utterance—*and Elohim said.* So perhaps the nuance is that this day began with a forceful declaration. The text, however, does not say that God spoke or worked on the seventh day. So it was by resting that God declared creation work finished.

There are seven words (in the Hebrew) in this line, and the middle word is *seventh.* In this way the narrator highlights the importance of the final day.

## B. Explanation (2:2b)

***And he rested on the seventh day from all his work that he had done.*** The verb *rested* (r. *šbt*) means "to cease, to desist." This is not the rest of weariness (Ps 121:4), but the cessation of the special work that was performed over the six-day week. The work ceased because it was finished. The divine rest is an exclamation mark to the phrase *it was very good* of 1:31. Creation lacked nothing. It was time for celebration and the enjoyment of the fruit of labor.

As in 2:2a this line also has seven (Hebrew) words, highlighting *the seventh day*. The resting of the Creator on the seventh day is a feature totally absent in other ancient Near Eastern cosmogonies.[204]

**C. Benediction** (2:3)

*1. Focus of the blessing (2:3a):* **Then Elohim blessed the seventh day and sanctified it.** The verb *blessed* (r. *brk*) again is in a form (Piel) that conveys declaration. God declared the seventh day *blessed*. The day was blessed because God *sanctified* the seventh day, i.e., he set it apart from ordinary work days by resting. This declaration stands in stark contrast to the Babylonian creation account in which the creator gods celebrated the completion of creation by building Babylon and a temple.[205]

Again in 2:3a the sentence contains seven words, with *seventh day* occupying the midpoint. Mentioning the seventh day for the third time in two vv highlights the importance of this day.

*2. Explanation of the blessing (2:3b):* **because in it he rested from all his work which Elohim had created and made.** The verb *rested* is repeated from the previous v for emphasis. *His work*, appearing for the third time in two vv, stresses that creation was divine work from start to finish. Referring to the creative acts of God as *work* (*melā'khāh*) provides the theological foundation to the biblical doctrine of work. Human labor is elevated and ennobled because it is patterned after God's work.

God *rested*, not because of fatigue, but because his creative work had ended. The concluding v of the first main unit of Gn brings together the two main verbs of

---

[204] Jaki, *Genesis 1*, 8.
[205] ANET, 68-69, lines 50-80.

the creation account: *created* (r. *bārā'*) and *made* (r. *'āsāh*). *God created* recalls the opening words of this unit. *Made* recalls all the "makings" reported in the rest of the unit.

In 2:3 *'āsāh* is in the infinitive form with *lamedh* (*to*) attached. Literally the clause with the duo of synonymous verbs is "which Elohim created to make." In this Hebrew construction the second verb serves to elucidate the sense in which the first verb is to be understood. In this case the infinitive *'āsāh* makes clear that the v is speaking of creation that is also a making, i.e., a wondrous work implying the making of things that never existed before (Cassuto). The verb *'āsāh* sometimes has broader connotation than *bārā'*; but in the creation account it is used of the making of something that did not previously exist (1:7, 16, 25, 26, 27; 2:2). Thus *'āsāh* is used as a synonym for *bārā'* in the first unit of Gn (cf. Ex 34:10).

*3. Implications.* There are at least three implications of the declarations regarding the seventh day. First, by sanctifying the seventh day God was indicating to man that rest as well as work is noble and holy. Second, by resting on the seventh day God was establishing a pattern of work and rest for those made in his image. Third, the blessings that are later to flow forth from that day for the good of mankind are potentially bestowed on that day by the declaration of God in 2:3.

## SEVENTH-DAY ISSUES

### A. Observance Issue

Some assume that humankind observed the Sabbath as a day of rest and worship from the beginning of time. As a matter of fact, there is no reference to any of God's people observing the Sabbath until the pedagogical days just before Israel reached Mount Sinai (Ex 16:26-29).

Crown of Creation

The Sabbath is not to be confused with the first day of the week when Christians assembled (Acts 20:7). The former celebrated deliverance from Egyptian bondage (Dt 5:15); the latter, deliverance from sin's bondage. The Sabbath celebrated the old creation (Ex 31:17); the Lord's Day celebrates the new creation (2 Cor 5:17; Gal 6:15). The former was observed with rest at home; the latter is observed with assembly for instruction, communion and worship. The two days have nothing in common except that they both are twenty-four hours long.

### B. Duration Issue

The absence of the temporal formula following day seven has led to the assertion that the seventh day had no termination. God has been in a Sabbath rest ever since the conclusion of day six. The words of Jesus in Jn 5:17 have been interpreted to mean that the creation Sabbath continues to the present. This passage was discussed in ch 6 in conjunction with the day-age view of the Gn days.

The formula *there was evening and there was morning* marked the end of the creative activity on each day. Since no work was performed on day seven the formula was omitted. Furthermore, the temporal formula is transitional from day to day. Since there was no eighth day there was no point in including the transitional formula.[206]

### C. Uniqueness Issue

In the Hebrew text day seven is set apart from the previous six days in several ways. First, it is the only day to be introduced before the day is described. Second, it is the only numbered day mentioned more than

---

[206] A. Dillmann, *Genesis Critically and Exegetically Expounded* (Edinburgh: T. & T. Clark, 1897), 1:92.

**175**

once. It is mentioned 3x in two vv. Third, it is the only day described in the Hebrew with a double article—lit., "on the day the seventh." The double article is used again in the second reference to the day. One article was used on day six, and the article is totally absent on the previous five days. Fourth, it is the only day that does not begin with the verb *said* (r. *'mr*). Fifth, the 6 + 1 pattern in the ancient Near East was designed to highlight the seventh item. The seventh day stands outside the pattern of paired days. No other day in the creation week corresponds to it.

In Mesopotamia the seventh, fourteenth, twenty-first and twenty-eighty days of certain months were considered cursed days. One text, for example, advises the king not to eat meat, change clothes, offer sacrifices, ride a chariot or render decisions on these days. The seer was not to give an oracle and the physician was not to attend the sick. In the biblical view, however, the seventh day is *blessed.*

The full moon in Babylonia was called *shapattu*—day of quieting the heart of the god. There is, however, no evidence that *shapattu* was a day of rest from labor, and no connection with the four monthly days that were considered cursed.

In Gn the threefold repetition of the phrase "seventh day" implies the day derives its special character solely from God. It has nothing to do with the phases of the moon. So the weekly biblical Sabbath was unique in the ancient world.

### D. Seven-Day Week Issue

For those who do not take the Gn 1 narrative seriously, the origins of the seven-day week are a mystery. The ancient Egyptians had a ten-day week; eight-day weeks are also documented. The seven-day week is frequently traced back to Mesopotamia. The ancient Babylonians recognized seven winds. The speculation is that originally one day was dedicated to each of these seven winds.[207] Others connect the seven-day week with the seven astral bodies thought by the ancients to revolve around the earth. The custom of naming the seven days after seven astral bodies, however, is attested only in the first century BC. Gn 1 gives the true origin of the seven-day week.[208]

# TABLET COLOPHON
## Gn 2:4a

*These are the generations of the heavens and the earth.* *Generations* (*tôl$^e$dôth*) means history, especially family history. It also means the origin of anything, i.e., the story of their origins. Most scholars render the word as "genealogical history, history, beginnings, origins, or chronicles." The plural reflects the notion that a history is made up a multitude of individual items. This is the first of eleven uses of this term in Gn.

The status of 2:4a in the text is in question. Some English versions regard 2:4a as introductory to what follows. The paragraphing of KJV, ASV, NASB, and NIV indicates this reading: "This is the account of the heavens and earth when they were created." Moffat regarded the phrase as misplaced, and put it as a heading before 1:1. Other versions, however, regard 2:4a as the conclusion to the first major section of Gn.[209] This approach is found in NJPS, NRSV and JB: "Such were the origins of

---

[207] Hildegard and Julus Lewy, "The Origin of the Week and the Oldest West Asiatic Calendar," *HUCA* 17(1942-43): 1-152.

[208] In Hebrew the seven day week was called *šābhua'* (Gn 29:27), from *šebha', seven*. In Greek it was called *sabbaton* (Lk 18:12). In the Bible the first six days of the week are simply numbered. The seventh day is called *Sabbath*.

[209] Mathews (*NAC*, 114) makes the case for regarding 2:4a as the heading for what follows, rather than the conclusion to what precedes.

**177**

heaven and earth when they were created." Current critics opt for this interpretation. They are supported by conservative scholars like Harrison.[210] This is the correct understanding of the function of 2:4a. It is also a clue as to how subsequent uses of the term $tôl^e dôth$ are to be interpreted. Following Wiseman, the term marks the conclusion of a tablet used by Moses in constructing the Book of Gn.

# CONCLUSION

Carl Henry[211] summarizes the biblical doctrine of creation rest in four conclusions. First, the creation of new kinds reached its climax and completion in the originally graded orders of being and life. Second, the laws and limits governing creation were fixed in the creation week. Third, the law of stability is now more fundamental in the space-time universe than that of changing forms. Fourth, man bears a permanent dignity and supremacy in the creation.

To this excellent summary, this concluding observation from Blocher is appropriate: "The Sabbath sums up the difference between the biblical and the Marxist visions. The essence of mankind is not work!"[212]

---

[210] R.K. Harrison, *Introduction to the OT* (Grand Rapids: Eerdmans, 1969), 548-49.
[211] Carl F.H. Henry, "Science and Religion," in *Contemporary Evangelical Thought* ed. C.F.H. Henry (Grand Rapids: Baker, 1968), 256.
[212] Blocher, *In the Beginning*, 57.

# 10
# PROVISION AND PROBATION
## Gn 2:4b-17

According to Dorsey, the second major unit of Gn is linked to the previous unit by the technique of "pearling." The writer picks up a topic introduced near the end of the previous unit—*mankind* (*'ādām*)—and makes it the new central focus.

The Gn 2 account of creation is extremely controversial. Leupold observed that every inch of the text is a battleground. Three serious allegations have been made against the account. First, it is alleged that this account of creation is full of mythological connections. Central in this account, however, is the tree of the knowledge of good and evil. No parallel to this concept has been found in the ancient mythological literature. The atmosphere of this ch differs profoundly from that of myth. The lucid narrative "is anything but a myth."[213]

The second allegation is that the narrative of Gn 2 reflects unsophisticated naiveté. Yet in truth there is a profound theological richness in this ch. It is "a religious and literary achievement of the highest order."[214]

The third and most common allegation is that Gn 2 contradicts Gn 1 at point after point. Critics dismiss both accounts because in the final analysis who can tell which of the two reports the truth. More recent study, however, has viewed the two accounts as part of a grand literary design by a very sophisticated writer/compiler. The supposed contradictions actually complement ch 1. The Bible presents a unified and integrated portrayal of crea-

---

[213] G. von Rad, *Genesis*, OTL Rev ed. (Philadelphia: Westminster, 1972), 88.
[214] R. Gordis, "The Knowledge of Good and Evil in the OT and the Qumran Scrolls," *JBL* 76 (1957): 129.

tion.[215] In the ancient Near East double accounts of the creation of man are not unusual.[216]

# PREPARATION FOR MAN
# Gn 2:4b-6

### A. Narrowed Perspective (2:4b)

Unlike Gn 1 the second account begins with a dependent clause that paints a picture of the circumstances at the time of man's creation.

*1. Creator (2:4b):* **When Yahweh Elohim...** Outside of Gn 2-3 this combination of divine names occurs only in Ex 9:30 in the Pentateuch.[217] *Yahweh* is used here for the first of 6,770x in the OT.[218] This is the name God is given when he visits his people and makes a covenant with them. Yahweh is the Creator's covenant name. Elohim is his creation name. Yahweh combined with Elohim refutes the old critical contention that the writer has employed two independent and contradictory "sources" that favored the names Yahweh and Elohim respectively. Careful students of the Gn text point out

---

[215] Randy Younker, "Genesis 2: A Second Creation Account?" in *Creation, Catastrophe, and Calvary,* ed. J.T. Baldwin (Hagerstown, MD: Review & Herald, 2000): 69-78. J.B. Doukhan, *The Genesis Creation Story: Its Literary Structure* (Berrien Springs, MI: Andrews University, 1978). Doukhan notes similarities in the structures of the two accounts.

[216] E.g., found in the Sumerian primeval history of Enki and Ninmah from ca. 2000 BC (Kikawada & Quinn, 39).

[217] The combination *Yahweh Elohim* occurs outside the Pentateuch 11x in the books of Chronicles, and 18x in the rest of the OT.

[218] The exact pronunciation of the special name *Yahweh* is debated. The rendering *Jehovah* is a sixteenth century Christian invention. After the Roman destruction of the temple, it became the practice of Jews to substitute the name *Adonay* (*my Lord*) when reading the four-letter name of God (YHWH). Orthodox Jews now go even further and use the substitute *Adoshem* for YHWH and *Elokim* for *Elohim* (God). They display respect for the divine name in written form by writing G-d and L-rd. Other than the ASV (1901) most English versions have followed the Jewish tradition and render YHWH as LORD (all caps) wherever it appears.

that these two names are used very carefully for theological purposes throughout Gn.[219] The contrast in the emphasis in the two names is displayed in Chart 13.

| Chart 13 |  |
|---|---|
| Dual Names for God in Gn 2 |  |
| Yahweh | Elohim |
| A proper name—denotes the God of a special people | A generic name for God. |
| Emphasizes God in his ethical aspect, as known by a holy people. | God as Creator of the material universe, ruler of nature, source of life. |
| God as perceived by simple faith. | God of the philosophically minded. |
| God in his personal involvement stands with his creation | God is a transcendent Being who is outside nature and above it. |
| Yahweh-Elohim |  |
| The combination is used to teach that *Yahweh* is to be fully identified with *Elohim* |  |

*2. Timeframe (2:4b):* **When Yahweh Elohim made the earth and the heavens.** Having given a new name to the Creator, the dependent clause introduces the timeframe for the creation of man: *When* is literally "at the time," not "in the day" (NASB; NRSV). Gn 1:1 declared that in the beginning God created *the heavens and the earth*, an idiom for the universe. Here the terms *heavens* and *earth* are in reverse position. This suggests that the writer does not have the universe in view, but the earth and its atmosphere, called *heavens* in 1:8. There is in 2:4b a shift in perspective. Context makes clear that the writer has narrowed his focus chronologically to the sixth day just before the creation of man.

*3. Location (2:5):* **in the land...** The writer next narrows his focus geographically to the future garden

---

[219]H.C. Brichto, *The Names of God: Poetic Readings in Biblical Beginnings* (Oxford: University Press, 1998).

area. The term *'erets* appears twice in 2:5. It probably should be rendered *land* rather than "earth" (NASB; NIV). Clearly the term refers to the future area of the garden.[220] The first use of the word *ground* (*ᵃdhāmāh*) in the creation narrative suggests that *'erets* has its restricted sense in this v.

## B. Negative Condition (2:5)

As the complex sentence that began in v 4 continues, the condition of the *land/ground*—the future garden area—is first described negatively. Three conditions of the future garden area are indicated.

*1. No special vegetation (2:5a):* **and every shrub of the field before it was in the land, and every plant of the field before it sprouted.** The noun *shrub* (*sîach*) occurs elsewhere only 3x, all apparently in reference to wild growth associated with uninhabited regions. Here the term is used in connection with *the field* (*hassādeh*). This term can refer to open country like pasture land. With the definite article it often refers to a definite, tillable portion of ground. The expression *shrub of the field* (*sîach hassādeh*) does not appear in Gn 1 in the list of vegetation that *the earth* (*hā'ārets*) brought forth on day three. This suggests that the expression refers to the special plants that God placed in the garden on day six.[221] *Was in the land* suggests the reference is to plants that are stable and continue from year to year.

The expression *plant of the field* (*'ēsebh hassādeh*), also missing in ch 1, refers to a grain-bearing plant that requires cultivation. It is mentioned (in the plural) in 3:18 in connection with the work penalty imposed on man because of the garden sin. *Sprouted* points to plants

---

[220]Youngblood, *BGIC*, 35.

[221]Others think *the shrub of the field* corresponds to *the thorns and thistles* of 3:18. These are desert plants that, on rare occasions of rain, spring up from seeds preserved in the dry soil.

that annually spring up anew, either as the result of the rains or of being sown by the hand of man.[222]

*2. No rain (2:5b):* **for Yahweh Elohim had not caused it to rain upon the land.** The writer next mentions the climatic conditions in the future garden area. The v declares that it had not rained prior to man's creation. The implication is that the particular vegetation mentioned in 2:5 needed rain.

Why had it not rained? Perhaps the garden was planned for a region of the globe where rain is not that common. Another possibility is that the conditions required to produce rain—especially the presence in the atmosphere of particles required as condensation nuclei for the formation of raindrops—were not present yet.

Does this statement prove that it did not rain until the time of Noah? Probably not. There is no biblical reason to think that natural weather conditions did not exist during the Antediluvian Period. The text certainly suggests that until the sixth day of creation and possibly until the Fall (if that occurred after the sixth day) the earth was rainless.

*3. No man (2:5c):* **and there was no man to till the ground.** The implication of the statement is that the sprouting of certain vegetation was retarded so that it might appear after man was already in possession of his domain. This particular vegetation needed rain; it also needed man's attention.

## C. Positive Preparation (2:6)

**But a fountain came up from the land and watered the whole surface of the ground.** God prepared the ground for the planting of the garden. The word *fountain* (*'ēd*) appears elsewhere only in Job 36:27. The translation *mist* (KJV; NASB) is a guess. The Greek version ren-

---

[222] Aalders, *BSC*, 83.

ders "spring" or "fountain." Speiser derived the word *'ēd* from the Akkadian *edu* = "flood, waves, swell." Other versions translate "streams" (NIV) or "flood" (NEB). Prior to the sixth day (and possibly the Fall) earth's vegetation depended on irrigation from subterranean waters.

The *fountain* came up from the *earth/land* (*'erets*). In 2:6 *'erets* is probably to be restricted to the garden area as in the previous v. The *fountain* watered *the ground* (*ᵃdhāmāh*). The word is repeated from the previous v. This watered ground is probably the location of the watered garden of 2:10.

## CREATION OF MAN
## Gn 2:7

The creation of man is related in a single v. This v, however, yields information that was not conveyed in the previous ch. Two aspects of man's creation are described in 2:7.

**A. Divine Action** (2:7a)
***Then Yahweh Elohim formed man***. The creation of man is attributed to *Yahweh Elohim* because his creation displayed the faithful mercy of Yahweh as well as the awe-inspiring power of Elohim.

The verb *formed* (r. *ytsr*) is used frequently in a creation context, often in conjunction with *create* (*bārā'*) and *make* (*'āsāh*).[223] Literally, the verb means "to mold, form or fashion." When used in the secular sense, it is most frequently used of the work of a potter (cf. Jer 18:2ff). The verb is not meant to describe the method of divine procedure.

---

[223] Isa 43:1, 21; 45:7; Pss 74:17; 139:16; Jer 1:5; Zech 12:1.

Provision and Probation

The implications of the statement are several. First, man is not an accident, but a designed creature. Second, man's body is a marvel revealing the artistry of the Creator. Third, God gave man a form. Fourth, the verb suggests special care and personal attention. Because of this connotation this verb is the equivalent of the divine contemplation in 1:26. The statement is theologically important because it shows that the body of man came from God as well as his inner being.

**B. Material Substance** (2:7b)
*1. Description (2:7b):* **of dust from the ground.** *Dust* (*'āphār*) is an accusative of specification, specifying material. The term is used 109x in the OT. It refers to any material broken down to its basic elements or parts.[224] It frequently is used of the substance of the earth. The term is used in conjunction with *ashes* (4x) and *clay* (3x). Some want to see in *'āphār* a reference to a "damp mass of the finest earth" (Leupold), presumable because of the association of the previous verb with a potter.

*From the ground* should not be taken to mean *out of* the dust of the ground, as if the Creator were molding a clay image. The idea is that the body of man was fashioned of basic substances similar to those found in the earth.[225]

There is a play on words in the Hebrew that is not evident in English. *Man* (*'ādām*) comes from the *ground* (*'adhāmāh*). Plaut tries to convey the word-play with this translation: "God fashioned an earthling from the

---
[224]Aalders, *BSC*, 85. It refers to scrapings from stones (Lv 14:41), the grindings of the golden calf (Dt 9:21); the pulverized pieces of idols (2 Kgs 23:12).
[225]Aalders, *BSC*, loc cit.

**185**

earth."[226] The earth is man's cradle, his home, and ultimately his grave.

*2. Implications.* Other Scriptures as well allude to the *dust/clay* origins of man. Paul wrote: "The first man was of the dust of the earth ... an earthly man" (1 Cor 15:47-48 NIV). Job's friend Elihu said: "from the clay I too have been taken" (Job 33:6). The reference to the *dust/clay* origins of man deflates any notion that man is a god in the making (contra Mormon theology). Furthermore, it was earth dust, not stardust from which man was made (contra extra-terrestrial theory of origin of life).

That the body was fashioned by God is the theological underpinning to the biblical doctrine that man must not abuse his body in any way. Asceticism, which mutilates, punishes, or humiliates the body and wanton profligacy are both forbidden. For Christians there is added incentive for body care. The body is God's temple.

Theistic evolutionists generally contend that the expression *dust of the ground* points to derivative creation, i.e., evolution. Man's body evolved; his soul was given to him by God. Actually the account makes clear that human beings have no biological antecedents. Both man's body and spirit come from God.

*3. Parallels.* Memory of the dust/clay origins of man survived in the two great cultures of the ancient Near East. At least three Mesopotamian compositions associate creation of man with *clay*. Egyptian paintings also make this connection (Sarna). Pagan parallels, however, are superficial when viewed holistically. The Bible emphasizes the superiority of man. At the same time, *dust* puts limits on human sovereignty.

---

[226] Plaut, *The Torah*, 19.

**C. Spiritual Aspect** (2:7c-e)

*1. Action (2:7c):* ***And [Yahweh-Elohim] breathed into his nostrils.*** Dust-man became living-man through a personal, vitalizing act of the Creator. The text need not be made to say that God put lips to nostrils of a clay image and breathed until respiration started. The statement is anthropomorphic. It simply means that God caused the vital breath to be in man's nostrils, i.e., gave him life. *Nostrils* are mentioned because these are the passages through which breath normally passes. The point of the v is that man received life-breath directly from the Creator. There is a divine *giving* to man, as well as a *shaping* of man. Though made of the same substance as animals (2:19), man is set apart from animals by this direct divine involvement in his creation.

*2. Spiritual nature (2:7d):* **the spirit of life.** God breathed into man *the spirit of life* (*nᵉšāmāh*). The term does not refer to breath or air but to the *spirit* of man—the aspect of man that is immortal. The term *nᵉšāmāh* is used 24x in the OT. The word is always used in connection with God and man, never in connection with animals.[227] The term *nᵉšāmāh,* however, is not a little piece of God. This human spirit is just as much created as is the human body (Zech 12:1). As in ch 1 man shares God's *image* (1:26f), so here man's correspondence to his Maker is expressed in terms of *breath* (*nᵉšāmāh*).

*3. Result (2:7e):* **and man became a living being** (*nepheš chayyāh*). The rendering of KJV and ASV ("living soul") is misleading. The term *nepheš* does not refer to the soul in the theological sense, but the being of the person. Paul declared: "The first man Adam became a living being" (1 Cor 15:45 NIV). Job's friend Elihu said:

---

[227]T.C. Mitchell defends the special meaning of *nᵉšāmāh. VT* 11(1961): 177-188. One possible exception to the word being used of animals: Gn 7:22.

"The Spirit of God has made me; the breath of the Almighty gives me life" (Job 33:6). Animals are living beings too, i.e., they have *nepheš* (Gn 1:21, 24, 28, 30). When God withdraws his life-giving power, creatures die (Job 34:15; Ps 104:29; Eccles 12:7). Apart from God, Abraham said, men are "nothing but dust and ashes" (Gn 18:27).

## WONDER OF MAN

### A. His Body

The human body as designed by God is priceless. It has been estimated that the raw materials of the human body—hormones, proteins, enzymes, etc.—are worth about six million dollars. The intricate work of fashioning the material into human cells might cost six thousand trillion additional dollars. Assembling these cells into a functioning human being would drain all the world's treasures. From just the physical standpoint each human being is priceless.[228]

The way the human body functions is perhaps the greatest wonder of creation. The human heart circulates five or six quarts of blood through the body once a minute. The heart beats 4,200x an hour; 100,800x a day; 36,792,000x a year; 2.5 billion times in a life time of seventy years. It circulates 650,000 gallons of blood through the body each year, enough to fill eighty-one railroad tank cars of eight thousand gallons each. The human digestive tract, if stretched out, would equal the height of a three story building. The kidneys hold more than forty miles of tubing that allows this organ to perform its function of cleansing the blood. One fourth of the body's total blood supply passes through the two kidneys every minute. The eye is a fully automatic, self-

---

[228]Harold J. Morowitz, Yale University biophysicist, writing in "Six-Million-Dollar Original," *Reader's Digest* (April 1977): 144.

focusing, non-blurring, color motion-picture camera that takes instant high resolution three-dimensional pictures. In the ear there are 24,000 hair cells that convert sound vibrations to electrical impulses. The human nose effectively filters more than five hundred cubic feet of air each day.[229]

### B. His Intelligence

Some facts about human intelligence are also worthy of contemplating. It has been estimated that the most brilliant genius uses but one tenth of one percent of his total potential brain ability. Men are perhaps ninety-five percent blind to the total color scheme displayed by nature and ninety-eight percent deaf to her many sound patterns. If Adam's five senses were tuned to perfection and he used the full potential of his intellect, he may have been a thousand times superior to any intellectual living today.[230]

### C. His Nature

Theologians debate whether man should be viewed as trichotomous (body, soul, spirit) or dichotomous (body and soul/spirit). The former position is based on 1 Thess 5:23; Dt 6:5; Mt 22:37; Mk 12:30; Heb 4:12.[231] The latter position is based on Mt 6:25; 10:28; Rom 8:10; 1 Cor. 7:34; Jam 2:26 et. al.

### D. Individual or Symbol?

It is popular in some circles to view Adam (man) as a symbol for mankind rather than as an actual person. This approach does not take the view of the writer of Gn

---

[229] Jerry Bergman, "Homo Sapiens: The Masterpiece of the Master Craftsman," *Bible Science News* 33 (Dec 1995): 1-6.
[230] Facts compiled by H.L. Willmington, *Willmington's Guide to the Bible*, 21
[231] This was the position of Alexander Campbell.

seriously. Adam is connected to Abraham by a genealogy. That genealogy later extends to David (Ruth 4) and ultimately to Christ (Lk 3:23-28). The NT always presents Adam as an historical figure (Mt 19:4-5; Rom 5:12-19; 1 Cor 15:21-22; 1 Tim 2:13-14). There is no legitimate reason to question that Adam was a real person.

# PROVISION FOR MAN
## Gn 2:8-14

If God is presented anthropologically as divine Potter in v 7, now he is presented as divine Gardener who prepares a beautiful area of foliage for the habitation of the first man.

**A. Garden Provision** (2:8)

*1. Planting of the garden (2:8a):* **And Yahweh Elohim planted a garden.** Rendering the verb *planted* as pluperfect (*had planted* NIV) in an attempt to harmonize ch 2 with the creation of vegetation prior to man in ch 1 is unnecessary. The garden was a special habitat created for man after man had been created. In respect to the garden several points require consideration.

*2. Name of the garden (2:8b):* **in Eden toward the east.** *Eden* is a location larger than the garden itself. Because of its situation *in Eden*, the garden came to be known as *the garden of Eden* (Gn 2:15 et al). The term *Eden* is related to a Sumerian word meaning "plain." Others think it is related to a Hebrew word denoting "bliss" or "delight." Elsewhere this garden is called the "garden of God" (Ezek 28:13; 31:9) or "garden of Yahweh" (Gn 13:10; Isa 51:3). These names do not suggest that God dwelled in the garden. Rather they reflect the fact that it was in the garden that God came to communicate directly and personally with man. The term "paradise" comes from the Greek rendering of *gan* (garden) in Gn 2:8ff.

*3. Purpose of the garden (2:8c):* **and there he placed the man whom he had formed.** The garden was created after man, and for man. Choosing the garden as the first habitat of man was an evidence of the gracious provision of God. The first man was not left to fight his way through jungle, or eek out a living from barren desert. The Creator not only gave man life, he placed him in an environment where he could experience abundant life.

*4. Localization of the garden.* Some think the whole earth was a paradise in the beginning (Leupold; Whitcomb). Others view that garden as a paradise within a natural environment (Ramm). The evidence seems to support this second position. First, the term *gan* (garden) always describes an enclosed area. Second, the garden was located *toward the east*. This means nothing more than that the garden was located east of where the writer of Gn resided. While vague, the expression helps to make the point that the garden was a real place, not merely a symbol. Third, *Eden* was a definite territory (Gn 4:16; 2 Kgs 19:12). Fourth, an angel was placed at the entrance of the garden (Gn 3:24). Fifth, man was placed in the garden (Gn 2:15). He knew the difference between the garden and the area outside.

## B. Garden Trees (2:9)

*1. Variety (2:9a):* **And out of the ground Yahweh Elohim caused to grow every tree that is pleasing to the sight and good for food.** God caused a variety of trees to spring up in the garden. *Every tree* is literally "the whole of trees," i.e., every kind of tree. The garden contained only trees that were either aesthetically attractive, or that produced eatable fruit. One must conclude that God did not permit any tree to grow in the garden that might produce fruit that was toxic to man. Among the garden trees were two special trees.

2. *Tree of life (2:9b):* **The tree of life was also in the midst of the garden.** The term *life* (*chayyîm*) appears in the plural form, the so-called plural of abstraction. A definite article is attached. It is not life in general, but a specific kind of life that is associated with the tree. Later it becomes clear that this tree related to eternal life (3:22).

All that is known about *the tree of life* is what can be deduced from the threefold use in Gn.[232] First, the tree of life was a real tree, as much as any of the other trees that grew in the garden. It is not to be given a symbolic interpretation. Second, the purpose of this tree was to confirm man in the possession of physical life and render physical death impossible (Leupold). Third, the tree was in the midst of the garden. This does not necessarily mean that the tree was in the middle of the garden. The meaning is that among the wide variety of trees this special tree grew.

Ancient pagan literature furnishes recollections of a "plant of life." The quest for this plant was an obsession in the ancient world, much like the search for the fountain of youth in western folklore.

3. *Tree of knowledge (2:9c):* **And the tree of the knowledge of good and evil.** Knowing good and evil is the theme of the narrative. It occurs here at the outset (2:9, 17); at the climax (3:5) and in the final survey (3:22). The idea that the tree of knowledge was an apple tree rests solely on a Latin word-play, *malus/malum*

---

[232]In Revelation John alludes 3x to an eschatological tree of life in the heavenly paradise (Rev 2:7, 22:2, 14). Proverbs alludes 4x to a tree of life in connection with what enhances life in any way (Prov 3:18; 11:30; 13:12; 15:4). None of these uses offers any insight into the use of *tree of life* in Gn.

(evil/apple). For the tree of knowledge there is no pagan parallel.[233]

Various explanations have been proposed as to the kind of knowledge that is referenced in the name of this tree. It was not sexual knowledge (Origen; Gordis), because God knows good and evil (3:5, 22) and he is asexual. It was not total knowledge (Cassuto), because Adam and Eve did not become omniscient when they ate. Wenham holds that the tree imparted divine wisdom such as legitimately can be obtained only through obedience.[234] All of these interpretations view the fruit of the tree magically.

The knowledge that resulted from partaking of the tree was experiential knowledge (Young). God forbade his creature to taste of the evil of disobedience in the concrete manner that man already was tasting (experiencing) good in the garden. Partaking of the tree brought moral discernment (Keil).

The main emphasis falls on the prohibition of eating from the tree rather than the properties of the tree. As long as he did not eat from the tree man had perceptive knowledge of good and evil. That is the kind of knowledge of good and evil that God possesses. When man ate from the forbidden tree he gained experiential knowledge of evil (disobedience) with all of its attending consequences.

Usage in the rest of the OT[235] of the phrase *knowing good and evil* suggests that the expression refers to the ability to decide between moral alternatives. Thus partaking of this forbidden tree was an assertion of moral autonomy (de Vaux), i.e., the right to decide for oneself

---

[233] Some want to equate the tree of knowledge with "the tree of death" attested in a Canaanite religious text. See M. Tsevat, "The Two Trees in the Garden of Eden," *Eretz-Israel* 12(1975):119 (English abstract).
[234] Wenham, *WBC*, 205. Wenham is followed by Mathews, *NAC*, 205f.
[235] 2 Sam 14:17, 20; 19:35; Isa 7:15-16; Dt 1:39; Gn 3:5, 22; 24:50; 31:24, 29; 1 Kgs 3:9.

about good (what enhances life) and evil (what is detrimental to life). The message of the tree of knowledge is that Yahweh reserves for himself the prerogative of deciding what is good and evil. He alone is autonomous.

### C. Garden Rivers (2:10-14)

*1. Configuration (2:10):* **Now a river flowed out of Eden to water the garden; and from there it divided and became four heads.** Apparently a single river flowed through the garden. The river *flowed out of Eden*, i.e., it had it sources in the territory of Eden. There is some dispute as to whether the four rivers were joined to the one river as upstream tributaries or whether the one river divided into four streams after leaving the garden. Those who emphasize *from there* take the latter view; those who emphasize the word *heads* take the former view. The term *heads* (*rā'šîm*) is used of eminent men (e.g., Ex 18:25), mountain heights (Gn 8:5) and military divisions (e.g., Judg 7:20); but it is never elsewhere used in the sense of headwaters. Whether one river became four or four rivers became one the point is that the garden is associated with abundant water.

Nearly all commentators flounder on the vv describing the four heads and the lands connected to them. In approaching these vv the interpreter must assume that the inspired writer was presenting accurate geography for the purpose of identifying more precisely the location of the garden. He was listing rivers, lands and products as they were known to him. While the geography was no doubt clear to the original readers, it is fuzzy to moderns. Two of the heads can be identified with some degree of certainty; two are a mystery.

*2. First head (2:11-12):* **The name of the first is Pishon; it winds through the whole land of Havilah, where there is gold. And the gold of that land is good; the bdellium and the onyx stone are there.** The phrase *winds through* (*hassōbhēbh*) comes from a root meaning, "turn around, go around, surround." In English versions it is rendered "flows around" (NASB; RSV); "encompasses" (NKJV). There are two areas called *Havilah* (sandy land) in the Bible (Gn 10:7; 10:29). It is probably the latter *Havilah* that was near the garden of Eden. *Bdellium* (*habbᵉdōlach*) is apparently some type of stone, not "aromatic resin" or "pearls" (NIV). Scholars also are not in agreement about how to identify the *onyx stone* (*'ebhen haššōham*). It is later mentioned in conjunction with the garments of the high priest (Ex 25:7) and with the temple (1 Chr 29:2).

In addition to his geographical intentions, the writer may have had another reason for reporting about the precious stones. Ancient pagan literature speaks of an idyllic garden where trees grew jewels. Perhaps the point is that the valuable stones actually were outside the garden.

Archaeologist Juris Zarins used LANDSAT satellite imagery to identify a "fossil river" that once flowed through northern Arabia. Modern Saudis and Kuwaitis know this river as Wadi Batin. This fossil river could be the biblical Pishon.[236]

*3. Second head (2:13):* **And the name of the second is Gihon; it winds through the whole land of Cush.** Like the first head the second also *winds through* a land. *Cush* usually refers to northern Sudan (called Ethiopia by the ancients) in Africa; Leupold takes that to be the meaning here. *Cush* in 2:13, however, cannot refer to Ethiopia because of the great distance between Africa

---

[236] D.J. Hamblin, "Has the Garden of Eden been Located at Last? *Smithsonian* (May 1987): 131f. Farouk El-Baz also has taken credit for tracing the partially underground, sand river channel from the mountains of Hijaz to Kuwait. He named this "fossil river" the Kuwait River. "Boston University Scientist Discovers Ancient River System in Saudi Arabia," in *Boston University News* (March 25, 1993): 1-2. See also James Sauer, "The River Runs Dry," *BAR* 22(Jul/Aug 1998): 52-57, 64.

and Mesopotamia (modern Iraq) where the garden seems to have been located.[237] Scripture also knows of a *Cush* in Mesopotamia during the days of Nimrod (Gn 10:8-12). Speiser has identified this *Cush* with the land of the Kassites (called *Kushshu* in the Nuzi texts) in Mesopotamia.[238]

Zarins identifies the Gihon River as the Karun River, which rises in Iran and flows southwesterly toward the Persian Gulf.[239] Until it was dammed the Karun contributed most of the sediment forming the delta at the head of the Persian Gulf.

4. *Third head (2:14a):* **And the name of the third river is Hiddekel; it flows east of Assyria.** *Hiddekel* without question is the Tigris River. The Tigris and Euphrates rivers were two of the greatest rivers of Western Asia. Both rivers originate in the Armenian mountains. The Tigris parallels the Euphrates in a shorter (1180 miles) and straighter course. This river is not as prominent in the Bible as is the Euphrates, but it is the site of a major vision of the prophet Daniel (Dan 10:4). Significant cities, like Nineveh and Asshur, were located on its banks.

5. *Fourth head (2:14b):* **and the fourth river is the Euphrates.** The Euphrates was known to the Hebrews as "the great river" (Gn 15:18; Josh 1:4) or simply "the river" (Nm 22:5). It flows on a somewhat winding course over twelve hundred miles to the Persian Gulf. Some of the great cities of the ancient world (Babylon, Mari) were located on its banks. It formed the northern boundary of the land promised by Yahweh to Israel (Gn 15:18; Dt 1:7).

---

[237] Youngblood, *BGIC*, 38.
[238] E.A. Speiser, *Genesis, The Anchor Bible* (Garden City, NY, 1964), 20.
[239] Hope Wozniak Graves, in private correspondence with the author, pointed out linguistic affinities between the biblical names *Pishon* and *Gihon* and their modern counterparts *Batin* and *Karun*.

**D. Garden Location**

*1. Non-geographical view.* More liberal commentators argue the *Gihon* is the Nile River; the *Pishon* is the Indus River. Together with the Tigris and the Euphrates rivers these were the four great rivers that supported life in the ancient world. According to these interpreters the point of Gn 2 is that the four great rivers of the ancient world have their origin in a single river.

*2. Promised Land view.* Because there is some uncertainty about the identity of the four heads, a number of locations have been proposed for the garden.[240] Sailhamer argues that the garden is actually the Promised Land that was between the Euphrates River and the Gihon, which he takes to be the River of Egypt.[241]

*3. Armenian view.* Some think the text points to an Armenian location near the headwaters of the Tigris and Euphrates. Those who argue for this northern location for the garden take the *Gihon* to be the Araxes River and the *Pishon* to be the Kur River.[242]

*4. Chaldean view.* More common is the view that the garden was located in Chaldea near the mouth of the Persian Gulf (Speiser), or perhaps what would now be under the Gulf (Harris).[243] In the light of the satellite discovery of the fossil river that once flowed through the Arabian Desert toward the Persian Gulf, this is perhaps the best suggestion.

Trying to locate the original Eden is futile due to shifting river beds, changes in configurations of the

---

[240] Numerous suggestions are listed in *ISBE* s.v. "Eden."

[241] Sailhamer, *Unbound*, 72f.

[242] Leupold, *Exposition*, 125f.; E.K.V. Pearce, *Who was Adam?* (Exeter: Paternoster, 1969), 51ff.

[243] Zarins believes that the original site of Eden vanished under the waters of the Gulf during a worldwide phenomenon called the Flandrian Transgression, which caused a sudden rise in sea level. See D.J. Hamblin, loc. cit.

land, and accumulation of enormous deposits of river silt.[244]

### E. Garden as Sanctuary

Wenham has developed at length the idea that the garden was viewed as the original sanctuary. The later Israelite tabernacle/temple was a symbolic representation of the original garden sanctuary. Wenham points out a number of parallels to later sanctuary terminology. First, the verb *walk to and fro* (*hithallēk*), used of God in the garden (Gn 2:8), is also used to describe the divine presence in the tabernacle (Lv 26:12; Dt 23:14; 2 Sam 7:6-7).

Second, the cherubim were stationed at the eastern entrance. The tabernacle/temple entrance faced the east. Cherubim symbolism guarded the approaches to the holy of holies (2 Kgs 6).

Third, the tree of life in the midst of the garden is paralleled by the idea that fullness of life is to be found in the sanctuary, a basic premise in Psalms. The tabernacle menorah (lampstand) may have been a stylized tree of life.

Fourth, Adam's job in the garden is described with a double verb *till and keep* (*le'obhdāh ulešomrāh*). The only other usage of this verb combination is found in Nm 3:7-8, 8:26, 18:5-6 where it is used of Levitical duties of guarding and ministering in the sanctuary.

Fifth, a river flowing out of Eden has its parallel in a river flowing out of the temple (Ps 46:4; Ezek 47). The *good gold* of Havilah (2:12) has its replica in tabernacle/temple furniture covered with pure gold (Ex 25:11, 17, 24, 29, 36).

Sixth, the precious stone *bedōlach* (2:12) is mentioned elsewhere only in Nm 11:7 where manna is com-

---

[244] M. Unger, *Archaeology of the OT* (Grand Rapids: Zondervan, 1954), 40.

pared to it. Manna was stored in or beside the ark (Ex 16:33).

Seventh, the onyx stone *šōham* (2:12) was widely used in decorating the tabernacle (Ex 25:7; 28:9; 20; 1 Chr 29:2). Two onyx stones, engraved with the names of the twelve tribes (Ex 28:9-14), were on the shoulders of the high priest.

Eighth, language describing the tree of the knowledge of good and evil (2:9; 3:6) is used of God's law (Ps 19:8-9). The law was kept in the holy of holies (Ex 25:16; Dt 31:26). Touching the ark or even seeing it uncovered brought death, just as eating from the tree did (2 Sam 6:7; Nm 4:20).

The thesis of garden/sanctuary parallelism is further supported by a study of the creation account. Kearney pointed out that there were six commands to Moses concerning the construction of the tabernacle, followed by a seventh ordering observance of the Sabbath.[245] These may correspond to the days of the creation week. It may be that God's rest on the seventh day (2:1-3) corresponds to his resting, i.e., dwelling, in the tabernacle (Ex 25:8; 29:45f).

# PROBATION OF MAN
# Gn 2:15-17

The focus now shifts to the first man. Five obligations are implied and/or set forth for Adam.

### A. Relationship to Cultivate (2:15a)
***Then Yahweh Elohim took the man and put him into the garden of Eden.*** In 2:8 the verb is the ordinary word for "put or place," with no special overtones. Here

---

[245]Kearney, *ZAW* 89 (1977): 375-87. The tabernacle commands are found in Ex 25:1; 30:11, 17, 22, 34; 31:1, 12.

the verb *put* (*yannichēhû*) is lit., "caused him to rest." This word is used in the OT to describe the rest or safety that God gives to his people (Gn 19:16; Dt 3:20; 12:10; 25:19). The same Hebrew word is used to indicate the dedication of something before the presence of the Lord (Ex 16:33-34; Lv 16:23; Nm 17:4; Dt 26:4, 10). Therefore, man was put into the garden sanctuary where he could rest and be safe in the presence of God, i.e., in fellowship with him.

## B. Task to Perform (2:15b)

Man was put in the garden *to serve and keep it* (2:15b). These two infinitives invite separate analysis.

*1. To serve it* (*le'obhdāh*). There is a question as to whether the suffix *it* was part of the original text. Several manuscripts have the word as a simple infinitive = "to serve." If the suffix is omitted, then man's life in the garden was to be characterized by worship. This is so because the root *'bd* is a regular way of indicating worship in the OT. Adam was to be a virtual priest, not merely a worker and keeper of the garden. The rabbis thought the word referred to sacrificial service.

The suffix *it,* however, probably is original. Then the question arises as to the antecedent of *it.* The ready explanation is that *it* refers to the garden. In Hebrew, however, this suffix is feminine; the word *garden* is masculine. Yet in spite of this difficulty nearly all commentators regard the reference of *it* to be to the garden. The LXX translators even changed the gender of the pronoun to make the reference refer to the garden.[246]

Assuming that the pronoun refers to the garden, the implication is this: man was to till or cultivate the garden. Work is essential to meaningful life, a gift of God and not a punishment for sin. Even in his relationship

---

[246]The only other suggestion in the commentaries is that *it* refers to the Torah, the law of God (which is feminine).

with the soil, man must maintain his humility. God planted the garden; man imitates God's work by devoting himself to horticulture. Perhaps this is intended as one illustration of *subdue the earth* (1:28).

2. *To guard it (lešomrāh).* The same problem exists with the suffix on this infinitive as was noted in the preceding word. The suffix is feminine; the natural antecedent is masculine. If the suffix were not originally part of the word, then the meaning would be something like "obey." Man was thus put in the garden to worship and obey God.[247]

Again most commentators take the pronoun *it* to refer to the garden in spite of the gender problem. In that case the word means that man was to guard or keep the garden. Some think the idea is that man should guard the garden from intrusion by the Evil One. Had they refused to listen to Serpent the first couple would have driven him out of the garden; but that was not to be.

While this is a possible interpretation, the language does not necessitate guarding the garden from some external enemy. The idea is that man is the keeper of the garden; he has responsibility for it. He is more than a mere servant. He has authority over the garden. It is his domain. Some authorities see in this verb the connotation "to look after it" (Meek; BDB). Adam had certain responsibilities to develop the potentialities of the garden.

3. *Combination.* Taken together the two infinitives have rich significance. The ideal state of sinless man is not one of indolence without responsibility. Work and duty belong to the perfect state. Leupold observes that "even though the garden was in every sense good, yet care was necessary to keep it from growing in exuberant disorder."[248] Man's authority over the garden, however,

---

[247] Sailhamer, *Unbound*, 76.
[248] Leupold, *Exposition*, 127.

was delegated, not absolute. The Creator's charge to keep the garden makes clear the place of man in God's scheme of things.

### C. Command to Obey (2:16)

***And Yahweh Elohim commanded the man, saying, From any tree of the garden you may eat freely.*** Chronologically these are the first words God spoke to man. The words in 1:28 were spoken after the creation of the woman. The verb *commanded* assumes moral accountability and freedom of choice on the part of man. The graciously provided gift of life in the garden paradise demands faithful obedience.

*1. Substance of the command. You may eat freely* is lit., "eating you shall eat." This is an infinitive absolute, the most forceful type of Hebrew expression. Some imagine a contradiction between this v and 1:29 where man was allowed to eat *every plant yielding seed.* This v is concerned only about what *trees* man could use for food. The two vv are supplementary. The trees of the garden are representative of all the riches of the earth that are placed at man's disposal.

*2. Significance of the command.* The significance of this command is threefold. First, the command obviously indicates fullness of permission—*you shall eat freely.* Second, the command also indicates obligation as well. There is an order here for man to enjoy the life God gives him, to explore the magnificent park and taste its fruits. By enthusiastically embracing his life in the garden and enjoying every one of its manifold wonders the man will show his gratitude to the Lord.[249] Third, God reveals himself in this first provision for man as the God of superabundant grace.

---

[249]Ibid.

### D. Prohibition to Observe (2:17a)

*1. Strength of the prohibition (2:17a)*: **But from the tree of the knowledge of good and evil you shall not eat.** Earlier in creation week God established boundaries for the components of the natural world and their inhabitants. So it is to be expected that God will draw boundaries for man as well. His boundaries are quite narrow. Only one tree is "off limits."

The Hebrew syntax expresses the strongest form of prohibition. The implication here is that enjoyment of God's good land is contingent on keeping God's commandments.

God addressed man personally and individually (*you*). Of all the creatures only man is so addressed. Man has personhood acknowledged by God. After the creation of the woman God will address the couple with the plural *you* (1:28f).

*2. Reason for the prohibition.* The prohibition does not imply that the tree itself was harmful physically, or that it was inherently evil. Everything that God had created was good (1:31). Later it becomes clear that the fruit of this tree was actually desirable for food. Why, then, is man forbidden to partake of it? The Creator does not announce the garden restriction in order to place a temptation before man. Rather the tree restriction served a practical purpose.

First, it presented man with a choice, hence defined for all time the kind of service that God desires from man. Second, the restriction served to strengthen man's faith and trust in Yahweh.[250] Man could have used that tree as place to worship, recall all his bountiful blessings and reflect on the seriousness of disobedience. Third, the prohibition demonstrated the nature of sin. Eating of the fruit of this tree was evil for one reason, viz., God pro-

---

[250]Youngblood, *BGIC*, 53.

hibited it. By implication not eating of the tree was *good*.[251] That is the point of the ch. It is God alone who has the wisdom and authority to proclaim what is good and what is evil.

*3. Common misunderstandings.* Batto is wrong to insist that man was created "to work the garden, apparently to relieve the deity—or perhaps better the gods."[252] Equally wrong are those who see in this narrative an effort on the part of a petty God to protect his turf (represented by knowledge = omniscience and eternal life) against encroachment by man. Yahweh is seen as the antagonist of man, rather than the benefactor.[253] This view is clearly incorrect for the following reasons.

First, it gives too much credence to the slanderous allegation of Serpent in 3:5. Second, Eve's motives for eating the fruit do not explicitly reference Serpent's remarks about the godlike character of knowledge (3:6). Third, man was not barred from the tree of life until he transgressed regarding the tree of knowledge. Fourth, God did not take away from man whatever he acquired by eating of the forbidden tree. Fifth, the trees were in an area intended for man's habitation and enjoyment, a strange place to put them if God were trying to protect his divine turf of knowledge and life. Sixth, by partaking of the fruit man became God-like in some sense (3:22); but he certainly did not become omniscient.

---

[251] Depending on one's interpretation of *guard* in 2:15 there may be a hint of good and evil. Man had a command to obey (good) and he was to guard the garden from external intrusion (evil).

[252] Bernard Batto, "Creation Theology in Genesis," *Creation in the Biblical Traditions*, ed. R. Clifford and J. Collins (Washington: Catholic Biblical Association, 1992).

[253] H.N. Wallace, "The Eden Narrative," (Ph.D. diss., Harvard, 1982), 235-36; W.M. Clark, "The Flood and the Structure of the Pre-patriarchal History," *ZAW*, 83(1971): 191. This notion is clearly refuted by Robert Di Vito, "The Demarcation of Divine and Human Realms in Genesis 2-11," *CBT*, 39-56.

### E. Warning to Heed (2:17b)

*For in the day that you eat from it you shall surely die.* God graciously warns the man what the consequences will be if he chooses to disobey. The Hebrew construction of this explanatory clause emphasizes three things. First, *in the day* stresses that the penalty will be instantaneous. Second, *you shall surely die* is literally, "dying you shall die." This idiom stresses that the penalty for disobedience regarding the tree is certain. Third, the language of this clause is a judicial penalty formula. It is found elsewhere in texts of condemnation both human and divine (e.g., Gn 20:7; Jer 26:8).

## CONCLUDING ISSUES

### A. Meaning of "Die"

In light of the fact that man did not immediately die physically, various explanations for this warning have been proposed. Some think that *die* means that afflictions will come upon Adam that will make him wish he were dead. Others think the threat is that man's life would be cut short of its allotted time of one thousand years. Another suggestion is that because of God's grace death was postponed.

The best explanation is that the sentence was executed as intended. At the tree of knowledge man declared himself independent from the will of God. He thus severed his vital connection with the living God, the source of all life. So the warning primarily focuses on spiritual death—separation from God. Furthermore, because of this man came under a judicial sentence of death. A similar warning in 1 Kgs 2:36-46 indicates that the expression *in that day you will surely die* (2:17) simply means "on that day you will fall under the power of a death sentence." Physical death, like birth, is a process.

The death process for man set in the minute man partook of the tree.

## B. Other Questions

Several interesting questions relating to the special garden trees are not definitely answered in the text. Could man have eaten of the tree of life before he had his confrontation with the tree of knowledge? Obviously God knew that man would not discover the tree of life first. Perhaps God even arranged that man could not discover the tree of life immediately.

Did man know also of the existence of the tree of life and did he know which tree it was? There is no indication in the text that the man was told anything about the tree of life.

Was Adam created physically immortal or was physical immortality possible only by eating the tree of life? Presumably the second alternative is correct, for otherwise what possible purpose would the tree of life serve? While in the garden man had access to the tree of life which, so it would seem, had some rejuvenating quality about it. One might say that by the sin in the garden man forfeited the opportunity for perpetual rejuvenation.

What is the relationship between Ezekiel 28:11-19 and the Gn garden narrative? Probably Ezekiel is alluding to a Canaanite myth that he sarcastically uses to describe the attitude of the king of Tyre. Apparently in some Gentile circles there was a remembrance (howbeit a garbled one) of a garden paradise from which the occupant was expelled because of sin.

# 11
# THE GARDEN MARRIAGE
# Gn 2:18-25

The remainder of Gn 2 focuses on man and his mate. Three basic themes run through this narrative, viz., the likeness and difference of the mates and the order that characterized the first marriage.

## MAN ALONE IN THE GARDEN
## Gn 2:18

**A. Divine Assessment** (2:18a)
***Then Yahweh Elohim said, It is not good for the man to be alone.*** Again the writer stresses God's knowledge of what is good for man and what is harmful for him. The creation of woman is a specific manifestation of this divine knowledge.

The plural pronoun in 1:28 suggests that woman was part of the divine contemplation preceding the creation of man. Yet the Creator delayed the creation of the female counterpart of the man for a time that he might accomplish several ends.

First, the delayed appearance of the first woman highlights her creation. Second, the delay created awareness in the man's heart of his need for a mate. Third, the delayed creation of woman helped the writer underscore her fundamental equality with her male counterpart. Fourth, the delayed creation helps to establish the foundations of the institution of marriage.

Yahweh Elohim assessed the situation of man without mate as *not good*. Obviously this assessment takes place prior to 1:31 where the Creator pronounced all that he had made as *very good*. The setting for the creation of woman is day six, after the creation of man. The Creator is not only noting the absence of something good, but is acknowledging a painful deficiency (Cassuto).[254]

There are several senses in which the situation of man without a mate was *not good*? First, it was not good *psychologically*. Man's life without a wife is devoid of joy, blessing and well-being. Second, not having a mate was *socially* not good. Man is a social being. In every way it is the normal thing for a man to go through life in fellowship with a wife (Leupold). Third, man without mate was not good *practically*. Providing for man's needs and comforts calls for a division of labors and partnership.

Did man perceive that his situation without a mate was *not good*? The text does not make his awareness explicit. Perhaps there was a growing awareness of loneliness, especially after he observed the gender pattern among the animals. Be that as it may, the statement in the text is not a subjective judgment. This is a statement of objective fact by the Creator. God himself declared that it was not good for the man to be alone!

Other Scriptures indicate that God calls some to a life of celibacy. There is no biblical reason to browbeat believers who choose to live in a single state, or those who cannot find a mate who measures up to biblical standards. The assessment of 2:18 was of *the* man, i.e., the first man, Adam. The v should not be taken to mean that this is the divine assessment of *every* man (or woman).

### B. Divine Solution (2:18b, c)

*1. General plan (2:18b):* **I will make a helper.** The solution to the *not good* situation of the man was to create for him a mate. The Creator never contemplated creating more than one such helper for the first man. It is in

---

[254]The Hebrew (*lō' tôbh*) is much stronger than the milder statement of something less than perfect (*'en tôbh*) would have been.

monogamous union that God's will is best carried out. God's stated intentions mirror the contemplation of 1:26. Interestingly, the creation of the man earlier in the ch is described in the third person. "The dignity of the woman is heightened by the monologue of God's creative contemplation."[255]

As part of the duality of man the woman possessed all that is implied in the concepts of image, blessing and dominion in 1:26-28. Yet the female component of the duality of man possessed another attribute. She was *a help* or *helper* (*'ēzer*). There are several implications in the use of this term.

First, Adam needed her. The first man can better fulfill the purpose of his creation in consort with a wife. Second, the word suggests interdependence. If he needs her, so also does she need him. Third, the word *help/helper* does not signal inferiority. In fifteen of the twenty-one occurrences of the word in the OT it is God who is the *help* or *helper*. One might even suggest that the woman was to be the divinely appointed *helper* to this man. Fourth, *help* states plainly that the duality should not entail any rivalry. Fifth, the term connotes what is plainly taught elsewhere, that the man is the leader in the relationship. The NT stresses that man is *head* and woman is *help*.

Specifically, how was the woman to be a help to the man? There may be some validity in the suggestion that she is to assist him in the management of the garden. More likely, however, her help is related to the bearing of children. It is through multiplying that man will be able to achieve dominion over the earth. So man cannot achieve that goal without his spouse.

*2. Specific aim (2:18c):* **suitable for him**. She is to be the exact counterpart of man in bodily structure, men-

---

[255] Mathews, *NAC*, 213.

tal ability, and spiritual make-up. Animals are *helps* to man, but they do not correspond to him. She is the helper par excellence.

Woman is suitable for the man because she is lit. "opposite" him. She supplies what is lacking in him. She is genuinely different. In order to fill the emptiness of his solitude, man must accept these differences.

The rabbis sensed a disharmony in the terms *help* and *suitable* (*opposite*). They concluded that if man is worthy, his mate will be a help, i.e., there will be unity. If not, she will be *over against him*, i.e., there will be disharmony. The choice belongs to man.

# MAN AND GARDEN ANIMALS
# Gn 2:19-20

### A. Creation of the Animals (2:19a)

*And out of the ground Yahweh Elohim formed every beast of the field and every bird of the sky.* How does this v relate to 1:25 where God made *cattle, creeping things and beasts of the earth*? Some think that this is another report of the animals created prior to man. The Hebrew verb form could just as easily be rendered as a pluperfect—*God had formed.* Here, however, a different verb is used and a different result is indicated.

The verb *made* in 1:25 has become *formed* (*yātsar*), the same word used of the creation of man in 2:7. Here the result is the *beast of the field*, not *beast of the earth* as in 1:25. In 2:5 there is reference to the *plant of the field*, where field seems to point to the garden. The verb *yātsar* and the word *field* suggest that this is a special creation of animals for the garden environment. No doubt the garden animals were those that were particularly useful, attractive and/or entertaining to man. Like the garden vegetation, the garden animals were those that thrived on human association.

## The Garden Marriage

**B. Assessment of Animals** (2:19b, c)

*1. Animals assembled (2:19b):* **And brought them to the man to see what he would call them.** A regular feature in Hebrew is to form proper names by adding an article to a common noun. Thus *hā-'ādām* (*the man*) could legitimately be rendered Adam. English versions differ as to the point in the text where they believe a proper name is intended. The expression *hā-'ādām* previously has appeared in 1:27, 2:7, 8, 15, 16, 18. It is here in 2:19, however, that the expression is rendered for the first time as the proper name *Adam* by the KJV. The NIV, NASB and NJPS begin to use *Adam* in 2:20, ASV in 3:17 and NRSV in 4:25.

In the Ebla texts from northern Syria the personal name *Adam* appears. This discovery strengthens considerably the traditional view that the biblical Adam was a real person and not simply a personification of mankind in general.[256]

*2. Animals analyzed (2:19c):* **and whatever the man called a living creature, that was its name.** It is a wrong interpretation of this passage to see here a series of unsuccessful attempts to create a mate for Adam. The view that Adam was merely providing a dictionary label for each animal is also incorrect. The point of the passage is not to explain how the animals got their present names.

The Hebrew indicates a precise case of identification. The text does not say "that became the name thereof." Adam identified each creature as to its nature—and that in fact was its nature. The v highlights Adam's intelligence and perceptiveness. He could see that each creature was inferior to himself and thus an unfit mate.

---

[256] Youngblood, *BGIC*, 39.

**C. Naming of the Animals** (2:20)

*1. Action (2:20a):* ***And the man gave names to all the cattle, and to the birds of the sky, and to every beast of the field.*** The giving of names implies the existence of language. God formed the first man as a communicating being. There is no clue in the text as to identity of this language or its relationship to any existing language. See further comments on ch 11.

What animals were named? How long did the process of naming take? Presumably the naming process was not of long duration for the following reasons.

First, only a limited number of animals were involved. The animals were not assembled from the various regions of the world. Excluded were probably marine animals, invertebrates and animals small enough to elude observation in the vegetation.[257] The text suggests that the garden animals formed in 2:19 were created specifically for the naming. Second, the purpose of the naming did not require a large number of animals. Third, Adam named the animals quickly on the basis of their obvious anatomical features; prolonged scrutiny of each animal to ensure that its name would be appropriate or permanent was not necessary. Fourth, the exercise may have been terminated by the Creator once its purpose had been accomplished.

*2. Result (2:20b):* ***but for Adam there was not found a helper suitable for him.*** There were at least four purposes for the naming.

First, there was a pedagogic (instructional) purpose. The exercise was designed to emphasize the fundamen-

---

[257]Even those who apply the naming to non-Garden animals limit the number of named animals. The animals named may have been representatives of a relatively small number of basic kinds originally created, not the wide variety now existing. See Frank Marsh, *Studies in Creationism* (Washington: Review & Herald, 1950).

tal differences between man and beast, especially between woman and inferior creatures.

Second, the psychological purpose was to arouse in Adam the awareness of not having a mate like the garden creatures.

Third, the polemical purpose was to condemn by implication bestiality. Man must not cohabit with animals.

Fourth, this was the beginning of man's exercise of lordship over the animals. It is true that the dominion mandate was given after the creation of woman, and to both the man and his wife. It appears, however, that man assumed dominion over animals even before the Creator formally put his stamp of approval on it. Just as the Creator expressed his sovereignty by naming various things in ch 1, so now the man expressed his sovereignty in a similar manner.

# MAN AND HIS MATE
# Gn 2:21-23

**A. Creation of the Woman** (2:21-22a):

*1. Passive role of man (2:21a):* **So Yahweh Elohim caused a deep sleep to fall upon the man, and he slept.** *Deep sleep* (*tardēmāh*) indicates an extraordinary sleep, perhaps even supernatural (LXX renders *ekstasis*). The point of the sleep is that man is totally passive in the mystery of the emergence of the woman. She is not, then, a creature of man—a mere extension of his body.

*2. Active role of God (2:21b):* **then he took one of his ribs, and closed up the flesh at that place.** The verb *took* (r. *lqch*) is used 3x in reference to the creation of the woman. Either the verb anticipates the marital union of the two,[258] or later use of the verb as an idiom for marriage is derived from this passage.

*Ribs* (sing. *tsēlāʻ*) is used 38x in the OT, over half that number in the account of the construction of the tabernacle. Only in this context is the word used in clear reference to part of man's anatomy. Here the standard English versions agree on the translation *ribs*. Some, however, argue that man's *side* (not *rib*) was used in the creation of Eve.[259]

The man was not left to heal on his own. God repaired the wound before he proceeded to create the woman. Whether Adam suffered any pain after he awoke is not indicated.

*3. Creative work (2:22a):* ***And Yahweh Elohim built the rib he had taken from Adam to (be) a woman.*** Since the word *ribs* is used so frequently in construction narrative, the verb *built* (*bānāh*) is appropriate. It implies great care and workmanship. In this term God is anthropologically depicted as the great Architect. It is significant that nothing is said about God breathing into the woman's nostrils the breath of life; she derived her life from that of the man. Precisely how God formed the rib into the woman is not revealed. It is the resulting oneness of the work that is important, not the mechanics of the process.

### B. Wrong Conclusions

*1. Etiological tale.* The story of the taking of one of Adam's ribs is not an etiological tale devised to explain why men have one less rib than women. As a matter of fact, both sexes have the same number of ribs. Though Adam lost a rib, this was not a trait that was passed on to his sons.

---

[258]Mathews, *NAC*, 216.
[259]A.T. Reisenberger, "The Creation of Adam as Hermaphrodite—and its Implications for Feminist Theology," *Judaica* 42(1993): 447-52.

*2. Androgynous tale.* The ancient Jewish view is that the first human was a hermaphrodite, i.e., part man, part woman. The rabbis based their argument on 5:2 which states that *God called them man* (singular). The two were one.[260] This Jewish legend could be cavalierly dismissed were it not for the fact that this bizarre notion has been endorsed by some modern scholars. Custance writes:

> Eve's *body* was clearly derived from Adam's *body*, and in this surgical process the two genders were separated and sexual dimorphism *in man* was initiated. In the original, the two sexes must therefore have in some way been fused. (emphasis his).[261]

Clearly the view that the first person was both male and female is incorrect. In 1:27-28 God contemplated making two persons, not one dual sex person. One must interpret 5:2 and 2:22 in the light of 1:27-28.

*3. Evolutionary imagination.* Theistic evolution struggles to explain the creation of the woman. One representative of this school states that Adam mated with a near-human. That union produced a female child that inherited Adam's image and soul. Then he married that daughter and thus Eve was formed from the body of Adam.[262]

## C. Positive Implications

The woman is the first of creation to come from a living being.[263] The description of the creation of Eve should be taken in a literal sense. Paul declares that

---

[260] *Genesis Rabbah* 8:1; Rashi.
[261] Arthur Custance, *The Seed of the Woman* (Brockville, Ontario: Doorway, 1980), 106.
[262] P.G. Fothergill, *Evolution and Christians* (London: Longmans & Green, 1961), 323-29.
[263] Hamilton, *NICOT*, 179.

"woman was made from (*ek*) man" (1 Cor 11:8, 12). There is, however, rich symbolism in the divine method.

The account underscores two things. First, the absolute unity of the human race is thus guaranteed. Second, the dignity of womankind is also guaranteed. She was not made out of inferior substance. She was not made from the head of Adam, or the foot. Being created from man's rib she is neither superior nor inferior; she is on the same level as a creature of God. A good wife is the rib of her husband. She is at his side to assist him in his work, to stand with him in his struggles, and to receive his love and support.[264]

### D. Presentation of the Woman (2:22b-23).

*1. Significance (2:22b):* **and [he] brought her to the man.** The woman was another benevolent provision of the Creator. She was a gift from God to a man who both needed and wanted her. Paradise was not complete—*very good* (1:31)—until the woman stood beside her man.

Earlier God *brought* the animals before Adam (2:19) to see what he would name them. Now he *brought* the woman knowing full well that Adam would immediately recognize her as one of his own kind. And so he did!

Marriage itself is not to be confused with the creation of the sexes. By presenting the woman to the man, however, God was inviting the couple to a form a union. God was in effect performing the first marriage. In this simple sentence the Bible sets forth three fundamental principles of marriage.

First, marriage is inter-sexual. In marriage a man and woman unite. Second, marriage is monogamous. God

---

[264]Cf. Thomas Aquinas, *Summa Theologiae* (1a, 92, 3c). Chauvinistic rabbis put a negative spin on the fact that Eve was created from Adam's rib. That is the only part of man's body that is covered (by hanging arms) when a man is standing naked! *Genesis Rabbah* 18:2.

created only one woman for Adam, although he certainly could have offered him an entire harem (Mal 2:15). Third, ideally marriage involves the blessing of the bride's father and the blessing of God. In the case of the first woman the Creator was also Father. By presenting the woman to the man God sanctioned and blessed the union. It was at that time that the Creator must have spoken the blessing found in 1:28.

2. *Acceptance (2:23a):* **This now at last....** Adam reacted to the presentation of the woman in an enthusiastic, poetic outburst. These are the only recorded words of man prior to the Fall. Adam was so excited that he said "I do" before he was even asked the question!

Adam's excitement over his new bride is indicated in the Hebrew by the thrice used word *this*. Literally the v is "This is now ... to this one ... it shall be called Woman because from man this one was taken." In marriage there must be cheerful and enthusiastic acceptance of one's mate.

3. *Assessment (2:23b):* **is bone of my bones, and flesh of my flesh.** Adam voiced a very perceptive assessment of his bride. This language in ancient times affirmed the family tie (Gn 29:14; Judg 9:2; 2 Sam 5:1; 19:12f.). Because they are of the same flesh, what affects the one affects the other. His assessment is also a commitment—a marriage vow. It is equivalent to a pledge to love, cherish and nurture his lovely bride.

4. *Designation (2:23c):* **she shall be called Woman, because she was taken out of man**. By naming his bride Adam was expressing his acceptance of her. He names her *'iššāh* (*Woman*). The writer explains that she was called *'iššāh* because she was taken from *'iš* (*Man*). In naming his bride Adam also names himself in relation to his wife. The words *Woman* (*'iššāh*) and *Man* (*'iš*) are etymologically unrelated; they are related only in sound. Moses was attempting to express the fundamental simi-

mental similarity between man and woman by the best terms available to him in Hebrew.

In biblical marriage there must be recognition of the spiritual leadership of the man. Naming the woman asserts possession and leadership. Her acceptance of the name indicates recognition of the leadership of her husband.

How did Adam know that the woman had been taken from his side? Perhaps there was soreness at the spot from which his rib was taken. Or perhaps God revealed it to him.

# GENESIS MARRIAGE LAW
# Gn 2:24-25

### A. Fundamental Principles (2:24)

There is some question as to whether it is Adam, Moses or God who is speaking in this v. In the final analysis the principle goes back to God, whether spoken by him or by another under inspiration of the Holy Spirit.

Some take 2:24 to be no more than a statement of fact regarding the nature of marriage. They translate it, "Therefore a man leaves his father and mother and clings to his wife and thus the two become one flesh." While this is a possible translation, treating the v in this manner ignores the fact that Jesus referenced this passage to establish the fact that marriage is an ordinance of God (Mt 19:5-6). Thus 2:24 is best taken as prescriptive, not merely descriptive. Paul referred to this v as the very foundation of the conjugal state (Eph 5:31).

*1. Marriage is independent (2:24a):* **For this cause a man shall leave his father and his mother.** The initiative for marriage independence must come from the man. He must be prepared to offer his wife a home, support and security. A new home unit comes into being through marriage. A couple should never expect parents on either side to sustain them during the course of their marriage. Primary obligations after marriage are to one's covenant spouse, not one's biological relations. This v diametrically opposes cultures that put parental obligations ahead of spousal obligations.

That *leaving* is mentioned as the first principle of marriage is remarkable since the presence of just one couple in the beginning might have caused it to be overlooked. Kidner puts the matter in proper perspective: "'Leaving' before 'cleaving'; marriage, nothing less, before intercourse."[265]

*2. Marriage is permanent (2:24b)*: **and [he] shall cleave to his wife.** The verb *cleave* (r. *dbq*) is used often in the OT of physical things sticking to each other, especially parts of the body. The verb is also used of clinging to another person[266] or to the Lord[267] in affection and loyalty. In marriage a man and a woman commit themselves unreservedly to one another.

The verbs *leave* and *cleave* are often used in the OT to describe faithfulness and unfaithfulness to a covenant.[268] The Bible presents marriage as fundamentally a covenant relationship (Mal 2:14).

*3. Marriage is sexual (2:24c)*: **and they shall become one flesh.** Becoming *one flesh* undoubtedly signifies the consummation of marriage in the physical joining of the bodies. Sexual expression is limited exclusively to the marriage relationship. In this fundamental principle are the seeds of the later strong condemnation

---

[265] D. Kidner, *TOTC*, 66 n. 1.

[266] The verb r. *dbq* is used of Ruth clinging to Naomi (Ruth 1:14), the men of Judah clinging to David during the uprising of the Benjamite Sheba (2 Sam 20:2), Shechem loving Dinah and clinging to her (Gn 34:3), and Solomon clinging in love to his wives (1 Kgs 11:2).

[267] The Israelites were to cleave to Yahweh in love and loyalty: Dt 10:20; 11:22; 13:4; 30:20; Josh 22:5; 23:8.

[268] E.g., Dt 10:20; 11:22; 13:18; 28:20; 30:20.

of premarital and extra-marital relations. In NT language they are *porneia*—illicit use of sexuality. Sexual intimacy, however, is a legitimate expectation within the marriage relationship (1 Cor 7:1-6).

Some think *one flesh* refers exclusively to the physical union.[269] More likely, however, *one flesh* refers to the "complete identification of one personality with the other in a community of interests and pursuits, a union consummated in intercourse."[270]

### B. Marriage Principles Illustrated (2:25)

*1. Openness (2:25a):* **And the man and his wife were both naked.** The word *naked* (*'ārôm*) appears 15x in the OT. In some poetic passages the term refers to total nudity or to improper clothing due to destitution. The term refers to a state of undress willfully chosen 7x. The point is that Adam and his mate had no inclination to conceal their bodies from one another.

*2. Without shame (2:25b):* **and were not ashamed before one another.** The verb *ashamed* (r. *bôš*) is used 125x in the OT, but only here in the Hithpael (reflexive) stem. So the connotation is that Adam and Eve were not ashamed *before each other*.

Some put a negative spin on these words, as if Scripture were condemning the couple for their brazen shamelessness. Nothing more is to be read into these words then the simple fact that in the idyllic conditions of the garden the man and the woman felt no sense of shame because of their nakedness. Adam and Eve were free of guilty hang-ups about sex. That is what God intends for those in the marriage state. In this case the absence of shame indicates innocence and sinlessness. In essence this v says the same thing as the concluding v of ch1. Everything was very good!

---

[269]See *Christianity Today*, Oct. 10, 1975.
[270]Leupold, *Exposition*, 137.

# OBSERVATION ON MARRIAGE

### A. Ingredients of Marriage
Marriage customs differ from society to society. There are no biblically mandated marriage ceremony rituals. There are, however, four main ingredients in biblical marriage: the blessing of God, sanction of society, consent of the partners; and release of the families. These four ingredients are implicit in the garden marriage account.

### B. Order in the Relationship
The text gives certain clues as to the structure of the first marriage. First, the woman was created to be Adam's *help* or *helper*. This does not mean, however, that women generically have been placed under the authority of men. See discussion on 2:18.

Second, the man has the role of initiating a new household (2:24). Third, the woman receives both her generic name (2:23) and her personal name (3:20) from her husband. Assigning a name to anything in biblical thought is an assertion of authority. Fourth, the woman is brought to the man, not vice versa (2:22). Fifth, the woman was created after man. Paul grounds his argument for the marriage headship of the man in the creation accounts. He points to the chronological priority of the creation of man (1 Tim 2:13). The man is the head of the woman (1 Cor 11:3) because he was not created *for her*, but she was created *for him* (1 Cor 11:9).

### C. Silence Regarding Fruitfulness.
The silence of the text at this point regarding offspring is surprising since the OT celebrates the gift of children. The text seemingly wishes to reserve for fruitfulness the status of an added blessing (1:28), without

linking it with the essence of marriage. Procreation is not the supreme purpose of marriage. For this institution the Lord gives only one reason: *It is not good that the man should be alone.*

# CONCLUSION

D.F. Payne[271] opined that Gn 1-2 give us "a doctrine of a Creator rather than a doctrine of creation." It is true that the emphasis throughout these chs is on the Creator. It is not true, however, that there is no doctrine of creation.

While there is much controversy among creationists about the details of the creation chs, the following nine points may be considered the irreducible truths of revelation in the account of creation. First, a sovereign, personal, ethical God is the voluntary Creator of the universe. Second, God created *ex nihilo* by divine fiat. Third, there are divinely graded levels of life. Fourth, man is distinguished from the animals by superior origin and dignity. Fifth, the human race is a unity. Sixth, man was divinely assigned the task of subduing the created world to the glory of the Creator. Seventh, everything that God created is good. Eighth, God ordained marriage between a man and a woman as the suitable and sole channel for expression of sexual energy. Ninth, the woman has fundamental equality with the man.

---

[271] D.F. Payne, *Genesis One*, 23.

# 12
# TEMPTER AND TEMPTATION
# Gn 3:1-8

The literary form of Gn 3 is hotly debated. Because an animal is supposed to speak in the account it has been branded as a fable by some. Where, however, is the punch line, lesson or entertainment value such as fables normally convey? Others regard this ch as a parable; but where is the moral or application? The ch cannot be considered legend. In legend the characters are fictitious. The main characters here already have been introduced in ch 2 in what the writer intends to be taken as sober history. In the light of the way this material is treated in the rest of the Bible it is best to regard Gn 3 as an actual account of the origin of sin, misery and death.

The presence of figures of speech in the ch does not negate the view that Gn 3 is dealing with actual events. No commentator who has received the story as the word of God has been satisfied with a completely flat literalistic reading. Among those who interpret the account most literally is E.J. Young. Even Young, however, thinks it would be ridiculous to picture God sewing the clothes in 3:21. Nonetheless, most evangelicals are not comfortable with the position of Pieters that only the temptation and F`+. -
all are actual historical events; all the rest is "part of the pictorial representation."[272]

Thematically considered, Gn 3 marks a turning point in the book. In the first two chs the writer has discussed creation, all of which was pronounced good by the Creator. In these two chs obedience to the Creator was fol-

---

[272]Albertus Pieters, *Notes on Genesis* (Grand Rapids: Eerdmans, 1943), 100.

lowed by blessing. Beginning in ch 3, however, the theme of "uncreation," as Blenkinsopp calls it, is introduced. Evil enters the world because of disobedience, which was followed by curse or judgment.

# TEMPTER
# Gn 3:1a

Sin is foreign to mankind. It comes from without. Man may be evil, but he is not the Evil One. This v brings center stage the archenemy of God and all that is holy—that being that hates all that the Creator loves. The writer does not pause to explain the origins of the tempter.

**A. Serpent Introduced** (3:1a):
***Now Serpent was more crafty than any beast of the field that Yahweh Elohim had made.*** Concerning the tempter these biblical facts stand out in 3:1. First, his name is in the emphatic position. Second, he is called *the Serpent* (*ha-nāchāš*). The addition of the article to a common noun often makes it a proper name in Hebrew. The writer already has employed this technique by calling the first man *hā-'ādām* (*the man*) or simply Adam. The word *serpent* likewise appears in Rev 12:9; 20:2 as a proper name. With but one exception the garden tempter is identified as Satan or the devil throughout Scripture. The exception is 2 Cor 11:3 where Paul says that Eve was deceived by *the serpent*. In the context, however, Paul warned the Corinthians about the wiles of Satan (2 Cor 11:14), thus seeming to equate *Satan* and *the serpent*.

The third fact related about the tempter is that he is a subtle or *crafty* foe. The term *crafty* (*'ārûm* from r. *'rm*) is a play on the word *naked* (*'arûmmîm* from the r. *'ûr*) in 2:25. Thus the first couple was nude, and Serpent was shrewd. The naked innocence of Adam and Eve is contrasted with the "malevolent brilliance" of Serpent (Kidner).

This is the only usage of the term *crafty* (*'ārûm*) outside the wisdom books. It is used 8x in Proverbs of a positive attribute. In Job, however, it is used as a negative (Job 5:12; 15:5).[273] In using the term of Serpent the writer of Gn clearly intended a negative connotation. Words such as tricky, shrewd, deceptive, cunning, and deceitful convey the intended meaning of *crafty*. The term elsewhere is never used of animals. This is the first clue that Serpent is not a biological reptile.

Serpent is said to be *more crafty than any beast of the field*. This statement falls short of saying that Serpent was one of the beasts of the field or that he had been made by God. In fact Serpent could not be part of this creation for two reasons. First, God had pronounced everything that he had made in this creation as very good (1:31). Clearly Serpent is a malevolent being. Second, Adam had demonstrated his intellectual superiority to all the beasts of the field (the garden animals) in Gn 2:19-20. Now, however, his wife is confronting a far more cunning being.

## B. Serpent and Satan

Regarding the relationship between Satan and the snake two positions have been taken. Some take the position that Satan took control of a serpent, or took the form of a serpent. But why? Because of the ugliness of the snake? Because of the loveliness of the snake? No logical reason has been offered why Satan would choose

---

[273] Aalders (*BSC*, 98) insists that the term should be taken in a positive sense. The prudence of the snake is manifested in ability to speak. Aalders seems to suggest that only the snake among the animals had the gift of speech. Others have suggested that all animals had the gift of language prior to the Fall.

to use a snake. Satan seems to have no trouble tempting human beings without mediation, so why would he use a dumb animal? These and similar questions create endless layers of speculation in an effort to make the narrative intelligible. The truth is that nowhere is the role of the snake presented as that of a disguise or of an instrument; nowhere does the Bible indicate that the tempter was twofold—Satan + snake. Nothing in the text requires that a biological reptile was present at all. The Bible simply does not teach that Satan took the form of a snake.

The second position is that Serpent is a proper name for the devil. No biological reptile was present.[274] The intertestamental literature supports this conclusion (Ecclus 25:33; Wis Sol 2:23f.) as does the NT.[275] Furthermore, the context of Gn 3 supports this conclusion as will be demonstrated shortly.

### C. Serpent Imagery

Why did the writer invoke the image of a snake when he called the tempter *Serpent*? Perhaps the key lies in how snakes were viewed in the ancient Near East. The snake in the ancient world was a symbol of pagan religion with its magic spells and divination. Perhaps the name Serpent was used of Satan to suggest that disobedience to the Creator was the root of all false religion. On the other hand, *Serpent* invites comparison between Satan's tactics and those of a dangerous snake. That Satan is given the name Serpent also suggests that man is to have dominion over him, just as over the animal domain.

---

[274] A strong defender of this position is J. Oliver Buswell, *Systematic Theology*, 1:264.

[275] Mt 12:29; Jn 8:44; 12:31; Acts 10:38; 2 Cor 10:4; Eph 6:12; 2 Thess 2:9; Rev 12:9; 20:2.

# TEMPTATION
# Gn 3:1b-5

### A. Serpent's Challenge (3:1b, c)

*1. Serpent's speech (3:1b):* ***And he [Serpent] said to the woman.*** Did a snake talk? If so, how was this possible? Could garden man understand "animal talk"? Did animals have the speech faculty before the Fall? Or was Eve's temptation merely an internal suggestion produced in her mind as she meditated on the snake? Why did Eve register no shock when an irrational creature spoke to her? Some have proposed that the serpent's speaking consisted of no more than this: Eve saw the snake near or in the tree, and temptation arose within her to transgress the command of God. All of the questions surrounding a talking snake become irrelevant once it is recognized that Serpent is a proper name for the devil.

The first man was using language as one of the tools for subduing the earth when he named the garden animals (2:20); Serpent used the tool to subvert the first couple. While Serpent communicated, it was not necessarily in verbal, audible words. Had Adam been in the vicinity there is no indication that he would have heard what Serpent was saying to the woman. Serpent communicates to the heart and mind, not the ear.

The target of the first temptation was carefully selected. The woman was not selected because she was inherently weaker than the man. Nonetheless, the woman in some respects was at distinct disadvantage. She had not heard directly from God the same prohibition and warning that her husband had heard. Secondhand prohibitions never have the same clout as those heard firsthand from the authority figure. Furthermore, the woman had never seen conditions outside the garden as had her husband (cf. 2:15).

In other respects the woman was equipped to deal with the devil. She had experienced the goodness of God in the bounty of the garden. She had received from her husband God's clear, simple, single prohibition to obey. She was a mature human with, no doubt, highly advanced intellect. She was pure and with no prior experience in disobedience that would make further disobedience easier.

2. *Serpent's approach (3:1c):* **Indeed, Elohim said, You shall not eat from any tree of the garden!** English versions render these words as a question that invites the woman to doubt the word of God. Justification for this translation is based on the response of the woman. The Hebrew phrase (*'aph kî*), however, with which the sentence opens is not an interrogative, but rather a strong affirmation. Luther suggests that in using this expression Serpent was turning up his nose, jeering, scoffing. Kidner renders: "So God has actually said...." Leibownitz renders "Even if God has said ... what of it!" Speiser comments: "The serpent is not asking a question; he is deliberately distorting a fact."[276] *From any tree* could be rendered "from every tree."

Serpent intended this ambiguous statement not so much to question God's word as to dispute God's goodness. The implication is that God's restriction is harsh and unloving. Serpent's intent is transparent. He aims to instill doubt in the woman's heart regarding the exact wording and intent of the divine prohibition.

In the conversation between Serpent and the woman the name Elohim is used 3x, but not *Yahweh*. The treachery that is being contemplated is an assault on the

---

[276]Speiser, *AB*, 23; Blocher (*In the Beginning*, 139) makes a similar comment: "The tempter makes a massive affirmation, adopting a tone of surprise and indignation or else of feigned compassion, because he wishes to make the fact seem outrageous."

divine/human personal relationship that the name *Yahweh* connotes.

**B. Woman's Response** (3:2-3)

*1. Her version of the provision (3:2):* **And the woman said to Serpent, From the fruit of the trees of the garden we may eat.** These words indicate that Eve is not firm in her resolve to obey Yahweh. First, she watered down the mandate: God *has said* vs. God *commanded* in 2:16f. Second, Eve minimized the privilege that she and her husband were experiencing by omitting *all* trees. Failure to appreciate *all* that God has provided leads men to rebel respecting what he has prohibited.

*2. Her version of the prohibition (3:3):* **but from the fruit of the tree which is in the middle of the garden, God has said, You shall not eat from it or touch it, lest you die.** Carefully examined the response of the woman was not very forceful. She repeated the words of the prohibition, but with certain modifications that likely indicate growing doubt, not memory lapse. First, the woman sharpened the prohibition by adding, *nor touch it*. Second, she generalized the punishment: *lest you die*, whereas God had said *in the day you eat you will surely die* (2:17). Third, she failed to refer to the particular tree by the name God had given to it. While it is true that the woman had not heard God speak the name of the tree, it is likely that Adam had passed on the prohibition verbatim. The tree is identified only as to location, which tends to place the tree of *the knowledge of good and evil* on a level with the other trees in the garden.

The criticism that the woman's comment contradicts the assertion of 2:9 that there were *two* special trees in the midst of the garden can be dismissed as mindless caviling. The focus is on the one tree. The tree of life is not within her purview at the moment.

**C. Serpent's Challenge** (3:4-5)

Serpent continued to challenge the tree prohibition by boldly contradicting God's word and by impugning the motives of the Creator. The irony of the passage is that Serpent more accurately reflects the Creator's words than did the woman.

*1. Contradiction (3:4)*: **And Serpent said to the woman, You shall surely not die.** Literally, "No! Not true that you shall surely die!" This is the strongest possible denial of the truthfulness of the divine threat that man will die if he eats of the forbidden tree. Serpent is suggesting that the Creator was merely using scare tactics. With this outlandish statement Serpent tears down the first great barrier to sin, viz. fear of punishment.

*2. Accusation (3:5)*: **For God knows that in the day you eat from it your eyes will be opened and you will be like God, knowers of good and evil.** The essence of sin is the perversion of godliness. Men are to be Godlike in ethical attributes; they are not to try to seize his power and wisdom. Serpent used a participial construction that suggests: "God knew all the time." Serpent attributes envy to God—makes him appear to be withholding good from his creatures. In this accusation Serpent tears down the second great barrier to sin, viz. the love of God.

Satan's accusation contains an implied threefold promise. First, Serpent promised enlightenment of the intellect. Satan recognizes the validity of the name of this tree: *tree of the knowledge of good and evil* (cf. 2:9). Second, Serpent promised equality with God. He promised that the man and the woman would become like God in respect to knowledge. In this instance Serpent is telling a half-truth. In 3:22 God acknowledges that man has become like God in respect to knowledge, but in a perverted sense. Third, Satan promised moral autonomy. The vassal was being pushed towards rebellion—going beyond defined limits. The rebel believes that he is bravely asserting his independence. At that very moment, however, he is being manipulated by another. He eschews being a servant of the Creator, only to become a slave of Serpent.

It is not clear whether Serpent said *like God* (ASV; NIV; NASB; NRSV; NKJV); or *like gods* (LXX; KJV) or *divine beings* (NJPS). The overall thrust of Serpent's assertion remains the same either way. The word *knowers* is plural, referring to Adam and Eve, not Elohim.

*Good and evil* are strange words on Serpent's lips. Heretofore *good* had been what Elohim declared was good—what enhances life and furthers the purposes of the Creator. Obviously Serpent defines the word differently. The temptation is to define *good and evil* by experience and immediate consequences. Serpent does not deny the existence of evil; he only refuses to acknowledge the right of the Creator to define the parameters of evil.

What entices a person to transgress a limit is not the sensual pleasure heightened even more by the prohibition, but the new possibilities of life that are apparently opened by the transgression. Gn points to the fact that people have the urge to transcend themselves by overstepping the limits God sets for them.[277]

## TRANSGRESSION
## Gn 3:6

Serpent's temptation was the occasion of the fall, not its cause (John Murray). The man and woman remain without excuse in this situation.

---

[277]Westermann, *Genesis 1-11*, 249.

### A. Steps in the Transgression (3:6)

There were three stages in the transgression of the woman.

*1. Contemplation (3:6a):* **When the woman saw that the tree was good for food, and that it was a delight to the eyes, and that the tree was desirable to make one wise.** This is not the first time the woman saw the tree; but now she saw it in a different light. The woman examined the tree at close quarters. Thus far the expression *saw that it was good* has been used only of God. Now the woman exercises her independent judgment. In her heart she began to agree with Serpent.

The tree was appealing physically (good for food), aesthetically (delight to the eyes) and intellectually. The tree was desirable to make one wise (*l<sup>e</sup>haskîl*). It was not philosophical or scientific knowledge that appealed to Eve, but experience that would put her in a position to determine for herself what was good and beneficial on the one hand, and harmful on the other. Hers was the mentality of the youth who says he must experience sin to decide for himself if it is wrong. She wanted nothing withheld that might bring her gratification.

The Bible knows of two kinds of wisdom. The wisdom that is from above (Jam 3:17) is freely given to all who ask God for it (Jam 1:5). Whatever wisdom that the woman gained through her disobedience is of a different kind, i.e., it is worldly wisdom (1 Cor 1:20).

*2. Capitulation (3:6b)*: **she took from its fruit and ate.** Paul sates that "Eve was deceived by the serpent's cunning" (2 Cor 11:3). The Apostle John (1 Jn 2:16) recognized three appeals in sin: the lust of the flesh (physical appeal), lust of the eyes (aesthetic appeal), and the pride of life (intellectual appeal). The garden temptation partook of all three of these appeals.

*3. Corruption (3:6c):* **And she gave also to her husband with her, and he ate** (3:6c). Did Adam approach the scene after the woman had partaken? Or did the woman seek out her husband? Or was Adam with the woman when she sinned? Certainly he was near, but the text does not indicate whether or not he witnessed her transgression. Did the woman realize her sin before she spoke to Adam? Or was she "as innocent as a child who has disobeyed but is not sure exactly in what way."[278] The text does not indicate. Certainly the dire consequences associated with the sin had not been experienced—yet.

Why did the woman offer the fruit to Adam? The psychology of most sinners is to drag others into their transgression. Did the woman use her femininity to tempt the man? The text does not share the details of the woman's approach to the man.

Why did Adam eat? Some think that Adam is following the path of conformity into sin. Custance thinks that Adam deliberately chose to follow his wife's lead so that she would not face the consequences alone, i.e., better to lose his life than lose his wife. Better to lose his fellowship with God than the companionship of Eve. Still others think Adam was emboldened by the fact that he could not observe any immediate repercussions from her transgression. The only Scriptural light that is shed on Adam's motivation is this: "Adam was not the one deceived; it was the woman who was deceived and became a sinner" (1 Tim 2:14 NIV). The implication is that Adam knew full well what he was doing.

The equivalent of a comma after *with her* is present in the Hebrew text. Adam struggled with the momentous decision that would affect all subsequent generations. At least some of the implications of what he was about to do must have been clear to him. He chose, in effect, to "poison" himself by disobedience. It is fruitless to spe-

---

[278]Custance, *Seed*, 114.

speculate what might have been the course of events had he chosen the path of obedience.

## B. Nature of the Transgression

Some writers contend that the sin in the garden was sexual in nature. Those who follow this approach put stress on the fact that the woman was *seduced* (1 Tim 2:14). The Greek verb, however, does not normally bear a sexual connotation, nor does the Hebrew verb in Gn 3:13. Another argument for the sexual interpretation is that the woman was punished as regards her sex life. The man, however, also transgressed. He was not punished in regard to his sex life.

If the sin was sexual in nature, what possible sin could it have been? By the nature of the case, homosexuality, incest and adultery would have been impossible. Was the sin their first act of intercourse? (Philo; Gunkel). This hardly seems possible. Sexual differences were created by God and pronounced *good* in ch 1. Sexual intimacy was encouraged in 1:28. Nakedness produced no shame in 2:25. Becoming *one flesh* describes one of the fundamental purposes of marriage.

Was the sin in the garden premature intercourse? No, because Adam and Eve are depicted as fully adult, married, and under commission to be fruitful. Did their sexual intimacy involve some illicit pleasure? (Gregory of Nyssa). No, because where is it ever suggested that the body should not experience sexual pleasure? Was the sinful sexual act bestiality? No, because Eve was by the side of her husband in 3:6, and man sinned without having anything to do with the snake (assuming there was a snake present). Serpent invited the woman to partake of the tree, not to have sex. Was the sin in the garden refusal to reproduce?[279] No, because there is no evidence

---

[279] Kikawada and Quinn, *Before Abraham Was*, 68.

that such was the case. The fact is that the offense was not *between* the man and the woman. They did not sin together, but separately.

# CONSEQUENCES
# Gn 3:7-8

Three immediate consequences of the sin of the first couple are spelled out in Gn 3.

### A. Intellectual Consequences (3:7a, b)

*1. Enlightenment (3:7a):* **Then the eyes of both of them were opened.** The effects of the transgression did not fall consecutively, first on the woman, then on the man. They both experienced the effects simultaneously. Open eyes are still a metaphor employed to indicate enlightenment. It is not clear that the enlightenment of Adam and his wife was due to direct action by the Creator. The opened eyes may be merely a way of describing the guilt and sense of failure that follows transgressing a simple command of the Creator.

*2. Shame (3:7b):* **and they knew that they were naked.** This was the only knowledge they acquired through their transgression. The word *naked* (*'ērōm*) is not the same word used in 2:25. This word is used 10x in the OT, It is not particularly associated with sexual arousal. Rather the term depicts the results of disobedience to God: dishonor, destitution, poverty, vulnerability and weakness. Adam and his mate realized that they were now under the judgment of God (cf. Dt 28:48; Ezek 22:29).

Children do not know good and evil (Dt 1:39; Isa 7:15). Innocence knows no shame. What happened to Adam and Eve is analogous to the attainment of maturity or adult responsibility. They experienced a sudden recognition that there was something inappropriate and distasteful in their nakedness. It is not so much shame before one another that gripped their heart, but shame before the Creator. It was this shame over nakedness that caused the couple to fear a confrontation with God.

Shame is a reaction to being unmasked or exposed. Prior to the transgression shameless nakedness indicated innocence. Sin preaches autonomy and self-sufficiency. Sexuality proclaims dependence and inter-relatedness. Nakedness proclaims creaturely weakness. Man is not a self-existing deity; he is human. He must reproduce to survive just like the animals.

### B. Practical Consequences (3:7c)

*And they sewed fig leaves together and made themselves loin coverings.* Because of their shame the couple made coverings for their bodies. Fig leaves were used because of their size and strength. This note about the leaves identifies at least one of the garden trees as a fig tree. Construction of the aprons was a tangible expression of their shame. The sinners are face to face with their own creaturely weaknesses.

### C. Spiritual Consequences (3:8)

*1. God walking (3:8a):* **And they heard the sound of Yahweh Elohim walking in the garden in the cool of the day.** The sinful couple heard their loving Creator approaching. *Sound (qôl)* means "clang, noise or voice." Probably the noise is that of footsteps[280] rather than voice. The participle *walking* points to customary action. Visitations between *Yahweh Elohim* and the first couple in the garden sanctuary were regular, perhaps daily. The *cool of the day* is the evening.[281] The description is anthropomorphic. The idea is that the first couple became

---

[280] As in 2 Sam 5:24; 1 Kgs 14:6; 2 Kgs 6:32.
[281] Sailhamer (*EBC*, loc) thinks the wind is the wind of judgment as in 1 Kgs 19:11 and Job 38:1.

aware of God's presence by some specific movement in nature.

*2. Couple hiding (3:8b):* **and Adam and his wife hid themselves from the presence of Yahweh Elohim among the trees of the garden.** Fear paralyzed the rebels as the Creator approached. Fear makes men flee from God; but flight is pointless (Amos 9:2f; Heb 4:13). The sinful couple hid *among the trees of the garden.* They were using God's excellent gifts as a screen or a shield from anticipated divine wrath. Man is not only powerless before God, he is ungrateful.

*3. Implications.* Theologians in the Middle Ages speculated about what would have happened had the couple passed the test regarding the tree of knowledge. They reasoned that God would have confirmed them in righteousness and made them not able to sin. It is inconceivable that God would have relentlessly put them through an endless series of tests, each one a bit harder than the previous one. The actual result of the Fall was a double negative. Man became not able not to sin. That universal tendency to disobey God became their awful legacy to the whole human race.[282]

## ALLEGED PAGAN PARALLELS

Certain aspects of the Gn 3 report find parallels, howbeit garbled ones, in the literature of the ancient Near East. Kramer translated one Sumerian myth he called a "paradise myth."[283] Supposedly Dilmun, a Mesopotamian name for Bahrain, was a paradisiacal abode. Other scholars have questioned whether Kramer

---

[282]Youngblood, *BGIC*, 55.
[283]"Enki and Ninhursag: A Sumerian Paradise Myth," in S.N. Kramer and J. Maier, *Myths of Enki, the Crafty God* (New York: Oxford, 1989), 22-30. "Enmerkar and the Lord of Aratta" has been interpreted by the same authority as "Sumer's version of a Golden Past" (88f).

is correct in regarding this as the Sumerian version of Paradise.[284]

There may be some hazy recollection of the tree of life in the Myth of Adapa.[285] Adapa fell into the sea while fishing. In the nether world Adapa was offered the "food of life." He refused to eat because the god Ea told him not to. Adapa lost eternal life and brought disease and mortality on the race.

The food of life aside, there is little in the myth of Adapa that compares with the Gn 3 report. Adam was seeking wisdom; Adapa already had it. Adam disobeyed; Adapa obeyed. Furthermore, Adapa is not connected with a paradise.

Likewise, allusions to the Fall of man into sin are non-existent in ancient pagan literature. In pagan literature there is no concept of a state of innocence from which man could fall. Two seals, however, have been discovered that display scenes that could be interpreted as depicting the temptation in Gn 3. One of these dates to about 3500 BC.[286]

# CONCLUSION

So far the narrative has indicated the immediate results of the sin of Adam and his wife. The Creator has not yet been heard from. The divine sentence upon the guilty pair is yet to come.

---

[284]B. Alster, *Dilmun: New Studies in the Early Archaeology and History of Bahrain*, ed. D. Potts (Berlin: Dietrich Reimer, 1983), 52-60; B. Batto, "Paradise Reconsidered," in *The Biblical Canon in Comparative Perspectives*, ed. K.L. Younger et al. (Lewiston, NY: Edwin Mellen, 1991), 33-66.
[285]A. Heidel, *The Babylonian Genesis*, 151.
[286]Both seals are documented, displayed and discussed by Custance, *Seed*, 126f.

# 13
# PUNISHMENT AND PROMISE
## Gn 3:9-24

In Christian theology the sin of the first couple is usually called the *Fall*. There is nothing in the text, however, to suggest this metaphor for Gn 3. Elsewhere in Scripture sin is a fall only in the sense of stumbling (*skandalon*), tripping as one walks or making a false step. It is better to refer to the sin of Gn 3 as transgression or disobedience. In the first sin man did not so much deviate from a prescribed path as cross a forbidden frontier. Cf. Hos 6:7; Rom 5:12, 14f, 17f, 19.

## CONFRONTATION
## Gn 3:9-13

### A. God's Search for man (3:9)

*Then Yahweh Elohim called to the man, and said to him, Where are you?* The question is addressed to Adam personally (sing. *you*) because it was to Adam personally that the prohibition had been articulated. This is the first question God ever asked man, and the first true question (in the Hebrew text) in the Bible. See notes on the alleged question of 3:1.

This question should not be interpreted theologically, i.e., to imply that God did not know the whereabouts of Adam. *Yahweh Elohim* does not use the ordinary word that is used for inquiring about one's location. The word used here scornfully emphasizes the absence of a person from a place he is expected or needed (cf. Ex 4:2; Gn 19:5).[287] The Garden Keeper was not at his post.

---

[287] B. Jacob, *The First Book of the Bible*. Ed. and trans. E.I. Jacob and N. Jacob (New York: Ktav, 1974), 26.

The question is pedagogical. It is designed by the master Teacher to force man to assess his condition now that he has disobeyed. This and the following questions in vv 11 and 13 suggest also that the divine Magistrate will not administer punishment without careful investigation. By conducting this inquiry God models the conduct that those who function in his name should display.

### B. Man's Fear and Shame (3:10)

*And he said, I heard the sound of you in the garden, and I was afraid because I was naked; so I hid myself.* In sinful man's response to the question of the Creator these points stand out. First, the reply is in the first person singular. "I" is the focus of concern. Second, God has only to call and the man answered him immediately. Third, the shallowness of man's response reveals the depths of his transgression. Fourth, because both are brought together in one sentence, the shame becomes the ground and formal expression for the fear. This fear is anguish arising from sin. Is it also fear of the reaction by the Creator? An action motivated by fear is not of faith, and cannot please God.[288]

The response of the man is emotional more than logical. Was he not naked when God gave him the prohibition? Had he not made an apron to cover his nakedness? His naked body was not nearly as big a problem for him as his naked disobedience.

### B. God's Interrogation (3:11)

*And he said, Who told you that you were naked? Have you eaten from the tree of which I commanded you not to eat? You* again is singular. No one hung a "guilt trip" on the couple; they experienced shame because of their transgression.

---

[288]Waltke, *GAC*, 93.

Adam had betrayed himself by his response to God's initial question. His awareness of his naked condition revealed that his state of innocence was over. He had transgressed the command of God. He was a sinner.

The purpose of these two questions is to lead man from shame to guilt. Only when sinners reach the state of guilt is there any possibility for forgiveness. The tree is no longer called the tree of knowledge; it is the tree they had been commanded not to partake of. It was the transgression tree!

### C. Sinners' Excuses (3:12-13)

*1. Woman blamed (3:12):* ***And the man said, The woman whom you gave to be with me, she gave me from the tree, and I ate.*** Adam's defense is thin and predicable. Immediate blame is placed on the woman. The wine of Adam's love for his wife has grown sour. The joyous reception of the woman in ch 2 turns to bitter acrimony. Ultimately Adam blamed God for the sin by mentioning that the Creator had given him the woman.

Adam's defense of himself before the Creator has two serious implications. First, freedom to defend oneself implies freedom to turn against God.[289] Second, "the effect of sin is the sin of denying sin."[290] The absurdity of the sinner's self-defense grows with the passage of time. Man has an amazing capacity to rationalize his conduct, however blameworthy that conduct may have been.

*2. Serpent blamed (3:13):* ***Then Yahweh Elohim said to the woman, What is this you have done? And the woman said, Serpent deceived me, and I ate.*** Eve's response was to blame Serpent. Her response is only three words in the Hebrew. Jacob observes: "Few words

---
[289] Westermann, *Genesis 1-11*, 255.
[290] Blocher, *In the Beginning*, 178.

are spoken when no escape remains."[291] In these three words the woman admitted that she had been deceived. Her culpability was in not being so firmly committed to the path of obedience that she could be deceived.

## CURSE UPON SERPENT
## Gn 3:14

Serpent was last to be accused, but first to receive the sentence for his part in the transgression.

**A. Nature of the Curse** (3:14)

*1. Direct address (3:14a):* **And Yahweh Elohim said to Serpent.** The text clearly says that the curse was directed to Serpent. Furthermore, the curse is couched in the second person. God is speaking directly to Serpent, not about him. The implication is that the one addressed is an intelligent being.

*2. Justification (3:14b):* **Because you have done this.** These words echo the question God asked the woman in 3:13. From these words the following conclusions are justified. First, the omniscient God knows the involvement of Serpent. Second, Serpent is justly punished. Serpent was judged for his actions, not his attitudes. Third, no explanations or rationalizations by Serpent are permitted. God knows what is behind the action of Serpent; but men are either incapable of understanding or are not intended to know the origin of evil. Fourth, though Serpent's involvement in the downfall of man is mysterious, his punishment is swift. Fifth, there is no hint of hope for Serpent. The text presents him as hopelessly irredeemable.

*3. Verb (3:14c):* **Cursed are you.** The author of the curse is *Yahweh Elohim.* Only here and in 4:11 is the

---
[291] Jacob, *First Book,* 27.

formula of cursing (*cursed are you*) used with God as speaker.[292] Serpent, who was introduced as *crafty* (*'ārûm*) in 3:1, now is *cursed* (*'ārûr*). *Cursed* comes from a root that is used 63x in the OT, most of which are in the Qal stem (54x), most frequently in the passive participle form (40x). The verb means "to bind, hem in with obstacles, render powerless to resist."[293] A curse invokes or announces forthcoming misery on a person. Use of the passive *cursed* to introduce a decree of doom is common. The execution of a curse requires divine intervention.

*4. Extent (3:14d)*: **more than all cattle and more than every beast of the field** is lit., "from all cattle." Some think this means Serpent is cursed out of the number of animals. He is set apart from all other animals for curse (Maas) or for additional curse (Morris). Probably the idea is that Serpent is cursed *above* all animals (KJV).

*5. Description (3:14e)*: **on your belly shall you go, and dust shall you eat all the days of your life.** Crawling on the belly indicates a lowly state. Eating dust is apt punishment for the one who led the woman to eat the forbidden fruit.

## B. Interpretation

*1. Various positions.* At least four different interpretations have been given to the curse on Serpent. First, more liberal scholars see Gn 3 as an etiological story (Westermann) designed to explain to simpletons how snakes came to crawl on their bellies.

Second, some conservative scholars believe that snakes underwent a biological transformation as a result of the curse (Keil; Morris). If God, however, changed

---

[292]The formula appears in Dt 28:16-19 and in the plural in Josh 9:23 where God is not the speaker.
[293]H.C. Brichto, *The Problem of "Curse" in the Hebrew Bible*, JBL Monograph Series, vol 13 (1963).

the structure of a creature that he created and pronounced "good," would he not be correcting himself?

Third, other conservatives question the biological transformation theory. They explain the curse to mean that a new significance was given to the condition of snakes (Kidner; Leupold). In other words, snakes always crawled on their bellies; but because of the garden sin man came to regard this condition as a punishment by the Creator.

Fourth, others see this curse as metaphorical description of the fate of Satan (Buswell).

*2. Relevant issues.* Addressing a series of questions relating to the curse of 3:14 may help in reaching a decision about what (if anything) happened as a result of it. First, was the object of punishment Satan alone, the snake he used, or both? Those who take the text of Gn 3 seriously recognize that Satan was directly involved in the temptation. If the curse did not involve Satan, then there is no indication of his punishment. In that case the snake was punished, but not the power behind the snake. The only way to involve Satan in the curse, however, is to view the crawling in the dust as metaphorical.

Second, if a biological snake was the innocent vehicle of Satan, why were the snake and all his kind punished? For those who believe that Satan made use of a biological reptile this is a difficult question.

Third, do snakes literally eat dust? Or is this a metaphor? If a metaphor, could it not as easily apply to Satan as to snakes? See Ps 72:9; Isa 49:23; 65:25; Mic 7:17.

Fourth, is there natural *enmity* (3:15) between snakes and humankind?

Fifth, if the curse was on a biological reptile how does one explain the Creator speaking to and cursing a non-intelligent, amoral creature?

Sixth, if the threats in 3:14 are applied literally to snakes, by what logic can 3:15 be interpreted as a reference to threats against Satan? If both vv refer to snakes, where is the punishment against Satan?

Having sorted through the issues relating to the curse on Serpent four conclusions are appropriate. First, the threat is against Satan himself. Second, the curse is cast in the language of literal snakes because that is the name given to Satan here: *Serpent*! Third, the basic idea is that the former angelic being was now debased in relationship to man and even to animals. Fourth, the implications of the curse on Serpent are spelled out in the following v.

# PROTEVANGELIUM
# Gn 3:15

Serpent's existence is one of lowliness and humiliation, his end is destruction. Ironically, he will be destroyed by a descendant of the very woman that he brought down.

### A. Initial Enmity (3:15a)
*And I will put enmity between you and the woman.* In the Hebrew the direct object *enmity* (*'ēbhāh*) stands first in the sentence for emphasis. The noun is used 4x (Nm 35:21, 22; Ezek 25:15; 35:5), but never of dumb animals. Only morally responsible beings can experience enmity. *Enmity* is not mere hostility. The term signals the beginning of the successful war—a life-and-death struggle—against Satan.

The subject of the sentence is the pronoun *I*. Yahweh Elohim is the speaker. The name *Yahweh* suggests this action mingles grace for man with judgment on Serpent.

The enmity is put between *you* (Serpent) *and the woman*. God does not arouse Satan against man for that would make him the author of evil. Clearly God did not need to generate any enmity in Serpent toward the wom-

woman. Had Serpent not hated the first couple he never would have participated in their downfall. So the enmity must be put in the heart of the woman.

She needed enmity toward Serpent. In the temptation she had been a pushover. She needed a stronger resolve to resist all temptation to disobey the Creator. That resolve grows out of hatred toward evil and the Evil One. The woman—first to sin—is given the strength and will to resist further temptation. The enmity that made Satan's mission more difficult was a gift of grace to the woman. No doubt this implies her desire to receive such help. Perhaps she had even asked for it. This is not to suggest that the woman thereafter was sinless. It only means that henceforth she would not be so easily deceived.

### B. Continuing Enmity (3:15b)

*[I will put enmity] between your [Serpent's] seed and her [woman's] seed.* The God-given enmity that aids the woman in her personal struggle with Serpent will surface in future generations. There will be enmity between Serpent's seed and woman's seed.

The term *seed* (*zera'*) cannot refer to physical *seed* (semen) for a woman possesses none. Metaphorically, *seed* refers to descendants or offspring. Theoretically the woman's seed could refer to the entire human race. Since the Bible generally emphasizes spiritual seed or progeny,[294] that is probably the meaning here. The first woman in her penitent state, fortified by the holy enmity put into her heart against the Evil One, is the mother of all those who love God, hate Satan, and embrace righteousness.

If the woman's seed are those who share the first woman's enmity toward Satan, then Serpent's *seed* must

---

[294]Isa 1:4; 57:4; Ps 37:25; Prov 11:21; Mt 3:7; 12:34; Lk 3:7; Jn 8:44; Rom 4:12.

be the children of the devil (Jn 8:44; Mt 23:33) and possibly evil spirits as well (Mt 25:41; Rev 12:7, 9). This in no way implies that Satan fathers demon spirits; but as humankind become Serpent's seed through choice, so also it is appropriate to include in the category of Serpent's seed those spirit beings who are aligned with Satan. The primary focus, however, is on humankind that enlists in Serpent's rebellion against God. Throughout the centuries unrighteous mankind will oppose and try to suppress the righteous and the godly.

The "ethical" interpretation of 3:15 is that Serpent is the embodiment of evil. In this view the v is speaking about how humanity struggles continually with this power.[295] On this interpretation, however, how would one explain Serpent's seed?

### C. Ultimate Victory (3:15c)

*He [woman's seed] shall bruise you on the head, and you [Serpent] shall bruise him [woman's seed] on the heel.* The conflict between righteous and wicked humanity comes to a climax in a showdown between Serpent and the woman's seed.

*1. Combatants.* The combatants in the final stage of the struggle between good and evil are identified in the text only with two subjective pronouns (*he* and *you*) and two pronominal suffixes (*you* and *him*). The second singular pronoun and suffix clearly refer to Serpent, the one being addressed. The defeat of Serpent is placed at the conclusion of a long warfare between the descendants of both Serpent and woman. Yet the defeat affects only Serpent himself. Serpent must then of necessity be a figure external to the human race that lives on while generations come and go.

---

[295] This view goes back to Philo. Modern interpreters holding this view are Dillmann, Vriezen, and von Rad.

The third person pronoun and suffix refer to the woman's seed. Context alone decides whether *seed* is taken in a collective or individual sense. When used as a collective *seed* is usually referred to by plural pronoun or suffix. Here the suffix is singular. So one Champion from among righteous humanity—those who oppose Serpent—will come forward to do battle. It is not the woman herself who enters into this showdown battle as suggested by the Vulgate.

The messianic interpretation of 3:15 is ancient. The Aramaic Targum and the LXX regarded 3:15 as messianic. Irenaeus and Justin Martyr were the first of the church fathers to expound the messianic interpretation.[296] While it is true that the messianic interpretation has lost favor in scholarly circles,[297] how else can the details of the prediction be explained? This Champion is born of woman biologically; he is also the progeny of the penitent first woman spiritually. No father of the Champion is named, hence the v harmonizes with idea of the virgin birth. Clearly 3:15 is announcing that someone will come forth from the seed of woman to defeat Serpent. If not Messiah, then who is this Champion?

*2. Head crushing.* Humanity's Champion and Serpent engage in deadly combat. The Champion aims to crush Serpent's *head* under his foot. Serpent retaliates by biting the Champion on the *heel*, delivering painful but not lethal wounds. The use of *head* and *heel* in the singular is further evidence that the conflict between the woman's seed and Serpent's seed ultimately is settled by one representative from each group.

The same Hebrew verb *crush* (*šûph*) is used to describe what the Champion will do to Serpent's head, and

---

[296]See H.P. Ruger, "On Some Versions of Genesis 3:15, Ancient and Modern," *BT* 27 (1976): 106.

[297]Westermann (*Genesis 1-11*, 260) asserts: "The explanation of Gen 3:15 as a promise has been abandoned almost without exception."

what Serpent will do to the Champion's heel. The verb *šûph* is used elsewhere only in Job 9:17 and possibly Ps 139:11 where the text is uncertain. Messiah delivered a mortal blow to the head of Serpent at the cross. The NT declares that a mortal wound has been inflicted on Serpent (Jn 14:30; 12:31; 16:11), the reign of the devil (Col 2:15; 1 Jn 3:8) and the reign of sin (Rom 5:21; 6:16-18).

2. *Heel crushing.* In the process of crushing Serpent's head, the Champion's heel is *crushed*. The translation of the word should not be watered down to something like "strike."[298] The blow against the heel of the Champion will be brutal; it would be a mortal blow were Serpent able to deliver it to the head. The thrust of the prediction is that the victory over Serpent will be achieved through suffering by Christ and his body the Church (Rev 12:13; Mt 13:25; Eph 2:2; et al).

## PUNISHMENT OF THE WOMAN
## Gn 3:16

In respect to the woman, two things are noticeably absence. First, the term *curse* is not used as it is with the punishment of Serpent and the man. Second, no specific cause is cited for the punishment of the woman as it is later with her husband. The text thus recognizes that the woman was deceived, but the man willfully disobeyed. The Creator announced a penalty on the woman that affected her in two vital roles that she plays in society, as mother and as wife.

**A. Her Role as Mother** (3:16a, b)
*1. Pain in childbirth (3:16a):* **To the woman he said, I will greatly multiply your pain in childbirth.**

---

[298] Aalders (*BSC*, 106) insists on translating the second occurrence of *šûph* with *strike* in keeping with the snake imagery in the passage.

From this announcement three facts can be deduced. First, God is directly responsible for what will transpire in respect to the woman, just as he was directly responsible for the enmity between Serpent and the woman in the previous v.

Second, there will be great pain associated with the birth process that will lead eventually to the Conqueror of Serpent. *I will greatly multiply* is lit., "multiplying I shall multiply." The verb *multiply* (r. *rbh*) is made emphatic by means of an infinitive absolute, and that in a form that occurs in only two other passages. These two passages (16:10; 22:17) use the term in a context of promising a blessing of many children. By using this form the narrator hints to his readers that there is a ray of blessing in this cloud of punishment.

Third, life will go on. The woman will not be physically slain for her sin. She will give birth to children, thus fulfilling the blessing of 1:28. Childbirth in this v is not the punishment. The pain associated with childbearing is the punishment.

Fourth, *your pain in childbearing* is lit., "your painful labor and your conception." The language is broad enough to include the sufferings of pregnancy, childbirth and the whole reproductive process. *Painful labor* (*'itssābhôn*) is used in the following v for the punishment of the man.

The brevity of the account results in questions that lead to endless speculation. Were there no female sufferings prior to the transgression? Would childbirth have been painless had the woman been obedient? The verb does not always have the narrow mathematical meaning of *multiply*. The announcement is simply that henceforth the sufferings associated with being female will be abundant, more than they would have been otherwise.

2. *Promise in childbirth (3:16b):* **in pain you shall bring forth children.** *Pain* (*'etsebh*) is parallel to *painful*

*labor* in the previous clause. Within the announcement of the punishment the gracious Yahweh has imbedded a promise: *you will bring forth*. The sentence seems to presuppose the woman's vocation to bring forth children, as stipulated in the mandate of the sixth day (Gn 1:28). Thus mankind retains the blessing and the power to procreate. With it, however, there is mingled bitterness. Because of disobedience unmitigated blessing becomes partially a burden.

### B. Her Role as Wife (3:16c, d)

In spite of the multiplied pain of her reproductive system, the husband-wife relationship will continue, but in altered circumstances.

*1. Her desire (3:16c):* **And yet your desire shall be for your husband.** Some think *desire (tᵉšûqāh)* refers to sexual desire as in Song 7:10. The idea is that the woman will not be able to escape pain in childbearing by sexual abstinence. She will be drawn to her husband. Others think the *desire* is psychological need for dependence on man. A third view is that of Susan Foh. She points to the use of *tᵉšûqāh* in 4:7 where sin, figuratively portrayed as a beast, desires take possession of Cain; but instead Cain should rule over sin.[299] So the woman's penalty is constantly to desire to gain control over the man in her life. Thus the relationship between the man and his wife, which knew no disharmony prior to the garden sin, now suffers disruption. The relationship between *'iššāh* (wife) and her *'iš* will be fraught with difficulty.

*2. His rule (3:16d):* **and he shall rule over you.** Though the woman will seek to dominate her man, the husband will rule over his wife. Here, as in 4:7, the verb rule (r. *mšl*) is used opposite the noun *desire*. This is the

---

[299] Susan Foh, "What is the Woman's Desire?" *WTJ* 37(1974-75): 376-383.

same Hebrew word used of the rule of a sovereign over his subjects. It is not, however, the same word used in 1:28 that authorized man's dominion over lower creatures. So man does not rule his wife in the same sense that he brings animals into submission. Furthermore, God does not say that he has *given* this rule to man over his wife. During the temptation Adam had submitted to her will; now she will submit to his.

History indicates that men abused their status, took advantage of their position and exploited women. In many cultures women were considered chattel. Penalty and prediction, however, are not to be confused with precept. What is described here is not the will of the Creator. The Bible calls upon mankind to combat the effects of evil as much as possible. Christian husbands are told to "love your wives as Christ loved the church" (Eph 5:25). Whatever leadership is inherent in the role of husband must be exercised in the greatest tenderness and compassion. A Christian husband's leadership is characterized by self-sacrifice and love.[300]

To escape the harsh realities of *rule*, some have pointed to a Hebrew homonym for the root *mšl* meaning "be like."[301] This root is used 7x. Thus "he [Adam] will be like you," i.e., there will be a mutual sexual desire thus insuring procreation and painful childbirth. There are three problems with this rendering. First, use of this root *mšl* in the Qal stem used here is not attested elsewhere. Second, other uses of "like" do not match the use here. Third, context hints of future martial disharmony in man's punishment in the phrase *because you listened to your wife*.

---

[300]M. Stitzinger, "Genesis 1-3 and the Male/Female Role Relationship," *GTJ* 2(1981): 23-44; I.A. Busenitz, "Woman's Desire for Man: Genesis 3:16 Reconsidered," *GTJ* 7(1986): 203-12.
[301]J.J. Schmitt, "Like Eve, Like Adam: *mšl* in Gen 3, 16," *Biblica* 72(1991)1-22.

Jacob rejects the usual interpretation that 3:16 is a statement of punishment. He points out that there is no statement directly connecting 3:16 with eating the forbidden fruit. Furthermore, procreation has heretofore been regarded as a blessing. So Jacob suggests that 3:16 is a parenthesis. Jacob paraphrases this way: "I need not punish you because enough hardship is in store for you." If there is any element of punishment at all in 3:16 it is the revelation of what the woman's lot will be. God takes responsibility for the pains associated with the female reproductive system because he created her as he did. Perhaps children are appreciated more because of the difficulties of bringing them into this world. Jacob does not see any change in the relationship between the man and the woman since 2:20. He sums up his position in these words: "Nothing would have changed for the woman had she not eaten of the fruit."[302]

Jacob's position is worthy of consideration. The context, however, does suggest that words spoken to the woman in 3:16 are directly linked to her involvement in the disobedience.

# PUNISHMENT OF THE MAN
## Gn 3:17-19

### A. Statement of the Curse (3:17a, b)

In 3:17 the writer sets forth the curse on the ground and the grounds of the curse in reverse order.

*1. Ground of the curse (3:17a):* **Then to Adam he said, Because you have listened to the voice of your wife, and have eaten from the tree about which I commanded you, saying, You shall not eat from it.** Adam had tried to deflect blame from himself by pointing to his spouse. Yahweh Elohim now turns Adam's excuse

---
[302] Jacob, *First Book*, 29.

into an admission of guilty. Marital harmony can never be used to justify transgression of a specific command of the Creator.

The sin of Adam was in eating; the punishment narrative uses this word in various forms 5x in three vv. The punishment fits the sin. The singular second person pronouns focus the blame for transgression squarely on Adam. There is no "wiggle room" in the accusation, nothing behind which Adam can hide.

*2. Curse on the ground (3:17b):* **Cursed is the ground because of you.** In 3:14 Serpent was *cursed* (*'ārûr*); here it is the ground. The woman was punished in regard to her relationship to the man. The punishment that falls upon *the man* (*hā'ādām*) is concerned about his relationship to *the ground* (*hā'ᵃdhāmāh*). Originally he was to *rule* over the ground; now the ground will resist his efforts. Some believe the ground itself changed because of this curse. Probably the threat was fulfilled by driving man outside the garden where the environment was harsh.[303]

## B. Result of the Curse (3:17c-19)

*1. Painful toil (3:17c):* **In pain you shall you eat of it.** The creation mandate to subdue the earth (1:28) remains after the Fall; but man's work will become much more difficult. The term *pain* (*'ittsābhon*) is the same word used of the labor pains of the woman in the previous v. The word is used only one other time (5:29), that in reference to agricultural toil. The abundance of the garden will no longer be available. Man must expend painful labor to secure his sustenance.

*2. Unrelenting toil (3:17d):* **all the days of your life.** Yahweh Elohim repeats the exact wording of the

---

[303]Lewis: "Nothing in the narrative suggests that the realm of nature has been altered in a fundamental way." "The Localization of the Garden of Eden," *BETS* 11(1968): 174.

curse on Serpent from 3:14. Toil is not confined to one period of life, or one project in life. It is part of the experience of life. Perhaps there is an element of grace even in this punishment. Too much leisure time gives too many opportunities for practicing old sins and inventing new ones. Jacob's view that the ground was cursed only for the duration of Adam's lifetime is incorrect.[304]

*3. Frustrating toil (3:18a):* **Both thorns and thistles it shall grow for you.** The word pair *thorns and thistles* (*qôts v$^e$dardar*) occurs elsewhere only in Hosea 10:8. In Jer 4:3 and 12:13 *qôts* refers to *thorns* among the grain. The idea seems to be *weeds* that make it difficult to raise crops. The text suggests that *thorns and thistles* (weeds) are the result of the curse. Perhaps *thorns and thistles* are metaphors for all pests that impede bountiful crop production. Certainly such annoyances were not part of the garden environment. They may not have been part of the original creation that God pronounced good. It may be that the propensity of the earth for producing such plants was now enhanced. Man must battle weeds (and perhaps other pests) to survive.

*4. Successful toil (3:18b):* **you shall eat the plants of the field.** Even in the midst of this negative announcement there is promise. These are the same plants that came into being on day six in connection with the garden (2:5). Man will find those food-providing plants outside the garden; but their growth and productivity will be hindered by the thorns and thistles.

*5. Wearisome toil (3:19a):* **by the sweat of your face you shall eat bread.** For man's entire life he is faced with the challenge of coaxing productivity out of the ground that God has cursed. The rigors of man's labor are graphically described in these words.

---

[304] Jacob, *First Book*, 28.

Biblical Protology

*6. Death (3:19b):* **till you return to the ground.** Long is life's struggle. At the end of the day life's only certainty is death. The pronouncement against the woman did not mention death. In the pronouncement against the man death is mentioned only at the conclusion of the sentencing. That man did not immediately die when he transgressed in the garden was a manifestation of God's grace. Nonetheless, the penalty announced in 2:17 was not cancelled. Until the Fall death was not the inevitable end for man. Exclusion from access to the tree of life brings death into the picture.

Paul wrote of death entering the world as a consequence of man's sin (Rom 5:12). Some take this to apply to animal death as well as human death. Before the Fall animals were not programmed for death. Animals were originally herbivorous, becoming carnivorous only after the Fall. Support for this view is supposedly secured from Rom 8:20-22.

The key phrase in Rom 8:20-22 is *the whole creation* (*pāsa hē ktisis*). This expression appears only in three other places in the NT (Col 1:15, 23; Mk 16:15) where clearly it refers to the human race. So in Rom 8:22 this phrase must mean that only the human race was subject to death as a result of the Fall of man.

Custance takes the fruit from the tree of knowledge to be toxic. He suggests that something analogous to grapes was the forbidden fruit, and something analogous to alcohol was the poison. Though Custance marshals evidence from pagan legend, Jewish tradition, and Scripture in support of his theory his case is not convincing.[305]

*7. Dust (3:19c):* **because from it [the ground] you were taken, for you are dust, and to dust you shall return.** This is a direct reference to the threat in 2:17 and

---

[305]Custance, *Seed*, 122-158. A similar view is advocated by Schneir Levin, "Cain Versus Abel," *Judaism* 53(2004): 51-54.

to the punishment of Serpent in 3:14. Return to the dust is necessary because of the constitution of man's body.

# AFTERMATH
# Gn 3:20-24

Four significant statements are made about the post-Fall situation.

### A. Naming of Eve (3:20)

*1. Adam's comment (3:20a):* **Now the man called his wife's name Eve.** Adam also exercised the prerogative of naming his spouse before the Fall. The name *woman* (*'iššāh*) recognized two things: her indebtedness to him for life, and her companionship. Now Adam gave his spouse the personal name *chavvāh*—an older form of *chayyāh* (*life*). This name acknowledged his indebtedness to her for the continuation of life.[306] So the woman's name points to one who continues to give life. In the NT and Latin Vulgate the name is *Heva* from which KJV derived *Eve*. This name can be regarded as Adam's statement of faith that the woman will produce new life as predicted in 3:15-16.[307] This statement of faith in turn is an indication of Adam's repentance.

*2. Moses' comment (3:20b):* **because she was the mother of all the living.** The Lawgiver is explaining the significance of the woman's name. At the same time he is reaffirming the unity of the human race.

### B. Clothing (3:21)

**And Yahweh Elohim made garments of skin for Adam and his wife, and clothed them.** The verb *made* (*'āsāh*) has hitherto been used only of the creative works

---

[306] Mathews, *NAC*, 254.
[307] There is no reason to conclude with Aalders that the naming of woman is out of place, that it probably took place much later.

of God. Only here in the OT is the verb used of manual labor on God's part; he fabricates something out of material at hand. The picture is anthropomorphic. The point is that God provided clothes of animal skins for the couple. Exactly how he went about doing this is not indicated.

Producing this clothing had several purposes. First, it was a response to Adam's expression of faith. Second, the clothing is tangible divine approval of the couple's sense of shame. God's intervention does not allow a return to the nudity of Paradise. It is the Creator's will that mature human beings be clothed. Third, on the practical level, the clothing provided protection for their bodies in the hostile environment into which they were about to enter. Fourth, the gift of the clothing was a manifestation of God's continued love for man in spite of his transgression.

Fifth, the production of the clothing from the skins of animals gave divine sanction to slaying beasts for man's needs. Sixth, some see in the clothing a forecast of atonement (covering) by the shedding of blood. Seventh, the clothing conveys the idea that only God can deal adequately with the shame generated by sin.

## C. State of Man (3:22)

*1. Evaluation (3:22a):* ***Then Yahweh Elohim said, Behold the man has become like one of us, knowing good and evil.*** Again the writer reveals a conversation within the godhead (cf. 1:26). *Behold* introduces a shocking development, in this case the ground for the action about to be taken. It is not clear whether the focus is on Adam or whether *the man* is understood in the dual connotation of 1:27 and 5:2.

Man had become like God but in a perverted sense. God knows good and evil by omniscience. Before the Fall man already knew about good and evil. He knew by

## Punishment and Promise

experience the bounty of the garden, a wonderful spouse, and a meaningful mandate. He knew through fellowship the goodness of the Creator. He knew that obeying God's commands was good. Before the Fall man also knew something about evil. He was informed that it was possible to disobey God. He was aware that there would be serious consequences if he violated God's command. After the Fall man knew good and evil in a different way—by experience.

The difference between God's knowledge of good and evil and that of post-Fall man may be likened to that of a male obstetrician and a mother. The obstetrician knows more about childbirth than the mother will ever know; she knows what childbirth means by personal experience. So the Creator knows all that there is to know about good and evil; man chooses to know evil through disobedience.

2. *Danger (3:22b):* **and now, lest he stretch out his hand, and take also from the tree of life, and eat, and live forever.** Gn 3:22 is an unfinished sentence, a fact recognized by KJV, ASV, NRSV, NASB, but unfortunately not by NIV or JB. It expresses what the godhead regards as unthinkable. The *tree of life* is mentioned again (cf. 2:8). Based on the comment of this v one can deduce the purpose of this tree. It apparently had the power to impart imperishable physical life.

The text need not be made to say that the tree produced some magical fruit that preserved life forever.[308] This tree probably had the property to impart life because God had appointed it to be so. Because man chose to reject God's command and experience evil, he must be barred from the tree of life.

Those who interpret this sentence to mean that God felt threatened by the new status of man are clearly read-

---

[308] Custance (*Seed*, 121) thinks the fruit contained antitoxins that cured every human ailment. .

ing between the lines, not the text itself.[309] Such a view is more in agreement with Serpent (3:5) than with the narrator. In view of 2:17 the removal of man from access to the tree of life is primarily a punishment for human disobedience "which is effected through alienation from God's presence."[310]

Prior to the garden transgression it was permissible for man to partake of the tree of life (2:16). The term *also* in 3:22 suggests that he had not done so. Had man chosen the path of obedience he would eventually have found and consumed the tree of life, thus escaping death. The two special garden trees were related to each other. Eating of the one precluded eating of the other (Aalders).

### D. Expulsion (3:23-24a)

*1. Explanation (3:23):* **Therefore Yahweh Elohim sent him out from the garden of Eden, to cultivate the ground from which he was taken.** The form of the verb *sent* (Piel) suggests that this was an order to depart from the garden. As Hezekiah, Josiah and Jesus cleansed the Jerusalem temple, so God cleansed the garden sanctuary of transgressors. The verb is used elsewhere of banishment (Gn 21:14; 25:6; Lv 16:10).

Expulsion from the garden was certainly an act of punishment; it was also an act of mercy. God knew that the worst condition imaginable is the state of physically living forever in a state of sinful rebellion. There is no indication how long the couple was in the garden before the expulsion. Estimates range from a few hours to a few years.

*2. Description (3:24a):* **So he [Yahweh Elohim] drove the man out.** Not only did *Yahweh Elohim* order man out of the garden, he *drove* him out. Does the writer

---

[309]Clark, "The Flood," 191-92; Wallace, "Eden," 228.
[310]Di Vito, "Demarcation," *CBT*, 48.

intend his readers to understand that it took force to remove the sinful couple from the garden? Probably not. Failure to obey God's command to exit would constitute additional sin. All the evidence, however, points to humility and penitence on the part of the couple following the announcement of punishment. Thus *drove* is to be interpreted as a more energized way of indicating that God ordered them out of the garden.

### E. Garden Guardians (3:24b-d)

*1. Position (3:24b):* **and at the east of the garden of Eden.** The east in the ancient Near East represented light and life. In Egypt, for example, all the gods of life were on the east bank of the Nile, while graves and gods of dead were on the west. In Gn, however, the east is usually negative, associated with judgment (3:24; 4:16), vainglory and greed (11:2; 13:11), and alienation (25:6).[311]

*2. Cherubim (3:24c):* **he [Yahweh Elohim] stationed the cherubim.** Cherubim are guardian angels (Ezek 1:5; 10:15; Ex 36:35), apparently of brilliant appearance (from root of the word). Those seen by Ezekiel had feet, hands, four faces and four wings (Ezek 10:21). It is not possible to know if the cherubim placed at the garden entrance resembled those described by Ezekiel.

*3. Sword (3:24d):* **and the flaming sword that turned every direction, to guard the way to the tree of life.** It is impossible to know whether the revolving sword-like flame functioned independently of the cherubim, or was a visible weapon in the hand of the invisible cherubim.

---

[311] Waltke, *GAC*, 85.

### F. Related Considerations

How long did the garden last after the expulsion? The text does not indicate. The implication in 2:5 is that the special garden vegetation needed man's attention. Presumably without that supervision the garden quickly lost its uniqueness and eventually blended into the surrounding environment. In any case all trace of the garden was erased by the great Flood.

# CONCLUSION

The curtain closes on this tragic act of human history. Sin separated Adam from God, from the garden, from nature's productivity; it even affected his interpersonal relationship. Man is a sinner under the sentence of death, yet clinging by faith to the hope that someday a Champion will come to crush Serpent and re-open access to the tree of life.

# 14
# RAPID "PROGRESS" OF SIN
# Gn 4:1-16

Fratricide is the central theme of this unit. This theme occurs in pagan mythology. In Egypt Seth killed Osiris; in Canaan Mot murdered Baal. These parallels, however, are quite remote from the Gn account. To date nothing corresponding to the Cain and Abel story has surfaced in the literature of the ancient Near East.

Among Bible critics (Gunkel; Mowinckel) this story is popularly considered an etiological tale explaining the mode of life of the Kenites. Cain supposedly represents a tribe. The Kenites were wandering metal workers who were despised by other peoples. The sign of Cain is some special mark of this wandering tribe; the curse on Cain is the reason for the lowly status of the Kenites.

The rebuttal to this approach is found within the text itself. First, there is no indication that Cain's descendants were wanderers like Cain himself. Second, the sign belonged to Cain personally, not to his descendants. Third, many tribes had tribal emblems, not just the Kenites. Finally, the Kenites were friends of the Israelites. Why would Moses deprecate them in this narrative with such an etiological tale?

## BEGINNING OF FAMILY LIFE
## Gn 4:1-2

In an effort to force the biblical text into agreement with a creation of man about 50,000 years ago, some proposed a novel theory about Cain. Farr has suggested that the references to Cain in Gn 4 might represent the condensation of a number of ancient traditions associated with several individuals: Cain the son of Adam; Cain the first murderer; and Cain the city builder and head of a clan.[312] These multiple Cains lived centuries apart. While there is not one shred of evidence in the text to support such a conclusion, some evangelicals are open to it.[313] A theory not required by the text, nor supported by the text must be considered the result of fanciful imagination.

**A. Birth of Cain** (4:1a)

*1. Intimacy (4:1a):* ***Now Adam knew his wife Eve.*** The unit begins with a beautiful euphemism. The expression has been accurately interpreted by NIV ("Adam lay with his wife") but at the cost of the rich implications of the word *know*.

*Know* (*yāda'*) means "to know by experience." The expression often refers to conjugal intimacy in the OT. The verb is used in this sense only of humans, not animals. This is another clue that the Bible regards human sexual intimacy as qualitatively different from the copulation of animals. Marital intimacy is not thought of primarily as physiological, but as personal. It is not the generation of a child that is primarily in mind, but rather an event between husband and wife which has its real meaning in community.[314] The fact, however, that the term is also used of such sexual perversions as sodomy (Gn 19:5; Jud 19:22) and rape (Jud 19:25) should prevent interpreters from reading too much tenderness into the term.

---

[312] F.K. Farr, *ISBE* (1915) 1:539 s.v. "Cain."
[313] J.J. Davis, "Genesis, Inerrancy, and the Antiquity of Man, in *Inerrancy and Common Sense* ed. Roger Nicole and J.R. Michaels (Grand Rapids: Baker, 1980), 146.
[314] Westermann, *Genesis 1-11*, 289.

Does this declaration of intimacy mean that Adam did not *know* his wife during their stay in the garden? Obviously if the stay in the garden was only a few hours or days there would not be time for procreation. It is difficult to believe, however, that there was no sexual intimacy during the garden stay. Certainly the Creator encouraged such intimacy (1:28). The statement regarding shameless nakedness also suggests marital intimacy.

Y.B. Smith, in conversations with the author, has proposed that several sons were born to Eve prior to the sin. These are *the sons of God* encountered in Gn 6:1. Whether or not this is the case, there is no intimation in the text of the connection between the garden sin and the martial intimacy here referenced. One thing for certain can be said: the verb *know* is not used only of the first sexual relationship between a man and his wife as 4:25 attests (cf. 1 Sam 1:19).

The verb *know* in 4:1 recalls the tree of knowledge that was so prominent in the previous two chs, and the twofold use of the verb *know* in ch 3 (3:5, 22). Use of the name *Eve* for the last time in the OT also ties this ch to what precedes.

2. *Conception and birth (4:1b):* **and she conceived and gave birth to Cain**. Sexual intimacy resulted in conception and birth.

The name *Cain* has various usages in the OT. *Cain* is a tribal name (Nm 24:21, 22; Judg 4:11). In other Semitic languages the same or a similar word means a smith or metal worker.[315] *Cain* is also a place name (Josh 15:57). In 2 Sam 21:16 the Hebrew equivalent of *Cain* is used as a common noun meaning "spear." The meaning of the name as used in Gn 4 can no longer be

---

[315]Ibid.

ascertained. Cassuto suggests that *Cain* means "one who has been formed."

## B. Birth Utterance (4:1c, d)

Commentators have very different opinions about the tone and meaning of Eve's birth utterance. Some think that she is boasting that she has created a man the same as Yahweh did earlier. It is equally possible to interpret her comment as praise. Almost every word in her statement is controversial. To understand what Eve said, her statement must be broken down into its components.

*1. Verb (4:1c):* ***And she said, I have gotten****.* The verb translated *I have gotten* (*qānîtî*) occurs 72x with the meaning "acquire" and a few places with the meaning "create."[316] Modern scholars are almost unanimous in the opinion that the name *Cain* (*qayin*) is unrelated to the root *qānāh* ("to get or acquire"). Cain (*qayin*), however, sounds something like *qānîtî*. Eve did not speak Hebrew. The biblical writer is attempting to reproduce in Hebrew the name and its meaning.

If the birth utterance is intended to explain the name Cain, then the woman is responsible for naming the first human ever born. It is not clear in the Bible what circumstances dictated whether the father or the mother was responsible for the naming of a child. In 4:26 it is the father who names the child.

*2. Object (4:1d):* ***a man****.* The term *man* (*'îš*) never is used of a male child. Hence it is unlikely that Eve used the word to refer to the baby. Eve may have used the term to express an irony and a profound truth. In 2:23 *woman* (*'iššāh*) was created from man (*'îš*); now man comes forth from woman. The sexes are mutually dependent on each other. The statement, however, may

---

[316] E.g., Gn 14:19, 22; Ex 15:16; Dt 32:6; Ps 78:54; 139:13; Prov 8:32.

go beyond irony to faith and hope. Eve may have seen in the child the future man, the Crusher of Serpent promised in 3:15.

*3. Prepositional phrase (4:1e):* **with the help of Yahweh.** The *'et* is taken by some to be the untranslatable sign of a definite direct object. Luther translated: "I have a man, Yahweh." It is not likely, however, that Eve believed her baby to be Yahweh. While it is true that later in biblical revelation the concept that Messiah is Yahweh in the flesh becomes clear, there is no indication that Eve had made this connection at the outset of history. Certainly there is no clue in Gn 3:15—the extent of messianic hope thus far—that the Champion will be divine. In any case, Eve was the first to use the covenantal name of God.

Probably *'et* should be read as a preposition, not the sign of the direct object. Even so the sense is still in dispute. Those (like Sellers) who interpret Eve's birth utterance as boasting take *'et* to mean "as well as." Her boast paraphrased is: "I, as well as Yahweh, have produced a man."

It is best to take the preposition *'et* to mean "with the help of Yahweh" (NIV; NRSV; NASB; NJPS). Taken in this sense, Eve's birth utterance is an expression of her thanksgiving and praise at deliverance from pain and danger. This is further evidence of her repentance and her faith in God's promises. The problem with this interpretation is this: God is frequently said to be *with* men; but no exact parallel has been produced where this preposition means "with the help of."

### C. Birth of Abel (4:2a)

***And again, she gave birth to his brother Abel.*** The name *Abel* (*hebhel*) means "breath, vanity, or vapor." Something had impressed Eve with the vanity of life. Was it conditions outside the garden? Was it the direction of Cain's life? In any case, Abel's birth name is an ominous foreshadowing of his fate.

The notion that Abel was a twin is based on two pieces of evidence. First, the text does not say that Adam knew his wife *again*, or that she conceived *again*. Second, the Hebrew text literally says: "she continued and gave birth to Abel."

## D. Occupations of the Brothers (4:2b)

*And Abel was a keeper of flocks, but Cain was a tiller of the ground*. The Fall did not cancel the mandate to subdue the earth. The sons of Adam are depicted carrying out that mandate of management. Cain followed in the footsteps of his father by becoming a farmer. Abel pastured sheep. If man was forbidden to eat meat in this early period, why raise sheep?

There are three implications in the statement about the occupations of the brothers. First, the cultivation of the soil and domestication of animals were practically coeval—a flat contradiction to evolution. Second, nowhere does the text intimate that one of these occupations is superior to the other. Third, nothing in the text supports the pagan notion that the skills of farming and shepherding were taught to men by gods.

The depiction of Cain and Abel as domesticators of plants and animals is a problem for those who think of the first family as Paleolithic (Old Stone Age) period primitives. Buswell, for example, suggests that Cain and Abel only *appear* to occupy these roles. Cain was really only a gatherer of natural fruit; Abel was a hunter. Both are described by Moses in terms that were understandable to his generation.[317] Moses, however, could write of gathering (Ex 16:16; Nm 15:32) and hunting (Gn 25:27; 27:3, 30). Had he wished to de-

---

[317]Cf. J.O. Buswell, Jr., *Systematic Theology*, 1:365-68.

scribe Cain and Abel as gatherer and hunter respectively he could have done so. If Moses wrote literal history, he had no need to make primeval culture look like his own day.[318] Furthermore, the beginning of agriculture and the beginning of animal husbandry appear simultaneous in the archaeological record as part of the Agricultural Revolution at about 8,000 B.C.[319]

## BEGINNING OF WORSHIP LIFE
## Gn 4:3-7

How did the concept of sacrifice originate? Some argue that the need for sacrifice was revealed to Adam. More likely, however, the practice arose spontaneously as a natural expression of a devout spirit (Leupold).

**A. Offerings of the Brothers** (4:3-4a)
The first account of sacrificial worship indicates that the material offered was determined entirely by the occupation of the worshiper.

*1. Time note (4:3a):* ***So it came about in the course of time.*** The opening phrase of 4:3 indicates a passage of time. The phrase is literally "it happened at the end of days" (*vay$^e$hî miqqēts yāmîm*). This exact wording appears elsewhere only in 1 Kgs 17:7. The phrase assumes something already has happened beforehand. It describes the continuation of an action, never its beginning. These facts lead to the implication that this is not the first time the brothers had brought their offerings.

*2. Cain's offering (4:3b):* ***that Cain brought to Yahweh from the fruit of the ground an offering.*** Cain brought a vegetable or grain offering. There was noth-

---

[318]Paul Seely, "Adam and Anthropology: A Proposed Solution," *JASA* 22(1970): 88.
[319]Aviezer, *In the Beginning*, 118.

ing inappropriate about that. *From the fruit,* however, has the connotation of "some of the fruit." The problem was that Cain made no effort to bring the best of his produce.

The term *offering* (*minchāh*) refers to the tribute that a subordinate should bring to a superior (cf. 1 Sam 10:27; 1 Kgs 10:25). Under Mosaic Law the term was usually reserved for grain offerings (Lv 2:1-16). In Gn, however, the term is not used in its legal and specific sense; it denotes a tribute offering of any kind. Waltke points out that Cain first failed at the altar. This can be traced to a failure in theology which in turn resulted in a failure in his ethics.[320]

*3. Abel's offering (4:4a):* **And Abel on his part also brought of the firstlings of his flock and of their fat portions.** The same verb is used to describe the bringing of Abel's sacrifice. Two key words, however, describe Abel's offering that were not used of Cain's. These are *firstlings* (*bekōrôt*; cf. Ex 34:19; Dt 12:6; 14:23) and *fat* (*chēleb*; cf. Nm 18:17). Both are significant words in later Mosaic sacrificial instruction. Abel's sacrifice is not mentioned again in the OT.

The account of the worship of Cain and Abel is full of uncertainties. First, what was the purpose of the offerings? For sin? or merely an expression of gratitude? Did the brothers use an altar? Are these fire offerings? There is no indication one way or the other. *Fat portions* seems to indicate that Abel slew the animals he offered. Beyond that deduction there is little that can be said with certainty about these offerings.

## B. Reception of the Offerings (4:4b-5a)

*1. Acceptance of Abel (4:4b):* **Yahweh had regard for Abel and for his offering.** The verb *regard* (*šāʿāh*)

---

[320]Waltke, *GAC*, 97.

## Rapid "Progress" of Sin

occurs 15x in the OT with God as subject. It means "to gaze on, or regard with favor." There are two prepositional phrases indicating the object of Yahweh's gaze. First, he gazed with favor on Abel. The determining factor in worship is the attitude of the individual. Second, Yahweh gazed with favor on Abel's offering. Abel's offering was a tribute offering (*minchāh*) like Cain's. Abel's *offering,* however, was a sacrifice in the truest sense of the word because it represented the best that he had.

2. *Rejection of Cain (4:5a):* **but for Cain and for his offering he [Yahweh] had no regard.** Yahweh did not look favorably upon the second worshiper. *Offering* (*minchāh*) is the same word used in the previous v for the offering of Abel. Clearly the two brothers had the same purpose in view as they brought their offerings. Both functioned as priests. Both desired God's acceptance. Cain's tribute offering, however, was not acceptable.

3. *Narrative symmetry.* The statement regarding the two worshipers is arranged symmetrically so as to highlight the contrast. The symmetry is such that the character of the worshiper gives credibility to the offering, and vice versa. Following the Hebrew word order the comments regarding the two worshipers can be diagramed as follows:

a. Had regard
  b. Yahweh
    c. unto Abel and unto his offering
    c. but unto Cain and unto his offering
  b. (he)
a. Did not have regard

4. *Means of communication.* How did God communicate his attitude concerning the offerings to the

two brothers? The answers to this question fall into two broad categories, the natural and the supernatural. Those who opt for the natural explanation think the acceptance was communicated by the way Abel was blessed in succeeding weeks, or by the happiness he experienced from his worship experience, or by the ascending of the smoke from the sacrifice.

In the supernatural category are such explanations as these: fire fell to consume Abel's offering;[321] Yahweh manifested himself to them (Skinner); a sign of some sort was given in the sacrifices themselves (Dillmann); a direct conversation took place between Yahweh and these worshipers.

## C. Basis of Evaluation

Why did Yahweh have a favorable attitude toward Abel and his offering but not for Cain and his offering? Commentators have drawn a wide-range of inferences from what is said, and not said, in the brief narrative. The suggested reasons why God smiled on Abel, and rejected Cain can be grouped under four heads.

*1. Procedural.* Some have proposed that something was wrong with Cain's offering procedurally. He offered it at the wrong time (Philo) or without proper ritual. The LXX rendering of 4:7 suggests that Cain did not divide his offering properly. The Greek text actually uses two different Greek words for the two offerings in 4:3f. Cain took part of his *sacrifice* (*thysia*) home with him while Abel left his entire *gift* (*dōron*). The Greek translators were interpreting, not translating. As noted above, the same Hebrew term is used for both presentations.

*2. Material.* Another view is that Cain's offering was inferior as to substance. It either was the wrong

---

[321]Judg 6:21; 1 Kgs 18:28; 2 Chr 7:11. This proposal was first made by Theodotion in the third century AD.

## Rapid "Progress" of Sin

substance (non-bloody), or of inferior quality or quantity.

Yahweh's attitude toward Cain's offering cannot be explained by arguing that any offerings from the cursed ground were unacceptable. Theologically more sophisticated is the contention that God had revealed to the first family that he wanted offerings requiring shedding of blood. The argument goes like this: By faith Abel offered a more excellent sacrifice (Heb 11:4). Faith comes by hearing the word of God (Rom 10:9f). Therefore, God must have revealed that he wanted bloody offerings.

This position, however, is based on assumptions and not on data in the record. It assumes that the offerings were sin offerings; that non-bloody offerings were never acceptable; that no concept of giving back to God could have arisen without revelation;[322] that faith has the same meaning in Heb 11:4 as it has in Rom 10:9f. Even if for the sake of argument one granted that Abel had received a revelation specifying a blood sacrifice that would not necessarily mean that Cain had heard the same revelation.

Others assume that it was the quality of Cain's sacrifice that was in question. Abel brought the best that he had—*the firstlings* [the best] *of his flock* [personal sacrifice] *and their fat portions* [their best parts]. Cain brought some of the fruit of his labor. Nothing indicates that he was concerned to bring the best.

Another view is that the quantity of Cain's sacrifice was inferior. Clarke understands the *more excellent* (*pleiona*) of Heb 11:4 to mean "more" or "greater." Furthermore, Clarke emphasizes the plural *gifts* (*dōrois*) in Heb 11:4 in reference to Abel's offering. So

---

[322]For arguments pro and con with respect to this matter, see discussion of H.H. Hobbs and J.D. Heck in *The Genesis Debate*, ed. R. Youngblood (Grand Rapids: Baker, 1991), 130-147.

Abel brought multiple offerings while Cain brought but one.[323]

*3. Spiritual.* A third category of answers points to the disposition of the worshipers as the key to the passage (Cassuto). It was Abel's sincerity, obedience, and/or faith that accounts for his acceptance. These interpreters point to the numerous OT texts that stress the importance of a proper spirit during sacrifice.

*4. Theological.* A fourth category of answers focuses on God rather than to two brothers. Thus God favors shepherds over farmers (Gunkel). This position can be dismissed rather easily by observing that God appointed agriculture as the occupation for Adam. Even more unacceptable are those who paint God as capricious and inexplicable (Westermann), or those who suggest that God preferred the smell of flesh cooking over that of vegetables (Levin). Believers must surely acknowledge that God had good reason to reject Cain even if he has not seen fit to reveal all the details in the narrative.

### D. New Testament Perspective

New Testament writers make two points that help in understanding the divine attitude toward the two offerings. First, the writer of Hebrews points to the *faith* of Abel (Heb 11:4). This does not necessarily mean that in his offering Abel was responding to a revelation from God. Several times in Hebrews people are said to have performed acts in faith where there is no specific command recorded for them to act in the way they did. Certainly obedience to a specific command is a demonstration of faith. But to argue that there can be no faith without obedience to a specific command is to mistake the evidence of faith for faith itself. The definition of

---

[323] Adam Clarke, *The Holy Bible...A Commentary and Critical Notes* (New York: Abingdon-Cokesbury, n.d.): 1:58-59.

faith given by Heb 11:1 says nothing about obedience. So the presence of faith in Abel was one factor in the acceptance of Abel and his offering. He had faith in the person of God, and probably faith in the Gn 3:15 promise of God.

New Testament writers also mention Abel's character. He was a righteous man (Mt 23:35) and his works were righteous (1 Jn 3:12). On the other hand, Cain is said to be *of that wicked one*, i.e., he was the seed of Serpent. His works are said to be *evil* (1 Jn 3:12).

The superiority of Abel's offering, then, is that it was offered by one who possessed faith and godly character. Abel worshiped God correctly, demonstrated faith clearly and pleased God fully.

### E. Attitude of Cain (4:5b)

*So Cain became very angry and his countenance fell* (4:5b). Cain was not pleased when he perceived that Yahweh had accepted Abel's offering. The verb *became very angry* (*chārāh*) and its derivatives are used 139x in the OT in reference to the anger of both man and God. It differs from other Hebrew verbs of anger in that it emphasizes the "kindling" of anger or the heat of anger once started. This inward burning anger of Cain manifested itself in his crest-fallen countenance.

Why did Cain seethe with rage? Cain's reaction shows the profound paganism of his worship. He had hoped by his sacrifice to manipulate God and thereby secure his selfish desires.

Cain's anger also illustrates another truth. Those who worship God superficially often harbor growing resentment toward those who are devoted in their adoration of God. Cain could not stand the thought that his brother had demonstrated the true meaning of being made in God's image, while he himself had no relationship with Yahweh.

### F. Education of Cain (4:6-7)

God dealt with Cain's growing anger in a three-stage approach designed to change his misguided perspective. Jacob refers to 4:7 as the most obscure v in the entire book.[324]

*1. Yahweh questioned Cain (4:6-7a).* **Then Yahweh said to Cain, Why are you angry? And why has your countenance fallen? If you do well, is there not a lifting up?** (4:6-7a). Three questions were designed to make Cain realize that his anger was unjustified. God had rejected his offering for good reason. Therefore, Cain should not be angry. The questions are designed also to elicit repentance. By failing to answer these questions Cain shows growing impudence and hardness.

In general the third question suggests that as long as Cain behaves himself he will have no reason to be angry over the way God responds to him. The implication is that even fallen man has a sense of right and wrong and the power to choose between them.

There is ambiguity in the word *lifting up* ($s^e$ '$ēt$ inf. from *ns'*). The verb is used in three ways that might be appropriate to this context. First, *lifting* is a metaphor for forgiveness (e.g., Ex 34:7; Nm 14:18; Ps 32:1, 5). When this is the case, however, the word *iniquity* or its equivalent is used with the verb. At this point Cain has not been charged with trespass, so forgiveness is probably not the intended meaning. Second, *lifting* is associated with *acceptance* (Gn 19:21). Yahweh would view with acceptance either the person of Cain (KJV; NIV; NRSV), or some future sacrifice by him. Third, to

---

[324] Jacob, *First Book*, 35.

lift up one's face (countenance) is an indication of a good conscience, confidence, and favor (2 Sam 2:22). In the previous v it was the *countenance* (lit., "faces") of Cain that had fallen, an indication of depression (cf. NASB). The conditional promise may be that if Cain will change his ways, he will have no reason to be downcast. His facial expression will be lifted up. Perhaps Yahweh intended the conditional promise to be gloriously ambiguous.[325]

2. *Yahweh warned Cain (4:7b):* **And if you do not do well, at the door is sin, a beast; and its desire is for you.** This is the first mention of *sin* (*chattā't*) in the Bible. The feminine noun is the most frequently used derivative (290x) from the root *cht'*, "to miss the mark; to fall short of the standard." In Lv and Nm the noun appears many times, sometimes referring to disobedience to God, other times to the sin-offering.

*At the door* is ambiguous. Does it refer to the door of Cain's house, or to the door of his heart? Or does the word *door* (*petach*) simply mean "opening," referring to the entrance to the lair of the crouching beast? In any case, danger was near. Aalders renders: "sin lies in wait."

*Beast* (*rōbēts*) has been much discussed. Literally the word means "a crouching one," hence a *beast*. The masculine suffix on the following noun requires that this word be taken as a masculine singular noun,[326] not a participle as in most English versions.[327] The verb root is used some 30x in the OT, almost always with the sense of "repose or rest from exertion." It is used

---

[325] NJPS renders "there is uplift," maintaining the ambiguity of the original.
[326] So argued by BDB, 308 s.v. #2403. Others argue that *his desire* refers to Abel's desire to displace Cain as firstborn, a desire that Yahweh will frustrate as long as Cain does what is right.
[327] *Crouching* (NIV; NASB); *crouches* (NJPS); *croucheth* (ASV); *lurking* (NRSV); *lieth* (KJV); *lies* (NKJV).

both of people and animals, both wild and domestic. Sometimes it is used of inanimate things as well.

What is the beast or crouching one at the door of Cain's life? The noun seems to be in apposition with the feminine noun *sin*. Thus *sin* is the crouching one or beast at the door. The following clause suggests that sin is not merely a potential stumbling block to Cain; sin is actively ready to pounce upon him.

Some contend that the root *rbts* can only refer to dormant rest, not crouching with some evil intent. The verb, however, does seem to have the crouching connotation in Gn 49:9. Certainly the following clause points to active intent to dominate. Hence in Gn 4:7 the writer metaphorically has compared sin to a crouching beast that intends to do harm to Cain.

*Its* (or *his*) *desire* refers to the *desire* (*t<sup>e</sup>šûqāh*) of the crouching beast for dominance over Cain. This is the same word used of woman's *desire* for mastery over her husband in 3:16. Sin will endeavor to have dominion—to drag down, to make one crouch or lie on the ground!

3. *Yahweh encouraged Cain (4:7c):* **but you must master it.** The Hebrew imperfect can be understood in three ways: "you *must* rule over it" (obligation); or "you *will* rule over it" (simple future); or "you *may* rule over it" (capability). The narrative that follows seems to rule out the simple future, for Cain succumbed to sin, he did not rule over it. It is hard to choose between the connotation of obligation and capability. Either understanding fits the context; but since the v appears to be intended as warning, a slight preference may be given to the obligation interpretation. As a man tames a wild beast, so man should be victorious over sin.

# BEGINNING OF VIOLENCE
## Gn 4:8-17a

Cain's actions toward his brother were his defiant response to the gracious probing by God. The term *brother* is used 7x in vv 2-11. In Cain's hostility toward Abel there is the first engagement of the eternal war between the seed of Serpent and the seed of woman forecast in 3:15.

**A. Fratricide by Cain** (4:8)

*1. Conversation (4:8a):* **And Cain said unto Abel his brother.** What Cain said is not recorded. This odd report opening is handled in two ways. First, some attempt to render the verb in such a way as to eliminate the difficulty. One finds the following: "And Cain told" (ASV; NASB) or "talked with" (KJV; NKJV) Abel.[328] Second, others, following some ancient sources,[329] supply what seems to be missing from the Hebrew text by inserting: "Let us go out into the field" (NIV; NRSV). Still others render the Hebrew text as is, and report the insertion found in the ancient sources in the footnotes (NJPS). The latter course is probably is best translation procedure.

*2. Murder (4:8b):* **And it came about when they were in the field, that Cain rose up against Abel his brother and killed him.** The crime of Cain was monstrous. Cain killed a brother, a righteous man (Mt 23:35; Heb 11:4; 1 Jn 3:12) and a prophet (Lk 11:50-51). Was the murder, however, premeditated?

---

[328] Some have proposed that *said* (r. *'mr*) had a homonym meaning something like "to fix a meeting place" (from an Arabic cognate) or "to watch for" (from an Ugaritic, Akkadian cognate). Others want to emend (alter) the Hebrew word to a different root.

[329] LXX, Vulgate, Samaritan Pentateuch and the Targum.

Youngblood argues that the murder was premeditated, since Cain carefully chose the time and place.[330] This interpretation goes beyond the explicit evidence.

### B. Interrogation by God (4:9-10)

*1. Yahweh's question (4:9a):* **Then Yahweh said to Cain, Where is Abel your brother?** Yahweh questioned Cain about his crime. This is the second time God approached sinful man with a question. The question directed to Cain corresponds to the one that God asked Adam, *Where are you?* (3:9).

*2. Cain's retort (4:9b):* **And he said, I do not know. Am I my brother's keeper?** Cain's response to God indicates an impudent and hardened disposition that is in stark contrast with Adam and Eve's fearful disposition after their garden sin. Cain told a boldfaced lie. A lie is too often the first refuge of a guilty conscience.

Some see Cain's rhetorical question as an ugly joke, i.e., "Does the keeper need a keeper?" Cain's attitude was diametrically opposite that of the Apostle Paul who felt an obligation to all men (Rom 1:14; 1 Cor 9:22).

*3. Yahweh's follow-up (4:10a):* **And he said, What have you done?** Abel's blood bore irrefutable testimony against the murderer. The question, which connotes divine outrage, elicits no response from Cain.

*4. Yahweh's indictment (4:10b):* **The voice of your brother's blood is crying unto me from the ground.** The word *blood* is plural suggesting many drops of blood bearing united testimony against Cain. The participle *crying* suggests that the protest of Abel's blood is continuous. *Unto me* emphasizes that there is someone to whom the blood of the victim cries out. Cain cannot hide his deed.

---

[330] Youngblood, *BGIC*, 62.

The writer of Hebrews uses Gn 4:10 as a launching pad for one of his great observations of contrast. Abel's blood cried out for vengeance. On the other hand, Jesus' blood speaks of salvation (Heb 12:24).

In the account of Cain a new dimension of sin is introduced. The garden sin was an offense against God. The sin of Cain is also an offense against God in that the dead man was made in God's image. Cain's sin, however, is primarily against his fellowman.

### C. Punishment of Cain (4:11-12)

The punishment of Cain was both swift and severe. The report revolves around three movements.

*1. Curse pronounced (4:11):* **And now you are cursed from the ground, which has opened its mouth to receive your brother's blood from your hand.** Adam was alienated from God but not cursed, but Cain was. He had chosen the path of the cursed Serpent; he will now live in a cursed state. *From the ground* could be rendered, "cursed more than the ground" [that was cursed after the garden sin]. Better, however, is the view that the curse is explained in the next sentence. Abel's blood was spilled on the $^{a}dh\bar{a}m\bar{a}h$; now Cain was driven from the $^{a}dh\bar{a}m\bar{a}h$.

*2. Curse explained (4:12a):* **When you cultivate the ground it shall no longer yield its strength to you.** From this time the *ground* will not give of its *strength* to Cain. Under the curse of 3:17-19 crop yield was curtailed; in respect to Cain it was totally cut off. The ground Cain formerly cultivated now became his enemy. In this sense Cain is cursed *from the ground*.

*3. Curse results (4:12b):* **You shall be a vagrant and a wanderer on the earth.** Because he can no longer make a living from the soil, Cain will be compelled to shift and stray about the earth. Far from being the settled farmer he always had been, he was to become a restless wanderer. Banishment and wandering are the culminating punishments threatened against Israel in Dt 28:15-24.

### D. Protest of Cain (4:13-14)

At this point Cain no longer denied his guilt; he only whimpered about his punishment. There are five aspects to Cain's protest.

*1. General protest (4:13):* **And Cain said to Yahweh, My punishment is too great to bear!** Most English versions present Cain's words as self-pity and protest. There are some, however, who think Cain is expressing repentance by saying that his sin is too great to be forgiven.[331] The term translated *punishment* ($^a v\hat{o}n$) can also mean "iniquity." Essentially the term refers to a crime that demands punishment. The term translated *bear* also has the meaning "forgive." Literally the text reads, "great my iniquity/punishment from forgiving/bearing."

*2. Banishment protested (4:14a):* **Behold, You have driven me this day from the face of the ground.** Cain protested banishment from the cultivated land. Repetition of the terms of Yahweh's sentence indicates that the murderer understood what the consequences would be. Cain is like a spoiled child who repeats the terms of punishment so as to expose, so he thinks, the harshness of it.

*3. Status protested (4:14b):* **and from your face I shall be hidden.** It is incorrect to think that either Cain or the writer viewed Yahweh's presence as limited to the area of productive land. That Yahweh exercises sovereign authority over all the lands to which Cain might wander is made clear in 4:15. Furthermore, Cain is not

---

[331] Jacob, *First Book*, 36. Also Luther and Sailhamer.

is not lamenting the interruption of his fellowship with Yahweh. He was not concerned about worship.

To be *hidden* from God's face means to be exposed to his wrath (Ps 139:7-12; Amos 9:3f.). Cain now sees Yahweh as the avenger of his dead brother. He fears an outburst of Yahweh's wrath at any moment.

*4. Lifestyle protested (4:14c):* **and I shall be a wanderer and a vagabond on the earth.** *Vagabond* comes from the root *nûd* — used 28x in the OT— which means "to move hither and thither." The root can have the meaning "flee." *Wanderer* comes from the root *nua'*. Essentially the two Hebrew terms are synonyms. Together they point to a life that is hunted and hounded by God's curse. Neither verb ever describes the life of a nomad.

*5. Endangerment protested (4:14d):* **and it will come about that whoever finds me will kill me.** The murderer knows that his fellows are capable of killing him. He senses that execution is the only appropriate response to his audacious crime that Yahweh has exposed. At the very least Cain intuits that expulsion from the community will make him a target. He will no longer enjoy the security of living in organized society.

Who was around to fear? Youngblood goes beyond the evidence when he writes: "The very fact that Cain had to keep on the move appears to mean that he feared far more people than the members of his immediate family."[332]

The abbreviated report about Cain and Able makes it appear that the two brothers were the only living humans besides their parents. A careful reading of the text suggests that almost 130 years had elapsed by the time Abel was murdered. At age 130 Adam fathered Seth

---

[332]Youngblood, *BGIC*, 65. For arguments pro and con with respect to the existence of hominids before the time of Adam, see H.W. Seaford, Jr., and G. Kufeldt in *The Genesis Debate*, 148-65.

(5:3). Seth was given to Adam and Eve as a substitute for the righteous Abel. It is reasonable to assume that Seth was born shortly after the death of Abel. That being the case a considerable number of human beings were living on the earth at the time of the murder.

If one presupposes children reaching seventeen before producing offspring, and three years between births, and assuming normal population growth, the human race would have reached a population of at least 800,000 in 125 years.[333]

### E. Mercy of God (4:15)

God showed mercy to Adam and Eve after their garden sin. So now he shows grace respecting Cain in two ways.

*1. Warning to Cain's enemies (4:15a).* **So Yahweh said to him, Therefore whoever kills Cain, vengeance will be taken on him sevenfold.** *Therefore* (*lāchēn*) is an adverb accompanied by a preposition. This term is used in conversation to reply to an objection, or to state the ground upon which an answer is made (BDB). Some modern translations follow the lead of the LXX in rendering the term as a strong negative, "not so" (NIV; NRSV). Others regard *lāchēn* as a positive affirmation of promise (NJPS).

*Take vengeance* (r. *nqm*) generally speaks of divine retribution against the enemies of God or his people. *Whoever kills Cain* is lit., "anyone killing Cain." If anyone slays Cain sevenfold he shall be avenged! This pronouncement serves two purposes: it forestalls vigilante justice; and it reassures Cain that he traveled about under immunity from execution. *Sevenfold* is to

---

[333] Mathematician Doug Brumbaugh in personal communication with the author. Brumbaugh made use of Fibonacci numbers. A Fibonacci number calculator can be found at http://javascript.internet.com/calculators/fibonacci.html

act as a deterrent. Cain stands under God's curse; but no human being has the right to step in and contravene God's sentence by killing Cain.[334]

2. *Sign for Cain (4:15b).* **And Yahweh appointed a sign for Cain, lest anyone finding him should slay him.** This v is commonly taken to refer to a mark on the person of Cain. A plethora of bizarre suggestions as to the nature of that mark have surfaced over the years.[335] More likely this v should be interpreted as a *sign*—usual meaning of the word *'ôth*[336]—given for Cain's benefit to confirm the verbal promise of protection just announced.

Certain questions about the mark or sign of Cain have been raised. Was this sign given once for all time, or was it repeated each time Cain's life was threatened? It appears that the sign was a one time event. Is the mark or sign meant for a single person or for a group (e.g., of the Kenites)? Only Cain is said to have received the sign. Is the sign a softening of the penalty on Cain? No, because Cain was not sentenced to death. The protection of his life in no way softened his punishment unless it would be in relieving the anxiety that accompanied it.

### F. Departure of Cain (4:16)

1. *Going out (4:16a):* **Then Cain went out from the presence of Yahweh.** Cain had no choice but to comply with the punishment for his crime. *Went out* has been taken to mean only that the confrontation with Yahweh was at an end. Others take *presence of Yahweh* to refer to the region near the garden where God had

---

[334] Westermann, *Genesis 1-11*, 311f.
[335] See James R. Conner, *Mistaken Views of Scripture* (Cincinnati: Monfort, 1923), 205-207. Recently Waltke proposed the mark was a "protective tattoo." Sailhamer thinks the sign was the city built by Cain that became for him a prototype of the cities of refuge.
[336] But compare Ex 12:13, 23; Josh 2:12.

manifested himself and communicated directly with his children. Since it is impossible to outdistance the presence of Yahweh geographically, some give to these words a spiritual connotation. Cain went out on his own to build a life without God. Under this view, Cain was the first secularist.

2. *Settling (4:16b):* ***and settled in the land of Nod, east of Eden.*** *Nod* is taken as a proper name by the LXX. Most modern commentators take the term to be a descriptive noun meaning "wandering."

The land of Nod or wandering for Cain was *east of Eden* (cf. vv 11, 14, 16). Where God previously had revealed himself, there Cain no longer can stay. He is shut off from God. *East of Eden* is not so much a piece of geographical information as a reference to a life of alienation from God.[337] The implication is that Adam and Eve and their family remained in the general area where the garden (or what was left of it) was located.

## CONCLUSION

God spared the life of Cain. Why? Is God inconsistent with his own insistence in the Law that murderers be executed? Does God require men to take the life of murderers (9:5) while he distances himself from capital punishment? Thoughts that God spared Cain because of the need to perpetuate the human race fail from the likelihood that over half-million people were already on the scene before Cain's sin. Cain was sentenced to a life of exile because his murder, though a serious crime and sin, was not premeditated.

Following the murder of Abel, the downward spiral of sin continued. Romans 1:28-31 takes up the story of sin where Gn 4 leaves off.

---

[337]Westermann, *Genesis 1-11*, 314. So understood in the novel by John Steinbeck.

# 15
# BEGINNINGS OF CIVILIZATION
## Gn 4:17-26

At this point the writer inserts a genealogy of the descendants of Cain. The following ch contains an even more detailed genealogy of the descendents of Seth. Since the record indicates that Adam begat other sons and daughters there must have been other family lines developing alongside the two that are detailed in Gn 4-5. It is possible that the unnamed family lines disappeared over time, or blended into the Cainite and Sethite lines. It is more likely, however, that the descendants of Cain and those of Seth are singled out because they are representative of two contrasting spiritual orientations.

The idea that this Cainite genealogy and the Adamite genealogy in ch 5 are variations of one original source emphatically must be rejected. First, both contain names that do not appear in the other list. Second, the names that appear similar are in fact different names. Third, both names that are identical are clearly identified as different individuals by the details recorded about them. Fourth, the positions of the identical names are different in the two lists. Enoch is third in the Cainite list, seventh in the Adamite list. Lamech was seventh in the Cainite list, ninth in the Adamite list. Fifth, the lists are not of the same length (eight vs. ten generations), although since Seth was born after Cain reached adulthood the first list should include one more generation.[338]

The similarities between the two lists may be explained by one of the following considerations. First,

---

[338] Aalders, *BSC*, 145.

287

both lists are probably selective in nature. The writer aims to highlight the names of the most prominent family members. Second, there may have been intermarriage between the various families of mankind. In any case, later biblical records contain similar names in families far removed from each other. How much more one should expect closely related families to display similarities in names.

## PRIMEVAL GENERATIONS
## Gn 4:17-18

The genealogy of Cain is "the genealogy of pride" (Youngblood). It has two major divisions, the first of which extends over seven generations. Westermann correctly observes: "The number seven obviously describes a totality; these seven designate the generations of the primeval period."[339] This part of the genealogy is similar to the Adamite genealogy in ch 5. Each of the seven names in the genealogy is matched by what appears to be a similar or identical name in Adam's genealogy through Seth in ch 5. The parallel lists of names are displayed in Chart 14.

| Chart 14 ||
| Cainite/Sethite Alleged Parallel Names ||
| Genesis 4 | Genesis 5 |
| --- | --- |
| Adam (4:1) | Adam (5:1) |
| Cain (4:1) | Kenan (5:12) |
| Enoch (4:17) | Enoch (5:21) |
| Irad (4:18) | Jared (5:18) |
| Mehujael (4:18) | Mahalalel (5:15) |
| Methushael (4:18) | Methuselah (5:25) |
| Lamech (4:18) | Lamech (5:28) |

---

[339]C. Westermann, *Genesis 1-11*, 324.

**A. Generations Two-Three** (4:17)

*1. Marriage of Cain (4:17a):* **And Cain knew his wife.** Biblical critics have used the reference to Cain's wife as a means of poking holes in the record. No women (beside Eve) heretofore have been named; therefore the writer has made a serious blunder by mentioning a wife that did not exist.

The identity of Cain's wife is really a non-issue. Clearly in the earliest days of the human race it was God's intention for close-relative marriages to take place. If the race was to spring from one pair, then brother-sister marriages were necessary for a time. There is no physical reason why such marriages could not take place. Adam had children not named in the text (5:4), so there was an available pool of sisters from which Cain could choose.

When the necessity for close-relative marriages no longer existed, the practice was forbidden by specific command of God (Lv 18). Close-relative marriages were quite common in royal families outside of Israel for many centuries. Today the risk of defective offspring is so high that every civilized country legislates against the marriage of close relatives. The first human beings, however, may have had a perfect constitution in which case brother-sister marriages would have been harmless.

*2. Birth of Enoch (4:17b):* **and she conceived, and gave birth to Enoch.** There are three others in the OT with the name *Enoch*. The more famous *Enoch* appears in the genealogy of Seth (5:18-24). There is also one in the family of Reuben (Gn 46:9), and one among the sons of Midian (Gn 25:4). The name is sometimes spelled *Hanoch* in English versions.

The verb *gave birth* (r. *yālad*) has the basic meaning "bring forth (children)." This form of the verb can be used of either the father or the mother. It is even used of animals. The Qal form of the verb is used 9x in Gn 4,

**289**

six in reference to mothers. The Qal stem may refer to something other than direct physical fathering of immediately succeeding offspring.

**B. Beginning of Urban Life** (4:17c, d)

*1. Building of the city (4:17c):* **And he was building a city.** The builder of the first city is ambiguous. The pronoun could refer to Cain (NIV) or to Enoch (Westermann; Cassuto). The following clause removes the ambiguity. Cain was the builder. The writer is making the point that cities originated outside the framework of God's people.

Personal safety may have been a motivating factor in Cain's actions. Building a city seems to be Cain's act of defiance to the punishment of perpetual wandering. The Hebrew participle (*was building*) implies that Cain may have commenced but did not finish his city. On the other hand, the city may have been intended as a place of safety for his extended family while Cain continued to move about.

What was this first city like? The term *city* (*'îr*) can refer to any settlement protected by a fortress or simple wall. Cain's *city* may have been nothing more than a walled enclosure with few houses. On the other hand, the population of Cain's descendants, by the most conservative estimates, may have been at least 100,000 by the time Cain was four hundred.[340] If Cain's city included any significant portion of this population then it may have been sizable.

*2. Naming of the city (4:17d):* **and called the name of the city Enoch, after the name of his son.** Waltke observes that instead of honoring God, unbelievers honor humanity.[341] The name Enoch has been traced to roots meaning "train up, dedicate." Possibly the son was

---
[340]Whitcomb and Morris, *Genesis Flood*, 29
[341]Waltke, *GAC*, 100.

named *Dedicated* because Cain dedicated the city to him.

In Mesopotamia the first city was Eridu, which sounds very much like the name of Enoch's son Irad. Mention of the building of the city by the murderer Cain may be intended to express a negative view toward cities. While the Mesopotamians gloried in their cities, the writer of Gn used this little note to point out the unsavory origins of the cities of that area.

What happened to the *city* built by Cain? The remains of this *city* 1) have been entirely obliterated; or 2) archaeologists have not yet found it;[342] or 3) it was of such a primitive form as to not leave remains.

## C. Generations Four-Seven (4:18)

Before examining the details of these generations, some general observations are in order. First, the descendants of Enoch down to Lamech (seventh generation) are enumerated with no comment (4:18). This may suggest that there was no progress in civilization during this period. Second, each generation is represented by one name. Third, nothing more is known about those who bear these names. Fourth, in one case the name itself has two forms. Fifth, the names are as good as beyond explanation. Commentators who try to explain the names on the basis of Hebrew roots forget that the Hebrew language most likely did not appear for centuries. Sixth, the names are not Hebrew. They probably are Babylonian in origin.

Three of the names in the line of Cain are compounded with the divine name *el* = *God*. Why? Some

---

[342]The remains of Jericho include the oldest ruins of a "city" found to date by archaeologists. The site was excavated by Kathleen Kenyon. She found the fortified walls (including a massive defensive tower) of a Neolithic (New Stone Age) city at the lowest level of the site. Conservative dating for the building of that city is estimated at about 7000 BC.

think these names show the influence of the Sethite line on the Cainites. Others think that along the way there may have been some in the line of Cain who were devout. On the other hand, the meaning of the names may have nothing to do with the religious standing of these men. Many of those who wear Christian names are anything but followers of the Nazarene.

*1. Fourth generation (4:18a):* **Now to Enoch was born Irad.** For what it is worth, Keil suggests that the name Irad means "Townsman." More recent authorities have traced the name to a root meaning "wild donkey."

*2. Fifth generation (4:18b):* **And Irad became the father of Mehujael.** In the Hebrew text there are two forms of the name representing the fifth generation in Cain's line. The difference in spelling of the names has not been preserved in the English versions. According to Leupold, *Mehujael* means something like "God gives life." *Mehijael* means something like "God is the fountain of life."

How these two variant forms of the name crept into the text is not clear. It may simply be the result of a scribal miscopying. On the other hand, it may be that Mehujael changed his name at or before the birth of his son. Changing names to mark significant milestones is documented in the lives of several biblical characters.

*3. Sixth generation (4:18c):* **And Mehijael became the father of Methushael.** The sixth generation from Adam in Cain's line is represented by *Methushael.* Again there is disagreement about the meaning of this name. Some think it means "Man of God" (Young); others propose "man of Sheol" (Tsevat).

*4. Seventh generation (4:18):* **And Methushael became the father of Lamech.** The name Lamech means something like "Overthrower, Wild Man" (Young). The seventh from Adam through Cain is the antithesis of Enoch, the seventh from Adam through Seth (5:21-24).

Lamech was a bigamist, a selfish, boastful, and violent man. Enoch walked so closely with God that he was "raptured" before experiencing death.

## LAMECH ELABORATIONS
## Gn 4:19-24

Part two of Cain's genealogy focuses on the seventh generation, that of Lamech. This part of the genealogical list has two elaborations. The first reveals the advancement of civilization through the efforts of the sons of Lamech. The second elaboration is a poem that reveals that while civilization in many ways was rapidly developing, in the moral area the spiral downward continued.

### A. General Observations

Before examining how the writer of Gn treats the origins of civilization a few general observations are in order. First, based on what is said in Gn one might conclude that civilization made greater strides among those who were alienated from God than among those devoted to him. Second, ancient peoples attributed the development of civilization to their gods. There were gods who gave the gift of writing, farming, domesticating animals, etc. The Bible, however, underscores that culture was created by human ingenuity. Third, in Cain's descendants violence escalates within civilization.

Fourth, some see Gn as anti-civilization because civilization requires population control, and the God of Gn is the deity of procreation.[343] This assessment, however, is not accurate. While there is a current of negative thought against overpopulation in the mythology of Mesopotamia, fertility cults doting on procreation were quite common in the Near East. While it is true that God

---
[343]Kikawada & Quinn, *Before Abraham Was*, 56f.

told the first couple to be fruitful, multiply and fill the earth, the writer of Gn does not dwell on the fulfillment of this mandate. He does not, for example, cite what must have been the enormous numbers of children fathered by the antediluvian patriarchs. The families he does describe are of modest size.

### B. Bigamy of Lamech (4:19)

*1. Two wives (4:19a):* **And Lamech took to himself two wives.** Why does the writer mention the two wives of Lamech? Some think it is simply the writer's way of subdividing the children of Lamech (Westermann). Others think that by mentioning the two wives the writer was hinting that the world was becoming more affluent. There may, however, be another reason for mentioning the wives. Since Gn 3 the writer has been developing his theme of the downward spiral of sin. The mention of Lamech's bigamy may be his way of indicating the increasing moral corruption in the line of Cain. Given all that the writer stressed about the garden marriage, he certainly must have regarded the brazen bigamy of Lamech as crossing over a line clearly set for the original marriage ordinance.

*2. Two names (4:19b):* **the name of the one was Adah, and the name of the other, Zillah.** Not much can be said about the wives of Lamech except what may be deduced from their names. Unfortunately these names cannot be explained with certainty.

The first wife was named *Adah*, which seems to mean something like "ornament" or "morning." Later one of Esau's wives bore this name (Gn 36:2).

The second wife's name *Zillah* has been taken by some to mean "shade," by others, "tinkle" (like a cymbal). On the basis of the names alone Leupold speculates that physical attractiveness may have been the governing motive in Lamech's sin.[344]

### C. Adah's Children (4:20-21)

*1. Jabal (4:20):* **And Adah gave birth to Jabal; he was the father of dwellers of tents and livestock.** The name *Jabal* means something like "wanderer." The phrase *father of* in this context means the first to excel in a particular skill or trade, not necessarily the biological ancestor. *Dwellers of tents and livestock* refers to those who reside in tents and alongside cattle. All three nouns in Hebrew are singular, used collectively. Jabal was the first to initiate the nomadic way of life. The text does not say, however, that Jabal was the first shepherd. Abel already has been presented as the first shepherd.

The term *livestock* (*miqneh*) comes from a root meaning "to buy, acquire or possess." So *miqneh* refers to possessions, especially animate possessions. This is not the same word for *cattle* used 4x in Gn 1-2. The term *miqneh* certainly can refer to cattle, but with the connotation of cattle legally owned for commercial purposes.[345] The term can embrace cows, camels and mules as well as sheep and goats. Hence Jabal was the father of "cattle barons and slave traders."[346]

*2. Jubal (4:21):* **And his brother's name was Jubal; he was the father of all those who play the lyre and pipe.** The name Jubal means something like "sound" (Leupold). Jubal was the father of musicians. The verb

---

[344] Leupold, *Exposition,* 219.

[345] Kikawada and Quinn (*Before Abraham,* 57) include slaves in *miqneh*. "Slave traders can claim descent from Cain through Jubal (*sic*)." The evidence they offer for this position is inadequate.

[346] Kikawada & Quinn, *Before Abraham,* 57. A novel suggestion concerning *miqneh* was advanced by T.C. Mitchell. He suggests that in the unvocalized Hebrew text this term may come from *qāneh* (*stalk, reed*) with a prefixed *Mem* indicating location. The meaning then is that Cain's descendants were dwellers of tents and *places of reed,* i.e., reed huts. "Archeology and Genesis I-XI," *FAT,* 91(1959); 41-42.

The verb *play* (*tāphas*) means "to manipulate or handle" (KJV). It describes the dexterity or art of the one who manipulates the instruments.

The instruments mentioned are meant to be the oldest and simplest musical instruments (Skinner). The *lyre* (*kinnôr*) was a stringed instrument mentioned frequently in the OT. Later the lyre became an instrument used in worship. What was invented by the ungodly was turned to the praise of the Creator. The *pipe* (*'ûgābh*) is elsewhere mentioned 3x in OT. (*Organ* in KJV connotes an instrument too far advanced.) The pipe too is mentioned as an instrument of praise in Ps 150:4. These two instruments also are mentioned together in a secular context (Job 21:12; 30:31). The brother of Jabal the wandering herdsman—the nomads—invented musical instruments. Throughout world literature nomads are associated with music.

Two clay cylinder seals dating to about 3,000 BC bear the imprint of a lute. This is the earliest archaeological evidence of stringed instruments. The earliest pipes or flutes consisted only of a hollow tube. Flutes fashioned with finger holes began to appear about 8,000 BC.[347]

### D. Zillah's Children (4:22)

*1. Tubal-cain (4:22a):* **As for Zillah, she also gave birth to Tubal-cain, a sharpener of all who work in bronze and iron.** The writer here notes the birth of technology. The name of Zillah's son is compound. *Tubal* appears in Ezek 27:13 as the name of a region important for metal work. *Cain* (*qayin*) may be a reference to his craft. His name means "Tubal the Artificer" (Cassuto). Leupold has a different take on the meaning of the compound name, suggesting "Iron Splinter."

---

[347] Aviezer, *In the Beginning*, 118.

Tubal-cain is said to be a *sharpener* (*lōtēš*). "Forger" (NIV) suggests the advanced technology of smelting that came along much later. The Hebrew root *ltš* means "to hammer or sharpen." The verb could be taken literally (depending on how the following word is translated), or figuratively of a teacher or instructor, i.e., one who sharpens students.

What did Tubal-cain sharpen? Was it "all implements" (NJPS; NASB) or "tools" (NRSV; NIV), or "cutting instruments" (ASV)? The Hebrew term *chōrēš* normally is rendered "artificer" (KJV) or "craftsman" (NKJV) in other contexts. So Tubal-Cain taught others the craft of metalwork. *Bronze* (*nᵉchōšet*) could also be rendered "copper" (NJPS); but not "brass" (KJV; ASV).

*2. Antediluvian metalwork.* The mention of metalwork in the Antediluvian Period raises a twofold problem. First, the text appears to represent a simultaneous development of copper (or bronze) and iron tools. This does not square with the clearly defined ages (stone, bronze, iron) postulated by archaeologists. In response it can be said that the evidence indicates that these ages were not nearly as uniform or as clearly defined as the general public has been led to believe.[348]

Second, the antiquity of metal work is a problem for some. The oldest known bronze artifacts date to about 3500 BC. The Iron Age is generally dated to ca. 1200 BC. In Anatolia, however, there is evidence for working in terrestrial iron as early as 6500 BC.

In response to the alleged anachronistic reference to metal work before the Flood five points can be made.

First, Adam—the first true human—may be relatively recent, closer in time to the documented metalwork mentioned above than is generally assumed. Second, the art of working metal may have appeared and

---

[348] Aalders, *BSC*, 132.

disappeared several times during ancient history. Third, if O'Connell is right about the pre-flood levels in Mesopotamia, then physical evidence exists of the use of hammered copper before the Deluge.[349] Fourth, the term *iron* in 4:22 may refer to an iron-like stone used for decoration and not to the metal later known by that name.[350] Fifth, there may be one or more time gaps in the line of Cain as recorded here.[351]

*3. Naamah (4:22b):* ***And the sister of Tubal-cain was Naamah.*** It is not clear why Naamah is identified as Tubal-cain's sister rather than Lamech's daughter. Perhaps her father died while she was young, and her brother became the head of the house. In any case, the name *Naamah* in Hebrew means something like "Beautiful" or "Pleasant." Some see in the naming of this daughter an indication that men now were selecting wives for their beautiful countenance rather than for their loving and pious hearts. Solomon had a wife with the name Naamah who was queen mother under Rehoboam (1 Kgs 14:21//2 Chr 12:13).

Since no particular contribution is attributed to Naamah the question arises as to why she is even mentioned. She may have been an important figure in the traditions of those who first received these narratives. For that reason the writer is exposing her ancestry. Jewish legend, for what it is worth, suggests that Naamah was a professional singer (*Tar Pseu Jon*) and that she became the wife of Noah (*Gen Rab* 23:3).

---

[349] P. O'Connell, *Science of Today and the Problems of Genesis* (2nd ed.; Hawthorne, CA: Christian Book Club, 1969), 2:29-46.
[350] R. Laird Harris, *Man, God's Eternal Creation* (Chicago: Moody, 1971), 83.
[351] Youngblood, *BGIC*, 69.

Beginnings of Civilization

### E. Lamech's Poem (4:23-24)

The brief poem attributed to Lamech is the first piece of poetry of which there is any record. The song manifests parallelism of thought and uses certain ancient poetic forms of words. This poem resembles in form those short songs that have been handed down from the earliest period of Israel's history (Ex 15:21; 1 Sam 18:7; Judg 15:16).

The theme of the poem is the glorification of the sword and the spirit of personal revenge.[352] For this reason Lamech's poem is often called "the sword song." The poem consists of six lines:

*1. Summons (4:23a):* **And Lamech said to his wives, Adah and Zillah, Listen to my voice, you wives of Lamech, give heed to my speech.** Lamech's poem is addressed to his wives. The poem begins with the summons to the auditors. The verbs *listen/give heed* occur 18x together in the OT in various types of speech (e.g., wisdom, prophetic). Paralleling *my voice* and *my speech* (or *what I say*) is very common in the OT.

*2. Explanation (4:23b):* **for I have killed a man for wounding me; and a youth for striking me.** The summons is followed by *for* (*kî*), which introduces the reason for the call to attention. It also serves the purpose of commanding attention (like *hinneh* = *behold*).

The verb *killed* is perfect tense. Most English versions render it as a past tense. This means that Lamech was boasting that he had slain a man. It is possible that the verb was intended as a "prophetic perfect," a declaration of certainty about the future. In this case Lamech

---

[352]Sailhamer (*EBC*, loc) argues that Lamech's words "appear to be an appeal to a system of legal justice." He anticipates the legal doctrine of *lex talionis* of Ex 21:24f, using some of the very words of the later Mosaic principle. According to Sailhamer, Lamech is pleading self-defense. Thus Lamech killed a man for wounding him, not because he "hated him" (Dt 19:4-6).

**299**

is boasting about something that he will do to anyone who wounds him (cf. NIV marginal reading).

If *man/youth* is synonymous parallelism, then Lamech had killed one person—a man who was in his youth. This is the best interpretation. The term *youth* (*yeled*) sometimes refers to the very young (Gn 21:8), but also to teenagers (Gn 21:16) and young adults (Ruth 1:5). "Boy" (NASB) and "lad" (NJPS) read too much into the term. Those who take the verb as a prophetic perfect see this as mounting parallelism. Lamech would show no mercy even to a lad.

The aggravation that provoked such a murderous response is called *wounding/striking*. These injuries were not lethal; but they were nevertheless a violation of Lamech's honor. The point of the song is that the singer has rendered retribution without limit for even the smallest injury. Lamech rejects the principle of societal authority expressed in law and law enforcement. He will be his own judge, jury and executioner. He and his descendants are committed to ever-increasing violence and vindictiveness. Mathews observes: "This is the first recorded incident in the Bible where crime is venerated by the culprit."[353]

*3. Boast (4:24):* **If Cain is avenged seven times, then Lamech seventy and seven.** The poem concludes with a boast. *Seventy and seven* symbolizes unrestrained retaliation, retaliation disproportional to the infraction. One incident of violence is reported of Cain; Lamech commits himself to a life of violence. When he killed his brother Cain was tight-lipped about it. On the other hand, Lamech celebrated his crimes and perhaps bragged of more to come. Cain was only able to use his fists or perhaps a stone to kill his brother. Lamech had access to weapons forged by his son Tubal-cain with

---

[353] Mathews, *NAC*, 290.

Beginnings of Civilization

which to deliver seventy-seven blows. Yahweh could only promise sevenfold vengeance on anyone who attacked Cain. Lamech threatens any who would attack him with seventy times that amount of retaliation.

# OTHER ISSUES

## A. Function of Lamech's Poem

Why has the writer included Lamech's poem in the record? Some think the poem is a bragging song intended to be hurled at enemies for the purpose of intimidation. That was certainly part of Lamech's motive for writing the poem. Given, however, the gap between the writer's time and Lamech, and given the antipathy that the writer shows toward the line of Cain, he could hardly have intended this song to be used for the purposes of intimidation by godly people. The song probably is intended to show that the march of civilization has its "down" side. Evil men learn through education to be cleverer in their schemes and more efficient in their brutality to their fellowman. The more progress in material things, the more potential there is for degradation.

## B. Chronological Placement

Archaeologists have documented a cultural revolution that dates to about 8,000 BC. This is sometimes called the Agricultural Revolution or the Neolithic (new stone age) Revolution. Every work of archaeology discussing this period remarks on these rapid and profound developments. Words like "explosive," "radical," and "revolutionary" are used to describe what transpired in a very short period of time. The following cultural innovations occurred during this revolution:[354]

---

[354] Aviezer (*In the Beginning*, 97-100) presents the documentation.

- beginning of agriculture.
- beginning of animal husbandry
- development of metalworking.
- invention of the wheel.
- first written language.
- development of ceramic pottery.
- origin of weaving.
- making of bread, wine, cheese and butter.
- development of musical instruments.
- advanced architecture.
- appearance of cities.

If Gn 4 reflects the Neolithic Revolution of about 8,000 BC then the creation of man must not be much earlier. The issue of how man relates to the man-like hominids that (supposedly) date back 250,000 years is an issue upon which creationists are divided. The various approaches to this problem are discussed in the following ch.

### C. Length of Cain's Genealogy

The genealogy of Cain is not carried down to the Deluge as is the line through Seth. There is no reason that it should be. The writer has made his point regarding the steady moral deterioration in the line of Cain. Lamech's belligerent boasting references the words of God to Cain and makes the connection between the two. If Cain is evil, Lamech is double-evil.

## A NEW BEGINNING
## Gn 4:25-26

### A. Seth the Substitute (4:25)

Having painted the bleak picture of the downward spiral of Cainite civilization, the writer now reverts to the birth of another son of Adam, one that reveals hope for ultimate salvation.

*1. Intimacy (4:25a).* **And Adam knew his wife again.** On this euphemism see on 4:1, 17. *Again* suggests renewal of intimacy after a period of abstinence. If Adam and Eve took God's mandate to be fruitful and multiply seriously, it is difficult to believe that they had no other offspring other than Cain and Abel for the 130 years prior to the birth of Seth (cf. 5:3). Yet the conception and birth of Seth are significant enough to be mentioned specifically.

*2. Birth (4:25b):* **and she gave birth to a son.** Seth is the first person to be called a *son* to Adam. Neither Cain nor Abel is called in Gn a *son* of Adam. The writer seems to invest in the word *son* a meaning beyond that of mere physical descent. This is made clear in 5:3 where the words *image* and *likeness* are used and the word *son* does not appear in the Hebrew. Seth was a true son of Adam spiritually as well as physically. He was also his son in the office of ruler of the earth.

*3. Naming (4:25c):* **And she [Eve] called his name Seth...** The significance of this birth is further underscored by inclusion of a birth comment by Eve. As was the case with her first named boy, Eve was responsible for the naming (4:1). The birth comment has no verbal introduction, the words *and she said* being supplied by English versions.

*4. Explanation (4:25d):* **for Elohim has appointed me another offspring in place of Abel; for Cain killed him.** Eve (presumably) linked the name *Seth* with a verb root meaning "to set or place." Hence *Seth* was the Substitute, set in the place of Abel. Eve's other children probably had gone in the way of Cain, leaving none to carry on the holy line. In the birth of this son Eve anticipates a new beginning. In faith she expects this son to be another Abel in respect to piety. Perhaps she foresaw

Biblical Protology

that, unlike Abel, this son would become the head of a godly family. The words *God has appointed me* contrast with the birth comment Eve made when her first son was born. She gives God alone the credit for the birth of this son.

The words *for Cain killed him* are the words of Eve, not the redundant comment of the narrator (cf. 4:8). Eve is recalling the terrible loss she experienced when Abel was taken from her.

The name *Yahweh* is used 9x in ch 4; but *Elohim* is mentioned but once, here in 4:25. If there is any place one would expect to find the covenant name Yahweh used it would be in connection with Seth. One cannot argue that Eve did not know the name Yahweh, for she used it in 4:1. If there is purpose here in her choice of divine names it is unclear. Perhaps her use was as unintentional as the interchange of divine names in the prayers of a modern believer.

### B. Enosh the Frail (4:26)

*1. Birth (4:26a):* ***And to Seth, to him also a son was born; and he called his name Enosh.*** For the first time the father gives the name. The name *Enosh* means something like "Frail Man" or "Mortal." Thus the first (Adam) and third names in this genealogy have essentially the same meaning.

The term $^e$*nôš* occurs 42x in the OT, but only in poetic texts. In thirty-two of the cases it is used of humans in their mortality and limitation or of a human being in contrast to God. The son of Seth, however, is the only person in the OT to have the name *Enosh*. He is referred to 7x by name (Gn 5:6-11; 1 Chr 1:1). That Seth gave his son the name *Enosh* indicates that he had begun to realize the feebleness and weakness of human flesh.

*2. A milestone (4:26b):* ***Then [men] began.*** Cain's descendants were noted for their contributions to technology and their ruthlessness; Seth's were remembered for contributions in the realm of faith. The verb *began* (r. *chll*) is used in Gn 1-11 to mark important milestones (6:1; 9:20; 10:8; 11:6). Here the form is Hophal perfect (*hûchal*), lit., "then it was begun."

The root *chll* sometimes refers to the action of polluting or defiling. For this reason the words of this half-verse have received a wide range of interpretations.[355] The root is used in some contexts where man is rebelling against God (6:1; 10:8; 11:6). For this reason some rabbis argued for a sinister interpretation of the final statement of ch 4. In the days of Enosh men profaned the worship of God into idolatry by calling idols by the name *Yahweh*. This negative interpretation is unlikely for two reasons. First, it requires the insertion of an object for the infinitive *to call* or *call on*. Second, the writer's intention seems to be to present the line of Seth in a positive light. For these reasons Gn 4:26 should not be interpreted as a reference to idolatry.

*3. Public worship (4:26c):* **to call upon the name of Yahweh.** In days of Enosh there was a major development in the history of biblical faith. This cannot be referring to private worship, for both Cain and Abel brought offerings to the Lord. The key to the passage is the infinitive *to call* (*liqrō'*). It seems to refer to invocation by prayer, especially in a public context, i.e., worship.[356]

Adam interacted directly with Yahweh (Gn 3:8-19), as did Cain and Abel (Gn 4:6f, 10-15). Perhaps as the original generations passed from the scene, public worship replaced direct interaction with Yahweh. On the

---

[355] See S.D. Fraade, *Enosh and His Generation: Pre-Israelite Hero and History in Postbiblical Interpretation*, SBLMS 30 (Chico, CA: Scholars Press, 1984). S. Sandmel, "Genesis 4:26b," *HUCA* 32(1961): 19-29.

[356] See Gn 13:4; Judg 15:18; 2 Sam 22:4; 1 Kgs 18:24, 25, 26; 2 Kgs 5:11; 1 Chr 4:10; Jer 10:25; Joel 2:32; Zeph 3:9; Zech 13:9.

other hand, perhaps it was increasing corruption, including the rise of idolatry, which drove the faithful to band together in public worship.

The object of this worship is *Yahweh*. The point of the v is that the name *Yahweh* is older than Moses. The use of this name goes back to primeval times. What, then, is the writer asserting in Ex 6:3 when he says: "I appeared unto Abraham, unto Isaac, and unto Jacob in (the name of) El Shaddai; but my name Yahweh was not known to them." Perhaps he means that the significance of the name was not known prior to Moses.

## TABLET COLOPHON
## Gn 5:1a

***This is the book of the generations of Adam*** (5:1a). The opening line of ch 5 is probably a subscription to the previous unit, not a superscription to what follows. The word *book* suggests that this unit was in written form, at least when Moses received it.

In the earliest days of writing it was often the practice to impress the name of the scribe at the end of the tablet. The name at the end of the *tôl$^e$dōth* formula may have been the writer or owner of the tablet containing the material, which in this case began in 2:4b. Moses probably added the formula *these are the generations of* before the name. There is nothing recorded in these chs that Adam could not have known about. Furthermore, Adam had the gift of language at the time of his creation. There is no reason to think that he could not have thought of a way in which to communicate his language in written form.

# 16
# ADAM'S SUCCESSORS
# Gn 5:1b-32

The third tablet employed by the writer consists largely of a genealogical listing of Adam's descendants (5:3-32). This genealogy is introduced by a prologue (5:1b-2) and it concludes with an epilogue (6:1-9a).

## GOD: CREATOR-FATHER
## Gn 5:1b-2

Ch 5 begins with transitional vv that make it clear that the writer is now doing some chronological backtracking. The patriarchs mentioned in ch 5 lived in the same timeframe as the leading figures of Cain's line mentioned in ch 4.

God is portrayed in these vv as the Father of mankind. First, the pattern of birth and naming continues from ch 4. Just as the first parents named their sons (4:25-26), so also God named Adam (v 2); and Adam, in turn, named his son (v 3). Second, the writer draws a parallel between creation and procreation as found in the reference to the image of God. Adam was created in that image, and passed that image on to his son. Third, the reference to Elohim's blessing ties in with the theme of the patriarchal blessing of sons that is found throughout Gn.[357] Whereas the Creator is not directly called Father, the wording of these vv supports that imagery.

In the transitional vv four great truths about creation are reiterated, and one new truth is revealed.

---

[357]Sailhamer, *EBC*, in loc.

### A. Old Truths Reiterated (5:1b-2b)

*1. Miracle of man (5:1b):* **In the day when Elohim created man.** Use of the divine name *Elohim* and the verb *created* (*bārā'*) tie these remarks to ch 1, and emphasize the tremendous power required to bring about the appearance of man. The phrase *in the day* probably is not referring to the sixth day of creation. This phrase appears 147x in the OT nearly always (if not always) as a general time reference equivalent to *at that time*.

Tablet Two began with the words, *In the day Yahweh Elohim made the earth and heavens....* So the beginning of the previous tablet has three things in common with the beginning of Tablet Three: 1) the phrase *in the day*; 2) the subject; and 3) the verb *made*. The catchword, occurring in the last line of Tablet Two and the opening sentence of Tablet Three is *Adam* (in both cases *'ādām* minus the article). Ancient scribes kept cuneiform tablets in proper sequence by two devices: 1) repetition of the key thoughts of the previous tablet; and 2) the use of catch lines, where the opening words of the first line of a tablet repeat a key word from the last line of the previous tablet. Gn 5:1b supports the theory that Moses was using a series of tablets as the source for the material in this book.

*2. Importance of man (5:1c):* **He made him [man] in the likeness of Elohim.** The transitional remarks underscore the supreme importance of man. *Likeness* (*dᵉmût*) reflects the language of Gn 1:26.

*3. Distinction in man (5:2a):* **He created them male and female.** The transitional remarks repeat the sublime distinction in man. Man is a duality. This repeats the truth expressed in 1:27. Woman received the divine likeness as much as her husband.

*4. Blessing of man (5:2b):* **and he blessed them.** The writer repeats the special blessing of man. God's original blessing on Adam and Eve (1:28) was intended for the whole human race.

### B. New Truth Articulated (5:2c)

*And he named them Adam in the day when they were created* (5:2c). The first man and his wife received a name from God. The name *Adam* means "Man" or "Human." In naming Adam and Eve the Creator is asserting his sovereignty over the couple. The name implies subordination on the part of man, recognition of the true nature of man, and limitation of the prerogatives of man.

# SUCCESSION LIST
# Gn 5:3-20

### A. Preliminary Observations

*1. Nature of the list.* Most writers refer to the contents of ch 5 as the record of the covenant family. Supposedly there was a perpetual conflict between the Cainites depicted in ch 4 and the Sethites depicted in ch 5. This approach is somewhat artificial. First, there is no record of any divine covenant with Adam's descendents through Seth. Second, this approach ignores the fact that the human race did not consist merely of Cainites and Sethites. Adam had numerous sons. Following conservative population models, before the Flood those sons must have generated descendants in the thousands. Third, only a handful of Sethites are named in ch 5. Fourth, the names are not presented as the descendents of Seth, but the descendants of Adam.

Ch 5 does not purport to list all the descendants of Adam through Seth, for each of the names listed fathered many sons and daughters. The list should not be interpreted to mean that there was but one faithful soul in each generation.

The ten names in Gn 5 appear to be a list of the most important members of the ruling family. The evidence of this will emerge in the discussion that follows. The idea, however, that these men were rulers is old, going back at least to the time of Josephus (*Ant.* 1.3.3, 4). The succession did not always devolve upon the firstborn son, for Seth clearly was not the firstborn of Adam.

*2. Framework.* With two exceptions (Enoch and Noah) the following pattern is followed throughout the genealogy: 1. Name. 2. Age at the birth of the eldest (or most important) son. To date no extra-biblical genealogies have been discovered which reflect this feature (Hess). 3. Name of this son. 4. Number of years he lived after the son's birth. 5. Statement that he begat sons and daughters. 6. Age at his death. 7. Death statement.

The phrase *he lived* followed by a number of years is important. Other biblical passages show that the use of *he lived* before or after an event indicates this event as decisive in the life of a person, dividing it into two periods.[358] The decisive event in these generations is the begetting of the son who will carry on the line of legitimate rulers descended from Adam.

*3. Textual problems.* Two ancient text traditions reflect significant variations in the numbers associated with the successors of Adam. The Samaritan Pentateuch reflects smaller numbers for some of the names; the Greek reflects larger numbers. These variations are displayed in Chart 15.

The debate about reconciling these numbers goes on. The consensus that seems to be emerging is that the Hebrew text is primary. The LXX (Greek) can be explained as "national" alterations of MT.[359] There are, however, a

---

[358] Jacob, *First Book*, 40.
[359] See G. Larson, "The Chronology of the Pentateuch: A Comparison of the MT and LXX," *JBL* 102 (1983): 401-9. See also R.W. Klein, "Archaic Chronologies and the Textual History of the OT," *HTR* 67 (1974): 255-63.

few modern voices that have been raised in support of the LXX reading of these numbers. Such a reading makes the time from Adam to the Flood about six hundred years longer, and thus harmonizes better with the early history of Mesopotamia.[360]

| Chart 15 Textual Variations in Gn 5 Genealogy ||||||||
| NAMES | AGE AT SON'S BIRTH ||| AGE AT DEATH |||
| | Heb. | Sam. | LXX | Heb. | Sam. | LXX |
| Adam | 130 | 130 | 230 | 930 | 930 | 930 |
| Seth | 105 | 105 | 205 | 912 | 912 | 912 |
| Enosh | 90 | 90 | 190 | 905 | 905 | 905 |
| Kenan | 70 | 70 | 170 | 910 | 910 | 910 |
| Mahalalel | 65 | 65 | 165 | 895 | 895 | 895 |
| Jared | 162 | 62 | 162 | 962 | 847 | 962 |
| Enoch | 65 | 65 | 165 | 365 | 365 | 365 |
| Methuselah | 187 | 67 | 187 | 969 | 720 | 969 |
| Lamech | 182 | 53 | 188 | 777 | 653 | 753 |
| Noah | 500 | 500 | 500 | 950 | 950 | 950 |
| To Flood | 100 | 100 | 100 | | | |
| Total | 1656 | 1307 | 2262 | 8575 | 8087 | 8551 |

*4. Ten generations.* By listing ten generations prior to the Flood and ten after the Flood the writer is highlighting the Flood as the great divide between Adam and Abraham. The antediluvian list culminates in a deliverer and a covenant, viz. Noah. The postdiluvian race also ends with a deliverer and a covenant, viz. Abraham. Ten in the Bible is the number of completeness.

*5. Comparisons.* Compared to the Cainite list of names in ch 4, the Adamite list is more detailed and stereotyped. Yet there are similarities. First, some of the names in the two lists are identical, suggesting some contact between the two lines. Second, both lists are structured similarly. The Cainite line contains seven

---

[360]Richard Teachout, "A New Case for Biblical Chronology," *Bible Science Newsletter* (Jan 1971): 1-3.

names, then a division into three sons. The Adamite line contains ten names, then a division into three sons. Third, the meaning of some of the names is uncertain.

**B. Adam** (5:3-5)

*1. Chronology (5:3a):* **And Adam lived 130 years...** This note is important for understanding the chronology of the primeval period. It removes the misconception that Abel was killed by Cain when the two were young men. It is not likely that God waited 130 years before giving Adam and Eve a godly child to take Abel's place. This note also explains why Cain might fear retaliation from numerous offspring of Adam when he was sentenced to a life of wandering.

*2. Verb (5:3b):* **and fathered [a son]...** The verb is the Hiphil stem of the r. *yld,* which is used 28x in this ch. (This use contrasts with the use of the Qal form of the same root in ch 4.) Later in the genealogy of Gn 11 it is used 27x. Outside Gn this form is used almost exclusively for direct physical offspring, i.e., biological father-son relationship. This, however, is not always the case as is indicated in Nm 26:58-59 where it is generally agreed that Kohath, son of Levi, could not possibly have directly fathered Amram the father of Moses.

Some regard the Qal stem of *yld* (when used in the masculine) and the Hiphil stem (that always has a masculine subject) as essentially synonymous. The evidence, however, suggests a different conclusion. The Qal form "evades or avoids any guarantee of actual fatherhood and legitimacy." The Hiphil form "designates the true physical father and progenitor."[361]

So the Hiphil is used in contexts where the issue of patrilineal descent is important to establish one's office or inheritance rights. It is therefore improper to insist

---

[361] B. Jacob, *Der Pentateuch* (Leipzig, 1905) cited in *TDOT* 6:79.

that the Hiphil form always indicates direct biological descent without intervening generations. The use of this form in Gn 5 suggests that a particular office is being passed on from father to son, the office of legitimate ruler. Of all of Adam's sons Seth was the designated successor as ruler. He inherited Adam's mandate to rule over the earth (Gn 1:26, 28).

*3. Transmission of image (5:3c):* **in his likeness and in his image...** In pagan cultures only the king was viewed as reflecting the image of some deity.[362] In the Bible, however, Adam was created in God's image, and Adam's son Seth bore the *image* and *likeness* of his father. The mention of the two terms from 1:26-28 suggests that through human procreation the image of God is replicated in the birth of every person.

The implications of this teaching are staggering. The concept of inherited image points to the inherent dignity of every human being. It requires respect for human life. It underscores the urgency for evangelizing the entire race. The fact that man bears the divine image is foundational to biblical morality (Jam 3:9; 1 Jn 4:20).

There is a link between image and sonship. In the ancient Near East royal persons were considered the sons or representatives of the gods (cf. 2 Sam 7:13-16; Ps 2:7). Luke can refer to Adam as *the son of God* (Lk 3:38) for two reasons. First, he was the appointed representative of the King. Second, he bore the image of his Creator even as a son bears the image of his father (Gn 5:3). Christ as the Son of God bears the title *Image* (Col 1:15; 3:10; Heb 1:3). Redeemed sons of Adam are enabled to conform to the image of the Son (Rom 8:29). Thus in Christ the image of God is refurbished, renewed and restored.

---

[362] For citations of pagan court literature see Blocher, *In the Beginning*, 86.

*4. Naming (5:3d): **and he called his name Seth**.* In 4:25 it was Eve who named the son. The former was an informal suggestion of a name, the latter the formal announcement of it.

*5. Conclusion (5:4-5):* **And the days of Adam after fathered of Seth were 800 years; and he fathered sons and daughters. And all the days that Adam lived were 930 years; and he died.** The text hints that the sons and daughters were born after Seth; but this is not a necessary conclusion. Adam's lifespan of nine centuries and three decades ranks him only fourth among the antediluvian patriarchs.

## C. Generations Two-Six (5:6-20)

*1. Seth (5:6-8):* **And Seth lived 105 years and he fathered Enosh. And Seth lived after he fathered Enosh 807 years; and he fathered sons and daughters. And all the days of Seth were 912 years; and he died.** The meaning of the name *Seth* was discussed in connection with 4:25. Seth might be appropriately titled the "Substitute." He became the Father of the righteous remnant.

*2. Enosh (5:9-11):* **And Enosh live 90 years and he fathered Kenan. And Enosh lived after he fathered Kenan 815 years; and he fathered sons and daughters. And all the days of Enosh were 905 years; and he died.** The name *Enosh* ("Frail Man") was discussed in connection with 4:26. Significant developments in the realm of public worship took place during his administration (cf. 4:26).

*3. Kenan (5:12-14):* **And Kenan lived 70 years and he fathered Mahalalel. And Kenan lived after he fathered Mahalalel 840 years; and he fathered sons and daughters. And all the years of Kenan were 910 years; and he died.** *Cainan/Kenan* means "Possession." The name appears only here and is generally regarded as a by-form of *Cain*.

4. *Mahalalel (5:15-17)*: **And Mahalalel lived 65 years and he fathered Jared. And Mahalalel lived after he fathered Jared 830 years; and he fathered sons and daughters. And all the days of Mahalalel were 895 years; and he died.** *Mahalalel* means "Praise of God." It occurs again as a proper name in Neh 11:4.

5. *Jared (5:18-20)*: **And Jared lived 162 years and he fathered Enoch. And Jared lived after he fathered of Enoch 800 years; and he fathered sons and daughters. And all the days of Jared were 962 years; and he died.** The name *Jared* means "Descendant."

# ENOCH AMPLIFICATION
# Gn 5:21-24

The number seven often symbolizes divine completeness. Enoch in the seventh generation from Adam is highlighted as an especially devout man. His name means "Dedicated." The writer departs from the stereotyped pattern in order to tell the story of the man who never died.

**A. Enoch's Walk** (5:21-22)

1. *Nature of his walk (5:21-22a)*: **And Enoch lived 65 years and fathered Methuselah. And Enoch walked with Elohim.** This passage is the starting point for the significance of Enoch in Jewish apocalyptic literature of the intertestamental period. Jewish legend interprets Enoch's walk as intimate communication in which God revealed all kinds of secrets about earth and heaven (*Jubilees* 4:17-21). Actually *walked* is used as a metaphor for life.

The spiritual quality of this man's life is indicated in the words *with God*. Abraham is said to have walked *before* God (Gn 17:1) and Israel is said to have walked *after* God (Dt 13:5); but only Noah is elsewhere said to have walked *with* God (Gn 6:9).

The walk of Enoch was not one that was moving toward a destination. The form of the verb (Hithpael) indicates walking to and fro. The form is used in 1 Sam 25:15f to describe friendly everyday conduct with regard to one's neighbors.

In this v *Elohim* has the definite article for the first of over 350x in the OT. The definite article stresses that the reference is to the one true and living God.

To walk with God was an important concept to the writer of Gn. He used this word in Gn 3:8 to describe God's fellowship with the first couple in the garden. Thus Enoch stood in a direct and immediate relationship to God similar to what was experienced by Adam and Eve before the Fall. Enoch's fellowship with God was morally and religiously perfect (Skinner).

*2. Beginning of his walk (5:22b):* **after he fathered Methuselah.** These words give a hint as to the event that triggered Enoch's devotion to God. What was his lifestyle before the birth of Methuselah? The text is silent. Perhaps, however, the writer means to suggest that Enoch's walk with God began after he became a father. Many a man has been jarred into serious involvement with the Lord by the birth of a son.

*3. Duration of his walk (5:22c):* **300 years.** The duration of Enoch's special relationship with God is clearly indicated. His was not an emotional commitment that faded in time. He was faithful to the end, which in his case, did not include death.

*4. Strain of his walk (5:22d):* **and he fathered sons and daughters.** Enoch did not hide from life in a monastery. His life was full of domestic duties. He must not have regarded his children as a burden. He did not use his children as an excuse for less than full devotion to the service of his Creator. Perhaps the mention of sons and daughters in connection with this man's walk is intended to suggest that he led his entire family in godly pursuits.

5. *New Testament perspective.* Apparently Enoch was a prophet who spoke out to the sinners of his generation and warned of judgment to come. See Jude 14-15.

**B. Enoch's Reward** (5:23-24)

*1. Disappearance described (5:23-24a):* **And all the days of Enoch were 365 days. And Enoch walked with Elohim, and he was not.** In comparison with the other antediluvian Sethites Enoch's earthly pilgrimage was comparatively short. He lived in this world less than half of the lifespan of the other nine names on the list. Shortness of life sometimes is taken as an indication of divine disfavor. That, however, was not the case with Enoch. To emphasize this point the narrator repeats the reference to Enoch's walk.

In the course of his daily walk with God, *he was not,* i.e., Enoch disappeared. These words describe a sudden, mysterious disappearance. These words alone do not explain where he went (as in 1 Kgs 20:40).

*2. Disappearance explained (5:24b):* **for Elohim took him.** Because of their overall theological position some insist that these words refer to premature death, or to physical removal from some immediate threat to his life. The apocryphal Wisdom of Solomon suggests that Enoch "was caught up, so that wickedness might not alter his understanding, or guile deceive his soul" (*Wis.* 4:11).

The verb *took* (*lāqach*) implies that the object taken is removed from a previous environment. It also implies being brought near to the one who is doing the taking. For this reason Aalders proposes the translation, "God

**317**

took him to himself." The term is also used of Elijah's departure from this world (2 Kgs 2:3, 5). This is not language that normally is used to describe death. The oldest recorded interpretation of the passage is that "Enoch pleased the Lord and was carried off to heaven" (Ecclesiasticus 44:16). The writer of Hebrews endorses this same view of what happened to Enoch (Heb 11:5). So Enoch experienced a protological rapture![363]

3. *Objections answered.* Two objections have been raised to the view that Enoch was translated out of his mortal body into the presence of God. First, Christ was the firstfruits of those who sleep (1 Cor 15:20); therefore Enoch could not have escaped death. But since Enoch never died he obviously could not be resurrected. In Enoch's case it is glorification not resurrection that is involved. So Enoch's translation does not in any way contradict 1 Cor 15:20.

Second, eight vv following the statement of Hebrews 11:5 regarding the translation of Enoch, the writer says this: "These (apparently including Enoch) all died in faith" (Heb 11:13). But Enoch is clearly the exception as the writer makes clear in 11:5. A similar situation exists in Gn 35:22b-27 where all the sons of Jacob are said to have been born in Paddan Aram whereas Benjamin is the exception.

# "PATRON SAINT OF GERIATRICS"[364]
## Gn 5:25-27

*And Methuselah lived 187 years and he fathered Lamech. And Methuselah lived after he fathered Lamech 782 years; and he fathered sons and daugh-*

---

[363] One stream of Jewish tradition disputed the conclusion that Enoch did not die (*Gen Rab* 25:1). Another even suggests that God killed him (*Targum Onkelos*).
[364] Hamilton, *NICOT*, 258.

*ters. And all the days of Methuselah were 969 years; and he died.* Methuselah was the eighth legitimate successor in the line of Adam. The name *Methuselah*, appearing only here in the OT, means something like "Man of a Dart." Years ago a "Believe it or Not" column pointed out that Methuselah was the oldest man in the Bible, but he was outlived by his father!

Assuming no gaps in the genealogical record, Methuselah died in the year the Flood came upon the earth, i.e., in Noah's 600th year. There is no evidence that he died in the Flood. He must have died a natural death before the waters came.

Cain walked away from God (Gn 4:16). Enoch and Noah walked with God (Gn 5:22; 6:9). Methuselah just walked in place marking time. In the longest life ever lived nothing was accomplished worthy of note in the sacred text. By contrast, Jesus lived but thirty-five or so years. All the books of the world cannot contain the things that he said and did (Jn 21:25).

## HOPEFUL FATHER
## Gn 5:28-30

**A. A Son Born** (5:28-29a)

*And Lamech lived 182 years and he fathered a son. And he called his name Noah.* The name *Lamech* means something like "Wild Man." The extreme age at which Lamech fathered a son suggests that physical maturity (and perhaps marriage) came much later than is the case today.

The name *Noah* is unique in the Bible. The name seems to be related, in Hebrew at least, to a root that means "to rest." Neither the writer nor Lamech pretends to be offering in the birth comment a technical etymological explanation of the name.

**B. A Hope Expressed** (5:29b-d)

Noah is highlighted in the genealogy by this birth comment, the only one included in Gn 5.

*1. Hope of comfort (5:29b):* **saying, This one shall comfort us.** *Comfort* (r. *nchm*) is closely related to the "rest" concept expressed in Noah's name. There is interplay between these two roots in the Flood account that follows.[365] The verb root seems to convey the idea of breathing deeply in outward display of one's feeling whether of sorrow, compassion, or comfort. In the Piel form used here, this verb describes active efforts to comfort by word or action the grieving after the death of a close relative. By way of prophetic anticipation Lamech announced that this son would bring *comfort* to the troubled race.

*2. Human struggle (5:29c):* **concerning our work and the toil of our hands.** *Work/toil* recalls the punishment of toilsome labor stipulated after the Fall in ch 3. Perhaps by this time these terms were used to describe all the hardships—physical, mental, moral, and spiritual—brought on by increasing sin.

*3. Divine curse (5:29d):* **because of the ground that Yahweh has cursed,** lit., "from the ground" (NASB). *Cursed ground* again references the penalty for the Fall stipulated in ch 3. Lamech anticipated some curse relief to come through Noah. Lamech himself may not have grasped fully the implications of the comfort he anticipated.

**C. Interpretation**

The comment of Lamech at the time of Noah's birth has evoked considerable discussion. The interpretations can be grouped into naturalistic and supernaturalistic.

---

[365]Mathews, *NAC*, 317. Mathews cites 6:6, 7, 8; 8:4, 9, 21.

*1. Naturalistic.* Some interpret Lamech's birth comment as merely human aspiration—a wish or possibly an expectation—that was not guided in any way by the Spirit of God. In this category are the following suggestions: First, Lamech was expressing his belief that his son would assist in the cultivation of the soil thus relieving the pain and toil of the curse. Second, since Noah was the first person reported to have been born after the death of Adam, Lamech calculated that the curse of 3:17 must now be over. Third, Lamech was boasting arrogantly that the advancements in human skills would nullify the effects of the Edenic curse. Support for this view is found in the numbers reported in the Samaritan Pentateuch that have Lamech dying in the 600$^{th}$ year of Noah, the year of the Flood. Since Lamech was not on the ark, he must have died among the unbelievers.

*2. Supernaturalistic.* Others view the birth comment of Lamech as prophetic. Under inspiration of God's Spirit Lamech anticipated the end of the Gn 3:17 curse. He expressed aspiration that his child would be the promised conqueror of Serpent (Gn 3:15), the one Jacob called the Rest Bringer (Gn 49:10). Perhaps similar aspirations were expressed by each generation of godly parents.

### D. Fulfillment

What comfort did Noah bring? One popular view is that the comfort was fulfilled in Noah's development of viticulture (vine growing) and viniculture (wine production) that lightened the burden and gladdened the heart.[366] This view understands *from the ground* to refer to the source of the comfort, not the source of the toilsome labor. The successful growing of the vineyard is

---

[366]Waltke, *GAC*, 115.

regarded as evidence that the Gn 3 ground curse had been mitigated. These interpreters take 8:21f (*I will not curse again the ground*) to be the confirmation their interpretation. See comments on 8:21.

This interpretation flounders at three points. First, it assumes, contrary to external evidence, that Noah's vineyard was the first ever grown. Second, toilsome labor is still necessary in order to make the ground productive. Third, NT teaching points to the eschaton as the time when the Gn 3 curse is removed (Rom 8:19-22).

Lamech's aspiration received a measure of fulfillment in the deliverance that God provided through Noah for the human race. It received further fulfillment in the covenant God made with Noah after the Flood (8:21-9:17). The comfort Lamech anticipated, however, was only possible after God cleansed the wicked world from sin in the waters of the Flood. This Lamech never anticipated. Nonetheless, the birth comment of Lamech makes an appropriate transition to the material that follows.

# TRANSITION TO NOAH
# Gn 5:30-32

### A. Lamech's Death (5:30-31)

*And Lamech lived after he fathered Noah 595 years and he fathered sons and daughters. And all the years of Lamech were 777 years; and he died.* Sethite Lamech stands in sharp contrast to Cainite Lamech in ch 4 at three points. First, Cainite Lamech was full of bluster, and focused on himself. Sethite Lamech was quietly optimistic, concerned about his fellows, and devoted to *comfort* with all that this word entails. Second, Cainite Lamech is famous for his *seventy and seven* utterance (Gn 4:24). Sethite Lamech is memorable for his 777 years of life. Third, whereas the earlier Lamech resorted to active violence to force his will on others (4:24), this Lamech waited in faith for deliverance from divine curse through his son.

## B. Noah's Progeny (5:32)

*And Noah was 500 years old, and Noah fathered Shem, Ham, and Japheth.* The text does not mean to imply that Shem, Ham, and Japheth were triplets. What is stated in 9:24 and 10:21 requires age differential between the brothers. It should not be assumed that the sons are named in the order of their births in 5:32. Probably Shem is mentioned first because of his spiritual priority. See 11:10. The order *Shem, Ham, Japheth* is euphonic. Actual order of birth was probably *Japheth, Shem* and *Ham.* The three sons of Noah are named because of the role these men will play in the Flood and in the postdiluvian world.

*Shem* in Hebrew means "Name." The name may suggest that his father aspired for him to make a name or reputation for himself. If so, his aspirations were fulfilled in ways Noah could never have imagined. Even to this day *Shemite* (modern *Semite*) concerns stand near the top of national agendas world-wide. The name *Ham* may be linked to the native term for Egypt, *Keme* (*the black land*), so called because of the soil of the Nile Valley. The name *Japheth* may be derived from the Egyptian *Keftiu* (Crete); but see on 9:27.

The concluding words of the antediluvian genealogy are not found until 9:28-29. The intervening material has been inserted as a parenthesis—howbeit a very important one—in the genealogy.

# ISSUE OF THE MACROBIANS

Macrobians are long-lived peoples. In Gn 5 all but three of the representatives of the line of Seth lived in excess of nine hundred years. Some find this biblical data to be contradicted by science. Anthropologists studying 187 human fossils found a death rate of from twenty to sixty years; only one case beyond sixty.[367] In the OT itself, apart from the patriarchs of Gn, only four men lived past the century mark.[368]

### A. Proposed Explanations

Two proposals have been put forward in an attempt to explain what are perceived to be the exaggerated numbers in Gn 5.

*1. Reduced years.* Various schemes have been proposed for the systematic reduction of the numbers in Gn 5. Some have proposed that in primeval culture the "birthday" was a sociological phenomenon and not a biological one as in western society. If this is the case, then the reckoning of years of a person's life would have no connection with solar years.

One suggestion is that the "years" were only thirty days long. To get people of nine hundred years to ninety years, however, would require a reduction factor of ten to one. No reduction factor can be consistently applied that does not result in some patriarchs having children when they were ridiculously young.

*2. Symbolic years.* Because of the use of ten generations and the emphasis on the seventh generation some have proposed that the numbers in Gn 5 should be viewed symbolically.[369] Enoch's 365 years (5:23) obviously equal the days of a year. Lamech's 777 years (5:31) are equivalent to the synodic periods of Jupiter + Saturn. (A synodic period is the time it takes a planet to return to the same place in the sky.) Jared's 962 years

---

[367] See Ramm, *CVSS*, 341, n. 53.
[368] Job (140), Moses (120), Joshua (110) and Jehoiada (130).
[369] M. Barouin, "Recherches numèriques sur la gènéalogie de Gen. V," *RB* 77 (1970): 347-65. Cited by Waltke, *GAC*, 111.

(5:20) are equivalent to the synodic periods of Venus + Saturn.

*3. Rhetorical years.* Dwight Young contends that the attribution of extraordinary length of life was a rhetorical devise to elevate these patriarchs.[370] Their ages were simply "grossed up" by "schematic increments based on a mathematical formula."[371] Nothing in the text, however, hints that Moses did not mean for *years* to be understood in the ordinary sense.

*4. Dynastic years.* Another way of getting rid of the embarrassment of macrobians is by pronouncing that the years apply to families, not individuals. "The longevity is the period during which the family had prominence and leadership. The age at the son's birth is the date in the family history at which a new family originated and ultimately succeeded to the dominant position."[372] This view, however, offers no credible explanation of Enoch. The record indicates that God took Enoch. Did God take a whole tribe?

*5. Real years.* The above explanations of the years of the Macrobians have not generated wide support. The writer appears to be reporting the fact that in the Antediluvian Period some people lived significantly longer than men are accustomed to live today.[373]

---

[370] Dwight Wayne Young, "The Incredible Life Spans of the Antediluvian Patriarchs," *JNES* 47 (1988): 123-129.

[371] R.K. Harrison, "From Adam to Noah: A Reconsideration of the Antediluvian Patriarchs' Ages," *JETS* 37(Jun 1994): 168. Harrison arrives at the actual numbers arbitrarily by dividing all of them by four.

[372] John Davis, *ISBE*, 1:139-143. Harold Camping has proposed a slightly different twist on this approach. He views the names in the list as reference points in an ancient calendar. All the days of X means that entire time that his name was used as a calendar reference point. At his death the calendar reference shifted to Y, a descendant of X. "The Biblical Calendar of History," *JASA* (Sept 1970): 98-107.

[373] J.L. Butler "Causes of Antediluvian Longevity," *BS*, 75:49-69. For arguments pro and con with respect to whether the pre-flood patriarchs lived for hundreds of years, see the treatments by J.A. Borland and D.L. Chris-

## B. Relevant Considerations

In considering the problem of the Macrobians several factors must be weighed. First, longevity is attributed only to the Sethite line. Apparently only those who were bearers of true religion lived these long lives. Second, perhaps the Flood made a radical difference in world conditions. Climate and degree of sunlight can increase disease and reduce life spans. Third, man coming right from the hand of the Creator was so free from disease that he could live much longer than contemporary man. Fourth, the Hebrew figures are modest compared to the tens of thousands of years attributed to the antediluvian kings in Sumerian tradition. On this, however, see below. Fifth, the aging process is not fully understood even today. The uncertainty of gerontologists about the mechanism of aging within the body should cause commentators to exercise caution regarding what may have been possible in earth's earliest ages.

# ANTIQUITY OF MAN

## A. Biblical Attempts at Dating

One of the major problems associated with the study of biblical protology is the issue of the antiquity of man. Bishop Ussher added up the figures given in Gn 5 and Gn 11 for the age of firstborn sons. Read from a western point of view and with a calculator, those numbers indicate that creation occurred in 4004 BC. Those who follow Ussher's methodology believe that the numbers in the Gn genealogies simply have to be added together to compute the time lapse from creation to the Flood (Gn 5) and from the Flood to Abraham (Gn 11). Since Abraham can be dated from other Scriptures with fair accuracy, computing the date of creation is as simple as add-

---

tensen in *The Genesis Debate*, ed. R. Youngblood (Grand Rapids: 1991), 166-83.

ing together the figures from the two Gn genealogies and the date of Abraham. Chart 16 illustrates the numbers that can be used for the first part of the computation.

## Chart 16
### Gn 5 Interpreted as Family Genealogy

| Adam YAC | Seth | Enos | Ken | Maha | Jared | Eno | Meth | Lam | Noah |
|---|---|---|---|---|---|---|---|---|---|
| 130 | **0** | | | | | | | | |
| 235 | **105** | 0 | | | | | | | |
| 325 | 195 | **90** | 0 | | | | | | |
| 395 | 265 | 160 | **70** | 0 | | | | | |
| 460 | 330 | 225 | 135 | **65** | 0 | | | | |
| 622 | 492 | 387 | 297 | 227 | **162** | 0 | | | |
| 687 | 557 | 452 | 362 | 292 | 227 | **65** | 0 | | |
| 874 | 744 | 639 | 549 | 479 | 414 | 252 | **187** | 0 | |
| **930** | 800 | 695 | 605 | 535 | 470 | 308 | 243 | 56 | |
| 987 | 857 | 752 | 662 | 592 | 527 | **365** | 300 | 113 | |
| 1042 | **912** | 807 | 717 | 647 | 582 | | 355 | 168 | |
| 1056 | | 821 | 731 | 661 | 596 | | 369 | **182** | 0 |
| 1121 | | 886 | 796 | 726 | 661 | | 434 | 247 | **65** |
| 1140 | | **905** | 815 | 745 | 680 | | 453 | 266 | 84 |
| 1235 | | | **910** | 840 | 775 | | 548 | 361 | 179 |
| 1290 | | | | **895** | 830 | | 603 | 416 | 234 |
| 1422 | | | | | **962** | | 735 | 548 | 366 |
| 1556 | | | | | | | 869 | 682 | **500** |
| 1651 | | | | | | | 964 | **777** | 505 |
| 1656 | | | | | | | **969** | | **600** |

Interpreting the chart: Column 1 gives the numbers for Adam and the years after creation. Thus 130 YAC is the year for the birth of Seth; 1656 YAC is the year for the Flood. The bold numbers in each column are those given in the text; the others are computed. The chart assumes that the names mentioned are individuals, and the years given are the actual years of their lives.

The assumption of those who use Gn 5 for chronological purposes is that the genealogy is consecutive, i.e., that every patriarch was the biological father of the son whose birth is reported. That may be the case, but not necessarily. Certainly context requires that Seth be the biological son of Adam, and Noah the biological son

Biblical Protology

of Lamech; but what of the others? Was Enosh, for example, the biological son of Seth? The text does not require this to be the case. The text says that at 105 Seth fathered Enosh. This may mean that at 105 Seth became the biological father of one of the direct ancestors of Enosh. It is a well known fact that biblical genealogies are more often than not selective, meaning that only key names are mentioned. If in any degree Gn 5 is selective, then it cannot be used for chronological purposes.

## B. Anthropological Attempts at Dating

Some anthropologists place the antiquity of man at 500,000 years; more conservative anthropologists place *Homo Sapiens* at 50,000 years. Even the most conservative anthropological estimates on the surface seem way out of line with the biblical numbers. This is probably the greatest single problem in harmonizing biblical protology with the data of science. How does one bridge the huge gap between what appears to be a straightforward reading of the biblical text and the conclusions of those in the sciences? To be more precise, the question is, how does biblical Adam relate to the fossil men whose bones have been recovered? Five different answers to this question have been proposed.

*1. No Adam view.* Some biblical commentators are willing to concede that evolution is a fact. No individual named *Adam* ever existed. The early chs of Gn are read as religious myth or parable, teaching great truths, but woefully lacking in historical accuracy. For example, Gn Adam symbolizes the unity of the human race. The Fall indicates that sin is universal in humanity.[374]

Most Bible believing Christians have serious doubts about the evolutionary approach to anthropology, believing that the theory is philosophy, not science. They are

---

[374] See E. Brunner, *The Christian Doctrine of Creation and Redemption* (Philadelphia: Westminster, 1952), 50-51.

quick to point out that the weaknesses of the evolutionary theory have been conceded even by some who espouse the theory. On the other hand, most students of the Bible rightly understand the author of Gn to be attempting to communicate records of what actually transpired in earth's earliest ages.

*2. Ancient Adam view.* Some Christian thinkers argue that fossil men were real men, the first of which was Adam who was made by special creation. Adam dates to at least 50,000 years ago.[375]

While even some of the most conservative writers grant that there may be some elasticity in the genealogies of Gn 5 and 11, 50,000 years stretches the elasticity to the breaking point. Furthermore, it is generally recognized that civilization began about 8,000 BC. Gn 4 seems to reflect the development of this civilization. It is hard to reconcile Adam's creation at 50,000 (or 200,000) years and the emergence of civilization at 8000 BC. Affinities between the Babylonian culture and biblical accounts in Gn cannot readily be harmonized with man being created 50,000 years ago. To state the matter another way, the world reflected in Gn 4 is relatively recent—about ten thousand years ago. Since no time gap is evident between Gn 3 and 4, man in Gn 3 must be comparatively recent as well.

*3. Two-Adams view.* In an attempt to bridge the gap between the 50,000 years ago origin of Adam with the ten thousand year old world of Gn 4 some have proposed the theory of two Adams. According to this view the Adam in Gn 4 is named after the original Adam who fell into sin thousands of years earlier.[376] One variation

---

[375] See W. Kornfield, "The Early-Date Genesis Man," *CT*, June 8, 1973; J.O. Buswell, "Adam and Neolithic man, *Eternity* (Feb, 1967): 29ff. Others of similar mind are found in the American Scientific Affiliation.

[376] See P. Seely, "Adam and Anthropology: A Proposed Solution," *JASA*, (Sept. 1970): 88-90.

on this two-Adams view are that the Adam created in 1:26 is the fossil man; the Adam created in 5:2 is the ancestor of modern man. This latter Adam is the one who fell into sin.[377] Another variation is that the Adam in ch 1 is different from the Adam in ch 2.[378] The problem with this view is that Gn 1:26, 5:1 and 9:6 seem to assume that from the beginning there was a basic continuity of men created in the image and likeness of God. Furthermore, Gn 3:20 explicitly calls Eve the mother of *all living*.

4. *Pre-Adamite view*. Another approach to the problem of the antiquity of man is to label all fossil men as "pre-Adamites." According to this view the biblical Adam is relatively recent. Fossil men are not true men. They are part of an earlier creation; or they simply evolved. The pre-Adamites were sub-human or pre-human.[379]

A major problem with this view is it does not offer a satisfactory explanation of how these pre-Adamites differed from Adam's race (*Homo sapiens*). Some say the pre-Adamite fossil men lacked spiritual capacity, or lacked linguistic capacity.[380] Others do not try to identify the differences. By definition pre-Adamites lived before Adam and therefore could not have been true men in the biblical sense.[381]

On the question of how Adam was related to the pre-Adamites the advocates of this theory again are of vari-

---

[377] See J.M. Clarke, "Genesis and its Underlying Realities," *FAT*, 93(1963): 146-154.

[378] Dan Vogel, "The Legacy of Two Adams," *JBQ* 33(2005): 3-12.

[379] See Gleason Archer, *SOTI*, 188-89; Derek Kidner, *TOTC*, 28-29; J. Stafford Wright, "An Examination of Evidence for Religious Beliefs of Paleolithic Man," *FAT*, 90(1958): 4-15; Robert Brow, "The Late-Date Genesis Man," *CT* (Sept 1972): 6-7.

[380] T.C. Mitchell, "Archeology and Genesis I-XI," *FAT*, 91(1959): 28-49.

[381] See Archer, *SOTI*; Murk, "Evidence for a Late Pleistocene Creation of Man," *JASA*, 17(1965): 37-49; R. Brow, "The Late-Date Genesis Man, *CT*, Sept. 15, 1972.

ous opinions. Some hold that Adam was a *de nova* creation possessing spiritual qualities the pre-Adamites lacked.[382] Others think that a pre-human became human (Adam) when self-consciousness evolved, or when God breathed into him the breath of life.

A variety of opinions has also been expressed in regard to the question of what happened to the pre-Adamites, if they ever lived. The most common answer is that they were destroyed before Adam (Archer). Others think they lived side-by side with Adam's race until the time of the Flood when they were all destroyed. Kidner subscribes to the view that they were all made truly human after the special creation of Adam and Eve. Evangelist C.C. Torrey saw evidence of the pre-Adamites in the biblical record. He was of the opinion that these sub-humans disappeared as a result of marriages to those who were truly human.[383] Some racist writers maintain that the pre-Adamites still exist today in the non-Caucasian races of the world.[384]

The pre-Adamite view has zero supporting evidence in the Bible. The concept of a pre-Adamic creature that looked like man, had many, if not most, of the skills of man, but which was not truly man appears to be an explanation born out of desperation.

*5. Recent Adam view.* The most conservative commentators like Whitcomb, Morris; and Leupold argue anthropology is completely wrong on the dates of fossil men.[385] Fossil men were true men, but they did not live

---

[382] A. Rendel Short, *Modern Discovery and the Bible* (1942; London: Intervarsity, 1954), 81; E.K. Pearce, *Who Was Adam?* (London: Paternoster, 1969); summarized in "Proto-neolithic Adam and Recent Anthropology," *JASA* 23(1971): 130-39.
[383] C.C. Torrey, *Difficulties of the Bible* (1907), ch 5.
[384] Charles Shields, *The Scientific Evidences of Revealed Religion* (New York: Charles Scribner's, 1900), 124.
[385] Whitcomb and Morris, *Genesis Flood*. Others of this opinion are Arthur Custance, British Evolution Protest Movement, Bible-Science Association, Creation Research Society and Institute for Creation Research.

upon the planet nearly as long ago as those in the sciences allege. Adam was created sometime between 10,000 and 4000 BC. Taken at face value the biblical data certainly point in this direction.

### C. Importance of the Question

The issue of the antiquity of man has not exercised the great theologians. B.B. Warfield judged that the issue is of no theological importance. No essential doctrine of the Christian faith is affected whether Adam lived 50,000 or 10,000 years ago.[386] Theologically it is the unity of the race rather than its antiquity that is of crucial importance.

In spite of differences on many issues relating to biblical protology, creationists are generally united on three points. First, God created the first man as an individual human being by supernatural means. There was an historical Adam. Second, man was created as a creature unique from all other creatures genetically, spiritually, and culturally. Third, man was created perfect and subsequently fell into sin.

Regarding the antiquity of man the Bible makes no plain declaration. For this reason the councils and creeds of Christendom have not sought to bind any particular view on the church as a whole. Those who set dates for creation do so on the basis of the genealogies of Gn 5 and 11.[387] The interpretation of these two chs is the basic issue between Creationists.

---

[386] B.B. Warfield, "On the Antiquity and Unity of the Human Race," *Biblical and Theological Studies,* (1911; Philadelphia: Presbyterian and Reformed, 1968), 238-61.

[387] See Frank Cramer, "The Theological and Scientific Theories of the Origin of Man," *BSac* 48 (1891) 510-516; M.G. Kyle, "The Antiquity of Man," *Journal of the Transactions of the Victoria Institute* 57 (1925):135.

# GENESIS GENEALOGIES

From a literary and historical standpoint the function of genealogies is to serve as bridges to span gaps in the biblical tradition. It is not sound methodology to employ these genealogies for chronological purposes. They were never intended to furnish data which can be used to compute the passage of time between creation and the Flood, and between the Flood and Abraham. The other functions of Gn genealogies can be summarized under three heads.

## A. Theological Purpose

Theologically Gn genealogies serve three purposes. First, they are evidence of divine blessing and the fulfillment of the creation mandate to be fruitful and multiply. Second, the genealogies underscore the power of death. The repetition of the words *and then he died* (a single word in Hebrew) 8x in the ch is a solemn reminder of the death penalty announced in 2:17. Third, the genealogies concretely argue for the unity of the human race. All people share the divine image; all have in common the failures of the past, and hope for a better tomorrow.

## B. Anthropological Purpose

Anthropologically the genealogies serve two purposes. First, the emphasis on the birth, procreation and death of those named stresses that they were real people, not gods, demigods, or ancestors worthy of religious veneration.[388] Second, genealogies give evidence of diminishing life spans after the Flood. The farther one moves from creation, the more deterioration there ap-

---

[388]Westermann, *Genesis 1-11*, 356.

pears to be in the physical constitution of the human family.

### C. Practical Purpose

Genealogies move from earlier to later. The past is not idealized. The promised seed of woman who will crush Serpent had not yet appeared at the time of Abraham. That destiny is yet future in Gn. Toward that destiny the genealogies point. God's people learn from the past so that they might deal with the present; but their eye is always on the hope.

# KING LISTS

There is nothing in the literature of the ancient Near East that matches the genealogies of Gn 5 and 11.[389] Having acknowledged the lack of direct parallels, an ancient document does exist that may shed some light on Gn 5. The Sumerian King List reports that eight kings ruled over five cities before "the Flood swept over the earth." The document reports that these kings ruled for 349,200 years, for an average of 43,650 years each.

For years scholars dismissed the numbers as the stuff legend is made of. In more recent years, however, scholars have looked for a reasonable mathematical interpretation to the preposterous numbers of the Sumerian King List.[390]

---

[389] M.L. West and J. Van Seters have drawn attention to formal similarities between the biblical genealogies and a Greek work known as the Catalogue of Women that comes from the sixth century BC. Richard Hess has shown that the comparisons are overblown. See "The Genealogies of Genesis 1-11 and Comparative Literature," *Biblia* 70 (1989): 241-54.

[390] See R.K. Harrison, "Reinvestigating the Antediluvian Sumerian King List," *JETS* 36(Mar 1993): 3-8. Harrison cites the foundational work in this area by D.W. Young in *JNES* 47 (1988): 123-129; *ZAW* 100 (1988): 331-361; *ZAW* 102(1990): 321-335.

Actually the reigns are expressed in the King List in terms of a unit of measurement called a *saros*. There is some evidence that the ancients assigned a value of 18.5 years to a *saros*.[391]

About 300 BC Berosus, a Greco-Babylonian priest, in his version of this King List has ten names. The last name in the Berosus' list is that of the man who survived the Flood (Ziusudra). In the biblical list the Flood came in the 600th year of the tenth representative in the list. The reigns of the ten kings listed by Berosus prior to the Flood add up to 120 *sari*. Calculated by the 18.5 equivalency the reigns of the ten antediluvian kings totaled 2220 years. This is not that far removed from the total one gets by adding the figures for the ten names in Gn 5 (1656 years).[392]

While the use of the smaller value of the *saros* (18.5 yrs.) in the calculation is controversial, Authur Custance presents a cogent defense of this procedure.[393] Certainly his methodology is more credible than the arbitrary formula employed by some that one week in Gn 5 equals five years in the King List. Converting the 1656 years of Gn 5 to weeks, then multiplying by five, gives a figure very close to the 432,000 years of Berosus' list (as computed by the formula 1 *saros* = 3600 years). There is, however, no justification for the formula one week = five years, other than the math happens to work out.[394]

Great differences exist between the Sumerian King List and Gn 5 that preclude any notion of "borrowing."[395] The existence of the King List in its various

---

[391] The standard value, which is generally used in translating the king list, is that a *saros* = 3600 years.

[392] Using the 3600 equivalence for the saros, the ten kings of Berosus ruled 432,000 years, an average of 43,200 years per reign.

[393] Arthur Custance, *Seed*, 482-88.

[394] Aalders, *BSC*, 147.

[395] T.C. Hartman, "Some Thoughts on the Sumerian King List and Genesis 5 and 11b," *JBL* 91(1972): 25-32; R.S. Hess, "The Genealogies of Genesis

**335**

permutations does seem to lead to some modest conclusions. First, in the Mesopotamian culture there was a strong tradition of a Flood that created a clear break in history. Second, various city states existed prior to the flood. Third, the tradition knew of people who lived enormously long lives prior to the Flood.

---

1-11 and Comparative Literature," *Biblica* 70(1989): 241-54; G.F. Hasel, "The Genealogies of Gen 5 and 11 and Their Alleged Babylonian Background," *AUSS* 16(1978): 361-74.

# 17
# CORRUPTION OF THE RACE
# Gn 6:1-8

The slippery slope of sin reaches total degradation in the opening vv of ch 6. So far the text has pointed primarily to the Cainites as those who were becoming ever bolder in transgression. Now the Sethites choose the path of sin. The result was a level of societal corruption that divine justice could no longer tolerate.

## SETTING FOR THE SIN
## Gn 6:1

The opening v of ch 6 sets the stage for a crisis in the development of the human family chronologically, geographically and demographically.

### A. Chronological Setting (6:1a)
*Now it came about, when men began to multiply.* Over time human population grew in accordance with God's blessing of 1:28. In the previous ch the writer noted 9x the birth of both sons and daughters. Population growth is seen in Gn as a blessing, but one that is fraught with dangers to the relationship between man and God. *Men* (*hā'ādām*) should not be taken as a reference to gender; it refers to mankind in general.

### B. Geographical Setting (6:1b)
*On the face of the ground.* This phrase (*'al pᵉnê ᵃdhāmāh*) restricts the locale of what is narrated in the succeeding vv. This is the same terminology used to describe the area from which Cain was banished (4:14).

## C. Demographic Setting (6:1c)

*And daughters were born to them.* The writer makes special note of the growth of the female population. This may suggest a sexual imbalance in population growth. At the very least it suggests that as more women were born marriage options became more complicated.

# SONS OF GOD
# Gn 6:2a

Those who precipitate the sin crisis are designated in 6:2 as *sons of God*. One of the thorniest problems in OT studies has to do with identity of this group. Three main views as to the identity of *the sons of God* have been put forward.[396]

### A. Angel View

Many identify the *sons of God* ($b^e n\hat{e}\ h\bar{a}'el\bar{o}h\hat{i}m$) as angels.[397] They are not called *sons of God* in the physical, genealogical or mythological sense; they are so-called because they belong to the world of Elohim (cf. Lk 20:36). According to this view angels transgressed their assigned bounds by cohabiting with human females. The following arguments are offered in favor of this view.

*1. Supporting arguments.* Three main arguments support the angel interpretation. First, the angel view is the oldest interpretation of *the sons of God*. The reading *angels* in Gn 6:2 is supported by one Hebrew MS from

---

[396]The two main views are debated by F.B. Huey, Jr., and J.F. Walton in *The Genesis Debate*, ed. R. Youngblood (Grand Rapid: Baker, 1991), 184-209.

[397]Kidner; Morris; Cassuto; See Rick Marrs, "The Sons of God (Gen 6:1-4)," *Restoration Quarterly* 23 (1980): 218-224; W.A. van Gemeren, "The Sons of God in Genesis 6:1-4: (An Example of Evangelical Demythologization?)," *WTJ* 43(1981): 320-48.

Qumran. One MS of LXX has replaced *sons of God* with *angels of God* here. This is the view reflected in some Jewish apocryphal literature such as Enoch 6:2 and Qumran Genesis Apocryphon.

Certainly the writer of Gn was familiar with angels. He mentions them at least 15x in the book. One wonders if the writer would employ such an ambiguous phrase as *sons of God* when he mentions angels for the first time.[398]

Second, the phrase *sons of God* is used of angels in OT poetic literature (Job 1:6; 2:1; 38:7 [LXX "angels of God"]; Dt 32:8 [LXX "angels of God;" MT "sons of Israel"]), as is the equivalent *bᵉnê 'ēlîm* (Ps 29:1; 89:6).

Third, those who hold to the angel interpretation of Gn 6:2 think that Jude 6-7 is the key to interpreting this passage.[399] They think that Jude links fallen angels to sexual immorality such as was practiced at Sodom. The text of Jude reads as follows:

> And angels who did not keep their own domain, but abandoned their proper abode, He has kept in eternal bonds under darkness for the judgment of the great day. (7) Just as Sodom and Gomorrah and the cities around them, since they [feminine] in the same way as these [masculine/neuter] indulged in gross immorality and went after strange flesh, are exhibited as an example, in undergoing the punishment of eternal fire (Jude 6-7 NASB).

According to v 6 "the angels did not keep their own domain;" they "abandoned their proper abode." This is not "a hunger for sexual experience" (Kidner) but a rebellion against God's authority. Furthermore, the antecedent of the feminine *they* in v 7 is the cities around

---

[398] See Robert Newman, "The Ancient Exegesis of Genesis 6:2, 4," *Grace Journal* 5.1 (1984) 13-36.

[399] Other NT passages alleged to point to the "supernatural" interpretation of Gn 6:1-4: 2 Pet 2:4; 1 Cor 11:10; 1 Pet 3:19-20 (the *spirits*).

Sodom and Gomorrah. These included Admah and Zeboiim (Dt 29:23).

What is the antecedent of the pronoun *these* in v 7? The pronoun *these* in form could be either masculine (in which case it would refer to *the angels*) or neuter (in which case it would refer to *Sodom and Gomorrah*, which are neuter in Greek. The law of nearest antecedent states that where there are two or more antecedents that are grammatically possible, the preference must go to the nearer one. Therefore, the reference must be back to Sodom and Gomorrah, not the angels of the preceding v.

There is yet another consideration that indicates that Jude is not referring to Gn 6. References to *darkness* and *judgment* are out of keeping with the context at the beginning of Gn 6.

*2. Opposing arguments.* Several relevant considerations weigh against the angel interpretation of Gn 6. First, the word *angels* in the Septuagint manuscript referenced above is not a translation of the original Hebrew text, but an unwarranted interpretation injected into the text.

Second, angels are spirit beings (Heb 1:14) without flesh and bones (Lk 24:39). They certainly cannot cohabit with females without taking on bodily form. There is no indication that they can take on bodily form without heaven's permission. Angels do not marry (Mt 22:30; Lk 20:34-36). (In fairness the angel supporters point out that Jesus is talking about angels *in heaven*.)

Third, those guilty of sin were *flesh*, not angels (6:3). Punishment fell on earth's inhabitants, not angels. If angels were involved, and in fact took the initiative, where is the reference to any consequences for their sin?

Fourth, the only defection of angels spoken of elsewhere in the Bible took place before the Fall.

Fifth, all the other angels mentioned in Gn are noble.

Sixth, the language used in the text is that regularly used in the OT for marriage. If demonic angels cohabited with human females one would think that stronger language would be used to described what transpired.

All of these considerations force the rejection of the angel interpretation of the *sons of God* in Gn 6:2.

## B. Kings View

The view that the sons of God were rulers is also ancient.[400] The text is taken to be a condemnation of kings that married indiscriminately and polygamously. Several pieces of evidence are used to support this view. First, a legitimate king in Israel might be designated as *son of God* (2 Sam 7:14; Ps 2:7; 82:6). Second, in the wider world of the ancient Near East kings were regarded as sons of various gods. For example, Benhadad (1 Kgs 20) means "son of the god Hadad." Third, the Sumerian King List pictures kings ruling cities prior to the Flood. Fourth, in Scripture occasionally the term Elohim is used for powerful men (Ex 21:6; 22:7, 8, 27; Judg 5:8 and possibly Ps 82:1, 6; 132:1), as is the related word *'ēl*.[401]

Kline saw these *sons of God* as corrupted rulers from the Cainite line who claimed deity for themselves, failed to maintain justice in society and built for themselves large harems.[402] He regarded the sons of God to be the same as the Nephilim of 6:4.

---

[400] Leroy Birney, "An Exegetical Study of Genesis 6:1-4," *JETS*, 13 (1970): 43-52.

[401] The word *'ēl*, usually translated *God*, refers to men in Ex 15:15; 2 Kgs 24:15; Job 41:17; Ezek 17:13; 31:11, 32:21. The exact relationship between the words *'ēl* and *'elōhîm* is disputed.

[402] M. Kline, "Divine Kingship and Sons of God in Genesis 6:1-4," *WTJ* 24 (1962): 187-204.

The weakness of this view is that the exact terminology *sons of God* is not used of kings elsewhere in the OT.

## C. Sethite View

A number of conservative writers (e.g., Leupold; Whitelaw; Keil) opt for the view that the sons of God were the godly descendants of Seth.[403] In support of this view the following arguments are advanced. First, a distinction between Sethites and Cainites has been developed since ch 4. A mixing of these lines in a culminating breakdown of human society fits the context of the book.

Second, warning against marrying with unbelievers a major theme of the Pentateuch.

Third, in the biblical concept Israel is God's son (Ex 4:22) and Israelites are the "children of God" or "children of Yahweh" (e.g., Dt 14:1). See also Dt 32:5; Ps 73:15; Isa 43:6; Hos 1:10. Fourth, Adam is called the "son of God" (Lk 3:38). It would be natural, then, to understand *the sons of God* to be godly successors of Adam. Certainly the NT writers did not hesitate to apply the terminology "children (sons) of God" to the godly both in this life (1 Jn 3:1, 2, 10) and in the resurrection (Lk 20:36).

Fifth, the term *'elōhîm* could be rendered as a genitive of quality, meaning, "godly sons."[404]

The problem of the Sethite view is that the exact terminology *sons of God* is not used of the people of God in the OT. Furthermore, this view seems to take the term *men* in 6:1 to refer to all mankind, whereas in

---

[403] For a complete delineation of this position, including a succinct presentation of the reasons supporting this view see John Willis, *Genesis* "Living Word Commentary," 164-65.

[404] Mathews, *NAC*, 330. This genitive can attribute a quality or condition to the construct so as to represent or characterize that person. The occurrence of this use is well attested with *bēn* (son). See GKC §128s-v.

6:2 *men* is limited to the Cainites. It does not seem reasonable that the same word would be used in different senses in two consecutive vv.

### D. Other Views

While most of the commentators have adopted one of the three views outlined above, there are other views on the table. Some have argued that the account is a vestige of a myth in which gods mated with humans. For those who embrace biblical theology such a notion is preposterous. Y.B. Smith in conversations with the author has proposed that the *sons of God* were pre-Fall children of Adam and Eve. She has proposed that Adam and Eve lived in the garden longer than is generally recognized. They had many sons prior to the Fall. Others have opted for a combination view. The sons of God were tyrant kings who were possessed by demonic creatures.[405]

### E. Relevant Considerations

The identity of the sons of God cannot be determined apart from the context of the genealogy of Gn 5. Those listed in that ch are most likely a selective list of rulers in the antediluvian world. Adam was created *according to the likeness* of God; he was commissioned to have dominion over the earth (Gn 1:26). Adam begat a son in his *likeness* and according to his image (5:3). Seth became the successor of Adam in his role as designated ruler of earth. Seth was not only *son* of Adam by birth, he was *son* of Adam by succession to rulership. So also with the other eight names listed in the genealogy of ch 5. Adam was *son of God* (Lk 3:38) in that he was created in God's likeness, and as such was

---

[405] A. Ross, *Creation and Blessing: A Guide to the Study and Exposition of the Book of Genesis* (Grand Rapids: Baker, 1988), 182. Also W.H. Gispen, VanGemeren, Waltke.

designated ruler. So the other rulers of the antediluvian era were *sons of God*, i.e., they traced the legitimacy of their rule back to Adam through Seth. So the *sons of God* were Sethites—at least a certain class of Sethites. The title in the context of Gn, however, has nothing to do with covenant standing, or moral stature but with rulership.

# DAUGHTERS OF MEN
# Gn 6:2

The identity of *the daughters of men* depends to some extent on the interpretation of *the sons of God*. Those who hold that *the sons of God* were angels see *the daughters of men* as any human females. Those who see *the sons of God* as kings see *the daughters of men* as commoners. Those who see *the sons of God* as Sethites see *the daughters of men* as descendants of Cain.

There is no contextual reason to limit *the daughters of men* to Cainite women. In fact, if anything the Cainite line is eliminated from the scenario by the geographical limiting phrase *upon the face of the ground*. The *men* who were multiplying were Sethites and families of the other sons of Adam mentioned in 5:4. All of these families were still living upon *the face of the ground* from which Cain was banished (4:14). The *daughters* born to these men were obviously from these same families. While some read into the phrase *daughters of men* a negative moral nuance, there is no clear indication in the text that these daughters were morally inferior to *the sons of God*. The phrase could just as well point to social inferiority. On the other hand, the phrase *daughters of men* may simply serve to link these women to the population explosion noted in v 1.

# SIN OF THE SONS OF GOD
## Gn 6:2b-3

### A. Temptation (6:2a)

*That the sons of God saw that the daughters of men were beautiful.* The complex sentence that began in v 1 continues. *Beautiful* (*tōbhōt;* sing. *tōbhāh*) has the nuance of physical beauty.[406] Targum Pseudo-Jonathan elaborates:

> And the sons of the princes saw the daughters of men; behold, they were beautiful, they wore mascara and facial makeup, and they went about scantily clad. Desiring licentious activity, they took for themselves wives of whomever they chose.

The implication is that lust was generated in the hearts of the sons of God. The marriages that ensued were based merely upon the attraction of the flesh.

This is the third time in Gn were physical beauty became a prime factor in arousing desire. Cf. 2:9; 3:6. This temptation is not referring to the enticement of naive angelic beings into wild licentiousness by alluring women (von Rad) for it is hard to imagine how creatures of a different realm would find humans physically attractive.

### B. Sin (6:2b)

*They took for themselves wives whomever they chose.* *Took wives* is never used of illicit sex.[407] The

---

[406] That the word *tōbhāh* can refer to physical beauty is established by Gn 24:16 (Rebekah); 2 Sam 16:12 (Bathsheba). Jacob (*First Book,* 45) takes the word to mean *strong* rather than *beautiful.* He cites 1 Sam 9:2 for justification where the term (in the masculine) is used of Saul. It is not at all clear in 1 Sam 9:2 that the word means *strong* rather than the usual rendering *handsome.*

[407] Contra Di Vito ("Demarcation," *CBT,* 49) who thinks that the text refers to rape.

language refers to legal marriage, without allusion to rape, adultery, or profligacy (Cassuto). There is no indication of any sin in the sons of God taking wives per se or in the daughters of men becoming wives. There is no indication that celestial beings (*sons of God*) defied God by transgressing their appointed boundaries with terrestrial women. The sin is spelled out in the next clause.

Insight into the meaning of the clause can be gained by a comparison of the various English versions. They took for themselves wives "whomever they chose" (NASB); "married any of them they chose" (NIV); "married all those whom they chose" (BV); "of all whom they chose" (NKJV). The sin is this: *the sons of God* (rulers) married polygamously. The bigamy of Cain's descendant Lamech now has escalated into widespread practice of polygamy among the legitimate successors of Adam. Birney summarizes the correct conclusion in these words:

> ... grammatically and exegetically the best interpretation is that the sin was not intermarriage between two groups—whether two worlds (angels and men), two religious communities (Sethite and Cainite), or two social classes (royal and common)—but that the sin was polygamy."[408]

Others suggest that the sin is the attempt on the part of humans to prolong and secure life by marrying gods. The following v is interpreted as thwarting the efforts of men to gain eternal life. This interpretation, however, can hardly be correct. *The sons of God*—considered by these interpreters to be immortal gods, angels or demons—are depicted taking the initiative in the sin. What they would gain by cohabiting with human females is unclear.

---

[408] Birney, op. cit., 49.

The sin is described in the Hebrew literally with the same trio of terms used in the account of the garden sin: *saw ... good ... took*. The use of these terms implies condemnation of the Gn 6 marriages. A fourth verbal parallel to the garden tragedy is the word *whomever*, lit., "from all" (*mikkōl*). This is the term used in 2:16 just before the prohibition regarding the tree of knowledge was stated. It is also used by Serpent in 3:1 to mock the garden prohibition.

The implication is that the Gn 6 marriages were ignoring established prohibitions. The original sin is replicated on a massive scale. The narrator previously used the word *know* to refer to the intimacy of marriage (4:1, 17, 25). One could say, then, that marriage to more than one woman transgresses forbidden boundaries of knowledge. So the sin in Gn 6:1-4 parallels the garden sin in yet another way.

### C. Divine Declaration (6:3)

This v reports divine reflection that leads to a decision (cf. 3:22).

*1. God's Spirit (6:3a):* **Then Yahweh said, My Spirit...** A number of views as to the meaning of *my Spirit* have been put forward. *My spirit* (lower case) has been taken to be the breath of life of 2:7 (Delitzsch) or power that bestows life (Childs). Others have proposed that *my spirit* refers to the angels of the previous v (Wellhausen). Still others think the text is referring to an ethical principle, the divine feelings that have been aroused, or the charismatic gift by which the *sons of God* become prophets, poets or heroes (Jacob). In truth *my Spirit* simply refers to the Holy Spirit that was first encountered in Gn 1:2.

*2. God's striving (6:3b):* **shall not strive with man forever.** The v announces the termination of some previous or customary action of the Holy Spirit. Unfortunately the verb translated *strive* (r. *dîn*) appears only here. Its meaning is debated.

The ancient translations rendered the verb *remain* or *last*. Cassuto offers some philological support for this meaning. The idea then is that God's Spirit will no longer *abide in* man (cf. NASB margin). Other etymologies of the term have been proposed: from a Hebrew root meaning "to judge or rule" (Delitzsch); from an Akkadian root meaning "to be strong or powerful" (Jacob); from Arabic and Ugaritic roots meaning to "be humbled or suffer loss of esteem" (Dillmann).

In support of the meaning *strive* or *contend* 1 Peter 3:20 can be offered: "God waited patiently in the days of Noah while the ark was being built" (cf. 2 Thess 2:7). The striving of the Spirit could be through the preaching of the word of God, in this case by righteous preachers like Noah (2 Pet 2:5) and Enoch (Jude 14). The striving could also be through direct influence on heart, mind and conscience.

The cessation of the action of the striving of God's Spirit signals judgment. *Not...forever* (*lō'...l$^e$ 'ōlām*) indicates that God's dealings with mankind are about to change. One must conclude that the striving of God's Spirit was a demonstration of God's compassion; the withdrawal of that striving indicates God's anger.

The cessation of Yahweh's striving demonstrated his anger *with man* (*bā'ādām*). If angels were the perpetrators of the illicit marriages with human kind, where is any indication of judgment on them? It is the human race that has become corrupt. The action of *the sons of God* (rulers) in marrying polygamously was the final straw in sealing the doom of the human family.

*3. Explanation (6:3b):* **because he also is flesh.** These words offer an explanation for Yahweh's decision regarding the striving of his Spirit with men. *Flesh* points to human weakness. The weakness could be physical, i.e., man's mortality (cf. 7:21), or moral, i.e., moral depravity (cf. 6:12). The latter sense is appropriate to this context. Man has sunk to the level of being *flesh,* i.e., completely devoid of the qualities that set him apart as a spiritual being.

*4. Grace (6:3c):* **nevertheless his days shall be 120 years.** The span of 120 years is not to be understood as a limit to the human life-span.[409] Such a notion is contradicted by Gn 11:10-26, which does not reflect any such limit. The only possible meaning of the clause is that Yahweh is granting a grace period before destruction (Delitzsch; Speiser). As long as the Spirit contended with them they had the opportunity to repent.

# NEPHILIM
# Gn 6:4

Now another group of transgressors—the Nephilim—is introduced. They are just as difficult to identify as the sons of God in 6:2.

### A. Identity of the Nephilim

*1. Ancient view.* Use of the definite article with *Nephilim* indicates that the writer was referring to an historical phenomenon that was familiar to his readers. The term *Nephilim* is used elsewhere only in Nm 13:33 where it refers to the Anakites who were giants. Based on the use of the term in the later passage the LXX translated the word in Gn 6:4 "giants." This was followed by the KJV and NKJV. NIV, NASB, NRSV and NJPS properly leave the word untranslated.

---

[409] Custance (*Seed*, 72) believes 120 years was to be the expected life span of man hereafter. This idea is supported by JB, "His life shall last no more than 120 years;" and by Mathews, *NAC*, 334f.

There is nothing in the etymology of the word itself to indicate stature. The word comes from a root that means "to fall." Some have proposed that the Nephilim were those who had "fallen" from heaven. Others connect the term with those who fall into Sheol as in Ezek 32 (Zimmerli; Cassuto), or those who have fallen into depravity. The context associates Nephilim with violence; so the word might refer to one who falls on others, i.e., a bully or tyrant. The Nephilim were not a race or ethnic group, but a class of men, equivalent in English to words like gangsters, tyrants, bullies, etc.

2. *Modern views.* Modern writers see the Nephilim as semi-gods (like Gilgamesh) or mythical beings. Sailhamer thinks the Nephilim were the great men named in ch 5. Some have suggested that the Nephilim were in fact *the sons of God* mentioned earlier (Birney). The most popular view is that the Nephilim were the product of the unions of the sons of God and daughters of men. The text, however, seems to present them as separate from the sons of God, but contemporary with them.

3. *Nephilim and Anakites.* In Nm 13:33 the Israelite spies say that "the descendants of Anak come from the Nephilim." If the Nephilim of Nm 13:33 and Gn 6:4 are the same group than the Nephilim and their descendants must have survived the Flood. Obviously that is not possible.

In approaching Nm 13:33 these facts need to be taken into consideration. First, the troublesome clause is absent from the LXX, raising questions about its authenticity. Second, the Anakites in Deuteronomy are listed among the residents of Canaan noted for their size and military skill (Dt 1:28; 2:10-23; 9:2). The Nephilim, however, are never listed in Deuteronomy among the Canaanite inhabitants. Third, the Israelite spies were clearly exaggerating in their statements about the inhabitants of Canaan in Nm 13:33 as the word "grasshoppers" indicates. Fourth, Nm 13:33 does not actually say that the Anakites were *sons* (descendants) of the Nephilim.

These facts lead to the conclusion that there was no intention in Nm 13 to connect ancestrally the Nephilim of Moses' day with the Nephilim of Gn 6. The term was used by anti-war Israelite spies as political propaganda in the same way the terms barbarians or Huns or Nazis might be used today to disparage a people or movement.[410]

**B. Origin of the Nephilim** (6:4a, b)

*1. Chronological note (6:4a):* **The Nephilim were in the land in those days, and also afterward...** The rise of the Nephilim is related to the actions narrated in the preceding vv. They were on the earth *in those days.* The text falls short of saying that the Nephilim *arose* in those days. *In those days* is a general expression referring to the days prior to the Flood. The *Nephilim* continued to be active *also afterward*, i.e., after the marriages of the sons of God and daughters of men. So the v suggests the Nephilim were in the land both before and after the union of the sons of God and daughters of men.

*2. Amplification note (6:4b):* **when the sons of God came in to the daughters of men, and they bore children to them.** Two more details about the marriages of the sons of God are related in Gn 6:4. First, *the sons of God came into the daughters of men.* This terminology is used in the OT to refer to a male who visits a woman's quarters (cf. Judg 15:1). Second, children were born to the unions of the sons of God and daughters of men. After the garden sin Adam and Eve lived

---

[410]Mathews, *NAC*, 337f.

on to have children. So those who transgressed in Gn 6 in respect to marriage were spared from immediate judgment. They lived on to have children. As noted above there is no direct connection between the marriages and the *Nephilim*.

### C. Ambiguous Phrases (6:4b)

***Those were the mighty men who were of old, men of renown*** (6:4b). Some think *the Nephilim* are being described in these phrases; others think these phrases describe the children of the sons of God and daughters of men. If the Nephilim and the children of the unions are one and the same (as is commonly assumed) then the question is not germane. The subject of the v, emphatic by position, is *Nephilim*. Most likely the pronoun *they* refers back to the emphasized subject in the v.

It is then the *Nephilim* who were *mighty men, men of old, men of renown*. Even Westermann admits that in these phrases there is nothing mythological. "All three statements describe human beings."[411] This threefold description presents a picture of powerful and skilled men of war who were famous in the lore of the ancient Near East. This description fits nicely with the proposed significance of the word *Nephilim* as meaning tyrants or bullies.

# DIVINE RESPONSE
# Gn 6:5-6

### A. Observation (6:5)

*1. Action of God (6:5a):* **Then Yahweh saw.** The action of Yahweh mimics the sons of God who *saw* the

---

[411]Westermann, *Genesis 1-11*, 379. In spite of this admission Westermann still presents the *Nephilim* as mythological beings. He explains the inconsistency of his own position by arguing that two different accounts have been fused together.

Corruption of the Race

daughters of men (6:2). The language also recalls the language of Gn 1 where God *saw* the goodness in his original creation. Now men have corrupted that goodness. The words *Yahweh saw* do not mean that God merely noticed something. This language portrays a judicial investigation that precedes an action by God.

*2. Actions of man (6:5b):* **that the wickedness of man was great on the earth**. *Wickedness* (*rāʻāh*) describes a situation, a state; not any specific action. Yahweh's judicial investigation found that "a state of corruption of mass proportions has come about."[412]

*3. Attitudes (6:5c):* **and that every intent of the thoughts of his heart was only evil continually**. The extent of the corruption is indicated in the reference to *every intent* (*yētser*) of men. The word appears elsewhere only in Gn 8:21 and Dt 31:21 in the Pentateuch. This word basically means the same as the following word, *thoughts* (*machšᵉbhōt*) *of his heart*. Human plans and intentions are contemplated action. The meaning is not so much what is within or hidden, but what humanity is striving after, planning, devising. The *heart* in Hebrew psychology was the center of thought, feeling, volition and morality. So their aspirations were *evil* (*raʻ*). *Continually* (*kol hayyôm*) is lit., "all the day." The phrase occurs only in elevated, emotional speech (Jacob).

**B. Lamentation** (6:6)

*1. Yahweh's sorrow (6:6a):* **And Yahweh was sorry that he had made man on the earth**. Several times in the OT Yahweh is said to be *grieved* or *sorry* (r. *nchm* in Niphal).[413] The KJV translates the term "repent" 38x; but this is not the word normally used for

---

[412] Westermann, *Genesis 1-11*, 410.
[413] The same expression occurs in Ex 32:14; Jer 18:7f. 26:3, 13; Joel 2:13; Jonah 3:10. This passage is very much like 1 Sam 15:11.

human repentance in which man turns from sin and error. God is immutable in his eternal purposes (1 Sam 15:29; Ps 110:4). "For he is not a man that he should repent" (Nm 23:19). Part of God's eternal purpose, however, is that he has the flexibility to respond to changes in circumstances or actions on the part of man. So in Gn 6: 6 it is not a change of purpose that is indicated but a change of feelings out of which a new course of action develops (Leupold).

2. *Yahweh's grief (6:6b):* **and he grieved himself unto his heart.** The second verb in the Hithpael form is even stronger than the previous verb. The only other usage of this form of the verb (Gn 34:7) describes the mixture of anger and grief that the brothers of Dinah experienced when they heard of the rape of their sister. This verb indicates deep-seated aggravation and indignation over what had become of mankind. The writer has purposely juxtaposed the conniving heart of man (6:5) with the broken and indignant heart of God (6:6).

## C. **Determination** (6:7)

1. *Devastating judgment (6:7a):* **And Yahweh said, I will blot out mankind whom I have created ...** *Yahweh* is the God of grace; but the grace period of 120 years was now over. *Said* does not necessarily mean that Yahweh was speaking to anyone. He may have simply said to himself, i.e., reached a decision.

Yahweh now has determined to *blot out* (*māchāh*) man. This term (also used in 7:23) is used 33x in the OT. It is used of the wiping of a dish (2 Kgs 21:13), the blotting out of a name from a register (Ex 32:32) or from memory (Dt 9:14). The term is used of the obliteration of a tribe from Israel in Judg 21:17. This strong term suggests the utter horror of Yahweh's decision to execute this judgment. At the same time it suggests the ease with which he will carry out the threat. It will be no more difficult for Yahweh to wipe the earth clean of people than it is for a person to wipe food residue from a plate.

The primary focus of the divine judgment is *mankind* (*hā'ādām*). *Whom I have created* recalls the special creation of humankind that sets man apart from all other creatures.

2. *World-wide judgment (6:7b):* **from the face of the ground, from man to cattle to creepers and to birds of the sky.** The extent of the contemplated judgment is made clear. The human population will be removed from *the face of the ground.* This is the special terminology used in these chs for the region occupied by the Sethites and other descendants of Adam, other than the Cainites who were driven from *the face of the ground* (4:14).

Besides *man* the judgment will include those creatures that God created for the use and pleasure of man. Using the technique of emphasis by enumeration or specification the writer mentions *cattle, creepers,* and *birds.* As with the previous listing of animal types (cf. 1:24, 25, 28, 30), the animals are broken down into three categories. This listing does not exactly correspond to any of the previous listings. The creatures are named in the order of their proximity to man. Clearly there is no anger with the animals.

3. *Justified judgment (6:7c):* **for I am sorry that I have made them.** Because of the horror of what is being announced, the explanation is repeated from 6:6.

### D. Exception (6:8)

***But Noah found grace in the eyes of Yahweh.*** This is the first occurrence of the word *grace* (*chēn*) in the

Bible. In Hebrew Noah's name spelled in reverse is the word for grace![414]

## TABLET COLOPHON
## Gn 6:9a

*These are the records of the generations of Noah* (6:9a). These words mark the conclusion of the third tablet that began in 5:1b. This tablet may have been written or preserved by Noah.

## CONCLUSION

The Antediluvian Period approaches its end. Morally the human race has been in a tailspin since man was expelled from Eden. Nonetheless, the Creator did not leave himself without a witness during this period. Of course, there was the continuing and powerful witness of nature (Rom 1:19f) and the witness of conscience (Rom 2:14f). Beyond that, however, Yahweh had given the special revelation of a promised Redeemer who ultimately will crush Serpent and all his seed (Gn 3:15). At times the antediluvians were exposed to the witness of public worship by the few who remained faithful (Gn 4:26), the preaching of Enoch (Jude 1:14f) and Noah (2 Pet 2:5), and the ministry of the Holy Spirit (Gn 6:3).

---

[414] J.M. Sasson, "Word-Play in Gen 6:8-9," *CBQ* 37(1975): 165-66.

# 18
# DELUGE ANNOUNCEMENT
# Gn 6:9-22

For the writer of Gn the account of the Flood is pivotal. Only snippets of history from the long centuries prior to the Flood have been narrated. For the most part the gap between Adam and Noah has been filled only by a few selected names. Now the writer focuses almost four chs on only about one year—the six-hundredth year of Noah's life.

## PRELIMINARY MATTERS

### A. Mesopotamian Parallels

Various alternatives have been proposed to explain the similarities between the biblical account of the Flood and certain Mesopotamian stories. W.G. Lambert reflects a popular view: "The flood remains the clearest case of dependence of Genesis on Mesopotamian legend."[415] There are, however, major differences in the two traditions that rule out the direct dependence theory.[416]

The biblical account of the Flood, when compared to Mesopotamian Flood accounts, displays certain distinct characteristics. First, these chs of Gn are marked by exactness of statement, as for example exact dating for crucial moments in the event. Five dates are given in the text. Working from those five dates, five more can be deduced.

Second, the biblical account is marked by sobriety and consistency. In the Babylonian Flood account the

---

[415] W.G. Lambert, "A New Look at the Babylonian Background of Genesis," *JTS* 16(1965): 291.
[416] Mathews, *NAC*, 100.

ark is said to be 3,000 x 1,200 feet, an obvious exaggeration. The biblical ark was huge, but only a fraction of the Mesopotamian figures. In the Babylonian account the Flood lasted only seven days. In the biblical account the waters prevailed for 150 days, and it was over a year before the earth was again habitable. In the Babylonian account the Flood resulted only from rain; in the Bible the fountains of the deep also burst open. The Bible carefully reports the gradual progress of the Flood in respect to its height, cessation, decline and complete withdrawal. The report of the construction of the ark with cells and light, and waterproofing bitumen passes the sobriety test.

Third, the biblical account is marked by pure monotheism. In the Mesopotamian accounts the Flood was brought upon the earth by petty gods who were annoyed by noise created by overpopulation. These gods were frightened by the Flood. After the Flood the gods gather around the sacrifice like a pack of hungry wolves.

Fourth, the biblical account of the Flood is also marked by personal participation on the part of the writer.

### B. Literary Structure

The Flood narrative has been artistically constructed. Following Cassuto, it consists of two acts of six paragraphs each. In Act One the picture becomes progressively darker until only one speck of light remains to illuminate the deathly flood, viz. the ark (7:23). In Act Two the light shines brighter and brighter until finally there emerges a tranquil and cleansed world with the hopeful light of the rainbow.[417]

---

[417]Cassuto, *CBG*, 2:30f.

Gordon Wenham demonstrates the chiastic arrangement of the paragraphs in the narrative,[418] refuting the old liberal idea of conflicting sources in the Flood account. Even within the narrative itself Wenham has demonstrated a chiastic arrangement of the various numbers of days.[419] Thus

A. 7 days of waiting for the Flood (7:4)
  B. 7 days of waiting for the Flood (7:10).
    C. 40 days of flooding (7:17a)
      D. 150 days of water prevailing (7:24)
      D' 150 days of water diminishing (8:3)
    C. 40 days of waiting (8:6)
  B. 7 days of waiting (8:10)
A. 7 days of waiting (8:12)

## C. Thematic Considerations

In terms of the overall theme of Gn the Flood marked the climax of *uncreation* that began with the garden sin in Gn 3. In the Flood God determined to *blot out man whom I have created* (6:7), *all in whose nostrils was the breath of the spirit of life* (7:22). The language clearly reflects that of the creation narratives. Again the world is covered with water as in Gn 1:2. Ps 104:6 even uses in reference to the Flood the word *t<sup>e</sup>hôm* (*deep*), which was used in Gn 1:2. In Gn 1 God's creative works are described in terms of separation and distinction; Gn 6 portrays the abolition of distinctions.

In Gn 1 the expanse of the heavens holds the waters above (1:6f); but in Gn 6 those waters are unleashed through the *windows of the heavens* (7:11). In creation God separated the land and waters (1:9f); in the Flood

---

[418] Gordon J. Wenham, "The Coherence of the Flood Narrative," *VT* 28(1977): 336-48. *WBC*, 158. See also W.M. Clark, "The Animal Series in the Primeval History," *VT* 18(1968):433-49.
[419] Wenham, *WBC*, 157.

account *the fountains of the deep* break through the earth (7:11). The outline of Flood destruction in 7:21 follows the same sequence as the creation in ch 1: earth, birds, cattle, wild animals, creepers and man. It seems that the writer is deliberately making the point that the Flood dismantled the original creation.

### D. Transition Structure

The transition from the corruption of the antediluvian world to the account of the salvation of Noah is bridged in 6:8-9 by a neat chiasmus[420] that can be displayed as follows:

Noah
    Found favor
        In the eyes of Yahweh
            These are the generations of Noah.
            **Noah was a righteous man.**
            **Blameless he was**
            In his generation
        With God
    Walked
Noah.

## WITNESS OF NOAH
## Gn 6:9b-12

Noah's name is used as a catchword to conclude Tablet Three and open Tablet Four. The unusual back-to-back presence of a proper name in the Hebrew text further supports the view that the first line of v 9 actually is the concluding sentence of the previous source tablet. So the third tablet begins with Noah's name, because he is the focus of it.

---

[420] Kikawada and Quinn, *Before Abraham*, 86.

Noah comes exactly half way in the genealogies between Adam and Abraham. He is a pivotal character in Gn 1-11.

### A. Noah's Character (6:9b-10)

Noah is the first person in the biblical narrative to be awarded special titles of distinction. The scope of Noah's godliness is spelled out in four ways.

*1. His personal life (6:9b):* **Noah was a righteous man.** This is the first use of the term *righteous* (*tsaddîq*) in the Bible. Noah satisfied the standards established for him by a holy God. He was in the right relationship with his Creator, and with his fellowman as well. This righteousness is cited in 7:1 as the reason God preserved Noah and his family through the Flood.

*2. Noah's public life (6:9c):* **blameless in his generations.** *Blameless* (*tāmîm*) comes from a root that means "to be complete or finished." It is used over 80x in the OT. The only person said to be *tāmîm* is Noah.[421] This adjective is found only in the plural.

The term *blameless* does not indicate absolute sinlessness. The proof of this is that those who claim to be blameless freely acknowledge their shortcomings (2 Sam 22:24). The basic idea of the word seems to be completeness. Those who are blameless are those who are wholehearted in commitment to God and his word. *Blameless* paired with the word *righteous* suggests that Noah was totally committed to righteousness.

The phrase *in his generations* probably means only that Noah did not give his contemporaries any excuse to criticize his conduct. The plural suggests that Noah was not only righteous among his contemporaries of the tenth generation; he stood out among all the generations that were on earth in his days.

---

[421] The closely related word *tām* is used seven times of Job.

3. *Noah's spiritual life (6:9d):* **with God did Noah walk.** Except for the prepositional phrase *with God* being in the emphatic position, this is the same statement made about Enoch in 5:22. See comments there. The emphasis on the phrase *with God* is probably designed to indicate how it was that Noah was able to be righteous and blameless in his generations. He chose to maintain close fellowship with the Creator. This was the secret of his spiritual power and exemplary life.

4. *Noah's family life (6:10):* **And Noah became the father of three sons: Shem, Ham, and Japheth.** Noah's godly life bore fruit in the lives of his sons. Noah's three sons were mentioned already in 5:32. The writer had no reason to take note of their births again in 6:10 if not for the connection between them and the godliness of their father. The implication both here and in the paragraphs that follow is that the three sons emulated the godliness of their father.

5. *Noah's stature.* While the Gn writer highlights the godliness of Noah, the rabbis attempted to belittle this Gentile lest Abraham lose some of his luster. The rabbis pointed out that Noah was only righteous *in his generations*; Abraham was as righteous as mortal man can be. Noah did not pray for the lost world; but Abraham did. Noah needed support in his walk with God; Abraham walked in his own righteousness before God. It is not said of Noah, "I have known him" implying God's choice. Noah was singled out for survival, Abraham for a mission.

This kind of comparison betrays ethnocentric exegesis at its worst. Probably an equally good case could be made from textual data that Noah's godliness was superior to that of Abraham. All such comparisons, however, are improper. Both men were used of God. Both men were godly. Both men played pivotal roles in the history of salvation.

Noah's godly life was celebrated in later Scripture. He along with Job and Daniel are a trio of righteous men (Ezek 14:14, 20). The writer of Hebrews emphasizes the faith of Noah (Heb 11:7-8 NIV). Peter calls Noah "a preacher of righteousness" (2 Pet 2:5).

### B. World of Noah's Witness (6:11-12)

The writer now further develops his description of the sin of the antediluvian world. He does this to justify the sentence of complete destruction just announced, and to highlight the environment in which Noah maintained his witness for God. Two new words are introduced into the discussion.

*1. Corruption (6:11a):* **Now the earth was corrupted before Elohim.** The term *corrupted* (*šāchat* in the Niphal) is repeated two more times in the following v for emphasis—7x total in the Flood narrative. The word means "perverted in its proper function." The term is used to describe physical objects (Jer 13:7), cities (Gn 18:28) and nations (Jer 4:7). The context indicates that the word refers to moral behavior. Mankind had destroyed the human world as God intended it to be. The rabbis thought that the word points specifically to sexual corruption.

*Before God* (*liphnê hā'elōhîm*) at the least suggests God's awareness of their corruption. The phrase, however, means more. They engaged in their corrupt conduct openly, i.e., defiantly. They had no sense of shame. Sometimes the phrase serves in Hebrew to indicate a superlative sense, as if to say the level of corruption was as high as the heavens.

*2. Violence (6:11b):* **And the earth was filled with violence.** *Violence* (*chāmās*) is not a general expression for sin; it is criminal oppression, bloodshed, and use of brutality, false accusation and unjust judgment. *Violence* seems to refer back especially to the mighty Nephilim in

6:4. The term is limited to human transgression; it is never used of animal violence. Man was commissioned to subdue the earth by filling it through procreation. Instead antediluvian thugs were filling the earth with violent deeds.[422] The song of Lamech (4:23f) illustrates the temper of the times.

3. *Investigation (6:12a)*: ***And Elohim looked on the earth, and behold, it was corrupt.*** As in 6:5 the divine *look* implies formal investigation. This investigation confirmed the shocking conclusion that the corruption was universal. Clearly this v is formulated as the counterbalance to 1:31. There *Elohim* saw that everything he had made was *very good*; now the world had become utterly corrupt.

4. *Explanation (6:12b)*: ***for all flesh had corrupted their way upon the earth.*** Does *all flesh* include animals under the verbal condemnation? Waltke argues that animals are included in the phrase *all flesh* throughout the Flood narrative. Animals as well as people had transgressed the boundaries established for them. Waltke sees in the postdiluvian regulations concerning animals (9:2-3) an implication that antediluvian animals had gotten totally out of control.[423] Hulst, however, studied the phrase *all flesh* in the OT and concluded that in contexts of guilt and judgment only humans are in view.[424]

# WORK OF ARK BUILDING
# Gn 6:13-22

### A. Announcement to Noah (6:13)

In the Mesopotamian Flood myth the plan of the gods to destroy the world by Flood was top secret. It

---

[422] Mathews, *NAC*, 359.
[423] Waltke, *GAC*, 134.
[424] A.R. Hulst, "Kol Basar in der priesterlichen Fluterzählung," *Oudtestamentische Studiën* 12(1958):28-68. Cited by Wenham, *WBC*, 171.

only leaked out accidentally to the Flood hero.[425] The biblical God, however, chose to make his intentions regarding coming judgment known to the righteous Noah (cf. Gn 18:17-21). The text is silent as to how this communication took place. Noah might have experienced a theophany, a vision or a dream revelation.

1. *Solemn (6:13a):* **Then Elohim said to Noah, The end of all flesh has come before me.** The decision of 6:7 is now made known to Noah. The gravity of the announcement to Noah is indicated in three ways. First, the announcement was made by *Elohim.* Second, the announcement pertained to *the end* ($q\bar{e}ts$) of all humankind. Third, the words *has come before me* (lit., "to my face") mean "near at hand."

2. *Justified (6:13b):* **For the earth is filled with violence because of them.** *Violence* is cited as justification for the Flood. The rabbis made the observation that their fate was only sealed when they put forth their hands to robbery. *Because of them* is lit., "from their faces." From their *faces* wickedness flooded upward (lit.,) toward God's *face* (v 11). Conditions on earth required the Creator to do what he had no desire to do, viz., destroy his creation. The forthcoming judgment was not sought by God, but was thrust upon him by man's conduct.

3. *Shocking (6:13c):* **And behold I am about to destroy them and the earth.** *Behold* introduces something shocking or unexpected. *Destroy* (*šcht* in the Hiphil) comes from the same Hebrew root translated *corrupted* in 6:12. Men have destroyed the moral foundations of the earth; just retribution requires that men be destroyed with the earth. The term *destroy* is a participle indicating impending action. The phrase *destroy them and the earth* is a zeugma, i.e., the participle governs two objects

---

[425] *ANET,* 95, lines 170-87.

*(them; the earth/land)*, but relates to the two in slightly different ways. The inhabitants will be wiped out; the earth/land will remain, but will be rendered incapable (temporarily) of fulfilling its intended purpose. Precisely how God planned to effect this destruction is not revealed at this point.

**B. Ark Instructions** (6:14-16)

God never trusts man's salvation to human invention. The Judge acts as Deliverer in specifying to Noah the means of his salvation. The writer is not so concerned about communicating a verbal picture of the ark as he is in underscoring Noah's meticulous obedience to the instructions of God.

*1. Materials (6:14a):* **Make for yourself an ark of gopher wood.** The word *ark* (*tēbhāh*) is used 14x in the Flood narrative, 7x in the preparation for the Flood, and 7x in the report of the diminishing Flood waters (8:1-14). It is used elsewhere only of Moses' *ark* (KJV; NASB) or *basket* (NIV; NRSV) in Ex 2:3, 5. Both Noah's ark and Moses' basket were coated with pitch; both saved life.

Moses chose an Egyptian word to describe the vessel Noah was told to build. In Egyptian the term translated *ark* refers to a ship that was square-cornered and chest-like in shape.[426] Such ships were primarily used for transporting grain or conveying the golden images used in religious processions across the Nile. These vessels were noted for their stability in rough waters.[427]

*Gopher wood* is not mentioned elsewhere in the OT. It is thought to be cypress (NIV). Because of its resistance to rot, cypress was used by the ancients in their shipbuilding enterprises. Others think that *gopher* describes the shape of the wood rather than its kind.

---

[426] A. Yahuda, *The Language of the Pentateuch in its Relations to Egyptian* (Oxford: University Press, 1933), 110.
[427] Aalders, *BSC*, 160f.

*2. Floor plan (6:14b):* **You shall make the ark with rooms.** *Rooms* is lit., "nests." Apparently numerous stalls or cages were installed to confine the various animals for their own protection and that of the others on board. By a slightly different vocalization of the key word the idea becomes "woven of reeds" (Jacob). For this reason some think the ark was constructed of reeds rather than planks of wood.

*3. Sealing (6:14c):* **And you shall cover it inside and out with pitch.** *Pitch* (*kōpher*) is not used elsewhere in OT; but is found in the same context in the Gilgamesh Epic. This *pitch* was most likely "a natural derivative of crude petroleum."[428] This may indicate that the world's oil deposits did not come into being as a result of the Flood as argued by Whitcomb and Morris.[429]

*4. Dimensions (6:15):* **And this is how you shall make it: the length of the ark three hundred cubits, its breadth fifty cubits and its height thirty cubits.** The cubit was the distance from the elbow to the tip of the longest finger. As time went on the cubit became standardized at about eighteen inches. There is no way to know, however, how long the cubit was in Noah's day. Assuming an eighteen inch cubit the ark was 450 x 75 x 45 feet. To put this in perspective, the ark was half again longer than a football field. The proportions were such as made it seaworthy. In the Babylonian Flood account the ark was a preposterous cube-shape![430]

The ark ranks along with some of the biggest ships today. Gross tonnage is estimated to have been 13,960. Its total deck space may have been as much as 97,700 square feet, equivalent to twenty standard college bas-

---

[428] T.C. Mitchell, "Bitumen," in *The New Bible Dictionary*, ed. J.D. Douglas (Grand Rapids: Eerdmans, 1962), 159.
[429] Whitcomb and Morris, *Genesis Flood*, 434.
[430] *ANET*, 93, lines 57, 58.

ketball courts. It was the largest ship ever built until AD 1884.

The difficulty of building a vessel of such enormous magnitude may be explained by 1) the extreme simplicity of its structure, 2) the length of time allowed for its erection, 3) the physical constitution of the builders, and 4) the facilities for obtaining materials which may have existed in abundance in the vicinity.

5. *A window (6:16a)*: **You shall make a window for the ark.** The word (*tsōhar*) occurs nowhere else in the OT, so its meaning is obscure. One etymology concludes that the word should be translated *window* (KJV; NASB) or "opening" (NJPS). Tracing the word to a different origin, NIV and NRSV render "roof." Even if the word does mean "roof," execution of the directive that follows would result in an opening in the ark. Egyptian houses and temples often had rectangular or semicircular openings above the regular doors and windows. These vents admitted light and air when the larger openings were closed.[431]

6. *Ventilation (6:16b)*: **Finish it to a cubit from the top.** Apparently the sides of the ship were finished to within one cubit (about eighteen inches) from the roof. Obviously there were supporting beams that extend to support the roof, which was probably flat. The space between the beans, however, was open. The roof probably extended about one cubit so as to prevent the rain coming in through the opening under the roof thus minimizing the danger of the vessel being swamped by the rain and waves. The opening near the roof provided light and ventilation to the vessel.

7. *Door (6:16c)*: **set the door of the ark in the side of it.** The word *side* (*tsad*) refers to the longer side of a structure. Apparently this door was the only means of

---

[431] Aalders, *BSC*, 162.

entering the ark. Undoubtedly the door was positioned above the water line, and thus rather high on the vessel. A ramp would have been required to gain access.

    *8. Decks (6:16d):* ***You shall make it with lowers, seconds, and thirds.*** These masculine plural nouns probably refer to the *rooms* or nests mentioned in v 14. The logical inference is that the vessel had three decks, all with various compartments. This helps to explain how Noah found room for all the animals.

    *9. Uncertainties.* The exact shape of the ark is not clear. Modern scholars think the vessel was more like a barge. In 1968 Meir Ben-Uri, an Orthodox Jew, produced a model of the ark that had a shape unlike any vessel known to man. Ben-Uri thought the ark was probably built of either bamboo or light weight wood, both common to southern Mesopotamia. His vessel is described as a "prismatic rhomboid," essentially a long bar whose cross section is shaped like a diamond. Such a vessel could have been built while lying at an angle on one side. Animals could easily climb a gentle incline on a side and enter through a door. As the ark began to float, it would right itself; as a result, the door would tilt and become a skylight in the roof, and water could not enter the craft from its sides. Ben-Uri's vessel would have had a capacity of some 5,500 tons.[432]

    Up to this point nothing has been said specifically to Noah about a Flood. Noah was asked to build a vessel before a Flood was mentioned. A righteous man will obey the Lord even when he does not fully understand all the whys and wherefores.

---

[432] Reported in *Jerusalem Post*, October 10, 1967; *Time*, (Feb 23, 1968): 76-79.

## C. Promise to Noah (6:17-18)

The announcement to Noah spells out the dimensions of the Flood and the how it will affect the patriarch and his family.

*1. Deluge (6:17a):* **And as for me, behold I am bringing Deluge as water upon the earth.** *Behold* indicates an unexpected turn in the announcement. The double first person singular subject underscores the certainty of the threat. The judgment cannot be evaded because it is the Creator himself who threatens it. The verb *bringing* is a participle, indicating impending action.

The term *Deluge* (*mabbûl*) is used 13x in the OT, all except two with the definite article. Here in the first usage of the term *Deluge* the writer adds the term *waters.* The word always refers to the Gn Deluge. Outside Gn the term is used only in Ps 29:10, "Yahweh sits upon the Deluge, indeed Yahweh is enthroned king forever." In Babylonian myth the gods themselves cowered before the raging floodwaters.[433] The God of the Bible, however, is depicted sitting serenely in sovereign majesty overseeing this event.

*2. Destruction (6:17b):* **to destroy all flesh in which is the spirit of life, from under heaven; everything that is on the earth shall perish.** *All flesh* is repeated from vv 12-13. The phrase appears 12x in the Noah chs, 26x in the rest of the OT. Outside the Noah chs the phrase refers only to humanity 23x. In the Noah chs context indicates that sometimes animals are included in the phrase.

The expression *spirit of life* (*rûach chayyîm*) occurs only 3x in the Bible, all in the Flood account (6:17; 7:15; 7:22). *Rûach* is the same Hebrew word used in 6:3 and 1:2 meaning "wind, spirit or breath." It is God's Holy Spirit that gives life to earth's creatures. This is not

---

[433] ANET, 94, lines 105-23.

the same terminology used in 2:7 when *Yahweh Elohim* breathed into man's nostrils the *breath of life*. The phrase here is broad enough to included both man and beast. God gave life; now he takes it away.

The phrases *under heaven ... on the earth* suggest that wherever those who have the breath of life dwell the Flood waters will overwhelm them. The result is that *all on the earth shall perish.* The verb *perish* (r. *gv'*) is used 12x in the Pentateuch and elsewhere only in poetry. It means "to pine away, to languish, breathe out." With one exception (Gn 7:21) the word is used of human death as opposed to animal death. The choice of this verb suggests that the focus is on the death of human beings. It points to the moment of transition from life to death, the cessation of breathing. It is variously translated "die, expire, breathed his last breath," etc.

*3. Covenant (6:18a):* **But I will establish my covenant with you.** This is the first use of the theologically significant term *covenant* in the Bible. Sometimes a *covenant* was an agreement between two parties, in which both accepted certain specified responsibilities. *My covenant* emphasizes that God is the author of this covenant.

Some think Gn 9:18 anticipates the *covenant* God made with Noah after the Flood in 9:9. Others think the covenant refers to God's promise, spelled out in the following line, to save Noah from the Flood. Probably both are included. The covenant with Noah began with the commitment to save him and his family; but it also included the provisions for preservation after the Flood.

Some think that the verb *establish* (*qûm* in the Hiphil) requires the confirmation of an existing covenant rather than the inauguration of a new covenant. The only thing resembling a covenant thus far is Elohim's creation week implied commitment to bless animal and human propagation (1:22, 28). So these scholars take the covenant in 6:18 to be that human habitation on earth will be preserved by Noah.[434] Through Noah God will again populate the earth (9:1). The weakness of this proposal is that the term *covenant* is not found in the first four chs of Gn. Furthermore, *establish* sometimes points to inauguration of a covenant (cf. Ex 6:4). In any case, in the covenant of ch 9 God renews the creation commitment to Noah.[435]

*4. Salvation (6:18b):* **And you shall enter the ark—you and your sons and your wife, and your sons' wives with you.** Because of Noah's righteousness God provided an opportunity for salvation to his family, and through them to the human race. Building the ark, provisioning it, entering it were acts of obedience that appropriated the salvation that God offered Noah.

For the first time God explains why the huge vessel had to be built. God ordained that salvation was to be found in the ark. In order to experience deliverance from the Deluge, Noah not only needed to build the ark, he had to enter it as well. The command to enter the ark implies salvation just as in 1:28 God's command implies blessing. God saves in commanding; man appropriates his salvation through obedience.[436]

The expression *you and your sons and your wife, and your sons' wives* occurs 5x in the Flood narrative (7:7, 13; 8:16, 18; cf. 7:1). Four of those times the family members are mentioned by their relationship to Noah. There are several implications. First, God intends to preserve humanity in its basic family structure.[437] Second, both Noah and his sons had married monogamously. Third, in this period family consisted not just of

---

[434]W.J. Dumbrell, *Covenant and Creation: A Theology of the OT Covenants* (1984; reprint, Grand Rapids: Baker, 1993), 15-26.
[435]Mathews, *NAC*, 367.
[436]Westermann, *Genesis 1-11*, 422.
[437]Waltke, *GAC*, 136.

Deluge Announcement

parents and children, but parents with their married sons and their wives and children if they had any. Fourth, the text gives the impression that Shem, Ham and Japheth were the only sons Noah ever had. Fifth, there is a hint that it was because of Noah's righteousness that God was showing consideration to the sons and wives.

Scripture declares that eight souls were saved in the ark (1 Pet 3:20). This directly contradicts the Babylonian myth that the Flood hero took an entourage of relatives and craftsmen on board. The Babylonian "Noah" even took with him a boatman to sail the vessel.[438]

**D. Obligations of Noah** (6:19-21):

In addition to building the ark (6:14-16) the responsibilities of Noah fall into two broad categories, viz. loading the animals and provisioning the ark.

*1. Loading the animals (6:19):* ***And of every living thing of all flesh, you shall bring two of every kind into the ark, to keep them alive with you; they shall be male and female.*** Noah had an obligation to make sure that a representative animal population was aboard the ark. Humans and animals stand together in face of catastrophes that threaten life. *Every kind* echoes Gn 1:20-23. The basic kinds of animals created in the beginning were to be preserved from the Flood. For discussion of the term *kind* (*min*) see on 1:20.

*2. Supporting promise (6:20):* ***Of the birds after their kind, and of the animals after their kind, of every creeping thing of the ground after its kind, two of every kind shall come to you to keep them alive.*** The command to bring the animals is made somewhat easier to obey by this promise. The language suggests that God will put the instinct into the animal kinds that causes them to come to Noah. In effect this also makes the

---

[438] ANET 94, lines 84-85, 94.

Creator responsible for deciding what animal lines were to be preserved, and what lines were left to perish. Apparently the animals will come voluntarily. This is the sixth listing of animals. Again it is not identical to any of the previous five. Expressions occurring in the creation story are repeated in order to emphasize that every kind of creature was deserving of preservation.

*3. Provisioning the ark (6:21):* **And as for you, take for yourself some of all food which is edible, and gather it to yourself; and it shall be for food for you and for them.** Animals cut down on eating when they have no physical exercise. Even so just gathering the food to be consumed on board the ark was a massive project.

### E. Obedience of Noah (6:22)

***Thus Noah did; according to all that God had commanded him, so he did.*** Years of hard labor and sacrifice, firm resolve and faith are packed into the simple words *Thus Noah did*. The command/obedience rhythm permeates the Gn narratives. It harks back to the creation fiat/fulfillment motif of Gn 1. Noah's obedience is praised by NT writers as well. Cf. Heb 11:7; 1 Pet 3:20.

## CONCLUSION

There is no indication how long the ark preparations took. The building of the ark and other preparations took place within the 120 years of grace that God granted prior to the judgment (cf. 6:3).

# 19
# WATERS PREVAILED
# Gn 7:1-24

The ark having now been built, Noah awaited further instructions from Yahweh. The date of the second communication with Noah can be computed from 7:11. There the narrator reports that the Flood began on the seventeenth day of the second month. According to 7:4 this communication came seven days prior to the beginning of the Deluge. Thus Yahweh's second communication to Noah came on the tenth day of the second month in Noah's $600^{th}$ year.

## PREPARATIONS
## Gn 7:1-9

**A. Boarding Command** (7:1)

*1. Specifics of the command (7:1a):* **Then Yahweh said to Noah, Enter the ark, you and all your household.** Presumably this command came directly from Yahweh at the end of the 120 years. How Yahweh communicated with ancient prophets and patriarchs is not indicated. The directive is for Noah and his family to board *the ark*. The definite article indicates that the vessel was prepared and was well-known to Noah.

*2. Explanation of the command (7:1b):* **For you alone I have seen to be righteous before me in this time.** These direct words from Yahweh serve three purposes. First, they confirm the appraisal of the narrator in 6:9 that Noah was a righteous man. Second, coming as they do after Noah has executed a number of precise and difficult instructions they commend Noah upon his obedient faith. Third, they communicate to Noah the reason he has been chosen to be delivered from the coming catastrophe. Up till this time Noah had not been told why he had been selected.

What is the relationship between *found favor* in 6:8 and this v? Three answers to this question have been offered. First, some hold that Noah found favor because he was righteous (Skinner). Second, others insist that Noah was declared righteous or given righteousness because he found favor (von Rad). Third, based on parallel language in 1 Sam 16:1; 2 Kgs 8:13 it has been suggested that Noah found favor in that God saw in him the potential to be righteous.

Whether the divine favor preceded or followed the righteousness in Noah cannot be clearly established from the text. Most likely, however, he found favor because he was righteous. The building of the ark was a test of his faith or obedience. Certainly Noah's righteousness was manifested through his obedient faith.

The words *you alone* do not imply that the other family members were not righteous. In the light of Ezek 14:20; 18:20 Noah's personal righteousness could not have saved his family. Therefore, one must conclude that the other family members must have followed in the footsteps of the righteous patriarch.

The words *I have seen* recall the words *God saw* in 6:5, 12. God saw a world of corruption and violence; but in Noah he saw something commendable. *Before me* (lit., "to my face") suggests that Noah's righteousness is being measured by God's, not man's, standard.

### B. Instructions: Clean Cattle (7:2a-d)

Commentators who see these words as contradictory to 6:19-20 have no feel for Hebrew narrative style. The initial command to take pairs of animals into the ark is now amplified.

*1. Obligation (7:2a):* **You shall take for you.** The verb *take* (r. *lqch*) indicates an action not commanded in

6:19-20. There Noah was told that animals will *come* to him; of those that came, he was to *bring* them into the ark. Here he is told to *take* the animals.

Though it may be coincidental, the verb *take* is commonly used when the preparation of animals for sacrifice is in view.[439] Perhaps the use of this verb hints at the purpose for the additional clean animals. The prepositional phrase *for you,* a phrase that also does not appear in 6:19-20, may point in the same direction. The animals gathered here may be in addition to the two of every kind specified in 6:19-20. On the other hand, these may be more specific instructions about one class of the animals mentioned earlier.

*2. Selection (7:2b): **of all clean cattle.*** One of the categories of animals that was to be preserved on the ark—the *cattle* ($b^e h\bar{e}m\bar{a}h$)—is now subdivided. *Cattle* are those animals closest to man, especially flocks and herds, and other domesticated animals. As the start of the Flood was but seven days hence, Noah was told to take action in respect to the clean cattle.

The cattle Noah was now told to take are designated as *clean* ($t^e h\hat{o}r\bar{a}h$). This is the first use of the word *clean* in the Bible. The distinction between clean and unclean animals antedated Moses. The Law of Moses made a sharp distinction between the two, with specific criteria that were to be applied (Lv 11; Dt 1). The Law served to formalized a concept that had a long pre-Mosaic history.

The fact that Abel offered sacrifices that were acceptable to God provides indirect evidence that a distinction of some kind already was known before the Deluge. Does this also imply that animals were acceptable for food prior the flood? In Mosaic Law it is this matter of suitability for food that is emphasized in connection with the clean/unclean distinction. There is no

---

[439]Cassuto, *CBG*, 2:73. Cassuto cites, for example, Gn 15:9-10; Ex 10:26.

direct evidence in Gn, however, that men consumed meat prior to the Flood. If they did so, they ate it without any specific divine authorization.

How did mankind come to recognize the distinction between clean and unclean animals? Was it by revelation? Human observation? Or perhaps simply general practice? What constituted the distinction between clean and unclean? It is possible that the distinction was revealed to Noah during his periods of fellowship with God. More likely, however, the distinction between clean and unclean is one that is based on their utility to humans, not on principles revealed later to Moses. Thus clean animals were those being raised by Noah and his sons.

3. *Numeration (7:2c)*: ***by sevens*** is lit., "seven, seven." Is the number *seven* repeated for emphasis, i.e., *seven, even seven*? Or was the number fourteen—seven pairs as interpreted by LXX? Another possibility is that the number was *seven times seven*, i.e., forty-nine, but this has not found widespread support. A majority of writers seems to favor the view that there were seven individual animals of each clean kind—three pairs and a spare. The phrase *a male and his female*, however, seems to point to seven pairs, not seven individuals.

Here is another example of a command without any rationale. Such commands test faith, and build greater faith. Two possible reasons for the command can be suggested. First, the extra clean animals would "jumpstart" reproduction in the new earth following the Flood. Second, additional clean animals may have been intended for sacrificial purposes. See comments above on the imperative *take* at the beginning of this v. Those who hold that there were seven individual clean animals of each kind suggest that the seventh animal was intended for sacrifice.

*4. Specification (7:2d): **a male and his female**,* lit., "a man and his wife." The language is strange, but necessary for precision. Had this phrase not been used, or had God said only *male and female* (as in 6:19), Noah would have regarded the gender of the seven pairs of clean animals as a matter of indifference. The *seven seven* were to be seven males and seven females. The stipulation anticipates the postdiluvian command to be fruitful and multiply (8:17; 9:1).

## C. Additional Instructions (7:2e-3)

*1. Unclean cattle (7:2e):* **And of the cattle that are not clean two, each male and his mate.** This communication stipulates that the principle of mated pairs also applied to cattle not considered clean, thus removing any potential ambiguity in 6:19. Though unsuitable for some purposes, unclean animals have the same right to life as clean animals. They are part of the goodness of God's creation. This stipulation only aims to divide cattle into two broad categories, viz. the seven pair category, and the single pair category.

*2. Birds (7:3a):* **Also of the birds of the sky, by sevens, each male and his mate.** It is a reasonable assumption that 7:3 is speaking only of clean birds. Birds are included in 6:20 among the pairs that were to come to Noah. So the seven mated pairs probably were clean fowl, i.e., those that were raised by mankind, and that were acceptable for sacrifice.

*3. Explanation (7:3b):* **to keep seed alive on the face of all the earth.** In the English these words mirror the last line of 6:20; but there is a subtle difference. The verb tense in the two vv is different. The former v uses the Hiphil form, stressing the responsibility of Noah in the preservation of the animals. This v uses Piel, indicating the purpose of taking the seven pairs on board. Perpetuation of the species of clean animals must be assured. *To keep seed alive* appears elsewhere only in the account of Lot's daughters (Gn 19:32, 34). There these words justify an act of human degradation; here they explain an act of divine salvation.

**D. Flood Alert** (7:4)

*1. Commencement (7:4a):* **For after seven more days, I will send rain on the earth forty days and forty nights.** Creation week consisted of six days of preparing the earth and positioning its inhabitants. The climax came on the seventh day of rest. So the week of final preparation and positioning of the animals on the ark climaxed on the seventh day with the commencement of uncreation. The impression is given that seven days were required for animal boarding. *After seven days* in English implies *on the eighth day*. Hebrew is not so precise. *After seven days* (lit., "to days yet seven") can mean after the seventh day has begun.

This v functions in three ways. First, it serves to justify the commission made to Noah to enter the ark. Years of anticipation and preparation were now condensed into a frantic week of last minute details and perhaps appeals to the lost. Second, it sets the deadline for the beginning of the Flood. Third, it stipulates for the first time how the Flood will begin, viz. with *forty days and nights* of rain.

*2. Consequences (7:4b):* **And I will blot out from the face of the land every living thing that I have made.** Although 6:13 was ominous, this v reveals to Noah for the first time the full scope of what God had determined to do in 6:7, viz. *blot* or *wipe out* every living thing. This verb (r. *mchh*) is used 33x in the OT, but only in the Flood account (6:7; 7:4; 7:23) with such all-encompassing breadth. Any ambiguity in the earlier conversation with Noah is now removed. *Living thing (hay$^\square$qûm)* occurs elsewhere only in 7:23 and Dt 11:6 (a context of general destruction). The word comes from a root that means to "stand up or arise." The noun refers to living beings, both man and beast, that arise on the earth, as opposed to creatures that inhabit the seas.

In 7:4 God makes three points. First, the Flood is a supernatural event. It does not just happen. The event is described as due entirely to God's action. Whatever resources he employed in bringing the Flood were secondary. Second, God takes full responsibility for the awful results of the Flood. Third, the words *that I have made* references the creation account (Gn 1-2). God is acting with the same directness and power in the Flood as in creation. These words declare God's right to orchestrate the Flood. At the same time they hint at the sorrow he experienced as he brought those devastating waters on the earth. The Creator destroys his own creation.

**E. Noah's Compliance** (7:5-9):

*1. General compliance (7:5):* **And Noah did according to all that Yahweh had commanded him.** The last compliance notice (6:22) referred to the building of the ark, the organizing of animals, and gathering of ark provisions. This compliance notice pertains to the entering of the ark as described in the following vv. The language here duplicates 6:22 except in minor details.

*2. Dating the Flood (7:6):* **Now Noah was six hundred years old. Now as for the Deluge, it came as water upon the earth.** The great Flood is dated according to the years of Noah's life. The 600$^{th}$ year of his life was crucial. This is the first of six specific dates relating to the year of the Flood. Someone—Noah himself or one of his sons—must have kept a record of the crucial events during that year. *Six hundred years old* means after Noah turned six hundred (cf. 7:6). This understanding is in accord with the ancient way of counting time. If

Noah was six hundred, his sons were approximately one hundred at the time (cf. 5:32).

*It came* (*hāyāh*) is lit., "came into being, happened." "Flood of water" or "waters" (KJV; NRSV; NASB), repeated from 6:17, is not exactly an accurate translation. Cf. NIV "floodwaters came." *Waters* is an accusative of specification. The Deluge came either *as* water or *with* water. The NJPS has an excellent rendering: "the Flood came, waters upon the earth."

*3. Entering the ark (7:7):* **Then Noah came, and his sons and his wife and his sons' wives with him unto the ark from the face of the waters of the Deluge.** Did the sailors come unto the ark at the beginning of the seven days mentioned in 7:4 or at the end of that week? Perhaps it took seven days to complete the entry. *From the face* (*mippnê*) suggests causality; it also suggests close proximity to the source of danger and the physical presence thereof. *From the face of the waters of the Deluge* suggests that the waters were already visibly rising when the family came to the ark. At the least the language suggests that the rain was pelting down.

If this interpretation is correct, then one would have to conclude that rains in the region had started even before the forty days of torrential downpour, or that the entering of the ark took place during the forty days. Others think the phrase means the family came to the ark just before the waters came. The phrase is rendered "because of the waters of the flood" (KJV; NASB; NJPS); or "to escape the waters of the flood" (NRSV; NIV). More light is shed on the ambiguous chronology by 7:10.

*4. Selected animals (7:8):* **Of clean animals and animals that are not clean and birds and everything that creeps upon the ground.** The narrator continues to emphasize the exact compliance of Noah. As commanded by God, Noah made the distinction between clean and unclean. For the basis of that distinction, see on 7:2. Along with the clean and unclean beasts the birds, presumably divided along the same lines, and creepers were included. Altogether the creepers are mentioned 16x in the creation and Flood narratives. The language here reproduces exactly that of 1:30.

Clean and unclean animals are mentioned together with no indication of a difference in the number of each as specified in 7:2-3. The general rule (two of every kind) was specified in 6:19. The additional clean animals specified in 7:2-3 constitute an exception to the general rule.

*5. Paired animals (7:9):* **There came into the ark to Noah by pairs, male and female, as Elohim had commanded Noah.** The narrator documents the fulfillment of the promise first made by Yahweh in 6:20 that the animals of both genders would come to Noah at the ark. In 6:19 Noah was to load the animals that came to him on the ark. So there was a divine action (bringing the animals) and a human action (boarding the animals) involved. *Came to Noah* recalls how God brought the garden animals before Adam (2:19).

Noah took a mate for each of the animals. *Pairs* is lit., "two two," the same construction found in 7:2 (*seven seven*). "Two two" has been rendered variously "two and two" (KJV; NRSV), "by two" (NASB), and "two of each" (NJPS). In the light of 6:19 (*two of every kind*), the Hebrew *two two* must be understood to mean *pairs* (cf. NIV). This in turn sheds light on the meaning of 7:2 where consistency argues that the translations should be *by sevens*.

*To Noah into the ark* suggests that Noah was in the ark when the animals came on board. The words could be translated "unto the ark to Noah," but 7:15 points in the former direction.

*As Elohim commanded Noah* is the third appearance of the compliance formula, repeating the language of

6:22. In 7:5 it was Yahweh whose instructions were obeyed. In biblical narrative repetition is a common form of emphasis. Biblical writers use repetition artistically to make their message perfectly clear. The repetition in the Noah narrative is "the result of an author seeking emphasis, not an editor fumbling with divergent tradition."[440] Repetition drives home the truth that Noah's salvation came through his obedience.

## BEGINNING OF THE FLOOD
## Gn 7:10-16

### A. Timing of It (7:10-11a)

*1. In reference to the entrance command (7:10):* **And it came about after the seven days that the waters of the Deluge came upon the earth.** *After the seven days* paraphrases the Hebrew "to (or for) seven days." The reference is to the seven days first mentioned in 7:4. The loading of the animals was now complete. *The waters of the Deluge came upon the earth* explains the ambiguous chronology of 7:6. The waters of the Deluge from which Noah fled did not appear until after the seven days. Therefore, Noah must have entered the ark on the first day of the forty days and nights.

*2. In reference to Noah's life (7:11a):* **In the six hundredth year of Noah's life, in the second month, on the seventeenth day of the month.** The beginning of the Deluge is precisely dated to the month and day of Noah's 600th year. Precise dates normally are associated in the Bible with actions of kings. Their presence in this narrative bears witness to the credibility of the account. They also indicate that this was a supreme moment in the history of man. Precise dating may also hint that Noah was the legitimate ruler of the time.

---

[440]Kikawada and Quinn, ***Before Abraham***, 92.

Attempts to identify the time of year are futile. There is no way of knowing what calendar Noah was using. Some in the ancient world celebrated the new year in the Spring (Mar/Apr), others in the fall (Sep/Oct). It could be that the second month refers to Noah's 600$^{th}$ year, not the second month of the calendar year.

### B. Sources of It (7:11b-12)

The narrator attributes the waters of the Deluge to three factors.

*1. Subterranean waters (7:11b):* **on the same day all the fountains of the great deep burst open.** *On the same day* refers to the day in the 600$^{th}$ year of Noah's life identified in the preceding v. This phrase is used to underscore significant events in biblical history. The verb *burst open* (r. *bq'*) is linked with *the waters* in many OT texts (e.g., Hab 3:9). The *great deep* (*t$^e$hôm*) refers to subterranean waters. Use of the adjective *great* (*rabbāh*) with *deep* elsewhere appears 4x in the OT. These waters were there before God shaped the earth (Gn 1:2); now they return.

Elohim was in the process of reversing creation. Forces beneath the earth's surface contributed to the great mass of water that covered the earth in such a short period of time. Earthquakes have been known to produce rivers of subterranean water. In recent years geologists have located subterranean oceans. Rough calculations suggest that a volume of water equal to that in the oceans on earth's surface may be trapped in the subterranean reservoirs.[441] Whether this is what is intended cannot be said. The Deluge was unique. Trying to produce analogies to what may have transpired are feeble at best.

---

[441] Carl Zimmer, "The Ocean Within," *Discover* (Oct 1994): 20-21.

*2. Floodgates (7:11c):* **and the floodgates of the sky were opened.** The noun and verb are used together several times (e.g., 2 Kgs 7:2). *Floodgates* are lit., "holes." *Floodgates* (windows) *of the sky* (heaven) appear 3x outside the context of the Flood account.[442] The writer employs a poetic expression to refer to the pounding rain, much as moderns talk about it "raining cats and dogs." Waters previously restrained by the expanse (1:7) are released. A virtual sea of water poured down from above.

*3. Forty days (7:12):* **and the rain came upon the earth for forty days and forty nights.** The word used for *rain* (*gešem*) is a different word than the one used in 7:4. The words, however, appear to be synonyms.

### C. Safety within the Ark (7:13-14)

Soon the door of the ark will be sealed (v 16), and all that is within will be lost to the view of the reader for over a year. Before that sealing takes place the narrator provides a glimpse within. The roster of those who will ride out the storm is reviewed as if to stress the importance of every occupant of that vessel.

*1. Eight souls (7:13):* **On the very same day Noah and Shem and Ham and Japheth, the sons of Noah, and Noah's wife and the three wives of his sons with them, entered the ark.** At the top of the list of those in the ark are Noah and his family. The expression *on the very same day* is used 13x in the OT. It marks significant days, especially days on which a divine command was carried out (e.g., Gn 17:23, 26; Ex 12:41). Entering the ark was a momentous day. The expression refers back to *on the same day* in 7:11.

Both the Flood and the entry took place on the same date. *On this day* of condemnation, *on this very same*

---

[442] 2 Kgs 7:2, 19; Mal 3:10.

*day,* Noah's family celebrated salvation by entering the ark. In connection with the Flood the family members previously have been mentioned in general, almost casual terms (6:18; 7:7). Here each son is listed by name. Previously Noah's spouse has been designated only as *your/his wife.* Now she is mentioned by her formal married name: *wife of Noah.* Previously the sons' wives have been mentioned, without any indication of how many women were involved. Here the *three* is added in a form that indicates that they are being considered as an entire group. So each son had his own wife.

2. *Animals (7:14):* **They and every beast after its kind, and all the cattle after their kind, and every creeping thing that creeps on the earth after its kind, and every bird after its kind, all sorts of birds.** Representatives of the animal kingdom were safe within the ark when the Flood broke loose. *They and every beast* means, not only Noah's household, but every beast. The v does not imply that the animals entered the ark on the same day as Noah's family. They entered the ark over the course of the week; Noah and his family entered on the seventh day. The point is that when the Flood began they were all together on the ark.

A fourth category—*beast* (*chayyāh*)—is mentioned for the first time among the animals safely residing on the ark. This term, without further definition, has not appeared since the creation account (1:24). It refers to the larger wild animals. *All sorts of birds* is lit., "every bird of every wing." Some imagine that the language includes insects as well as birds. In Hebrew, however, "bird of wing" always refers to birds proper. So regarding birds, there are two expressions (*every bird*), the second (*every bird of every wing*) clarifying the first.

For those in Noah's world that special day began like any other. Jesus indicated that the people were carrying on business as usual when the Flood waters carried them all away (Mt 24:37-39).

**D. Sealing of the Ark** (7:15-16)

*1. Grand entrance (7:15):* ***So they went into the ark to Noah by pairs of all flesh in which was the breath of life.*** The narrator must have anticipated that his account of the animals on the ark would be a major stumbling block to his credibility. So by way of further explanation he stresses three points. First, the animals came of their own volition, so the entrance was orderly. Second, a relatively small number of animals came, for they came by pairs. Third, the pairs that came were literally representatives of all living creatures. *They went into the ark to Noah by pairs* repeats the wording of 7:9 except that *by pairs* appears at the end, rather than beginning of the clause. Clearly the words here refer to entering into the ark. This sheds light on the ambiguity of 7:9. *Breath of life* is repeated from 6:17.

*2. Noah's obedience (7:16a):* ***and those entering were male and female of all flesh. They entered as Elohim had commanded him.*** The animals that entered the ark were not just animal pairs, but mated pairs. This was necessary to fulfill God's long-range intention for the world. The emphasis for the fourth time is on the compliance Noah. The command concerning the animals was issued to one person, viz. Noah. Obviously Noah had something to do with orchestrating the grand entrance into the ark, but his precise role is not clarified.

Those who claim that such a vast throng of animals could not have entered into the ark in one day are quibbling. First, in emergency situations, and obviously impelled by the power of God, who can say how long it would have taken? Second, there is no statement in the text that the process of loading the ark took only a day.

The statement v 16 can be read to mean that this was the day on which the grand entrance into the ark concluded.

3. *Door closed (7:16b):* **And Yahweh closed (it) behind him.** The verb *closed* (r. *sgr*) was previously used in reference to the closing of Adam's flesh after the removal of the rib (2:21). The direct object *door* is implied. *Behind him* (*ba"dô*) following verbs of shutting means "to shut doors behind or upon." In this case Yahweh shut the door of the ark *behind* or *upon* Noah from the outside, i.e., shut him in. Since this was an act of special mercy and direct involvement with mankind, the name *Yahweh* is used rather than *Elohim*.

While sealing those who were being saved inside the ark, Yahweh was also barring entrance to anyone else who might try to enter. No genuine salvation can exist without discrimination between saved and lost.

## POWER OF THE FLOOD
## Gn 7:17-24

The description of the actual Flood is sober, simple, scientific and unadorned with graphic details that might prove emotionally heart-wrenching. At the same time the description is artistically presented in carefully crafted sentences. The expressions *flood/waters* appear 7x in this paragraph as does the ominous expression *upon/over* (*'al*) *the earth*. Clearly the narrator aimed to paint a picture of the dominion of the waters.

### A. Waters Rising (7:17-20)

The narrator describes four stages in the rise of the Flood waters.

*1. Ark floats (7:17):* **Then the Deluge came upon the earth for forty days; and the water increased and lifted up the ark, so that it rose from upon the earth.** The duration of the Deluge of rain already has been noted in 7:12. Here this fact is reiterated as an explanation of how the massive ark with its heavy cargo was lifted off the ground. Forty days was the time required for the water to reach its maximum height.

2. *Ark moved (7:18):* **And the water prevailed and increased greatly over the earth; and the ark floated on the surface of the water.** Not only was the ark lifted by the water off the ground, it floated on the water away from its original position. The verb *prevailed* (r. *gbr*) is used 4x in this ch. This word comes from the context of battle. The roaring waves attacked creation and destroyed what God had made, like a mighty warrior vanquishes his opponent. *Prevailed* in the context of water is defined by the phrase *increased greatly*.

3. *Mountains submerged (7:19):* **And the water prevailed more and more over the earth, so that all the high mountains everywhere under the heavens were covered.** The previous two vv have depicted the power of the Flood in terms of the floating of the ark. Now the narrator depicts the strength of the Flood in terms of the mountains. The Flood conquered the heights of earth. *More and more* is lit., "greatly, greatly," thus doubling the intensity of the previous v. *All/every* (*kol*) translated various ways appears 9x in this ch. The devastation was all-encompassing.

4. *Fifteen cubits (7:20):* **As for the waters, they prevailed fifteen cubits higher, and the mountains were covered.** As battle casualty reports reveal the extent of a military victory, so a concrete depth figure reveals the extent of the Flood's victory over creation. Fifteen cubits (over 22 feet) was sufficient depth to prevent the ark from smashing into one of the mountains.[443] If the mountains were covered to this extent, then all lower terrain of necessity must have been covered as well. The

---

[443]The ark was thirty cubits in height. Even if only half of its height floated above the water, the ark would have cleared the tallest mountain.

earth as formed and filled by God in Gn 1 ceased to exist.

## B. Flood Mechanics

Speculation abounds regarding what mechanisms God might have used to produce the world-wide catastrophe. Donald Patten[444] suggests that the Flood was produced by a near-pass of some heavenly body that interacted with earth over the course of a year. He speculates that the gravitational pull of this heavenly body produced tidal waves on the earth's water, with perhaps tides of 5,000 to 10,000 feet. Patten believes that tidal activity explains the manner of flotation of the ark, the direction of flotation, and daily increase of the waters.

In a quarry in England a hundred foot log lies at a forty degree angle piercing through strata after strata each (supposedly) laid down millions of years apart. Patten alleges that tidal activity would explain this. Enormous tides would fossilize animals and petrify forests in a matter of hours.

According to Patten the gravitational pull of the heavenly body would also cause tidal pulls beneath the earth's crust in the fluid magma. This created enormous pressures of mega tons per square inch, leading to mountain uplift.[445]

## C. Waters Destroying (7:21-22)

While Scripture does not discuss the mechanics of the Flood in any detail, it does portray the devastating result of the Deluge. The language of 6:17 is repeated in these vv to stress that God fulfilled his threats concerning his creation.

---

[444]Donald Patten, "Noachian Flood and Mountain Uplifts," in *Symposium on Creation*, ed. Henry Morris (Grand Rapids: Baker, 1968), 93-118.
[445]Donald Patten, "The Biblical Flood: A Geographical Perspective," *BSac* (Jan 1971): 36-49.

*1. General statement (7:21a):* **And all flesh that moved on the earth perished.** *Flesh* (*bāsār*) refers to all forms of living things that are perishable. *Moved* is the root *rms* which generally heretofore has been rendered "to creep." Here the root must have the broader connotation of 1:21. *Perished* (r. *gv'*) indicates precise fulfillment of the warning of 6:17.

*2. Emphasis by enumeration (7:21b):* **birds and cattle and beasts and every swarming thing that swarms upon the earth and all mankind.** Each category is introduced in the Hebrew by the preposition *Beth*. The idea is that all flesh within the category of birds, etc. perished. The list covers all animals that God created, except water creatures. The list of animals given at this point is different from the lists in 6:7 and 7:14. This list reflects the order of creation.

The winged creatures that normally soar above the earth could not escape the disaster. *Cattle*, cherished by man and protected from the elements were wiped out as well. Wild *beasts* (*chayyāh*), in places remote from man, drowned in bush or cave or tree. *Every swarming thing* was used in 1:20 to describe water creatures. Here the phrase may describe a new category of land creatures not heretofore mentioned; on the other hand the swarmers may be the countless kinds of land creatures that are not specifically included in the other categories.

The climax of the list of Flood victims is *man* (*hā'ādām*). The categories of animals were introduced by the preposition *Beth*. No preposition is used with *man*. There are no subdivisions or species within the category of man.

*3. Emphasis by description (7:22):* **All that had the breath of the spirit of life in its nostrils from all that was on the dry land died.** The language here is not the same as in 2:7 where *Yahweh Elohim* breathed into man's nostrils *the breath of life* (*nišmat chayyîm*). Here the language is broader. It refers to the breath by which God's Holy Spirit animated living creatures, both man and beast. The phrase beginning with *from all* limits the previous all-inclusive designation to land animals. Double use of the word *all* in this v is another device used to stress the dimensions of the Flood. The use of *perished* in 7:21 pointed to the moment of death; *died* (r. *mût*) indicates the condition that follows the moment of expiring.

### D. Waters Cleansing (7:23)

Previous vv have described the physical result of the Flood. This v portrays the twofold purpose of the Flood as punishing and purging.

*1. Punishment (7:23a):* **Thus he blotted out every living thing that was upon the face of the land, from man to cattle to creeping things and to birds of the sky, and they were blotted out from the earth.** A Hebrew verb without a stated subject can be rendered as a passive in English. That is the course followed by KJV; NIV; and NJPS. It is better, however, to follow NASB and NRSV and render the verb active, *he blotted out*. Thus the great initiator of the Flood suddenly is introduced, howbeit without specific name at this point.

The verb *blotted out* (r. *mchh*) has previously been used in 6:7 and 7:4. In 6:7 Yahweh resolved to blot out living things. In 7:4 he revealed his intention to do so. Now the narrator affirms that Yahweh has executed his resolve. In this v the verb *blotted out* appears first in its active form, then in its passive form. This construction is common in the Hebrew Bible.[446] *Every living thing* mirrors the threat God made in 7:4.

Because this v views the Flood from its moral purpose, man is given first place on the list of the creatures

---

[446]E.g., Jer 17:14; 21:4; Ps 19:12-13; 69:14.

affected. On the list in 7:21 birds came first, man last. Here their positions are reversed. The thrust of this v is that God brought the Flood as an act of judgment against mankind. The other creatures were affected because they share the dry land with man.

2. *Purging (7:23b):* **and only Noah was left, together with those that were with him in the ark.** The earth was cleansed by the waters of the Flood. Evil was blotted out. A new start for mankind was now possible.

### E. Water Prevailing (7:24)

***And the water prevailed over the earth 150 days.*** For the fourth time in this ch the verb *prevailed* (r. *gbr*) is used. The term *greatly* ($m^e\,'\bar{o}d$) is not used here as in 7:18-19, indicating that the reference is not to the maximum depths of the water. Still the waters were deep enough to cover the earth and thus be said to have *prevailed.* "Flooded" (NIV) is unneeded and potentially misleading. It might imply that the waters kept increasing for 150 days. The facts seem to be these: The waters rose for forty days. Storms continued for the next 110 days, but with less intensity. These would serve to keep the water at its height. Then the waters began to recede.

Comparison with 8:4 indicates that the 150 days did not follow the forty days. The forty days are included within the 150 days of prevailing.

# CONCLUSION

The Flood marked the end of God's patience with the progression of sin. It constituted a gigantic cleansing operation, a kind of "de-creation."

# 20
# EXTENT OF THE FLOOD

Discussion of the extent of the Flood must begin with a definition of "universal" Flood. Those who take the Bible seriously generally believe that the Flood was anthropologically universal, i.e., it wiped out all mankind, except the eight on the ark. Whether the Flood was geographically universal is another question. Believing scholars take opposite positions on the geographical extent of the Flood.[447]

## UNIVERSAL FLOOD VIEW

### A. Abundant Use of *kōl*

In the space of four chs—eighty-five vv—the Hebrew term *kōl* (*all*) is used 72x, an average of 18x per ch. This compares to the rest of Gn where *kōl* is used on average of 5.8x per ch. This concentration of the use of *kōl* in the Flood narrative by itself does not define the extent of the disaster. It does appear, however, that Moses is going out of his way to stress universality of the Deluge.[448]

### B. Flood Purpose

God sent the Flood to destroy corrupt mankind (6:5, 11-12). Therefore every single man, except Noah and his family, must have been destroyed, else the Flood failed to accomplish its stated purpose. It is highly unlikely that the population of the earth at that time

---

[447] For detailed arguments pro and con with respect to the universality of the flood, see S.A. Austin and D.C. Boardman, *The Genesis Debate*, ed. R. Youngblood (Grand Rapids: Baker, 1991), 210-29.

[448] Mike Kruger, "Genesis 6-9: Does 'All' Always Mean All?, *CEN TJ* 10(1996): 214-218.

could have been confined to the small region of Mesopotamia. Even the most conservative estimates of population growth show such a population concentration to be impossible. It is ironic that advocates of a local or regional Flood tend to accept dates of 50,000 years and higher for the creation of Adam. Such a view requires that by the time of the Flood humankind had spread far beyond the Mesopotamian Valley.

How large was the human population at the time of the Flood at least 1656 years after creation? Whitcomb and Morris calculate the population of the world at over a billion at the time of the Flood.[449] Wright calculated that a single couple could increase to a million in 500 years, and 500 thousand million (200 times the present world population) in 1,000 years if there were no wars, famines etc.[450] The Catholic conservative O'Connell (who dates the Flood to about 7000 BC) thinks man had reached all parts of Europe that were free of ice—all parts of Africa, and Asia west of the Himalayan mountains. He doubts that man had yet reached the western Hemisphere, India, China or Australia.[451]

Limited Flood advocates respond to the population growth argument in two ways. First, some simply deny that the Flood was anthropologically universal. They think the text is speaking from Noah's perspective. It refers to all the sinful people who lived in the region of the ancient Near East with which Noah was familiar. Second, they argue that the population had not spread far out of the Near East. So if the Flood is dated early enough, then even a large regional flood would have wiped out all human population. In any case the Flood would only need to reach the regions to which man had

---

[449] Whitcomb and Morris, *Genesis Flood*, 26.
[450] G.F. Wright, *The Origin and Antiquity of Man*, (Oberlin, OH: Bibliotheca Sacra, 1912), 483.
[451] O'Connell, *Science*, 2:69-72.

migrated to serve the purpose of wiping out sinful mankind.

Some think that *all flesh* in 6:12 includes animals. Animals, as well as men, were corrupt as a result of the Fall. They grew more violent. So God destroyed all animals (except those on the ark) in the Flood. If this were the case, then certainly there would be no reason to think that only the animals in the Mesopotamian Valley were corrupt, or that animals had not spread beyond the Mesopotamian Valley at the time of the Flood. How is it possible to argue that *all flesh perished* (7:21) means that all men perished, but not all animals?

### C. Statements Regarding the Waters

Statements in the text regarding the depth of the Flood are thought to be strong evidence that the Flood was geographically universal. *All the high mountains everywhere under the heavens were covered. As for the waters, they prevailed fifteen cubits higher, and the mountains were covered* (7:19-20).

In response those who hold to a limited Flood point out that universal language is often best interpreted phenomenally or optically—that is, from the limited standpoint of the eyewitness who writes the account. This allows the *high mountains* to be those known in the experience of Noah, i.e., those that could be seen by him in the Mesopotamian region. *Earth* in the narrative may mean *land.* Universal language is also often the language of hyperbole, the language of deliberate exaggeration for literary effect. Cf. Col 1:23; Gn 41:57; Joel 3:2.

The duration of the Flood argues for world-wide catastrophe. Noah was on the ark a total of 370 days. A local or regional Flood would not have impacted the land so the survivors could not leave the vessel for so many months. Limited Flood advocates, however, argue that had the Flood risen to heights of thousands of feet it would have required far longer than a year to subside.

The geology of the Flood—*the fountains of the deep; the floodgates of heaven* (7:11; 8:2)—is put forward as evidence of the worldwide scope of the Flood. Limited Flood advocates, however, point out that the text does not indicate the duration of the geological phenomena described in these vv.

### D. Statements Regarding the Ark

Two considerations concerning the ark are thought to argue in favor of a geographically universal Flood.

*1. Size of the ark.* Why would such a huge vessel be necessary to protect a few animals from a narrow region of the planet? The very size of the vessel argues in favor of a large variety of animals on board, animals from various regions and distant places.

The limited Flood advocates, however, point out that scholars cannot be sure that the size of the cubit in Noah's day was the same as in later OT history. A shorter cubit would make for a much smaller vessel. A smaller vessel would have been more easily serviced by eight people.

*2. Need for an ark.* If the impending Flood were local, Noah and his family (and whatever animals were threatened with extinction) would have had plenty of time to move to a safe place out of reach of the floodwaters. This may be the strongest argument supporting a geographically universal Flood.

The response of the limited Flood advocates is threefold, but painfully weak. First, the ark was part of Noah's witness. It served as a graphic warning to the wicked that they could choose either to heed or to ignore. Second, a migration by Noah and his family would not have had nearly the same powerful effect. Others might have joined in the migration (as in the Exodus).

Third, the ark was the best way to make absolutely certain that only Noah and his family survived.

### E. Postdiluvian Words

The commission to postdiluvian man to *be fruitful and multiply and fill the earth* (9:1) must be interpreted as broadly as the same words in Gn 1:28. The same is true of the dominion of man over *every beast of the earth* (9:2; cf. 1:28). If *the earth* in Gn 9:1 refers to the entire planet, why would *earth* in 8:13 refer only to the Mesopotamian region?

In Gn 9:9-10 God declares his covenant to Noah, his descendants, and all the animals that came off the ark. Can any conceive of an interpretation that says that this covenant was with the descendants of a local Mesopotamian Flood hero and his small stock of animals, but not with the millions of humans and animals that may have descended from those outside the Flood area? God's covenant was with the whole planet! If that is the case, does that not require that *the earth* in the preceding Flood description must refer to the entire planet?

If context defines the scope of *the earth* in the Flood chs, how could Moses have made his intentions any clearer?

### F. New Testament Allusions

Another argument for universality is that the inspired writers of the NT allude to the Flood in ways that suggest its geographically universal scope.

The Book of Hebrews affirms:

> By faith Noah, when warned about things not yet seen, in holy fear built an ark to save his family. By his faith he condemned the world and became heir of the righteousness that comes by faith (Heb 11:7 NIV).

In this v *the world* clearly refers to the world of mankind in Noah's day. The writer believed that the Flood was anthropologically universal.

In both of his epistles Peter referred to the Gn Flood account. Concerning the generation of Noah, he wrote:

> ...who disobeyed long ago when God waited patiently in the days of Noah while the ark was being built. In it only a few people, eight in all, were saved through water, 21 and this water symbolizes baptism that now saves you also—not the removal of dirt from the body but the pledge of a good conscience toward God (1 Pet 3:20-21 NIV).

This passage establishes that Noah was real, the ark was real, the waiting was real, and the salvation of eight people was real. That *only a few* were saved suggests that the rest of mankind perished. Clearly the Flood was anthropologically universal.

Perhaps the most powerful NT statement bearing on the issue of the Flood's extent is found in Peter's second epistle:

> First of all, you must understand that in the last days scoffers will come, scoffing and following their own evil desires. 4 They will say, "Where is this 'coming' he promised? Ever since our fathers died, everything goes on as it has since the beginning of creation." 5 But they deliberately forget that long ago by God's word the heavens existed and the earth was formed out of water and by water. 6 By these waters also the world of that time was deluged and destroyed. 7 By the same word the present heavens and earth are reserved for fire, being kept for the day of judgment and destruction of ungodly men (2 Pet 3:3-7 NIV).

Since creation (the subject of v 5) was universal, and since the coming judgment (the subject of v 7) will be universal, the Flood (the subject of v 6) must also be universal. If this were not so the comparison would break down. Limited Flood advocates respond: the language of v 6 could simply be taken to mean *the world of mankind*. In fact the language of v 6 seems to differentiate the *world* that was flooded from the earth and heavens of vv 5 and 7.

Jesus alluded to the Flood of Noah's day in language that suggests universality:

> For in the days before the flood, people were eating and drinking, marrying and giving in marriage, up to the day Noah entered the ark; and they knew nothing about what would happen until the flood came and took them all away. That is how it will be at the coming of the Son of Man (Mt 24:38-39 NIV).

The following facts are clearly inferred from Jesus' teaching. First, Noah was a real person. Second, Noah entered the ark. Third, the Flood came and destroyed the people who were routinely going about their business. Fourth, Jesus used the Flood as an illustration of the lack of preparation of most at the time of his coming in judgment.

Beyond these four facts the words of Jesus cannot be pressed. If it is argued that in Mt 24 Jesus spoke of the Flood in the context of universal judgment, it can be argued that in Lk 17:26-30 he spoke of it in the same breath as the local judgment on Sodom. Thus Jesus cannot be made to support either position regarding the extent of the Flood.

## G. Universal Flood Traditions

Some cite the existence of Flood traditions throughout the world as proof that the Flood must have been an event of world-wide significance. There are about 150 such accounts. If Noah's Flood were local, why would flood stories of all sorts be so widespread?[452] One extreme example of a Far Eastern Flood tradition is re-

---

[452] Nelson, *Deluge Story*, 169.

ported by C.H. Kang.[453] It is alleged that the Gn Flood story is told within the pictographic characters of the Chinese language.

Limited Flood advocates point out that some of these stories are simply local adaptations of the biblical story. Others bear little resemblance to the biblical account. In all these stories it is a local group that survived the flood. Would not this contradict the biblical account that only one family survived? Therefore, one would have to conclude that these stories are either fiction, or based on local floods in the areas of their origin, or are corruptions of the biblical story.

If the world-wide Flood traditions do reflect the biblical event a nucleus of truth may have been brought to the far corners of the earth by descendants of Noah. The widespread distribution of Flood accounts, therefore, says nothing about whether the Flood was universal or local.

## UNIVERSAL FLOOD PROBLEMS

Ramm[454] has identified several scientific problems attending the view that the Flood was geographically universal. These problems fall into five categories.

### A. Geological Problems

Christian geologists insist that although there is evidence for extensive local flooding in ancient times, no geological evidence whatever exists in the crust of the earth to prove the universal-flood theory. Countless layers in the earth, however, have been discovered. In some of these layers remains of ancient animals and plants (fossils) have been found. Can these layers be explained

---

[453]C.H. Kang, *Genesis and the Chinese* (1950); and C.H. Kang and Ethel Nelson, *The Discovery of Genesis* (Concordia, 1979).
[454]Ramm, *CVSS*, 163-67.

only by an endless slow process of change and evolvement, or can they also be explained, at least in part, by sudden catastrophes of exceptional power?

Formation of fossils actually requires a change of conditions by which animal and plant life are suddenly cut off from the atmosphere by a layer of some kind. Sea creatures, that normally live at great depths, are found in the same layer with creatures that lived in the shallow waters near the coast. At some sites fossils of numerous species are heaped together in great numbers. This argues for a great catastrophe in the history of the earth. There are fossils indicating that certain groups of animals were wiped out suddenly and with great violence.

## B. Archaeological Problems

While Flood levels have been found in several cities in the region of Mesopotamian, generally these levels are not dated by archaeologists to the same time. Some of these cities, according to Mesopotamian tradition, existed before the Flood. The evidence, however, shows that one city was thriving at the same time that a nearby city was destroyed by water. So there is no evidence of a universal Flood. The problem with this argument, however, is that the archaeological evidence also has been read to indicate simultaneous inundation of Mesopotamia.

## C. Hydrological Problems

*1. Amount of water.* Ramm contends that to cover literally the highest mountains on earth requires eight times more water than the world now contains. Furthermore, waters flooded the earth for 150 days (7:24). If the Flood waters covered the whole earth they rose at least a hundred feet per day during those five months. Such swiftly rising waters would have generated powerful currents that would have smashed the ark to smithereens against a cliff wall or mountainside.[455]

All of this assumes that the mountains at the time of the Flood were equivalent in height to the mountains on earth today. Geological evidence points to relatively recent elevation of some of earth's highest mountain ranges. Given the uncertainty about earth's terrain in Noah's day, how can any person claim there is not enough water in ocean, sky and below earth to fulfill the terms of the biblical description? Water covers 71% of the earth's surface already. The Pacific Ocean averages three miles in depth, the Atlantic averages two. One fifth of dry land is flat desert area easily inundated by rising water. The total cubical contents of the land above sea level is only $1/36^{th}$ that of the waters that are below that level. If the ocean today were to rise three thousand feet, three fourths of the present land area would be under water. Obviously when the highest elevations were much lower it would have taken considerably less.[456]

Those who are looking for additional water sources speculate that a large mass of ice drifted into the earth's atmosphere from outer space and poured out an enormous volume of water upon the earth in a short space of time. Whatever the explanation for the amount of water required, scientific theories, discoveries and speculation should never become a basis for faith.

*2. Other water problems.* The mixing of fresh and salt water would have caused irreparable damage to nearly all forms of marine and freshwater life. A Flood so deep as to cover the highest mountains would have created such pressure that all forms of life at the bottom of the sea would have been snuffed out. A Flood so deep

---

[455] Youngblood, *BGIC*, 109.
[456] For documentation of these points see William Springstead, "The Dying of the Giants," *JASA* (Sept 1970): 91-97.

that it covered earth's highest mountains would have had no place to recede. Where did all the water go?

### D. Zoological Problems

*1. Distance.* A world-wide Deluge would have required some animals to travel enormous distances to reach the ark. How did tens of thousands of species from all over the world get to the ark from their distant habitats? How did large land animals from other continents cross the oceans?

*2. Number.* It is alleged that there are so many species of animals on the earth that even a boat the size of the ark could not house representatives of them all. This problem, however, is not difficult to answer. There are about a million species of animals, 95% of which could have lived outside the ark. It has been estimated that there are about 50,000 species which might need protection within the ark. These average the size of a sheep. They could have been housed on one floor of the ark with food storage on the other two decks. It has been estimated that a modern freight train hauling 150 boxcars could easily handle these animals. But the ark had a carrying capacity of more than 520 stock cars.[457]

*3. Maintenance.* Once in the ark, how could only eight people feed and care for all the animals? How would they provide their varied diets and environments? Hibernation—where normal functions are suspended or greatly retarded for long periods of time—may have eased the maintenance problems. If that were the case, however, why does 6:21 speak about taking every kind of food on to the ark? Youngblood retorts: "It would seem that the animals on the ark were to masticate rather than hibernate."[458]

---

[457] Whitcomb and Morris, *Genesis Flood*, 67-69.
[458] Youngblood, *BGIC*, 111.

*4. Dinosaurs.* Were dinosaurs on the ark? They may have become extinct before the Flood. Some evidence exists, however, that dinosaurs were contemporary with mankind. Cave paintings seem to depict dinosaurs. There are dinosaur footprints in the same rock strata as human prints near Glen Rose, Texas. Noah may have taken baby dinosaurs on the ark, or even dinosaur eggs.

A careful reading of 6:19-20 suggests that Noah was to bring on the ark two of every kind that came to him. He was under no obligation to take aboard any animals that God did not cause to come to him. Several species of animals may have been obliterated in the Flood.

*5. Animal fossils.* If animals of the world came to Noah, then one would expect to find some fossil evidence that these animals once passed through Asia. Kangaroos are an example. The only place where there are either fossil or living kangaroos is in Australia. If the fossil evidence means that there never have been kangaroos in Asia, then kangaroos were not in the ark or if they were, they hurried from Australia to meet Noah, and as rapidly returned to their native land. Limited Flood advocates ask, Is it not easier to believe that kangaroos were never in the ark, and hence were in an area untouched by the Flood. This means that the Flood occurred only in the area inhabited by man.[459]

In response to the fossil argument these points can be made. First, fossils are only formed under unusual conditions; apart from these conditions, all dead animals rapidly decompose and disappear. Second, there is no fossil evidence of lions in Palestine, but they are mentioned frequently in the OT. Buffalos by the millions roamed the western plains less than two centuries ago. Yet those animals have left scarcely a trace. "The flesh

---

[459] Russell L. Mixter, *Creation and Evolution* (Wheaton, IL: American Scientific Affiliation, 1950), 15.

was devoured by wolves and vultures within hours or days after death, and even the skeletons have now largely disappeared, the bones dissolving and crumbling into dust under the attack of the weather."[460]

*6. Postdiluvian distribution.* If all animals worldwide were wiped out by the Flood, how does one account for the redistribution of the species to their various natural habitats after the Flood? Two proposals have been made. First, some animals may have traveled quickly to distant lands on floating debris. Two citations from authorities who are not defenders of the biblical account establish the potential of floating debris.

> In times of flood, large masses of earth and entwining vegetation, including trees, may be torn loose from banks of rivers, and swept out to sea. Sometimes such masses are encountered floating in the ocean out of sight of land, still lush and green, with palms twenty to thirty feet tall. It is entirely probable that land animals may be transported long distances in this manner. Many tropical ocean currents have a speed of at least two knots; this would amount to fifty miles in a day, 1000 miles in three weeks.[461]

> It seems certain that land animals do at times cross considerable bodies of water where land connections are utterly lacking. . . . floating masses of vegetation, such as are sometimes found off the mouths of the Amazon, may be one means of effecting this type of migration.[462]

Second, land bridges may account for the postdiluvian redistribution of animals. Marsh writes:

> One glance at a world map will show that, with the exception of the narrow break at the Bering Strait, a dry land path leads

---

[460] Carl Dunbar, *Historical Geology* (New York: Wiley, 1949), 39. Cited by Whitcomb and Morris, *Genesis Flood*, 83.
[461] P.A. Moody, *Introduction to Evolution*, 262.
[462] Alfred S. Romer, Harvard University, *Vertebrate Paleontology* (2nd ed.; Chicago: University Press, 1955), 513. Cited by Whitcomb and Morris, *Genesis Flood*, 85, n 2.

Biblical Protology

from Armenia to all lands of the globe except Australia. In the case of the latter (Australia) the East Indies even today form a fairly continuous bridge of stepping-stones to that southern continent. As regards the Bering Strait, there is no doubt that a land connection once existed between Asia and North America.[463]

### E. Anthropological Problem

The primary anthropological problem relating to the universality of the Flood is this: no Mongoloid or Negroid peoples are named in Gn 10 as descendants of Shem, Ham and Japheth. This is taken by some to indicate that these people were not descendants of Noah's sons. Therefore, the peoples of southern Africa and the Near East must have been unaffected by the Flood.

# LIMITED FLOOD VIEW

For the limited Flood advocates the issue is not a matter of what God can do, but what he did do; not a question of inspiration, but of interpretation.

The limited Flood theory is based on two assumptions. First, the theory assumes that members of the human race had not reached all principal countries of the world before the Deluge. Second, advocates further assume that the total submergence of even one continent is impossible.

The limited Flood approach exists in several variations. Some, like Ramm, argue that the Flood did not destroy all mankind, only those in the area of Mesopotamia. LaSor and Sutcliffe see the Flood as a judgment only on the Sethites. Others hold that all mankind was destroyed, but man had not yet spread beyond the Mesopotamian valley (H. Miller). Some include all animals in the destruction, but argue that only a small por-

---

[463]Frank L. Marsh, *Evolution, Creation, and Science* (Washington: Review and Herald, 1947), 291-92.

tion of the earth was occupied by "living creatures" at the time. G.F. Wright links the Flood with the ice age. Humans that had spread into Europe were driven back into the Mesopotamian Valley by the Ice Age. Still others envision a Flood that overwhelmed Mesopotamia and regions further to the south in Arabia and Africa (O'Connell).

The universal mode of expression, not uncommon in Scripture, indicates only that the then-known world and the then-populated parts of the earth were covered by the Flood. Similar expressions are found in Joshua 4:24; 1 Kgs 4:34; Jer 34:1; Dan 2:39; Rom 10:18. It is in keeping with the usage of Scripture to limit the extent of the Deluge to the then known world. There is no need to assume that the waters of the Flood were fifteen feet above Mount Everest.

## DATE OF THE FLOOD

To some extent the issue of the geographical extent of the Flood and the date of the Flood are related. The earlier the date, the less territory was occupied by mankind.

### A. Biblical Data

A few have attempted to date the Flood by using the genealogy in Gn 11. If that genealogy is consecutive (no gaps), Abram was called by God 425 years after the Flood. By other biblical data the call of Abram can be date to about 2092 BC. This means the Flood occurred about 2517 BC.

There are problems with a massive Flood at about 2517 BC. The Abraham narratives give the impression that Ur of Chaldees was a highly developed civilization, as was Canaan, and Egypt. Could all this have happened in only four centuries?

## B. O'Connell's Dating

Patrick O'Connell points to a number of interesting coincidences at the end of the Ice Age—the so-called Late Pleistocene period—ca. 7000 BC. First, there were massive extinctions of large animals world-wide. "A sudden wave of large animal extinction, involving at least 200 genera, most of them lost without phyletic replacement, characterized the late Pleistocene."[464] "About 95% of the North American mega fauna became extinct during a short period some 8,000 years ago."[465] The same was true of Europe. "All these extinctions coincided with the presence of man."[466]

Second, O'Connell calls attention to the migratory instincts of animals. "Migratory behavior is instinctive. The origin of migration is little understood, although the habit may have evolved at the time of the retreat of the last ice age."[467]

Third, land bridges appeared throughout the world.[468]

Fourth, geologists point to the Pleistocene period as the time when mountain building took place upon this planet. "Mountain uplifts amounting to many, many thousands of feet have occurred within the Pleistocene epoch itself."[469]

O'Connell summarizes his conclusions in this paragraph:

---

[464] Paul S. Martin and H. E. Wright, *Pleistocene Extinctions* (New Haven: Yale, 1967), 75.
[465] *Ibid.*, 105. Citations of Martin and Wright by W. Springstead, "The Dying of the Giants," *JASA* (Sept 1970): 91.
[466] N.J. Berrill, *Inherit the Earth* (New York: Dodd and Mead, 1966), 40. Citation by Springstead, loc cit.
[467] J.L. Cloudsley-Thompson, *Animal Behavior*, (New York: Macmillan, 1961), 106. Citation by Springstead, op. cit., 92.
[468] For documentation, see Springstead, op. cit., 92-93.
[469] Richard Flint, *Glacial Geology and the Pleistocene Epoch* (New York: Wiley, 1947), 4. Citation by Springstead, op. cit., 91.

...there is sufficient evidence to show that (a) the end of the Last Glacial Period, (b) the *hiatus* at the end of the Mousterian Period, (c) the destruction of the ancient settlements of Jericho in Palestine, of Ur, Kish, Tepe Gawra etc., of Mesopotamia, and the early settlements of Iran, and (d) the Deluge, all occurred at the same time, which was about 7,000 B.C.; and that this date can be a landmark scientifically established from which to begin the calculation of the length of the period from the deluge to the creation of Adam and Eve.[470]

Since O'Connell wrote, additional evidence has been published suggesting that the Flood transpired in the time span of 7000 to 5000 BC. Ryan and Pittman found evidence that when the European glaciers melted about seven thousand years ago the Mediterranean Sea overflowed into what was then a smaller freshwater lake to create the Black Sea.[471] In 2000 Robert Ballard, underwater explorer, found evidence of human habitation beneath three hundred feet of water about twelve miles off the coast of Turkey.[472] Apparently before the great Flood there were villages located near the shore of what became the Black Sea. Sub-specialists in the field of archeology have concluded that a global wet phase began around 7500 BC. This phase, though probably interrupted by some dryer periods, was predominantly wet until at least 3500 BC. There were lakes, rivers and grasslands in what today is called the Empty Quarter, the largest sand desert in the world until about 3500 BC when the dryer pattern observed today began.[473]

---

[470]P. O'Connell, *STPG*, 2:133.
[471]W. Ryan and W. Pittman, *Noah's Flood* (New York: Simon & Schuster, 1997).
[472]Robert Ballard, *The Quest for Noah's Flood* (Washington, D.C.: National Geographic Video, 2001).
[473]James Sauer, "The River Runs Dry," *BAR* 22(Jul/Aug 1998): 57, 64.

## C. Other Dating

William Hallo, curator of the Yale Babylonian Collection has gone on record regarding the Mesopotamian Flood traditions. He believes that recent discoveries "make it seem possible that a specific historic flood provided the original inspiration for the Mesopotamian version of the deluge, and that this particular flood occurred about 2900 B.C." He sees a linguistic connection between two of the five antediluvian cities mentioned in Sumerian literature and two persons named in the Bible as having lived before the Flood. The antediluvian city Eridu corresponds to Irad (Gn 4:17) and the antediluvian city of Larak can be compared to Lamech (Gn 4:18).[474]

# CONCLUSION

The purpose of this ch has been to survey the positions that have been taken with respect to the extent of the biblical Flood. While there are still some issues to be resolved by further research, the preponderance of the evidence favors a geographically universal Flood at about 7000 BC. This is not an issue, however, upon which Bible believers necessarily must walk in lockstep.

---

[474]William Hallo, "Antediluvian Cities," *Journal of Cuneiform Studies* 23(Oct, 1970). Similar conclusions can be found in M.E.L. Mallowan, "Noah's Flood Reconsidered," *Iraq* 26(1964): 62-82; R.I. Raikes, *Iraq* 28(1966): 52-63; S. Kramer, *Expedition* 9(1967): 12-18.

# 21
# RE-CREATION AFTER JUDGMENT
# Gn 8:1-22

The theme of chs 8-9 is "Re-creation" after the Flood. These chs were structured with Gn 1 in mind. Comparison of the terminology used during the six creative days in Gn 1 and the terminology used to describe the earth emerging from the Flood waters indicates clearly that the writer viewed the Postdiluvian world as a re-creation.[475] Some of the parallels are the following:

- Spirit/wind passes over the scene (1:2; 8:1).
- Sea separated from dry land (1:9; 8:4-5).
- Dry land appears (1:9; 8:4-5).
- Birds fly about (1:20; 8:7-12).
- Land animals and man go about (1:24-27; 8:18-19).
- Creation mandate renewed (8:17).
- Permanence of created order promised (8:22).
- Creation ordinances modified (9:1-7).
- Man begins to be re-created (by procreation, ch 10) and to fill the earth as God commanded (10:32).

## FIRST RAYS OF LIGHT
## Gn 8:1-5

Gn 7 focused on the prevailing of the waters over the earth. A new topic is now introduced, viz. the first stage in the deliverance of the Flood survivors. These vv pre-

---

[475] This comparison has been noted by a number of writers, but is most convincingly displayed by Mathews, *NAC*, 383.

sent five increasingly bright and hopeful signs that all will be well for the ark dwellers.

### A. God Remembered (8:1a):
*But Elohim remembered Noah and all the beasts and all the cattle that were with him in the ark.* When used of God the verb *remembered* (r. *zkr*) does not imply prior forgetfulness. To *remember* is to act upon a previous commitment. In this case the previous commitment is to save Noah and his family. It implies mercy toward one dealing with a negative or threatening situation (cf. Gn 19:25). The word looks to the future as much as to the past. God's saving action is set in motion when he remembers. The God who remembers makes justice possible and fulfills promises.[476]

Youngblood indicates the literary importance of the v.

> Genesis 8:1 functions as the hinge of the flood story, the fulcrum on which the story is balanced. Up to this point things were getting progressively worse, but from this point on things gradually improve."[477]

It is not the covenant Elohim remembered, but Noah, and by implication, his family. He also remembered the animals. God's concern for the well-being of the animals is an underlying theme throughout the OT (cf. Jonah 4:11). The twofold classification of ark animals is unique in the Flood account.

When did Elohim remember and begin to act on behalf of the ark dwellers? Probably the actions reported in 8:1 antedate the concluding comment of ch 7. It was after the forty days and nights of torrential rain that God began to act. Though the waters continued to prevail for

---

[476]Cf. Plaut, *Torah*, 72.
[477]Youngblood, *BGIC*, 101.

## Re-creation after Judgment

another 110 days, Elohim already had set in motion the mechanisms that would bring the Flood to an end.

**B. God Acted** (8:1b-2):

*1. Wind sent (8:1b):* **And Elohim caused a wind to pass over the earth, and the water subsided.** *Wind* (*rûach*) is the same word translated *spirit* in Gn 1:2. There the Spirit of God hovered over the face of the waters; here the wind passed over the earth, which at this time was still covered with water. The wind aided evaporation, but that is probably not the main idea in the narrator's mind. As in Gn 1:2 the *rûach* prepared the earth for life. This is not the last time that God will use the wind to aid the cause of his people (e.g., Ex 10:13, 19; 14:21; 15:10).

The verb *subsided* (r. *škk*) is used only three other times in the OT. Three of the four uses refer to allaying of anger. Ordinary wind stirs up angry seas; in this case Elohim sent a wind that calmed the ferocious waters.

*2. Water restrained (8:2):* **Also the fountains of the deep and the floodgates of the sky were closed, and the rain from the sky was restrained.** At the same time he sent the wind, Elohim stopped the sources of the Flood water. The *fountains of the deep,* no longer called *great,* and *the floodgates,* reference the sources of the Flood in 7:11. Because *rain* is vital to productiveity it was *restrained,* but not cut off completely.

**C. Water Receded** (8:3):

*1. Commencement (8:3a):* **And the water returned from upon the earth, going and returning...** As in 7:17-20 where waters gradually rose, so now they are depicted gradually receding. The twice-used verb *returned* (r. *šûbh*) suggests that the waters returned to the places whence they came, i.e., both to the heavens and to the great deep. *Going and returning* is a Hebrew id-

415

iom meaning *little by little*. What is happening in this v is parallel to the third day of creation when the waters were gathered into their place.

2. *Observation (8:3b):* **and at the end of 150 days the water decreased.** The duration of the period of drifting on the waters is stated in days (rather than months) to indicate how agonizingly stressful that time must have been to those on the ark. Even the promises of God do not make sailing rough seas any less stressful!

Only at the end of the 150 days when the ark ran aground was Noah aware of the waters' abatement (cf. 7:24). The process lasted another 163 days beyond that. *Decreased* (r. *chsr*) is lit., "lacked." The idea is that the water lacked the strength that it formerly had when it covered the mountains by fifteen cubits (cf. 7:20).

**D. Ark Rested (8:4):**

*1. Date (8:4a):* **And in the seventh month, on the seventeenth day of the month...** A comparison with 7:11 indicates that 150 days—five months of thirty days each—had elapsed from the beginning of the Deluge. Since the waters prevailed for 150 days (7:24), the ark must have lodged on this mountain peak almost immediately after the water began to recede.

*2. Location (8:4b):* **the ark rested upon the mountains of Ararat.** The verb *rested* (r. *nûach*) plays off the name *Noah* (*nōach*). The hopes expressed by Lamech at Noah's birth (5:29) had been fulfilled in a most unexpected way.

The place of the grounding was *the mountains of Ararat* north of Assyria. The pattern of mountains in this area is like a swirl of ranges called a "knot." The Armeanian Knot is 1500 miles from the nearest ocean (the Indian Ocean), about as far from a major ocean as is possible on the face of the earth. Today this range is 8,000-12,000 feet above the postdiluvian sea level, the second highest complex in the Eastern Hemisphere. The highest peak in the region is 17,000 feet. The region was located in what now is eastern Turkey, southern Russia and northwestern Iran. The ancients called the region Urartu. The Ararat region is mentioned elsewhere in 2 Kgs 19:37; Isa 37:38; Jer 51:27. The specific landing spot is not identified in Scripture. In the intertestamental *Book of Jubilees* the specific site is called Mount Lubar.

### E. Land Sighted (8:5):

*1. Process (8:5a):* **Now as for the waters, they were going and decreasing until the tenth month;** Whereas the ark ceased to move about, the waters were not locked in place. *Going and decreasing* means "steadily decreasing." The verb is repeated from 8:3. Apparently the waters receded every day. The preposition *until* (*'ad*) does not mean that the waters ceased to diminish on the first day of the tenth month, only that a special milestone in the process was reached on that date.

*2. Milestone (8:5b):* **in the tenth month, on the first day of the month, the tops of the mountains appeared.** There is a parallel to day three of creation week when dry land *appeared* (cf. 1:9). If one assumes the ark landed on one of the higher peaks of the region, being able to see the mountains round about could indicate that the level of the water had declined hundreds of feet by this time. Assuming months of thirty days, seventy-four days have elapsed since the ark was grounded. Noah had been on the ark for 224 days.

By way of practical application, one might note that troubles come flooding over life with devastating intensity (forty days and nights); but they dribble away at an agonizingly slow rate.

# BIRDS DISPATCHED
## Gn 8:6-12

The Flood trauma is over; but the recovery mode lingers on for five more months. The narrator now relates how Noah at intervals dispatched four birds from the ark. There is no indication that he was following divine command. Apparently before men learned to navigate the seas by using the stars, they determined the location of land by dispatching birds (cf. Pliny, *Nat. His.* 6:83). In any case, in the Babylonian Flood account the hero also dispatched birds—dove, swallow, raven—from his vessel after the Flood.[478]

### A. Window Opened (8:6)

*Then it came about at the end of forty days, that Noah opened the window of the ark that he had made.* The Deluge reached maximum strength over a forty day period (7:12). So after he first saw the mountain tops Noah gave the earth forty days to dry out. He seems to have waited the forty days by logic or instinct, not by divine command. The forty days obviously follow the period mentioned in 8:5. Assuming months of thirty days, the window was opened on the 264th day that Noah resided on the ark.

The *window* was not specifically mentioned during the ark construction. Some have reasoned that the window must have been in the roof since Noah could have had adequate intelligence of the situation from a side window. He would not have needed to send out the birds. Such reasoning, however, does not take into the account the rugged terrain in the landing region. From Noah's vantage point atop one of the peaks of Ararat he

---

[478] *ANET* 94-95, lines 145-54.

was not able to see conditions down on the lower elevatios where man needed to relocate.

**B. Raven Dispatched** (8:7):

*1. Action (8:7a):* ***And he sent out the raven...*** The *raven* refers to the particular raven Noah had selected. The reason Noah sent out the raven is not explicitly stated in the text. Perhaps he merely wished to see how it would behave, to see what he could learn from its movements. The raven is a strong bird. Ravens normally seek a home territory that is desolate and uninhabited. Their keen eyesight enables them to see for miles around. They can eat almost anything. It made good sense to dispatch the raven before the gentle, low-flying dove.[479]

*2. Result (8:7b):* ***and it flew here and there until the drying up of water from upon the earth.*** The bird *flew here and there*, lit., "going and returning." The picture is one of the raven flying about for a time, then returning to the ark again and again. This aimless flight continued *until the drying up of water from upon the earth.* The earth did not reach the condition of being *dried up* (r. *ybš*) until the 27$^{th}$ day of the 2$^{nd}$ month of Noah's 601$^{st}$ year (8:14). Therefore, the raven displayed the pattern of flitting back and forth to the ark for 107 days. The movements of the bird obviously were inconclusive. Noah learned nothing from the raven.

Some see in the release of the unclean raven a symbol that impurities had been removed; the world had a fresh start.[480] This reads too much into the raven episode for two reasons. First, there is no indication that what was aboard the ark was impure. Second, the symbolism breaks down in that the raven was released into the new world.

---

[479]See George Howe, "The Raven Speaks," *JASA* (March 1969): 22-25.
[480]Mathews, *NAC*, 387.

Ravens are mentioned elsewhere 10x in the Bible. The raven is expressly mentioned as an unclean bird (Lv 11:15: Dt 14:14). This bird is likely to eat carrion (Prov 30:17). The Creator provides food even for the insignificant raven (Job 38:41; Ps 147:9; Lk 12:24). Ravens brought food to Elijah (1 Kgs 17:4, 6). A maiden might compare the hair of her beloved to the blackness of a raven (Song 5:11).

### C. First Dove Dispatched (8:8-9)

*1. Action (8:8a):* **Then he sent out a dove from with him...** The text is not clear as to the time Noah dispatched the first dove. Probably he waited seven days as in 8:10. *From with him* (*mē'ittô*) employs a Hebrew preposition that implies intimate association. This phrase was not used in connection with the raven.

Doves are mentioned 42x outside the Flood account in the Bible. They were considered the epitome of beauty and gentleness (e.g., Song 2:14; 5:2).

*2. Purpose (8:8b):* **to see if the water was abated from the face of the ground.** Noah's purpose in sending out the raven may have been unclear even to himself. That was not the case with the dove. This bird was to serve as Noah's eyes, to see where he could not see from the ark. At this point Noah did not know whether or not the waters had continued to recede since the tops of the mountains became visible forty-seven days earlier.

*3. Result (8:9a):* **but the dove found no resting place for the sole of her foot, so she returned to him into the ark;** Doves prefer clean, dry and sheltered conditions. Noah knew that if the dove could find no place to nest, there was no land suitable for human habitation in the immediate vicinity.

*4. Explanation (8:9b):* **for the water was on the surface of all the earth.** When the dove returned to the ark Noah concluded that the water remained on the surface of the whole earth, except the uninhabitable mountain tops visible from the ark window.

*5. Retrieval (8:9c):* ***Then he put out his hand and took her, and brought her into the ark to himself.*** Noah's tender concern for this creature is evident in this action. Perhaps this dove was a pet.

### D. Second Dove Dispatched (8:10-11)

*1. Interval (8:10):* ***So he waited yet another seven days; and again he sent out the dove from the ark.*** The verb *waited* (r. *chûl*) means "to dance, twist, or writhe in pain (as in childbirth), in anguish, or in contrition." The verb pictures Noah pacing, wringing his hands, rushing from time to time back to the window anxious to take the next step in gathering intelligence. *Yet another seven days* suggests that Noah had waited seven days before sending out the first dove. The seven-day increments in this narrative suggest that time was reckoned by the seven-day week.

*2. Evidence (8:11a):* ***And the dove came to him toward evening; and behold in her beak was a freshly plucked olive leaf.*** The bird finally returned at *evening*, the time of day when birds normally return to their nests. The term *behold* expresses the exhilarating joy and excitement that Noah experienced when he saw what the dove carried in its beak.

The *plucked olive leaf* has evoked considerable discussion. The adjective *plucked* (*tārāph*) emphasizes that the olive leaf (or leaves if the word is collective as in 3:7) was fresh and green. Clearly some vegetation survived the Flood. Youngblood reasons that if an olive tree on some relatively low hill survived, the Flood must not have been geographically universal.[481] Olive trees,

---

[481] Youngblood, *BGIC*, 114.

however, are capable of sprouting shoots under water, and thus could have survived the Flood.[482]

Others argue that the leaf proves that the ark did not land in the heights of Mount Ararat where olive trees do not grow. This inference, however, fails to give weight to the length of time the bird was gone. Its mission was not completed until evening. The dove would have had plenty of time to descend to lower elevations to fetch the leaf. Wherever the leaf was secured it gave promise that the waters were continuing to diminish at lower levels outside the range of Noah's vision. It was encouraging to see that life was still possible on the planet.

*3. Deduction (8:11b): So Noah knew that the water was abated from the earth.* Using the powers of deductive reasoning Noah *knew* that lower hills where olive trees were cultivated already were free of water. This is precisely what Noah wished to learn when he sent forth the first dove in v 8.

### E. Third Dove Dispatched (8:12)

*Then he waited yet another seven days, and sent out the dove; but she did not return to him again.* The verb *waited* (r. *ychl*) is a synonym of the verb used in v 10. A week later—the 284th day on the ark—Noah dispatched a third dove. The fact that it did not return indicated that it had found a place to nest and start a new life.

# LAND DRYING
## Gn 8:13-14

### A. Water Removed (8:13a, b):

*1. Date (8:13a): Now it came about in the six hundred and first year, in the first month, on the first*

---

[482]Aalders. *BSC*, 176.

*of the month...* The 601$^{st}$ year refers to Noah's life as in 7:11. The setting is the first day of a new year; but whether this is calendrical new years or Noah's birthday cannot be determined. In either case the first day of the new year signaled a new beginning for the human race. Thirty days have elapsed since Noah sent out the third dove.

2. *Report (8:13b):* **the water was dried up from upon the earth.** The verb *dried up* (r. *chrb*), used twice in this v, means "freed of water." The earth had dried up but was not completely dry as the following v indicates. Noah was not yet aware of what the situation was because of the narrow view he had from the window in the side of the ark.

### B. Covering Removed (8:13c)

***Then Noah removed the covering of the ark.*** Noah now took action that no doubt was an occasion of great celebration for man and beast alike. Just what is meant by the term *covering* is not clear. Some think that the roof is intended. If so, then this was the first step in dismantling the ark. Yet Noah still lived in the ark for another two months. So why did he remove the roof?

Aalders points out that the term *covering* (*miksēh*) always refers to a cloth covering. This covering must have been a deck cloth, probably made of the skins of animals fastened over the roof to make it more waterproof. Its removal would facilitate the drying out of the atmosphere inside the ark. To remove this covering Noah and his sons would have to climb on to the roof of the ark from which they would have had a better view of the surroundings.[483]

---

[483] Aalders, *BSC*, 177.

## Biblical Protology

**C. Delightful Observation** (8:13d)

*And looked, and behold, the surface of the ground was dried up.* The survivors surveyed the scene from the roof of the ark. *Behold* indicates the delight and excitement of the viewers when they discovered what the narrator declared to be the case earlier in the v.

**D. Thorough Drying** (8:14)

*And in the second month, on the twenty-seventh day of the month, the earth was dry.* The final date in the Flood narrative documents the day when the earth could be declared completely *dry* (*yābh$^e$šāh*). The ground is back in the condition it was in Gn 1:9.

# ARK EXIT
# Gn 8:15-19

**A. Command** (8:15-17)

*1. For humans (8:15-16):* **Then God spoke to Noah, saying, Go out of the ark, you and your wife and your sons and your sons' wives with you.** Now that the earth was thoroughly dry, Noah and his family were told to leave the ark. This is the first recorded communication with Noah since 7:1. A most eventful year has elapsed in the interim. The exit command (*go out of the ark*) parallels the entrance command (*go into...the ark*) in 7:1. In three previous references to Noah's family his sons are listed before his wife (6:18; 7:7, 13). This may simply indicate that the narrator was not a slave to form. On the other hand, the time on the ark may have brought Noah and his wife closer together.

*2. For animals (8:17a):* **Every living thing of all flesh that is with you, birds and cattle and every creeping thing that creeps on the earth bring out with you.** Noah was told to bring forth the animals. *Living thing* (*chayyāh*) previously in the Flood narrative indicated wild animals (7:14, 21). Here the term refers to animals generically. Three categories of animals are named, each introduced by the preposition *Beth*. The meaning is, "every living thing ... in the category of such and such."

*Birds* stand first in the animal list as in 6:20; 7:8, 21. Perhaps they were the easiest creatures to release. The second category was *cattle* ($b^e h\bar{e}m\bar{a}h$), those animals closest to man and most useful to him. Finally, the creepers are named, those smaller animals that hug the earth when they walk or crawl. The larger wild animals are not named, perhaps because with their pens unlocked they would exit quickly on their own without any assistance from Noah. The verb *bring out* (Hiphil impv. r. *yts'*) stands last in the clause, which permits the focus to be on the animals rather than on the action of Noah. The prepositional phrase *with you* is used 3x in 8:17. The phrase suggests not merely accompaniment, but intimate companionship. A bond grew between all the ark dwellers during the harrowing time of the Deluge.

*3. Explanation (8:17b):* **that they may breed abundantly on the earth, and be fruitful and multiply on the earth.** What was said on the third day of creation week to the sea creatures (1:20, 22) is here applied to the land creatures.

**B. Compliance** (8:18-19)

*1. Human exit (8:18):* **So Noah went out, and his sons and his wife and his sons' wives with him.** Noah led the eight souls forth in orderly fashion. The language again mirrors the description of the Noah's obedience in entering the ark (7:1, 7). The list of family members reverts to the order used most frequently in the narrative (6:18, 7:7, 13).

*2. Animal exit (8:19):* **Every beast, every creeping thing, and every bird, everything that moves on the** *earth, went out by their families from the ark.* The animals also exited in orderly fashion. Others question whether the intention of this v is to depict an orderly exit. Aalders contends that *by their families* has nothing to do with the order in which they left the ark. It only indicates that the various kinds of animals returned to their natural habitat.[484]

| \ | \ | **Chart 17** <br> **Flood Chronology** | \ |
|---|---|---|---|
| Y/M/D | Cum. | Event/Intervals | Ref. |
| 600/2/10 | | Loading the ark | |
| | | 7 days | 7:4 |
| **600/2/17** | 1st | Deluge begins | 7:11 |
| | | 40 days | 7:12, 17 |
| 600/3/27 | 40th | Forty days end; 150 days continue | 7:24 |
| | | Bal. of 150 days = 110 days | 8:3 |
| **600/7/17** | 150th | 150 days end; ark grounded | 8:4 |
| | | 74 days | |
| **600/10/1** | 224th | Mountains visible | 8:5 |
| | | 40 days | 8:6 |
| 600/11/10 | 264th | Raven dispatched | 8:7 |
| | | 7 days ? | |
| 600/11/17 | 271st | 1$^{st}$ dove dispatched | 8:8 |
| | | 7 days | 8:10 |
| 600/11/24 | 277th | 2$^{nd}$ dove dispatched | 8:10, 11 |
| | | 7 days | 8:12 |
| 600/12/1 | 284th | 3$^{rd}$ dove dispatched | 8:12 |
| | | 30 days | |
| **601/1/1** | 314th | Covering removed | 8:13 |
| | | 57 days | |
| **601/2/27** | 371st | Exit from ark | 8:14 |

Reading the chart: Firm dates are indicated in bold type. Dates are indicated in terms of the year, month,

---

[484] Aalders, *BSC*, 179.

and day of Noah's life. Column two gives a running total of days. Column three indicates the significant events and intervening time. Column four indicates the textual basis for the items in column two.

# FLOOD CHRONOLOGY

The chronology of the Flood can be worked out with great specificity because of the five firm dates that are in the text. Comparing 7:11 with 8:14 indicates that the Flood lasted exactly one year and ten days. But how long were the months? How many days were in the years as counted by Noah? Was he using a solar year equivalent to the 365 days of the present calculation or a lunar year of 354 days? These uncertainties make it impossible to determine with mathematical precision how many days the Deluge lasted. Assuming, however, that the months consisted of thirty days, Noah was in the ark for a total of 370 days. The Flood itself lasted 313 days.

# A NEW ERA
# Gn 8:20-22

**A. Worship** (8:20)

Man was created on the sixth day. The seventh day was a day of restful celebration and worship. So Noah began his life in the re-created world with worship.

*1. Construction (8:20a):* **Then Noah built an altar to Yahweh.** The first work in the new life was a work dedicated to Yahweh. *To Yahweh* is the standard language used later to describe the altar-building practices of the patriarchs (e.g., Gn 12:7-8; 13:18).

*2. Selection (8:20b):* **and took of every clean animal and of every clean bird.** Noah set apart some of the clean animals that had been preserved from the Flood. The valuable and precious are to be offered to God. The

## Biblical Protology

verb *take* (r. *lqch*) was used in 7:2 in the instructions concerning clean animals, suggesting a connection between those instructions and what now transpired. The Hebrew suggests that Noah offered some of every kind of clean animal. On the definition of *clean,* see on 7:2.

*3. Sacrifice (8:20c):* **and offered burnt offerings on the altar.** In *burnt offerings* the whole animal (minus the hide) was burnt. This is not the same word used in 4:3-5 for the offerings of Cain and Abel. Their offerings were tribute offerings. *Burnt offerings* symbolized the total commitment of the worshiper.

Through he is not called a priest, Noah was acting as priestly intercessor for his family in this episode.

Since the text offers no explanation for Noah's sacrifice, scholars have offered a plethora of opinions. He offered sacrifice to remove what remains of God's anger (Gunkel) or to inaugurate a new course of events (Dillmann) or to free the earth from the burden of the curse (Procksch). Others suggest propitiation (Skinner) or confession of sin (von Rad) as the motive. On the other hand, perhaps Noah offered up the burnt offerings out of natural desire to thank God for deliverance (Cassuto).

Under Mosaic Law the burnt offering was not primarily associated with propitiation for sin. Job, however, proves that in patriarchal times the burnt offering could be offered up as atonement (Job 1:5). So Noah's offering is best taken as offered for the purpose of thanksgiving and atonement.

Scripture celebrates the institution of regular public worship in the days of Enosh (4:26). Likewise Scripture celebrates this spontaneous act of worship on the part of Noah. Both types of worship are pleasing to the Lord.

**B. Acceptance** (8:21a)

**And Yahweh smelled the soothing aroma.** Critics regard such language as a sign of theological primitivism. Yet smelling is no cruder than seeing or hearing.[485] The language is anthropomorphic as any description of God in human language must be.[486] Examination of the passages where God is said to *smell* (or not smell) the odor of sacrifices indicates that the expression is metaphorical for acceptance.[487] The same metaphor also is used of NT offerings. See Eph 5:2; Phil 4:18.

By way of contrast to the dignified picture painted here, the Babylonian Flood story has the gods swarming from all sides "like flies" to enjoy the sacrifices. They squabble among themselves about who should enjoy the offering.[488] The God of the Bible does not consume sacrifices. Only the odor reaches him. The pleasing odor does not come from the unpleasant smell of burnt meat. What makes the sacrifice pleasant to Yahweh is the attitude of the heart of the worshiper.

*Soothing aroma* (*rêach hannîchōach*) or "odor of rest" is another word play on the name *Noah* and the idea of rest. Again the expectations of Lamech (5:29) were fulfilled in ways that he could not have imagined. The anger of Yahweh (displayed in the Flood) is assuaged, in part at least, by this sacrifice. The sincere worship of Noah led to a compassionate commitment on the part of the Lord.

### C. Yahweh's Decision (8:21b-d)

Yahweh reaches a decision that affected all generations that lived on this planet since the Flood.

*1. Curse cancelled (8:21b):* **And Yahweh said to his heart, I will not curse again the ground on account of man.** Clearly these words reveal a heart full of pain

---

[485] Jacob, *First Book*, 60.
[486] R. McKenzie, "The Divine Soliloquies in Genesis," *CBQ* 17(1955): 155-58. McKenzie argues that even *God is spirit* (Jn 4:24) is anthropomorphic, albeit more refined and therefore less obvious anthropomorphism.
[487] E.g., Ps 50:13f; Amos 5:21.
[488] ANET, 95, lines 160-80.

because of the world-wide catastrophe (cf. 6:6). *Not curse again* is lit., "I will not add to cursing again." Some take this to be a reference to the curse on the ground in 3:17. The meaning is then, "I will not add to that curse," i.e., place any additional burden upon securing man's sustenance than already exists. The verb *curse* (r. *qll*), however, is not the word (*ʾrûrāh*) used in the earlier passage. The verb *curse* here refers to the Flood itself. There was a time when Yahweh cursed *the ground* (*hāʾdhāmāh*) with a Flood because of man (*hāʾādām*). That will not happen again.

In polytheistic Flood accounts a dispute among the gods triggered change in relations with mankind. In the Bible this is the sovereign decision of the one God. No power can challenge it.

2. *Explanation (8:21c):* ***for the intent of man's heart is evil from his youth***. The reason for the decision not again to curse the earth is stated in these words. The divine judgment of the Flood did not alter in any way man's tendency toward evil. Cf. 6:5. People gravitate toward transgression. *From his youth* (NIV "childhood") indicates the early age at which the tendancy toward lawlessness manifests itself. The evil impulses of mankind must be controlled by law. This is why postdiluvian law begins to be enacted immediately.

3. *Limitation (8:21d):* ***and I will never again destroy every living thing, as I have done***. The decision not to destroy the world is limited by these words. The thought may be paraphrased this way: "I have brought judgment upon the evil inclinations of men's hearts by sending this great Deluge. I will not again bring such a judgment upon the earth for this cause."

The verb *destroy* (r. *nkh*) is not one that is used in reference to the Flood elsewhere. It previously was used in reference to killing Cain (4:15). It is the common

# Re-creation after Judgment

word used for slaying a person or beast or unleashing a plague.

What motivated God to make this decision regarding another all-destructive judgment on the earth is not specifically stated. Contextually, it is connected to the sweet aroma of Noah's sacrifice. The fact that Noah expressed his thanksgiving and consecration after his salvation moved the Lord. God's decision appears to be his response to Noah's devotion.

In essence God's decision is to put up with man's evil until the day of final accountability. The era of God's patience now begins. Cf. Rom 3:26.

### D. Commitment to Order (8:22)

This v spells out some of the positive ramifications of the decision of God not again to send a world-wide temporal disaster upon the earth.

*1. Duration of earth (8:22a):* **While the earth remains** is lit., "until (*'ōd*) all the days of the earth." The expression does not occur elsewhere. This phrase qualifies *never again* in the previous v. The earth is providentially preserved until final judgment (1 Pet 3:20-21; 2 Pet 2:5-12). In 8:21 *again* (*'ôd*) is used twice in presenting what would *not* be permitted to happen in the future. Beginning as it does with the same Hebrew word (*'ôd*), 8:22 serves to introduce the positive aspect of God's decision.

The text does not mean that the earth in its present form will continue forever. The commitment relates only to temporal divine judgment, similar to the Deluge. The final judgment will be something entirely different. It will bring this world and its history to an end. Cassuto observes: "The earth is not eternal, only the creator is eternal. Since the earth had a beginning, it stands to reason that it will also have an end."[489]

*2. Rhythm of nature (8:22b):* **seed time and harvest, and cold and heat, and summer and winter, and day and night shall not cease.** During the interim between the Flood and the day when the curtain falls on earth history there will be a rhythm to nature. It is not the intention of this v to stipulate the seasons of the year. This is a list of four opposite phenomena that portray nature's rhythm.

*Seed time and harvest* indicate the whole year. The orderly alternation between the one and the other guarantees a continuing food supply, hence preservation of mankind. This commitment parallels the provision of vegetation for man's food supply on the sixth day of creation week (1:11-12). Some think *cold and heat* is another description of the whole year (Delitzsch; Cassuto); but it could just as well be a description of the ordinary day as experienced in the Near East. *Summer and winter* may again point to the whole year. The alternation of *day and night* is the most fundamental rhythm of life. Every living creature exists in and requires this alternation. The language recalls that of the fourth day of creation (1:14).

---

[489]Cassuto, *CBG*. 2:121.

# 22
# POST-FLOOD WORLD
# Gn 9:1-17

One would expect that the first communication to the inhabitants of the new world would reveal the divine decision mentioned in 8:21-22. God's first priority, however, was to provide for the inhabitants of the new earth what they needed in order to survive and prosper.

## COVENANT CONDITIONS
## Gn 9:1-7

### A. Provision for Increase (9:1)

*And Elohim blessed Noah and his sons and said to them, Be fruitful and multiply, and fill the earth.* This is the third blessing on mankind (1:28; 5:2). The blessing consists of a repetition of the creation mandate of 1:28. The command is repeated in 9:7 at the end of a series of commands. This suggests that the purpose of the intervening commands is to enhance the rapid reproduction of the human race. By way of contrast, in Mesopotamian myth population growth was viewed with disfavor by the gods; they sometimes inflicted women with sterility to retard growth.[490]

### B. Provision for Protection (9:2)

*1. Nature of the provision (9:2a):* **And the fear of you and the terror of you shall be ...** In effect this provision renews the dominion promise of 1:26, 28, and takes it a step further. *Fear* (*môrā'*) is used 12x, and *terror* (*chat*) is used 4x in the OT. The two words mean

---

[490] ANET 106, lines 51-61.

essentially the same thing. These synonyms are used for emphasis. The implication of this provision is that prior to the Flood there was no instinctive fear of mankind. Animals were now considered dangerous to humans.

*2. Extent of the provision (9:2b):* **on every beast of the earth and on every bird of the sky, together with everything that creeps on the ground, and together with all the fish of the sea...** Four categories of creatures are listed to emphasize the extent to which the instinctive fear of man will manifest itself. Heading the list is *every beast of the earth,* the wild animals. Because of location, size and nature these creatures might have less reason to fear man. In second position is *every bird of the sky.* Even those creatures that soar far out of the reach of man will possess the instinctive fear of man. *Together with* translates the preposition *Beth.* The sense is that while fish and small animals are expected to have fear of man, birds and wild beasts are not. Yet the instinctive fear of man will be in them all. This provision guarantees man a measure of safety as he multiplies upon the earth.

*3. Obligation of the provision (9:2c):* **into your hand they are given.** This is the language of the holy war. The phrase suggests that humanity is given the power of life and death over animals. Humans may kill animals for mankind's good. Man lives under the tension of knowing the Creator has positive good will toward every living being, yet the Creator has given man the right to take the life of the animals. This requires a solemn stewardship on man's part.

### C. Provisions for Sustenance (9:3-4)

*1. Permission (9:3):* **Every moving thing that is alive shall be food for you; as the green plant I have given to you everything.** A new element is added to the supremacy of human beings. Prior to the Deluge man was authorized to slaughter animals for sacrifices and for making clothes from the hides. Now permission is granted for man to make meat a part of his diet.

Several aspects of this permission call for comment. First, *every...all* indicates that no restriction was yet made regarding clean and unclean food. Dietary restrictions were introduced as a badge of Mosaic covenant (Lv 11; Dt 14:3-21). For this reason the Mosaic dietary restrictions were abolished in NT (Mk 7:19; Acts 10:9-16; 1 Tim 4:3).

Second, the permission to eat meat applies to moving, living animals. They must be killed for the purpose of eating. Animals that die of themselves or that are killed by other beasts are excluded (cf. Lv 11:40). This restriction was later modified in the Mosaic code. An animal found dead could be given to an alien or sold to a foreigner (Dt 14:21; Cf. Lv 17:15-16). *Moving thing* (*remes*) is used in the broad sense of 7:21. The meaning is clarified by the phrase *that is alive*.

Third, *I have given* indicates the gracious nature of the provision. Wherever *I give/have given* (*nātan*) is used in the Pentateuch with God as subject it means "bestow, appoint, assign" (Milgrom). The context is always that of God effectively bestowing blessing. This means that in the present passage the gift of the blessing implies the possibility of taking animal life for man's needs.

Fourth, the words *shall be food for you* and *as the green plant* is a reference to the original statement of provision to Adam (1:29).

Fifth, the breadth of the provision (*everything*) recalls the provision of the garden where man could eat of every tree except one (cf. 3:16f).

There is a hint of the rationale for permitting man to slay beasts for his own needs in the words *that is alive*. The animal population survived the Deluge because

435

Noah partnered with God in building the ark. Thus animals owe their lives to man as well as to God their Creator.

*2. Diet change.* Four opinions have been expressed about the relationship between 1:29 and 9:3 in respect to the diet of man. First, some hold that animal food was expressly prohibited before the Flood. Now for the first time eating meat is permitted (Leupold; Candlish). Second, others hold that animal food was permitted from the beginning, but was not used until now when men were explicitly directed to partake of it (Luther). Third, another view is that animal food was used prior to the Flood, but is here for the first time formally sanctioned (Keil; Alford). Fourth, there are those who contend that animal food was permitted before the Fall. Now that grant is expressly renewed (Bush; Whitelaw).

Before reaching a conclusion regarding the relation of 1:29 to 9:3 certain facts must be processed. First, the language of 1:29 does not explicitly forbid the use of animal food. Second, if 1:29 is interpreted to mean that man was not permitted to eat meat before the Fall, then the same must be said of wild animals (1:30). Yet the carnivorous animals seem to be designed by the Creator to be meat eaters. One would have to speculate that the very nature of these beasts was changed as a result of the Fall. Third, before expelling Adam and Eve from the garden, God provided them with animal skins for a covering (3:21). Would not this action teach by example that man had the right to slaughter animals for his own needs? Fourth, shortly after the Fall animals were slain for sacrificial purposes (4:4). Yet there is no record of God specifically authorizing such slaughtering. Does this not suggest that man interpreted his dominion over the animals to include the right to slaughter them for his own needs?

Now for the assessment of the four views of the relationship between 1:29 and the present passage. The first of the views is hermeneutically weak. A positive grant of vegetation does not necessarily exclude animal food. The second and fourth views suffer from the lack of any positive statement in the text indicating permission to eat animal food. Though it cannot be proved, the likelihood is that man did eat meat prior to the Deluge as postulated in the third view.

So why does God explicitly sanction the eating of meat here if man had already been eating meat? First, the purpose of specifically granting permission to eat meat at this time was to introduce the restriction that appears in the following v. Second, the severely reduced animal population might make man reluctant to slay animals for meat.

*3. Restriction (9:4):* **Surely flesh together with its life—its blood—you shall not eat.** *Surely* (*'akh*) is a strong adversative rendered "but" (KJV; NKJV; NIV), "only" (NRSV; NASB), "however" (NJPS). Man may eat meat, but the permission is restricted. In form this prohibition has the appearance of the prohibitions of the Decalogue.

The connection between *life* (*nepheš*) and blood is made throughout Scripture (e.g., Lv 17:11, 14). It is the pulsating life-blood which is forbidden to be eaten immediately after wounding or killing. *You shall not eat* repeats the language of 2:17 regarding the tree of knowledge except here *you* is plural.

Eating of animal flesh is limited to such flesh as no longer has its life in it. This restriction forbids two practices: First, it forbids eating meat taken from a living animal—something that may have been practiced in pre-Flood days, and which has been observed in certain remote tribes. Second, it forbids eating of meat taken from slaughtered animals from which the blood has not been properly drained.

Why does God impose this restriction on meat eating? There are several possible reasons. First, it may be to guard against cruelty to animals (Calvin). Second, the restriction may be designed to build a hedge around human life by showing the inviolability that God attached to even the lives of the lowly creatures (Poole; Murphy; Kalisch). Third, God may have imposed this restriction to illustrate the intimate connection that even in the animal world exists between the blood and life. Fourth, the prohibition may be designed to teach the sanctity of blood (Keil; Delitzsch). Finally, it is possible that God's purpose was to instill a respect for the sacredness of life by preventing wanton abuse. The killing of animals carries within it the danger of blood-lust, of killing for the sake of killing, of blood-thirstiness.

### D. Provisions for Government (9:5-6)

*1. Value of human life (9:5a):* **And surely your lifeblood I will require.** *Surely* (*'akh*) is the same particle with which the previous v began. It introduces a second restriction regarding taking life. *Lifeblood* is lit., "your blood to your lives," i.e., the blood of you yourselves as opposed to animals. This direct object in the Hebrew is positioned before the verb in the sentence for emphasis. Life and blood are again linked as in the previous v. All life is valuable, and human life uniquely so.

The verb *require* (r. *drš*) means "to seek, revenge or demand an accounting." The idea is that God will come looking for blood in recompense for the blood of an innocent victim slain. The threefold repetition of this verb emphasizes the value that God places on human life and the certainty of divine retribution for murder. God will exact compensation for every life taken. The nature of that compensation is spelled out in the following v. The implication of this warning is that before the Flood the lack of capital punishment led to blood vendettas (Gn 4).

*2. Destruction of beasts (9:5b):* **from every beast I will require it.** So valuable is human life that recompense will be exacted even of animals that take human life. No sanction is stated, however, for taking animal life. Why are animals mentioned first? The entire paragraph deals with relations between men and animals. Animal blood may be shed for food; but human blood may not be shed at all, except in recompense for homicide. The point is that ultimately God vindicates the life of one whose life is violently taken.

A legal principle is established in 9:5. The beast that slays a man should be destroyed. This statute was later incorporated into the Law of Moses (Ex 21:28-32). In Christian times this principle also was followed. The purpose was not to punish the animal. The aim was twofold: to rid the world of a creature that had become a menace to man, and to warn humans about the sanctity of human life. If a beast slays a person because of natural instincts it must be killed. How much more a human who is capable of moral discernment?

*3. Execution of murderers (9:5c):* **And from every man, from every man's brother I will require the life of man.** The word *brother* (NIV "fellow man") recalls 4:8-11. In the case of Abel God did not exact blood for blood. From now on he will. Some hold that *two* individuals are here spoken of: a suicide and a murderer (Murphy); or a murderer and his kinsman (Bush); or a murderer and the civil authority (Candlish). Probably, however, *one* individual is in view. The murderer is first generically distinguished from the beast, and then characterized as the victim's brother (Keil). Murder is the ultimate violation of the brotherly relationship of humankind. Anyone who commits murder has gone the way of Cain.

Jacob offers the following cogent insight on 9:5. "Man is compensated for refraining from animal blood by having the sanctity of his own blood guaranteed by God."[491]

*4. Legal principle (9:6a):* **Whoever sheds man's blood, by man his blood shall be shed.** *Whoever* (lit., "the man shedding blood") makes clear that the legal principle applies to all regardless of wealth or rank. The Mosaic code inculcated this principle. No redemption by monetary payment for a murderer was permitted in Israel as in other law codes of the ancient world (Nm 35:31).

*Sheds blood* does not refer to accidental bloodshed. The later law of the manslaughter makes this clear (Nm 35:11). It does not refer to judicial executions, for that is commanded in the present statute. The phrase can refer to killing in war (1 Chr 28:3); but that is excluded here on grammatical and legal grounds. The singular envisions an individual acting alone. Legally, war is viewed as an extension of the state's right to take life in order to squelch evil. Under Mosaic Law blood shed in war was not considered murder (1 Kgs 2:5). What is in view in Gn 6:9 is premeditated murder. Prior to the Deluge there was so much violence and bloodshed that there was a special need for a provision to prevent the return of such conditions.[492]

*By man* indicates that humans are God's agents in exacting recompense by capital punishment. The preposition *Beth* when used with the Niphal form of the verb indicates agency. That there is a societal obligation to execute murderers is emphasized by the chiastic parallelism where the second half word order reverses that of the first half.

---

[491] Jacob, *First Book*, 62.
[492] Aalders, *BSC*, 185.

This is not observation or prediction but prescription. It is the will of God that man should shed the blood of a murderer. The principle should not be interpreted narrowly on either end. If a man strangled someone he should face the death penalty as surely as though he literally shed blood. By the same token, the execution of murders need not be literally by shedding blood. Under Mosaic Law the execution generally was by stoning. That, however, was not meant to be a paradigm for all societies for all times.

Two major questions regarding this passage remain, one historical and one practical. Does the v sanction family revenge? In a sense it does. Only one family existed at the time. Thus execution of murderers by the family is authorized. As the human family grew the execution of murderers by a victim's family members only led to retaliation and an endless cycle of violence. It did not take the human race long to discover that the execution of murderers must be left to society as a whole. Later God reveals that among his people only those who have received a fair trial may be executed. The Mosaic code severely curtails—some would say, eliminates—the principle of family revenge (Nm 35:19-21; Dt 19:12).

The second remaining question is this: Does Gn 9:6 sanction capital punishment for all time? The answer to this question lies beyond the scope of the present study. It is more appropriately addressed by ethical theorists.[493]

*5. Implications.* In 9:6a God authorizes man to be his agent in the execution of murderers. In this authorization is the germ of the concept of human government. If men have been given power over the lives of other men, then also over all lesser things as well—property, taxes, etc. (Rom 13:4).

---

[493] See discussion pro and con between C.F.H. Henry and M.A. Reid in *The Genesis Debate*, ed. R. Youngblood (Grand Rapids: Baker, 1991), 230-50.

*6. Explanation (9:6b):* **For in the image of Elohim he made man.** Some think the image is in man as judge. This is what gives men the warrant to sit in judgment on their fellows and shed the blood of murderers. More common is the view that this clause explains the sanctity of life. Murder is regarded as an attack upon the image of God, hence is disrespectful of the Creator.

The conjunction *for* (*kî*) need not refer only to what immediately precedes it. Grammatically it can also apply to what is further removed from it. In this case grammatically *for* could refer to everything in this paragraph.

There are three clues in the text that the final clause applies to the entire paragraph. First, in Gn 1:26-28 a close connection is established between man being created in the image of God, the blessing of fruitfulness and man's dominion over the animals. Here the creation blessing is being repeated. So this suggests that the connection is between the final clause and all that precedes in the paragraph. Second, the first half of v 6 is in a unique chiastic form that distinguishes it from the rest of the passage. It is not likely, then, that the final clause was meant as an extension of the first. Third, there is a shift in the last clause from God speaking in first person (vv 1-5) to the third person speaking about God.

For these reason 9:6b is best taken as a comment of the inspired writer, not part of the direct speech of God himself. The writer is pointing out the motivation for the words of God that precede in vv 1-6a. This clause explains why the human race was spared from the destruction of the Deluge, why God blessed humanity with fruitfulness and why he protected people from the threats of wild animals and other human beings. It is because man is made in the image of God.[494]

---

[494] Aalders, *BSC,* 187

Post-Flood World

The growth and spread of humankind, as it unfolds in Gn 10, needed the civilizing restrictions of 9:4-6. Only with these restrictions does human dominion become really human.

### E. Reinforcement (9:7)
*And as for you, be fruitful, and multiply; swarm in the land, and multiply in it.* *As for you* (plural) addresses Noah and his family. The paragraph ends on a happy note by this repetition of the blessing of fruitfulness in 9:1. The repetition gives a pro-life tilt to the entire passage. This v serves the purpose of bracketing the restrictions of vv 4-6 with blessing. The rabbis used this v to place a strong judgment upon anyone who did not try to produce a family. The verb *swarm* (r. *šrts*) previously in Gn is used only of lower creatures (1:20f; 7:21; 8:17).

# COVENANT PROMISES
# Gn 9:8-17

These vv consist of three words that Elohim communicated to Noah. The subject of all three is the postdiluvian covenant.

### A. First Word (9:8-11)
The first of the three divine communications to Noah emphasizes the scope of the covenant and the contents of it.

*1. Introduction (9:8-9a):* **Then Elohim spoke to Noah and to his sons with him, saying, Now as for me behold....** These words serve to focus on the setting up of the covenant that dominates the whole passage. The divine decision, revealed to readers in 8:21f, is now announced to Noah. On three previous occasions Elohim communicated to Noah alone. Here he spoke also with

Noah's sons. For the fifth time in the Flood narrative (ninth time in the text thus far) the word *behold* is used to introduce something unexpected and exciting.

*2. Scope (9:9b-10):* **I am about to establish my covenant with you, and with your descendants after you and with every living creature that is with you, the birds, the cattle, and every beast of the earth with you of all that go out of the ark, even every beast of the earth.** On *establish my covenant* see comments on 6:18. In this case the term *covenant* does not refer to an agreement between two parties. It is called *my covenant* because God takes the initiative in setting this covenant in place.

This covenant is more dissimilar than similar to the covenant with Abraham (Gn 17). Abraham responded in word and action; there was no specific response to God's covenant with Noah. This covenant is best regarded as an unconditional promise given in response to Noah's offering. God takes full responsibility to preserve the earth.

The covenant has a wider application than what was intimated in 6:18. The one-sidedness of this *covenant* is seen in that it included animals as well as all the descendants of Noah. It confirms Elohim's prior relationship with all creatures implied in the blessing in Gn1.

Since no general destruction will come upon humanity, it follows that none will come upon the creatures as well. *Living creature* (*nepheš chayyāh*) is used for the ninth time in the text to refer to any animal. This general term is immediately given a unique threefold breakdown: *birds, cattle* (domesticated animals) and *beast of the earth* (wild animals). The twice used *with you* identifies all these animals as Flood survivors. This is clarified by the concluding expression, *of all that go out of the ark. To every beast of the earth* reiterates that the covenant extends even to the wild animals although they are the most distant from man.

*3. Gist (9:11):* ***And I establish my covenant with you; and all flesh shall never again be cut off by the water of the Deluge, neither shall there again be a Deluge to destroy the earth.*** This v confirms that the *covenant* is nothing more than divine commitment. This covenant is even described by Isaiah with the word "oath" (Isa 54:9).

The word *cut off* (r. *krt*) occurs only here in the Flood account. Elsewhere the term refers to cutting someone off from God's providential care, hence delivering them over to the realm of death. The twice-used *Deluge* makes clear that Elohim is not promising a floodless earth, only that no future floodwaters will be equivalent to the Deluge experienced in the days of Noah.

The last sentence of the v goes beyond the first. No Deluge will cut off *all flesh*. In fact, God says there will never again be a world-wide Flood at all. *Destroy* (r. *šcht*) is used 7x in the Flood narrative.

## B. Second Word (9:12-16)

The second divine word focuses on the covenant sign. It also further amplifies the commitment made in the previous word.

*1. Announcement (9:12):* ***And Elohim said, This is the sign of the covenant that I am giving between me and you and every living creature that is with you, for everlasting generations.*** God usually certifies his covenants with signs. Cf. Gn 17:11; Ex 31:13, 17; Lk 22:20. It is not clear whether the clause *that I am giving* refers to the sign or to the covenant itself. The verb can be used with the word *covenant* (cf. Nm 25:12). The following v, however, makes clear that it is the covenant sign that God is now giving. So the fivefold use in the

Hebrew of the preposition *between* (*bîn*) in vv 12-13 refers to the covenant sign.

A rainbow has no special significance of itself; but by divine appointment it has very special meaning to the parties of the covenant. The sign is to last *for everlasting generations*, i.e., until new generations cease to appear on the earth.

*2. Description (9:13):* **My bow I have given in the cloud, and it shall be for a covenant sign between me and the earth.** In pagan theology the bow was found in the constellations of stars. In Gn the *bow* is associated with *cloud* 3x to make clear that God's *bow* is a rainbow. Rainbows are produced by refraction, reflection, and dispersion of the sun's rays against drops of water or mist. A rainbow appears when the sun is behind the viewer and a gathering of moisture is in the air in front of him.

The fact that God makes use of the rainbow as a covenant sign does not mean that this is the first rainbow that mankind ever saw. Some think the possessive pronoun *my* points to prior existence of the rainbow. Others understand *I have given* to indicate that God initiated the rainbow phenomenon for the first time. The phrase, however, could be understood to mean that from now on the rainbow will be a sign of the covenant.

There is no evidence in the text that it never rained prior to the Deluge. The appeal to *God had not caused it to rain upon the earth* (Gn 2:5) has no implications on the question at hand one way or the other. It says nothing about conditions in the world between the time of creation and the Flood.

If there was rain prior to the Deluge, then rainbows must have been common. There is no inherent reason why God could not have chosen a previously existing phenomenon and designated it as a sign for the purpose of this covenant. A family heirloom may be placed on the finger of a bride-to-be as a token of a new commitment. Circumcision can be documented in the world prior to Abraham; yet circumcision became a covenant sign to him (Gn 17:10).

The sign of the covenant is between God and *the earth*, i.e., all who reside on the earth. This is another indication of the one-sidedness of this covenant. A rainbow stretches from earth to heaven. It is therefore an appropriate symbol of the bond between God and the earth. A rainbow stretches from horizon to horizon. This also makes it an appropriate symbol of a universal commitment.

Outside Gn 9 the rainbow appears in only three passages, all as part of symbolic vision. Ezekiel saw a rainbow in connection with the throne-chariot of God (Ezek 1:28). John saw one over the throne and over the head of a powerful angel (Rev 4:3; 10:1).

*3. Implementation (9:14):* **And it shall come about, when I bring a cloud over the earth and the bow shall be seen in the cloud.** This v indicates the way that the covenant sign will work. *Bring a cloud* is lit., "in my clouding with a cloud." Elohim takes responsibility for bringing rain clouds over the earth. The Hebrews did not think of rain pouring through celestial windows; they knew very well that rain came from clouds (cf. Isa 5:6; 1 Kgs 18:44). So the covenant sign appropriately appears in rainy conditions.

The denominative verb (r. *'nn*) is used only here. The KJV and NASB set up a needless scientific conflict by making it appear that whenever the sky is cloudy a rainbow appears. Rainbows do not appear every time the sky is cloudy. NIV, NRSV and NJPS recognize v 14 as the protasis for a conditional statement that is completed in the following v.

*4. Commitment (9:15):* **Then I will remember my covenant, which is between me and you and every liv-**

*ing creature of all flesh; and never again shall the water become a Deluge to destroy all flesh.* The verb *remember* is anthropomorphic. It does not imply that God has faulty memory. See on 8:1. The preposition *between*, used of the covenant sign in vv 12-13, is now used of the covenant itself. In v 11 it was *the earth* that God would not again *destroy*; here it is *all flesh*.

5. *Reiteration (9:16):* **When the bow is in the cloud, then I will look upon it to remember the everlasting covenant between Elohim and every living creature of all flesh that is on the earth.** The switch from first person to third in this v is designed to underscore that it is *Elohim* who makes this covenant or commitment. *Look* suggests that God deliberately chooses to focus on the sign of hope, not the on-going and escalating sin of mankind. *Remember* is repeated from the previous v for emphasis. The concept of *everlasting covenant* (*bᵉrîth 'ôlām*) is common in the Pentateuch. *Everlasting* is limited in 8:22 to as long as the earth endures.

## C. Third Word (9:17)

*And Elohim said to Noah, This is the sign of the covenant that I have established between me and all flesh that is on the earth.* In typical Hebrew style the concluding v of the section repeats the key thoughts of the previous vv. The repetitions hammer home the truths.

As a sign the rainbow is unique. Other signs in the OT involve something made by man or done by man in order to remind him of obligations to God (Ex 13:9f; 31:13, 17; Nm 15:37ff). Man, however, does not make the rainbow nor does he look upon it to remind him of covenant obligations.[495]

---

[495] Jacob, *First Book*, 66.

## "ARKEOLOGY"

From time to time there have been reported sightings of the ark frozen in ice in one of the mountains of Ararat. These accounts are difficult to evaluate. They are full of intrigue, mysterious deaths, lost photographs, and other oddities that fuel conspiratorial theories. Owing to the geographical isolation and political and religious sensitivity of the area thorough exploration has been impossible. To date no physical or photographic evidence of the remains of the ark have been produced that have gained widespread acceptance among archeologists. The following bibliography will provide a good basis for those who might desire to look into the matter further.

**Bailey**, L.R., "Wood from 'Mount Ararat': Noah's Ark?" *Biblical Archeologist* 40(1977):137-46. _____, *Where Is Noah's Ark? Mystery on Mount Ararat.* Nashville: Abingdon, 1978. Points out discrepancies and improbabilities of the various sighting accounts. **Balsiger**, D. and C.E. **Sellier**, *In Search of Noah's Ark.* Los Angeles: Sun Classic Books, 1976. **Berlitz**, C., *The Lost Ship of Noah.* New York: G.P. Putnam, 1987. **Cummings**, V.M., *Noah's Ark: Fact or Fable?* San Diego: Creation Research Center, 1972. **Fasold**, D., *The Ark of Noah.* New York: Wynwood, 1988. Everyone has been looking in the wrong place. Fasold believes he has found the ark on a much lower hill to the south of Mount Ararat. **LaHaye**, T.F. and J.D. **Morris**, *The Ark on Ararat.* Nashville: Thomas Nelson, 1976; *Life* magazine, September 5, 1960. Aerial photographs of a large, canoe-shaped structure the dimensions of which approximately match those recorded in Genesis. **Montgomery**, J., *The Quest for Noah's Ark.* Minneapolis: Bethany Fellowship, 1972. An account of earlier searches for the ark on Ararat, and the author's own expedition. **Navarra**, F., *Noah's Ark: I*

*Touched It*. Plainfield, NJ: Logos International, 1974. **Noorbergen**, R., *The Ark File*. Mountain View, CA: Pacific Press, 1974. Shows a fine critical sense in doubting a large number of alleged sightings and finds. **Parrot**, A., *Journey to Ararat*. London: Longman, Brown, Green, & Longmans, 1845. **Shea**, W., "The Ark-shaped Formation in the Tendurek Mountains of Eastern Turkey," *CRSQ* 13(Sept 1976). **Wyatt**, R., *Noah's Ark Found*, 1980.

# CONCLUSION

The Flood narrative is interpreted typologically by the Apostle Peter. He declares:

> God waited patiently in the days of Noah while the ark was being built. In it only a few people, eight in all, were saved through water, 21 and this water symbolizes baptism that now saves you also--not the removal of dirt from the body but the pledge of a good conscience toward God (1 Pet 3:20f NIV).

Noah and his family were saved by passing through the waters of the Flood into a renewed world. The analogy with Christian baptism is that believers pass through the waters of baptism into a new life.

The Flood narrative also illustrates several great truths concerning God's judgments. First, they are not arbitrary. Second, they are announced in advanced. Third, those who are in danger are given opportunity to repent. Fourth, God's judgments result in death. Fifth, divine judgments are a manifestation of God's justice.[496]

---

[496] Following Youngblood, *BGIC*, 99-100.

# 23
# SIN AND PROPHECY
# Gn 9:18-29

The tendency toward "uncreation" noted in ch 3 began almost immediately after Noah's family left the ark. In this section the narrator focuses on three dark episodes: Noah's drunkenness, the sin of Ham, and the defiance of Babel that led to the disintegration of mankind. The first two of these episodes will be discussed in this ch.

## INTRODUCTION
## Gn 9:18-19

The opening vv of this unit set forth the theme of postdiluvian history. The section concludes with a similar comment in 11:9.

### A. Change of Focus (9:18)
***Now the sons of Noah who came out of the ark were Shem and Ham and Japheth; and Ham was the father of Canaan.*** The focus now shifts from Noah to his sons and their future. Noah's sons already have been mentioned 3x (5:32; 6:10; 7:13). Here the note is added that Ham was the father of Canaan. This anticipates the prophecy regarding Canaan in 9:25-27.

A person who manifested deep-rooted tendencies, good or bad, was called "son of X" by the Hebrews. For example, a murderer was called "son of a murderer" (2 Kgs 6:32), a wise man "son of a wise man" (Isa 19:11). Ham, of course, could not be called the son of a sinner. So the writer did the next best thing. He twice called him the *father* of Canaan, the worst of sinners (cf. 9:22).[497]

### B. Change of Theme (9:19)

***These three were the sons of Noah and from these the whole earth was spread abroad.*** *Spread abroad* (r. *pûts* in Niphal) implies divine blessing. God made them fruitful. The concept of being spread abroad over the earth is further described and explained in chs 10-11.

## POSTDILUVIAN FALL OF MAN
## Gn 9:20-24

In Gn 3 two individuals sinned—a wife and her husband—and thereby brought profound repercussions upon the family of man. In postdiluvian "paradise" (a cleansed world) two individuals—a father and his son—sin. Likewise their sin had profound repercussions upon the family of man.

### A. Noah's Sin (9:20-21)

*1. A vineyard (9:20):* **Then Noah, the man of the earth, began and planted a vineyard.** The phrase *the man of the earth* is usually taken to refer to someone who works the ground, i.e., a farmer. It is true that *the earth* (*ha'adhāmāh*) sometimes refers to cultivated ground. The word, however, also is used for the earth in general. In this phrase there is nothing to suggest that Noah worked the soil. Noah is *the man of the earth* in a very different sense. He is the patriarchal head of the only family on the earth.

Only in Ezra 3:8 is the exact expression *began...and* used. The language does not presuppose that husbandry and vine cultivation were now practiced for the first

---

[497] Jacob, *First Book*, 70.

time.[498] The NRSV mistranslated "Noah was the first to plant a vineyard." Out of forty occurrences of the expression *began to* only four can be rendered *was the first to* (Kidner). Much to be preferred is NIV "Noah proceeded to plant a vineyard." Other translations are "Noah began to be a husbandman" (ASV); "Noah began farming" (NASB).

Since Lamech, Noah's father, was a farmer (Gn 5:29), it is likely that this also was Noah's occupation before his call to be the ark builder. Perhaps the idea is that until this time Noah had not personally been involved in grape production and winemaking.[499]

Why is this detail about Noah noted in the narrative? First, the writer may simply be completing the picture of Noah as the new Adam (cf. 2:7). Second, this note may be intended to contradict the pagan notion that wine making originated with the gods. Third, planting the vineyard is mentioned to signal a time lapse between this paragraph and the preceding one. The length of the interlude, however, cannot be determined. Fourth, the vineyard story may serve only as the backdrop to the final prophetic pronouncements of Noah.

The view that Noah's vineyard and wine production is the fulfillment of Lamech's expectation (5:29) concerning his son is surely not correct. Lamech anticipated relief from the curse on the ground. That curse was not alleviated by the Flood or by the wine. See comment on 5:29.

*2. Drunkenness (9:21a):* **And he drank of the wine and became drunk.** The purpose of planting the vineyard now becomes obvious. Noah was not looking for

---

[498]Waltke (*GAC*, 148), however, thinks the v implies a new, not a renewed activity. Skill in growing grapes and producing wine was introduced by Noah. This new technology, however, was quickly perverted, as in ch 4.
[499]C.T. Francisco, "The Curse on Canaan," *CT* (Apr 1964): 8.

fresh fruit for the breakfast table. He drank *of the wine*, i.e., some of the wine (NIV; NRSV).

Much has been made of the fact that there is no word of condemnation of Noah for his drunkenness. Yet one can hardly ignore the implication of vv 28-29. See comments there. Some even attempt to put a positive spin on Noah's drunkenness. They dismisses his nakedness as a private affair.[500] This position, however, can hardly be correct.

This is the first mention of *wine* in the Bible. This does *not* mean, however, wine had never before been extracted from grapes or that Noah was unacquainted with the nature and effects of this intoxicating beverage. The definite article before *wine* (*hayyayin*) suggests that Noah was familiar with the use and treatment of the grape. Furthermore, evidence abounds in ancient literature to document drunkenness before the Flood (cf. Mt 24:38).

The drunkenness cannot be excused as the result of age and inadvertency. Noah's actions should not be whitewashed with assertions that drunkenness as such was not regarded as reprehensible in antiquity (Westermann).

Some argue that Noah lost his ability to hold liquor while on the ark or that he was in deep depression. Some even use Noah's drunkenness as evidence that the earth's conditions were very different before the Deluge. Supposedly before the Flood there was a vapor canopy over the earth that affected air pressure. It was a virtual oxygen chamber in which it was nearly impossible to get drunk. The implication is that Noah did not know the

---

[500]"Noah: Sot or Saint?" in *The Way of Wisdom: Essays in Honor of Bruce K. Waltke*, ed. S.K. Soderlund (Grand Rapids: Zondervan, 2000, 36-60). Waltke (*GAC* 148) rightly takes this position apart.

potency of the grape juice in the post-Flood environment.[501]

Still another theory is that Noah had been told to be fruitful and multiply (9:1), but he was an old man. He produced the wine because he thought it would increase sexual desire and lessen inhibitions.

The truth is that Noah's drunkenness was inexcusable and sinful. Since Noah's drunkenness was only incidental to the prophetic announcement to follow, the narrator does not comment on his culpability.[502]

*3. Nakedness (9:21b):* ***And he uncovered himself inside his tent.*** To be uncovered was regarded as a disgrace (Ex 20:26; 2 Sam 6:26; 10:4f.). Wine makes fools of even the most righteous men. The NIV and NRSV rendering "he lay uncovered inside his tent" does not do justice to the nuances of the Hebrew. The verb is Hithpael, normally reflexive. He was not disrobed by Ham; he disrobed himself. Noah did not passively lay uncovered; he actively made himself naked (cf. NJPS; NASB). Drunkenness and nakedness are elsewhere connected in Scripture (Hab 2:15). Nakedness is associated with shame (3:7, 21).

The form of the suffix on the word *tent* (*'oh$^o$lōh*) raises a question as to the location of Noah's sin. This is an archaic masculine ending that in the consonantal text might be mistaken as a feminine suffix.[503] Rabbinical scholars prefer the feminine reading, suggesting that Noah was in his wife's tent for marital relations. There is, however, no compelling reason to read the suffix as feminine. In either case, Noah's sin of exposing himself

---

[501] *Bible-Science News*, "What Shall we do with a Drunken Sailor," 31(January 1994): 1-2.
[502] Mathews, *NAB*, 417.
[503] Cassuto (*CBG*, 2:161) provides several parallels. This same noun and suffix are used in Gn 12:8; 13:3; 35:21.

is mitigated somewhat by the fact that it did not occur in public.

### B. Ham's Sin (9:22-23)

*1. Its nature (9:22a):* ***And Ham, the father of Canaan, saw his father's nakedness and told his two brothers outside.*** For the second time the text notes that Ham was the father of Canaan (9:18). The fact is mentioned again because it was in respect to this type of behavior that Canaan and his descendants followed in the path of their father Ham. To express the matter a different way, by acting as he did Ham showed himself to be the true father of Canaan.

Ham demonstrated parental disrespect in four ways. First, he invaded the privacy of his father. He had no business in his father's (or mother's) tent. It is possible, of course, that the tent opening was not covered. If that were the case Ham could have gazed upon his father without entering the tent. The wording, however, suggests that for whatever reason Ham had entered the tent.

Second, Ham saw the nakedness of his father. This was not a mere harmless glance, but "he looked at" (BDB)—he gazed with satisfaction (Leupold) at his father's nakedness. Was this "homosexual voyeurism"?[504] Other passages in the Mosaic code forbid looking on another's nakedness. A priest was not evev to go up steps to offer sacrifices lest his nakedness be exposed (Ex 20:26).

Third, Ham dishonored his father by failing to cover him. In the ancient Near East it was a familial obligation for a son to care for a drunken father.[505]

Fourth, Ham told (with obvious delight) his brothers outside about his father's condition. He should have kept this knowledge to himself. Ham, however, at-

---
[504] Waltke, *GAC*, 149.
[505] ANET 150, lines 32-33.

tempted to make his father an object of derision. In the actions of Ham one can see in the bud the parent-dishonoring Canaanite perversions of Moses' day.

*2. Speculation.* Where narrative is straightforward and simple, commentators rush in with speculative theories. Did Ham commit a carnal act in the tent? Other passages in the Pentateuch use the expression *see the nakedness* in such a way as to suggest that more than a blatant look is involved in this expression. An Israelite was not to take his sister so that he "sees her nakedness" (Lv 20:17). On the other hand normally Gn speaks of illicit sexual encounters in plain language. Why would the writer in this case hide some terrible deed behind the metaphor of nakedness?

If Ham did commit a carnal act, with whom did he commit it? Some think Ham committed a homosexual act with his drunken father. It is true that the verb *saw* sometimes means "to lust" (Gn 6:2; 34:2). This meaning, however, must be derived from context. There is nothing in the text to suggest that Ham's look was in fact lust.

Since the episode may have taken place in the tent of Noah's wife, some argue that Ham must have committed a carnal act with his mother.[506] In the Mosaic Law to "uncover the father's nakedness" is a euphemism for having a sexual relationship with the mother. See Lv 18:8. The text, however, does not say that Ham "uncovered his father's nakedness;" he only looked on it. Furthermore, the *nakedness* here is literal, not metaphorical for sexual activity.

---

[506]See F.W. Bassett, "Noah's Nakedness and the Curse of Canaan: A Case of Incest?" *VT* 21(1971): 232-37. Kikawada and Quinn (*Before Abraham*, 102f): "Ham committed incest with his mother after Noah was rendered incapable by drink."

It has even been suggested that Ham castrated his father.[507] This speculation is fueled by the absence of any reference to progeny of Noah born after the Flood. There is no hint of castration in the account, unless it is the comment of the narrator in v 24.

*3. Its rebuke (9:23):* **But Shem (along with Japheth) took a garment and they laid it upon both their shoulders and walked backward and covered their father' nakedness; and their faces were turned away, so that their father's nakedness they did not see.** The previous v in Hebrew began with the verb *saw*. This v ends with the same verb, for lit. the last words are "they not saw."

As God covered the nakedness of Adam in the garden (3:21), the two brothers covered the nakedness of their father. The writer wished to draw attention to the pious conduct of Shem and Japheth. He does so in a series of concrete action verbs. *They took—put it—walked backwards—so covered—were turned away—did not see.* The first verb is singular; the following verbs are plural. Does this suggest that Shem took the lead?

The two rebuked the conduct of their brother by walking into the tent backward, not daring so much as to glance at their father. Repetition of *their father's nakedness* echoes *his father's nakedness* in the previous v, thus emphasizing the nature of the sin. Cassuto comments: "If the covering was an adequate remedy, it follows that the misdemeanor was confined to seeing."[508] There is no indication that Ham had brought Noah's garment out of the tent in order to verify his story as proposed by Jacob.[509]

---

[507]Talmud, *Sanhedrin* 70a. Perhaps the rabbi was influenced in his opinion by the old Canaanite myth that told how the god El-Kronos had emasculated his father. A similar myth was told in Hurrian circles. See Plaut, *Torah*, 85.
[508]Cassuto, *CBG*, 2:151.
[509]Jacob, *First Book*, 67.

## C. Noah's Enlightenment (9:24)

*When Noah awoke from his wine, he knew what his youngest son had done to him.* How did Noah know what had happened to him? By revelation? intuition? interrogation? Did Shem and Japheth volunteer the information?

*His youngest son* is lit. "his small son." Ham is always listed before Japheth when the three are mentioned together. Perhaps the reason is that people prefer in a short list like this to pronounce the longer name last. So the order *Shem, Ham and Japheth* is euphonic. Another possible explanation for Ham's name being given priority is that the Hamites maintained a closer affinity with the Shemites than did the Japhethites.

Jewish tradition understands *his youngest son* to be a reference to his grandson, implying that Canaan was involved in the despicable act of his father. One suspects that the rabbis were driven to this conclusion by the fact that Canaan is cursed in Noah's last words.

Those who think Ham committed a carnal act in the tent emphasize the verb *had done*. Robertson comments: "It seems very unlikely that Noah would have had any remembrance of a mere look from his son while he was in a state of drunkenness."[510] The verb, however, could just as well refer to the parental mockery outside the tent.

# NOAH'S PROPHECY
# Gn 9:25-27

The closing vv of ch 9 do not express Noah's last will and testament or merely prayerful requests. Patri-

---

[510] O. Palmer Robertson, "Current Critical Questions Concerning the "Curse of Ham" (Gen 9:20-27)," *JETS* 41(June 1998): 179. See also D. Atkinson, *The Message of Genesis 1-11: The Dawn of Creation* (Leicester: Inter-Varsity, 1990), 169.

archs, like Noah, were also prophets (Ps 105:15; Gn 20:7). As in the case of Abraham, Isaac and Jacob, the last words of Noah were prophetic.

A. **Curse on Canaan** (9:25)

*1. Nature of the curse (9:25a):* **So he said, Cursed be Canaan.** The focus on Canaan gives a future cast to the words. Noah is not describing how things were in his day, but how they will be in future generations. The Canaanites will become the curse-bearers in the new world. The curse on Canaan links him with the curse on the Serpent (3:14) and on Cain (4:11).

A curse is a negative prophecy pertaining to temporal life. The text has nothing to do with racial origins as contended by the pro-slavery groups before the Civil War. The proof is found in depictions of the Canaanites in the monuments of ancient Egypt. They definitely did not display Negroid features. So there is no justification for putting a racial spin on this passage.

*2. Object of the curse.* Why was the curse placed on Canaan when it was Ham who committed the sin against his father? Some recensions of the Septuagint read "cursed be Ham;" but the Hebrew manuscripts do not support this reading. Neither is there support for the view that the v really means, cursed be *the father of* Canaan. The other sons of Ham are ignored. There is no evidence that the other sons of Ham are cursed in their youngest brother (Keil), or that the absence of a word about the other sons of Ham is an ill omen about their future (Delitzsch).

Various answers have been proposed as to why Noah cursed Canaan. Some say it was because Ham (the youngest son of Noah) was punished by the knowledge of what would happen to his youngest son (Delitzsch). Others argue that Canaan himself was involved in some manner in the sin of his father. The proposal even has been made that Canaan was the illicit product of sexual intercourse by Ham.

The truth is that Canaan inherited his father's propensity for decadence. That decadence only grew over the centuries. Eventually it called forth the judgment of Yahweh. Noah foresaw that the character of Ham would manifest itself in the Canaanites. In 10:19 the narrator makes a point of mentioning that the descendants of Canaan inhabited Sodom, Gomorrah, Admah and Zeboiim, infamous centers of homosexual activity. Furthermore, during the days of the patriarchs the iniquity of the Amorites (a portion of Canaan's descendants) was ever-increasing (Gn 15:13, 16). Moses warned the Israelites that they should not follow the sexual abominations of the Canaanites (Lv 18:3).

*3. Omission of Ham.* Another question that has haunted commentators is why Ham is omitted from the curse. An old Jewish opinion is that Ham is omitted because he was already blessed, along with Shem and Japheth, in 9:1. Another possibility is that Ham was already dead. Noah lived 350 years after the Flood. The text does not state how long Ham lived. It is conceivable that he died during that period.

Perhaps the curse did not immediately follow the incident as in Gn 49. A long gap existed between the commissions of crimes by Levi, Simeon and Reuben and Jacob's deathbed negative prophecy against these sons. The mention of Noah's death immediately following his utterances concerning his descendants suggests that these words were spoken near the time of Noah's death. This looks like the kind of deathbed prophecy one finds in Gn 49.

*4. Content of the curse (9:25b):* ***A servant of servants he shall be to his brothers***. *Servant of servants* is the Hebrew way of expressing the superlative degree, i.e., the lowest of servants. Such a servant was subjected to the most humiliating type of slavery. Parallel utterances indicate that these words do not just apply to Canaan as a person, but to a wider group. The curse is more on Canaan's descendants than on Canaan himself. There is a hint of this in the text in the plural *tents* used in reference to Shem in v 27.

In this initial curse statement Canaan is said to be a servant to *his brothers,* i.e., other Hamites. From this one may deduce that Canaan differed in character from his brothers. Canaan's brothers are designated as *Cush, Mizraim, and Put* in Gn 10:7, names associated with North Africa.

Canaanite tribes throughout history were in a position of subjection to the great powers. Before Israel occupied the land the area of Canaan was subject to Egypt. Egyptian subjugation of Canaan in the 15th century BC is probably to be viewed as the fulfillment of this prophetic word concerning Canaan.[511]

Canaan's slavery is political, but it is spiritual as well. The disgrace is that he must live in servitude to his own brothers. The closest parallels are Gn 27:29, 40.

### B. Blessing of Shem (9:26)

*1. Doxology (9:26a):* **He also said, Blessed be Yahweh, the Elohim of Shem.** Shem is identified by his relationship with God and vice versa. The fact that Yahweh is blessed suggests that Shem was already in proper covenant relationship with Yahweh. The implication is that Shem will be blessed, and this blessing will come from Yahweh. Blessing a person's divine protector represented or reinforced the blessing of the person himself (cf. 1 Sam 25:21).

Noah foresaw rich blessings to be experienced by the Shemites. He was so overwhelmed by what he saw

---

[511] See Robert Brow, "The Curse of Ham—Capsule of Ancient History," *CT* (Oct 26, 1973): 8-10.

that he burst forth in a doxology of praise for Yahweh. Not every individual Shemite would be blessed, any more than all of Abraham's posterity were included in the blessing pronounced on him. In these words there is a hint that the promised Seed—the Crusher of Gn 3:15—would come through the line of Shem.

2. *Subjugation (9:26b)*: **And let Canaan be his servant.** Noah prophesied that the Canaanites will be subjugated by the Shemites. This prophecy was fulfilled in the invasion of Canaan by the Israelites in the late fifteenth and early fourteenth centuries. The language is tamer than is used in the preceding v to describe the servitude of Canaan to his brethren.

*Be his servant* is lit., "be a servant to him" or "to them" (*lāmô*).[512] Since the reference is more to Shem's descendants than to Shem personally, it could be argued that the plural reading is preferred. The meaning is not materially affected either way.

### C. Enlargement of Japheth (9:27a)

*May Elohim enlarge Japheth.* The verb *enlarge* (*ypht*) sounds very much like the name Japheth. The idea is that God will enlarge the inheritance of Japheth whose name means "the one who spreads abroad." This is not a prophecy of personal gain for Japheth, but rather an abundant increase in the case of Japheth's descendants. The enlargement includes material blessing, especially in the extension of territory. *Elohim* (not *Yahweh*) does this for Japheth. No special relationship to God is mentioned in respect to Japheth.

---

[512] On the grammatical ambiguity of the suffix on the preposition see GK §103 g note 3.

## D. The Tent-dweller (9:27b)

*And let him dwell in the tents of Shem.* Because of the ambiguity of the pronoun *him,* three major approaches to this brief prophecy have emerged.

*1. Non-messianic views.* Most take the ambiguous pronoun (*him*) to refer to Japheth in which case Japheth is to dwell in the tents of Shem. The NIV incorporated this interpretation into the text as a translation.

Some see dwelling in the tents as a metaphor for displacement, citing 1 Chr 5:10 and Ps 78:55 where the expression has this meaning. In this context, however, dwelling in tents implies friendly sharing of Shem's hospitality. Shem was blessed in the preceding v. It would not be likely that Shem here received what is tantamount to a curse.

Others think that dwelling in tents means no more than that they would be good neighbors. The prophecy is that there will be friendly relations between descendants of Shem and descendants of Japheth as in Ps 84:10; 120:5. These passages, however, refer to someone being a guest in a home. Here there is no mention of good relationships between the parties involved.

*2. General messianic view.* Others think the basic idea of dwelling in someone's tent means sharing their lot. Japheth will share the blessings of Shem. Since Shem's blessing centered in his relationship with Yahweh, the Japhethites also will be included in that relationship. The fulfillment involves Gentiles being grafted into the Olive Tree. Shem's spiritual heritage belongs to Gentiles (Eph 3:6; Gal 3:26ff.). If the tent-dweller here is Japheth, then this interpretation is to be preferred.

*3. Personal messianic view.* Still better is the view that takes the pronoun *him* to refer to *Elohim*.[513] Four facts support this view. First, the subject of the first verb

---

[513]Charles Briggs defends this view. *Messianic Prophecy* (1886; Peabody, Mass.: Hendrickson, 1988), 82.

in v 27 is *Elohim*. No subject is indicated for the second verb. It is natural to take both verbs in the v to have the same subject.

Second, the verb *live* or *dwell* (r. *škn*) is associated with Yahweh's presence in the camp of Israel (e.g., Ex 25:8; Lv 16:16), being semantically related to "tabernacle" (*miškan*).

Third, the Hebrew *tents of* (*'oh°lê*) *Shem* forms wordplay with the parallel *God of* (*'elōhê*) *Shem* in v 26. A mere transposition of letters alone distinguishes the two.[514]

Fourth, understanding the second half of v 27 to refer to the coming of Elohim makes for a more appealing literary pattern in the passage: three curses on Canaan, two blessings on Shem, and one blessing on Japheth.

If the above analysis is correct, this is the second messianic prophecy in the Bible. God is coming to dwell in the tents of Shem, i.e., among the Shemites. The fulfillment is when Christ became flesh and *dwelled* (lit., "tented") among the Jewish people (Jn 1:14).

### E. Further Canaanite Subjugation (9:27c)

***And let Canaan be his servant.*** For the third time Noah refers to the curse on Canaan. Canaanites will be the servant of Japhethites. Descendants of Japheth included the Greeks and the Medes. The fulfillment came in the conquest of Canaanite Tyre and Sidon by the Greeks and the fall of Carthage, a Phoenician (Canaanite) city state, in the Punic wars.

### F. Silence Regarding Hamites

Ham is not mentioned in Noah's declarations. He is not cursed; hence he is not under the judgments mentioned in connection with the Canaanites. Ham, how-

---

[514]Mathews (*NAC*, 424) makes observations two and three, but fails to see the significance of his observation.

ever, is not blessed either. One must conclude that the rest of the Hamites are neither blessed nor cursed. The conditional nature of prophecy always leaves the door open for Hamites to be converted and then to share in Shem's blessing. Later promises of salvation are extended to the Hamitic Egyptians (Isa 19:18-25; Zech 14:18). Not even all Canaanites are under the curse. Those, like Rahab, who cast their lot with the people of God found salvation.

## DEATH OF THE PROPHET
## Gn 9:28-29

**A. Report** (9:28-29)

*And Noah lived 350 years after the Flood. So all the days of Noah were 950 years, and he died.* *After the Flood* suggests that the narrator regarded the Flood as the great line of demarcation of eras. Before the Flood, Noah walked with God (6:9) like his predecessor Enoch (5:22). Enoch was taken to heaven; Noah's death notice is reported in nineteen words. Would Enoch's translation have been repeated for Noah had he continued the righteous and intimate walk with God after the Flood?

The genealogical record that started in 5:32 is completed in the pattern of ch 5. Assuming no gaps in the genealogy in ch 11, Noah lived until the 58$^{th}$ year of Abram. It cannot be proved from scriptural data that Noah was no longer alive when God called Abraham. The Abraham narrative, however, gives the impression that considerable time had passed since Noah.

In the Babylonian tradition the one saved from the Flood is divinized. Here the Flood hero dies like all other humans.

Sin and Prophecy

### B. Retrospect

A number of parallels between Adam and Noah suggest that the writer viewed Noah as the head of the postdiluvian world. Warren Gage[515] has identified these parallels in convincing manner. Here are a few of the observations he makes. First, Adam and Noah are the only two individuals associated directly with the terminology *image of God* (1:27; 5:1-3; 9:6). Second, Adam walked with God in the garden (3:8); Noah is also said to have walked with God (6:9). Third, Adam asserted his authority over animals by naming them (2:19), Noah by preserving them (7:15). Fourth, the mandate to multiply is given almost verbatim to each (1:28-30; 9:1-7). Fifth, both Adam and Noah worked the ground (3:17-19; 9:20). Sixth, Adam sinned against God by eating (3:6), Noah by drinking (9:21). Seventh, both men experienced shameful nakedness (3:7; 9:21). Eighth, both Adam and Noah have three named sons (4:1-2, 15; 6:10).

## TABLET COLOPHON
## Gn 10:1a

*Now these are the generations of the sons of Noah.* Those responsible for the record of the Flood and perhaps the custodians of the tablet upon which the Flood account was written were Shem, Ham and Japheth. After the Flood they had sons. This forms the transition to the Table of Nations that follows. If they had any sons before the Flood those sons must have been destroyed by the Flood.

---

[515] Warren Gage, *The Gospel of Genesis: Studies in Protology and Eschatology* (Winona Lake, Ind.: Carpenter, 1984), 9-15.

# 24
# DESCENDANTS OF NOAH
## Gn 10:1b-32

*S**hem, Ham and Japheth; and sons were born to them after the Deluge* (10:1b). The naming of the three sons is not be regarded as being in apposition with *sons of Noah* in the first half of the v as in most English versions for were that the case the sentence would have read like this: "And these are the generations of Shem, Ham and Japheth, the sons of Noah," the order into which the English versions have forced the Hebrew. Rather, the three names stand alone. The Table of Nations opens in the same format as the first v of 1 Chr, with simply a listing of names.

Gn 10 is called segmented genealogy. It lists descendants of all three sons of Noah for several generations. Apparently these various families are tracked through the years because many of them were still influential at the time Gn was written.

While the sons of Noah are listed here in the usual order, the Table of Nations presents their descendants in reverse order. The Table is organized into three major divisions, which begin in 10:2, 6 and 21. The Table is conveniently summarized in 1 Chr 1:5-23, which lists the names in exactly the same order as here.

## JAPHETIC PEOPLES
## Gn 10:1b-5

The sons of Japheth are named first for three reasons. First, Japheth was the firstborn son of Noah. See on 11:10. Second, Japheth's descendants were of less theocratic significance. Third, the Japhetic peoples settled in regions more geographically remote from Israel.

The Israelites had the least contact with the descendants of Japheth, at least up to the time Gn was written. The Japhethites settled in the distant north and west, mostly in the areas of Asia Minor and Armenia. They spoke Indo-European languages.

### A. Sons of Japheth (10:2)

*The sons of Japheth: Gomer, Magog, Madai, Javan, Tubal, Meshech, and Tiras.* Seven sons of Japheth are named. The number seven is symbolic of completeness. There were probably many other sons of Japheth that settled in regions far removed from Israel, e.g., in India and the Far East. Only those peoples that were on the political horizons of Israel are selected for inclusion in the Table. The Japhetic peoples are not arranged in any geographical order.

*1. First son. Gomer* is elsewhere mentioned 3x. In Ezek 38:6 Gomer is listed as an ally of Gog. The name is known in cuneiform and in classical authors where the Gomerites were known as the Cimmerians. They originally were found on the northern coast of the Black Sea. After being conquered by the Assyrians these people disappeared from history.

*2. Second son. Magog* is elsewhere mentioned 3x (Ezek 38:2; 39:6). Josephus identified Magog as the Scythians. Delitzsch accepted this identification, but modern scholars prefer to identify Magog as Lydia.[516]

*3. Third son. Madai* is the common name in the OT for the Medes or their land. These people were located east of Assyria in mountains of modern northwest Iran. They helped overthrow the Assyrians in 612 BC. The Medes developed a sizable kingdom in the sixth century BC. They were finally absorbed into the Persian Empire.

---

[516] NIDOTTE 4:685-87.

*4. Fourth son.* Javan refers to the Greeks. The term is used many times in the OT. It is also attested in cuneiform.

*5. Fifth son.* Tubal is mentioned elsewhere 7x. They also are mentioned in cuneiform literature and Herodotus, who calls them Tibarenoi. They were known for their military prowess. They lived in the mountains southeast of Black Sea.

*6. Sixth son.* Meshech refers to a people of Asia Minor. Elsewhere they are mentioned 7x. They were known for trading in copper vessels (Ezek 27:13). Frequently they are associated with Tubal (Ezek 32:26; 38:2-3; 39:1). Meshech is identical to the Assyrian Mushki and the Greek Moschoi. There was also an otherwise unknown Aramean tribe by the same name (1 Chr 1:17), perhaps identical with Mash (Gn 10:23). Waltke identifies Meshech with Phrygia.

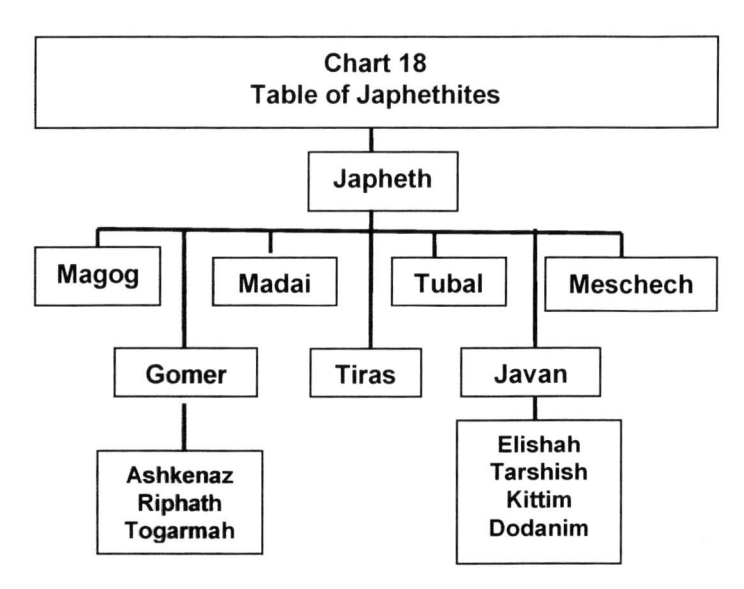

**Chart 18
Table of Japhethites**

- Japheth
  - Magog
  - Madai
  - Tubal
  - Meschech
  - Gomer
    - Ashkenaz
    - Riphath
    - Togarmah
  - Tiras
  - Javan
    - Elishah
    - Tarshish
    - Kittim
    - Dodanim

*7. Seventh son.* Tiras is not mentioned elsewhere in OT or cuneiform. There is, however, a similar name in Egyptian literature. The term appears to refer to one of the Sea Peoples, perhaps the Turusa from the region of the Aegean Sea. They may have been the same people known to the Romans as the Etruscans.

### B. Grandsons of Japheth (10:3-4)

The Table lists grandsons of Japheth through only two of his sons. Seven grandsons are named. This is an indication that the writer is being selective. The names he selects are representatives of all the grandsons of Japheth.

*1. Grandsons through Gomer (10:3):* **The sons of Gomer: Ashkenaz, Riphath and Togarmah.** *Ashkenaz* is mentioned elsewhere only in 1 Chr 1:6 and Jer 51:27 in a summons against Babylon. These people are associated with two other kingdoms known to have existed in the Armenian highlands. Modern writers equate them with Scythians who lived north of Black Sea.

The identification of *Riphath* (*Dipath* in 1 Chr 1:6) is uncertain. Josephus identified this people with the Paphlagonians who lived between the Black Sea and Bythinia.

*Togarmah* is elsewhere mentioned 3x. These people were a trading partner with Tyre (Ezek 27:13f; 38:3-6). They are also mentioned in Hittite and Assyrian texts. They were located somewhere in the region of Urartu (Armenia).

*2. Grandsons through Javan (10:4):* **The sons of Javan: Elishah, Tarshish, the Kittim and the Rodanim.** Again the organizing principle is not geography. *Elishah* is mentioned 1 Chr 1:7 and in Ezek 27:7. These people exported purple and copper. They are mentioned in Akkadian and Hittite texts. Their identity is uncertain.

*Tarshish* is mentioned elsewhere 10x in the OT. Older works identified Tarshish as a Phoenician colony in Spain. New data points to a North African location, near modern Tunis.

The *Kittim* (a plural form) are elsewhere mentioned 7x. The Kittim came from Cyprus.

*Dodanim* (*Rodanim* in 1 Chr 1:7) probably inhabited the island of Rhodes.

*3. Migrations (10:5):* **From these the coastal lands spread into their lands each to its tongue, to their clans in their nations.** From these refers to the whole Japhethite stock. *Coastal lands* refers to the Greek coastal regions with the adjoining offshore islands, possibly also the entire territory surrounding the Caspian Sea and the Black Sea. *Each to its tongue* indicates that these migrations took place after the division of languages reported in ch 11. The initial impulse to dispersion was the confusion of languages.

*Clans* and *nations* indicate that there were further divisions after the initial dispersion according to language. The terms in this v indicate that the descendants of Noah's three sons are being divided by their ethnicity, geography, language and politics.

The words of 10:5 function as a kind of refrain (cf. 10:20, 31). "It closes a section in a solemn, monotonous way like the close of each of the days of creation."[517] The point of the v is that throughout the whole time span after the dispersion, people were subdividing and ramifying (branching out).

The v contains certain basic elements common to all that indicate that they are part of the human race— language, families or clans that perpetuate life.

The Japhetic peoples have contributed much to the progress of civilization. From these peoples come the scientific method, philosophy, democratic government, and advancements in legal theory.

---

[517] Westermann, ***Genesis 1-11***, 508.

# HAMITIC PEOPLES
## Gn 10:6-20

In 9:18 four descendants of Noah are named; but in Noah's prophetic words (9:25-27) only three are mentioned. One is passed over in silence. The same pattern is followed in the Table for the sons of Ham. Four sons are named. Descendants are listed for three of these. Put, however, is passed over in silence. This pattern indicates that the Table is selective.

Furthermore, the selectivity is indicated in that seven Cushite nations are named, and seven nations descended from Mizraim. Seven is the number of completeness. These two sets of seven names are separated by a narrative describing the Cushite kingdom of Nimrod. The list of Hamitic peoples concludes with the naming of eleven nations descended from Canaan.

Most of the Hamitic peoples were located to the south of Israel. The Hamites are treated in the second place so that the list might conclude with the Shemites. Hamites were Israel's closest and most bitter neighbors. Thirty Hamitic names are on the list, only four of which are direct descendants of Ham.

**A. Sons of Ham** (10:6)

*The sons of Ham: Cush, Mizraim, Put and Canaan.* *Cush* is generally the land south of Egypt, i.e., Nubia or Ethiopia. Cush is mentioned in Egyptian writings and 26x in the OT; but it is not always clear that in each case it refers to the same land. In view of what is reported in vv 8-12 about Nimrod it is unlikely that this is African Cush. There was an area in central Arabia called Kosh that mighty have been called Cush by the Hebrews. Nations descended from Cush are enumerated in v 7.

Descendants of Noah

```
                    Chart 19
                Table of Hamites

                       Ham
         ┌──────────┬─────┴──┬──────────┐
       Cush       Mizraim   Put        Canaan
        │           │                    │
        │     Ludites Anamites Le-   Sidon Hittites Jebusites
        │     habites Naphtuhites    Amorites Girgashites
        │     Pathusites Casluhites  Hivites Arkites Sinites Ar-
        │     Caphtorites            vadites Zemarites Ha-
        │
   ┌────┬──────┬──────┬──────┐
  Seba Havilah Sabtah Raamah Sabtechah
                       │
                    ┌──┴──┐
                  Sheba  Dedan
```

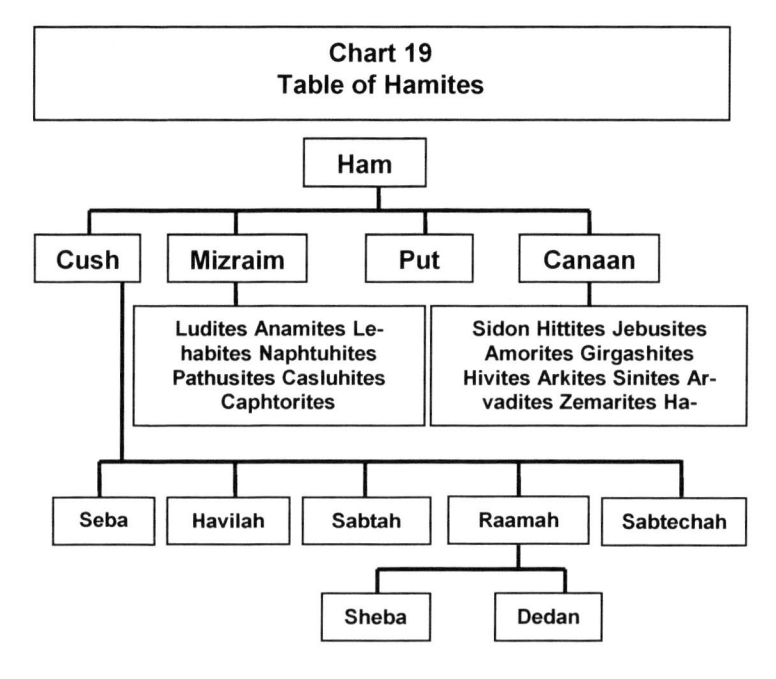

*Mizraim* refers to Egypt. The dual ending on the Hebrew word probably refers to the two great divisions of Egypt, i.e., Upper and Lower Egypt. Mizraim (Egypt) is mentioned many times in the OT. Nations descended from Mizraim are enumerated in vv 13-14.

*Put* is elsewhere mentioned 6x. Put is probably the area known to the Egyptians as Punt. It is supposedly located in the coastal areas of the Red Sea, opposite the SW point of Arabia, extending as far south as Somaliland. Josephus, however, understands Put as Libya.

*Canaan's* descendants occupied the area stretching from southern Syria to the Mediterranean Sea, including Phoenicia and Palestine. Nations descended from Canaan are enumerated in vv 15-18.

### B. Cushites (10:7)

The writer has selected for inclusion on the list of Cushites seven names. No doubt other names were

475

passed over. Seven served his purpose for indicating completeness.

*1. Cush's sons (10:7a):* **The sons of Cush: Seba, Havilah, Sabtah, Raamah and Sabtecah.** *Seba* was identified by Josephus as Meroe, the ancient capital of Ethiopia, between the white and blue Nile in Africa. The Greek geographer Strabo, however, refers to a people called Saba on the coast of the Red Sea. Elsewhere these people are mentioned 4x in the OT (Isa 43:3; 45:14).

*Havilah* (*sandy land*) is a stretch of land in southwest Arabia.

*Sabtah* is elsewhere mentioned only in 1 Chr 1:9. Possibly Sabtah was the old Arabian commercial city of Sabatah within the borders of modern Yemen.

*Raamah* is elsewhere mentioned 2x in the OT. Ezek 27:22 mentions them as a commercial people. A south Arabian city with a similar name is known from ancient texts. Strabo confirms the existence of an Arabian people called Raamanites.

*Sabtecah* is elsewhere mentioned only 1 Chr 1:9. The location is unknown. Some place this people on the Persian Gulf, others on the Red Sea.

*2. Cush's grandsons (10:7b):* **The sons of Raamah: Sheba and Dedan.** The grandson Raamah produced two great grandsons for Ham: *Sheba* is elsewhere mentioned 12x in the OT. The Sabeans were a people of southern Arabia. A queen from this land once visited Solomon.

*Dedan* is elsewhere mentioned 9x in the OT. The name also appears in ancient inscriptions. Dedan was located in northern Arabia on the border of Edom. Dedan was a caravan center for incense trade (Isa 21:13). Jeremiah warned merchants from Dedan working or staying in Edom to flee the country because God was bringing judgment on it (Jer 49:8). Ezekiel warned Edom that their soldiers fleeing even to Dedan would be struck down (Ezek 25:13). Ezekiel noted that Tyre traded with Dedan (Ezek 27:15, 20).

### C. Kingdom of Nimrod (10:8-12)

The list of Hamitic descendants is interrupted by a narrative detailing the origins of Babylonia and Assyria, two future enemies of Israel.

*1. Biblical data regarding Nimrod (10:8-9):* **Now Cush became the father of Nimrod; he began to be a mighty one on the earth. He was a mighty hunter before Yahweh; therefore it is said, Like Nimrod a mighty hunter before Yahweh.** The name *Nimrod* means "we shall rebel." The phrase *began to be* (4:26; 6:1; 9:20; 11:6) signals an important development in history. In this case, the innovation is naked aggression.

Four important facts are reported about Nimrod. First, he was *a mighty one* (*gibbōr*)—a tyrant. cf. 1 Chr 1:10. The terminology links Nimrod with the antediluvian tyrants mentioned in 6:4.

Second, Nimrod was *a mighty hunter* rather than a shepherd of his people. Some take this to mean that he was a hunter of game. Assyrian kings saw themselves as protectors of their people when they hunted wild game. More likely, however, Nimrod was a hunter of men. He was a slave trader who forced his captives to build his cities. Assyrian kings are said to have "hunted" people.

Third, Nimrod was a mighty hunter *before* (*liphnê*) *Yahweh*. Scholars differ over the meaning of this expression. At the very least it means Nimrod acted openly, almost defiantly. Aalders thinks "all we have here is an acknowledgment that God was aware of Nimrod's skill."[518] Jacob understands *before Yahweh* as a form of superlative. Even God could not have found a mightier hunter.[519] It is best to understand *before* in the

---

[518] Aalders, *BSC*, 225
[519] Jacob, *First Book*, 72.

sense, "in opposition to Yahweh." Cf. Gn 6:11. The LXX translates "against the Lord."[520]

Fourth, Nimrod's actions gave birth to a proverb in Israel that described other "hunters" or ruthless kings.

The importance of Nimrod lies in the fact that he was the founder of imperialism. With Nimrod patriarchal tribalism gave way to empire.

*2. Extra-biblical data.* The Assyrians deified Nimrod. They made him the god Ninurta, god of hunting. Ninurta was the titular deity of Kalach (Calah), a city founded by Nimrod. The land adjacent to Assyria was later called "land of Nimrod" (cf. Mic 5:6). The name Nimrod is perpetuated in several place names in Mesopotamia (e.g., Birs Nimrud, southwest of Babylon). Josephus identifies Nimrod as the builder of the tower of Babel (*Ant.* 1.4, 2).

Attempts to identify Nimrod with some king mentioned in the ancient Mesopotamian records have not met with widespread acceptance. Some suggested identifications of Nimrod are: Gilgamesh (ca. 2600 BC), Lugalzagisi, first empire builder (ca. 2350 BC); Sargon of Akkad (ca. 2345 BC); the Cushite Amenophis III (1411-1375 BC); and Tukulti-Ninurta I, the first Assyrian to rule over all Babylon (1246-1206 BC).

*3. Founding of his kingdom (10:10):* **And the beginning of his kingdom was Babel and Erech and Accad and Calneh, in the land of Shinar.** Babel was the original seat of Nimrod's empire. It was regarded as the first city of the world. Babel (Babylon) was located on the Euphrates River south of the point at which the Tigris and Euphrates rivers come closest together. Babylon was the conqueror of Judah. The city became for the Jews the symbol of all that was evil.

---

[520]Michael Akpa rejects the notion that Nimrod's actions were anti-God. "Did Nimrod Build the Tower of Babel?" *AASS* 7(2004):103-12.

Biblical *Erech* is the ancient city of Uruk located about 125 miles south of Babel on the Euphrates River. This was the city of the legendary hero Gilgamesh. In the Sumerian King List Uruk was one of the first cities mentioned after the Flood. Centuries later the inhabitants of this area were deported to Samaria by Assyrians (Ezra 4:9-10).

*Akkad* was in northern Babylonia. This was the city of the famous Sargon I (ca. 2500), arguably the greatest king of the third millennium BC. The exact location of Akkad is unknown. It is mentioned only here in the OT.

*Calneh* has not yet been identified. Some think it is the same as the important northern Babylonian city of Nippur.

The phrase *in the land of Shinar* refers to all four of the previously mentioned cities. Shinar was the whole land of Babylonia, the southern part of modern Iraq. Because of its association with Nimrod and the tower of Babel, Shinar came to connote evil (Dan 1:1; Zech 5:11).

*4. Expansion of his kingdom (10:11-12):* **From that land he went forth into Assyria, and built Nineveh and Rehoboth-Ir and Calah, and Resen between Nineveh and Calah; that is the great city.** From the land of Shinar (Babylonia) Nimrod went to *Assyria.* This fact harmonizes with Mic 5:6 where Assyria is called "the land of Nimrod." Over the centuries the Assyrians became one of the cruelest of nations. In the eighth century BC the Assyrians conquered Israel's northern kingdom.

Nimrod prided himself on building cities, not temples. In Assyria he built *Nineveh.* This became the base of his operations in northern Mesopotamia. Nineveh was located on the east bank of the Tigris River opposite modern Mosul in northern Iraq. *Rehoboth Ir* was one of the suburbs of Nineveh known to the Assyrians as Rebit-Ninua, lit., "broad places of the city." It was located where the modern city of Mosul stands.

*Calah* was located at the junction of the Tigris and Zab rivers. It was a royal city for many years. Later Calah was called Nimrud, probably because of its early connections with Nimrod. Calah was approximately twenty miles south of Nineveh.

*Resen* was about 2.5 miles northwest of Nimrud where the modern city of Selamiyeh stands. *The great city* could refer to Calah; but the phrase probably refers to the complex of all four neighboring cities (Jonah 1:2; 3:2-3; 4:11).

At the time the earliest books of the Bible were written Mesopotamia was dominated by Shemitic peoples (Babylonians; Assyrians). No one living in Moses' day and later could have imagined a day when a non-Shemitic empire had existed in Mesopotamia. Yet Gn 10 declares that in its earliest history Mesopotamia was dominated by Hamites.

Ancient records verify the accuracy of this portrayal of facts. The Sumerians, who made such substantial contributions to civilization, were a Hamitic people. Furthermore, the representation that Babylonia had an older civilization than Assyria is also historically accurate.

Finally, the Nimrod narrative is now known to be historically accurate on another point that probably would have been counterintuitive to anyone living in the Mosaic era. Side by side with conquest peaceful colonization played a role in the earliest history of Mesopotamia.

### D. Descendants of Mizraim (10:13-14)

*Mizraim was the father of the Ludites, Anamites, Lehabites, Naphtuhites, Pathrusites, Casluhites (from whom the Philistines came) and Caphtorites.* The writer again selects seven nations to illustrate descent from Mizraim. The number is symbolic and indicates completeness.

Lud or *the Ludites* are elsewhere mentioned 5x in the OT (cf. Jer 46:9; Ezek 30:5). Some identify the Ludites as the Lydians of Asia Minor, others (reading Lubites) as the Lybians of North Africa. See also under *Lehabites*.

The *Anamites* are mentioned elsewhere only 1 Chr 1:11. They are possibly to be identified as the Kenamites who occupied a large oasis west of Egypt.

The *Lehabites*, mentioned elsewhere only in 1 Chr 1:11, are probably the same as the Lubites found in 2 Chr 12:3; 16:8; Dan 11:43 and Nahum 3:9. Therefore this is a reference to the Lybians of North Africa.

The *Naphtuhites* appear elsewhere only in 1 Chr 1:11. They are probably to be identified with the Napatoech mentioned in Egyptian texts—a people who lived in the Nile Delta.

The *Pathrusites* are mentioned elsewhere only in 1 Chr 1:12. They were the inhabitants of Pathros or Upper (southern) Egypt mentioned 5x in the OT.

The *Casluhites*, also mentioned in 1 Chr 1:12, were possibly those who dwelled near Mount Cassius to the east of the Nile Delta.

The *Philistines* are probably not to be counted as one of the nations in the Table. They are mentioned parenthetically to identify Israel's bitter foe from about 1200 to 1000 BC. One wave or division of the Philistines came from Caphtor or Crete (Amos 9:7); but that does not mean that Crete was their original home.

The *Caphtorites* are mentioned elsewhere twice. Their land iz also mentioned twice. These people are the inhabitants of the island of Crete.

### E. Canaanites (10:15-19)

Because the Canaanites were so intertwined in the history of Israel, the writer abandons his use of the symbolic number seven. He aims here at completeness. Eleven peoples are traced back to Canaan, the grandson of Ham. The text further puts emphasis on the Canaanites by outlining their borders.

*1. Most powerful Canaanites (10:15):* **Canaan was the father of Sidon, his firstborn, and of Heth.** Sidon is said to be Canaan's firstborn. This may simply mean that the inhabitants of Sidon were the first branch of Canaanites to establish an independent nation. Perhaps the term Sidon represents the entire Phoenician people. Sidon was older than Tyre as a leading city in Phoenicia. In the literature of the ancient Near East Phoenicians are called Sidonians (cf. Judg 18:7; 1 Kgs 5:20; 16:31).

*Heth* was the ancestor of the Hittites. In patriarchal days the Hittites lived around the region of Hebron in the tribal territory of Judah. By the time of Moses, however, they had established a powerful kingdom in the heart of Asia Minor. Thousands of tablets from the royal archives of this people were located near the Turkish town of Boghazkoy. Their idolatry was repulsive to Isaac and Rebekah; but Esau married two of them (Gn 26:34-35; 27:46).

*2. Neighboring Canaanites (10:16-17a):* **Jebusites, Amorites, Girgashites, Hivites.** The Table now lists several subdivisions of the Canaanite peoples who lived in Palestine. The *Jebusites* were pre-Israelite inhabitants of Jerusalem and environs (Judg 19:10-11; 2 Sam 5:6-9). They were of Amorite and Hittite origins according to Ezek 16:3, 45.

The *Amorites* are mentioned frequently in Assyrian and Egyptian documents. In OT the term designates the inhabitants of the mountain range of central Palestine. In Moses' day they controlled as well the Transjordan region (Dt 3:8; Judg 11:22). The term sometimes is used of the pre-Israelite population of Palestine as a whole.

The *Girgashites* are mentioned elsewhere 4x in the OT, in Phoenician texts and possibly Egyptian inscriptions. It is uncertain where they lived.

The *Hivites* are frequently interchanged with Horites, the ancient Hurrian people. They lived in central Palestine around the towns of Shechem (Gn 34), Gibeon (Josh 9:1, 7), and in the Lebanon mountains near Mount Hermon (Judg 3:3; Josh 11:3; 2 Sam 24:7).

*3. Distant Canaanites (10:17b-18a):* **Arkites, Sinites, Arvadites, Zemarites and Hamathites.** The Table next lists the people who occupied certain cities in the territory of Phoenicia. The *Arkites* are mentioned elsewhere only in 1 Chr 1:16. These are the inhabitants of the Phoenician city of Arka or Irkata mentioned in Egyptian and Akkadian inscriptions. The city was located north of Tripoli Lebanon.

The *Sinites* are mentioned elsewhere only 1 Chr 1:15. These are the inhabitants of a Phoenician city known in the tablets as Sianoe, and to the Greek geographer Strabo as Sinna. The place is also attested in the Ugaritic texts. The city was not far from the city of Arka mentioned above.

The *Arvadites* are elsewhere mentioned only in 1 Chr 1:16, but their city is mentioned in Ezek 27:8, 11. These people occupied an island city just off the coast of Tripoli Lebanon. The city, known in the tablets as Arwada, is modern Ruwad. Arvadites are the most northern of the Phoenician peoples mentioned in the Table.

The *Zemarites* elsewhere are mentioned only in 1 Chr 1:16. These people inhabitant a Phoenician city named Samar in Egyptian texts, Soemoer in Amarna Tablets, and Simirra in Assyrian inscriptions. The modern name is Soemra. It is located between Tripoli Lebanon and Arvad.

The *Hamathites* appear elsewhere only in 1 Chr 1:16; but the famous city of Hamath on the Orontes River is mentioned over 30x. Hamath is the only inland city of this Phoenician group.

*4. Canaanite boundaries (10:18b-19):* **Later the Canaanite clans scattered and the borders of Canaan reached from Sidon towards Gerar as far as Gaza, and then toward Sodom, Gomorrah, Admah and Zeboiim, as far as Lasha.** The narrator sketches a verbal map of the territory occupied by the Canaanites because that is the region that God will give to Israel as their inheritance. The border of Canaan follows the seacoast highway from *Sidon* in the north to *Gaza* in the south. From there it extends to *Sodom and Gomorrah* south of the Dead Sea. A more detailed description of Canaanite territory is found in Nm 34:2-12. Cf. Gn 15:18; Ezek 47:15-20; 48:1-28.

Exact location of *Gerar* is disputed. *Gaza* is still a town to this day. *Sodom and Gomorrah* are named 15x in the OT. *Admah and Zeboiim* were located near Sodom and Gomorrah. They were destroyed at the same time as their more famous sister cities (Gn 14:2, 8; Dt 29:23; Hosea 11:8). *Lasha* was the region of the Dead Sea, perhaps the northern end.

The term *scattered* anticipates the Babel episode in ch 11.

### F. Conclusion of Hamite Table (10:20)

***These are the descendants of Ham by their clans and languages, in their territories and nations.*** The Hamitic peoples made substantial contribution to the progress of civilization. These peoples get the credit for some of the basic technological inventions. Hamitic peoples were the founders of modern civilization.

# SHEMITIC PEOPLES
## Gn 10:21-31

Shem was blessed by Noah. The chosen line of legitimate rulers came through him. The mention of the Shemites is the climax of the Table. The Shemites listed in the Table are twenty-six in number of which five are sons.

**A. Introduction** (10:21)

The genealogy of Shem is introduced by two statements, the first looking back to the previous narrative, the second looking forward to the genealogy yet to be presented.

*1. Backward link 10:21a):* **Sons were born to Shem whose older brother was Japheth.** This translation follows that of NIV and NRSV. Another rendering is "the older brother of Japheth" (NASB; NJPS). The Hebrew is ambiguous. The ambiguity is maintained in KJV which reads, "the brother of Japheth the elder." The chronological note in 11:10 necessitates that Japheth be the older. See comments there.

*2. Forward link (10:21b):* **Shem was the ancestor of all the sons of Eber.** *Ancestor* is lit., "father of." At the very least Shem was four generations removed from Eber. Clearly the narrator wished to highlight Eber by mentioning his name out of order. Again his name is highlighted by being repeated as the son of Shelah (v 24) and as the father of Peleg and Joktan (v 25). So why are Eber's *sons* mentioned here? Perhaps it is because this was the last generation before a major division took place in the descendants of Shem.

Biblical Protology

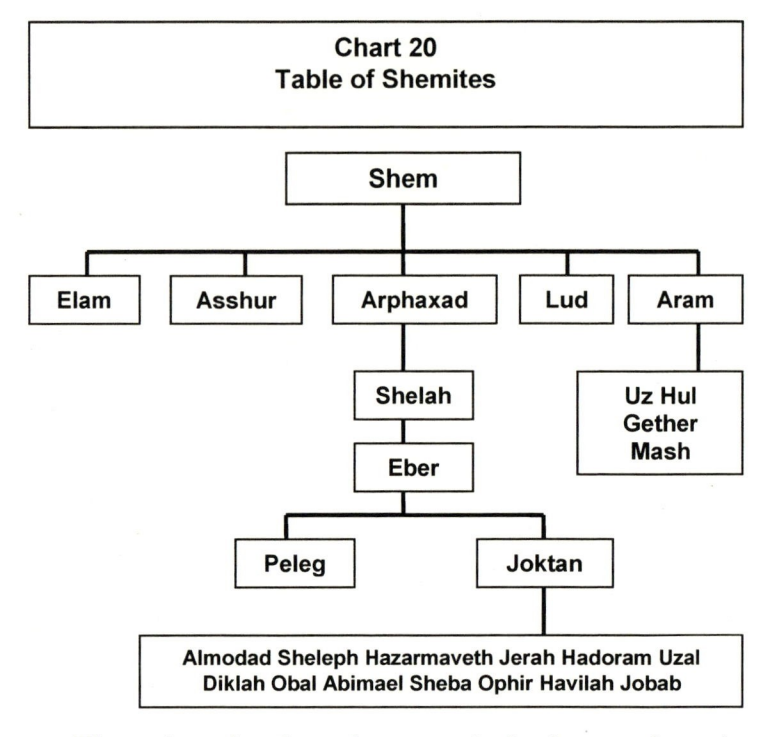

**Chart 20
Table of Shemites**

```
                    Shem
  ┌────────┬────────┼────────┬────────┐
 Elam   Asshur   Arphaxad   Lud     Aram
                    │                 │
                  Shelah           Uz Hul
                    │              Gether
                   Eber             Mash
                    │
              ┌─────┴─────┐
            Peleg       Joktan
                          │
        Almodad Sheleph Hazarmaveth Jerah Hadoram Uzal
        Diklah Obal Abimael Sheba Ophir Havilah Jobab
```

The writer abandons the numerical scheme of previous lists. Shem's descendants are traced down to the two sons of Eber, Peleg and Joktan. From that point the list displays the line of the second son, Joktan (vv 26-29). Then the writer inserts the Babel narrative (11:1-9). Then a second Shemite genealogy appears, this one tracing the descendants of the first son of Eber (11:10-32).

Babel not only divided the peoples in the confusion of tongues; it also led to a bifurcation in the line of Shem. The descendants of Eber through Joktan terminate at Babel; the descendants of Eber through Peleg lead to Abraham. The first group sought to make a name (*shem*) for themselves by building a city (11:1); the second group produced that one for whom God promised to make a name (12:2).

In this introduction to Shem there is no mention of Ham. The reference to Shem and Japheth together without Ham may be intended to recall Noah's final blessing of Shem and Japheth (9:26-27) where Ham is also excluded.

### B. Sons of Shem (10:22)

*The sons of Shem: Elam, Asshur, Arphaxad, Lud and Aram.* Five men (or people groups) are said to be the sons (descendants) of Shem. *Elam* is a people and country mentioned a number of times in the OT. The country was located east of Babylon, in the southwestern part of modern Iran. The Elamites were a power in third and second millennia BC. Some Elamites were among the audience that heard Peter preach the first gospel sermon on the day of Pentecost (Acts 2:9).

*Asshur* gave his name to the land of Assyria, mentioned twice previously in 2:14; 10:11. The Assyrians were located along middle course of the Tigris River. Assyria was a strong, independent kingdom as early as 2000 BC. Both the land and the people are often mentioned in the OT. The earliest inhabitants of Assyria were, however, Hamitic Sumerians, not Shemites.

*Arphaxad* is thought to be Babylon, though the exact explanation of the name is uncertain. Aalders, however, links Arphaxad to territory that the Greeks called Arrapachitis that was in the hills of the upper part of the great Zab River.[521]

*Lud* may refer to a people called *Lubdu* in cuneiform. They were located on the Upper Tigris near Armenia. Others think the reference is to the Lydians in Asia Minor.

*Aram* refers to a people widely dispersed in Syria and Mesopotamia. The Arameans are mentioned both in

---

[521] Aalders, *BSC*, 234.

OT and Assyrian texts. They migrated into those locations from Kir (Amos 9:7), probably in southern Babylonia near Elam. The Aramean kingdom that centered in Damascus became especially important in later Israelite history. The Aramaic language and script began to spread in the Near East before 1000 BC. By the sixth century BC Aramaic was widely used in the area. After the Babylonian exile Aramaic displaced Hebrew as the popular language in Palestine. Portions of the books of Daniel and Ezra are written in the Aramaic language.

### C. Grandsons of Shem (10:23-24a)

*1. Through Aram (10:23):* **The sons of Aram: Uz, Hul, Gether and Mash.** *Uz* is mentioned 8x in OT. As a place name Uz was the homeland of Job, but the site is unknown. It was east of the Jordan River, but whether in the north in Aramean territory or in the south near Edomite territory is debated. Perhaps there were two peoples, one located near Syria, the other to the south between Egypt and Arabia.

*Hul* and *Gether* are mentioned elsewhere only 1 Chr 1:17. Their identity is unknown.

*Mash* is read *Meshech* in the Greek version and 1 Chr 1:17, and that is the reading followed by NIV. If this is correct, then both Japheth and Shem had sons name *Meshech*. Mash may be connected with Mount Masius of northern Mesopotamia or with the Lebanon mountains.[522]

*2. Through Arphaxad (10:24a LXX):* **Arphaxad was the father of Cainan.** These words dropped out of the Hebrew text at some early stage of manuscript copying. The Greek version adds these words here and in 11:12-17. The addition supplies the anticipated ten names between Shem and Abraham. It is easier to explain the

---

[522]Waltke, *GAC*, 173

omission as due to haplography than to explain why these words were added by the Greek translators. This Cainan was part of the lineage of Christ (Lk 3:35-36).

**D. Third-Sixth Generations** (10:24b-29)

*1. Third generation (10:24a):* ***[And Cainan] was the father of Shelah.*** *Shelah* probably means "sprout, branch, or descendant" (cf. 38:5, 11). This may be an abbreviated form of the name Methushelah.

*2. Fourth generation (10:24c):* ***And Shelah was the father of Eber.*** *Eber* is the last of the legitimate postdiluvian rulers before the Dispersion. From what the writer says in 10:21 it is clear that he regarded the sons of Eber as the most important branch of the Shemites. *Eber* is related to the word "Hebrew."[523] His name has also turned up in the Ebla tablets that were excavated in northern Syria. These tablets date to about 2400 BC. A king named *Ebrium* ruled over Ebla for twenty-eight years. Could this king be the same as biblical Eber? At the very least, the name Eber is ancient.

*3. Fifth generation (10:25):* ***Two sons were born to Eber: one was named Peleg, because in his time the earth was divided; his brother was named Joktan.*** The name *Peleg* means "division." His name is appropriate because of something that transpired in his days. Five views have been put forward regarding the meaning of the phrase, *the earth was divided* (r. *plg*).

First, some apply these words to a dispersion of people prior to Babel.[524] According to this view Babel only involved the Shemites.

Second, some have proposed that the clause points to a division of the world into areas or maps.[525] Peleg was an ancient cartographer!

---

[523] Gn 14:13; 39:14; 40:15; 41:12; Ex 2:11; 3:18.
[524] W.S. LaSor, *Eternity*, December, 1960.
[525] Albert Ferguson, *Bible-Science Newsletter*.

Third, some see here a reference to the drifting of the continents into their present locations.[526] This view is based on the usage of the noun *peleg* in ten passages where it is associated with water; hence division by water.

Fourth, it has been proposed that the v refers to the widespread canalization of the land of Mesopotamia, a major development in the civilization of the region.[527] This understanding is supported by the OT usage of the noun *peleg*, and by cognate words in both Ugaritic and Akkadian that mean "canal."

Fifth, a majority of scholars see in this note a reference to the dispersion at Babel. This means that chronologically the Table of Nations comes after the dispersion account in ch 11. This is the most likely interpretation of the passage in view of the fact that in Ps 55:9 the same Hebrew verb (r. *plg*) is used alongside the phrase "confounded their speech." Furthermore, in three other places in ch 10 there is a foreshadowing of the division of mankind according to languages (10:5, 20, 31).

Joktan is an Aramaic name meaning "watchful." Joktan was the forefather of the tribes of south Arabia.

*4. Sixth generation (10:26-29):* **Joktan was the father of Almodad, Sheleph, Hazarmaveth, Jerah, Hadoram, Uzal, Diklah, Obal, Abimael, Sheba, Ophir, Havilah and Jobab. All these were the sons of Joktan.** Practically nothing is known about the tribes mentioned as the sixth generation of Shemites. *Almodad* was an ancestor, region or tribe in Yemen. *Sheleph* was probably a Yemenite tribe. *Hazarmaveth* may refer to the

---

[526]D.G. Barnhouse, *Genesis: A Devotional Exposition* (Grand Rapids: Zondervan, 1970): 1:68; B. Northrup, "Continental Drift and the Fossil Record," *Repossess the Land* (Minneapolis: Bible-Science Association, 1979), 165-170.

[527]Skinner, *ICC*, 220; Hamilton, *NICOT*, 345; D.M. Fouts, "Peleg in Gn 10:25," *JETS*, 41(Mar 1998): 17-21.

south Arabian region of Hadramaut. *Jerah* is a yet unidentified region. *Hadoram* is an Arabian tribe.

*Uzal* traditionally is the pre-Islamic name of Sana'a, capital of Yemen. *Diklah* is an oasis in southern Arabian. The name means "palm-land." *Obal* was in SW Arabia. *Abimael* is unidentified. *Sheba* may be the same location as Seba in 10:7. *Ophir* was between Sheba and Havilah in SW Arabia in the region now known as Oman. This area was famous for its gold (Job 22:24). It possibly included the coast of Africa opposite this area of Arabia. Ophir may be called the land of Punt in Egyptian sources. *Havilah* may be the same location as the Havilah of 10:7. *Jobab* is in southern Arabia.

### E. Other Shemite Details (10:30-31)

*1. Joktanite boundaries (10:30):* **The region where they lived stretched from Mesha toward Sephar, in the eastern hill country.** The reference is to the region of Joktan's sons. Mention of these boundaries shows the importance of the Shemites to the narrator. Neither of the two names can be definitely located. *Mesha* was a territory in northern Arabia, far south of Hadramaut. *Sephar* was a city in what is now Oman or Yemen.

*2. Refrain (10:31):* **These are the sons of Shem by their clans and languages, in their territories and nations.** This is essentially the same note that closed out the listing of Japhetic (10:5) and Hamitic (10:20) peoples.

Like the other two great families of the human race, the Shemites have made lasting contributions to the development of civilization. It is among the Shemites that the original revelation of the Creator God has been preserved. The world's three great monotheistic religions have Shemitic roots.

## CONCLUSION OF THE TABLE
## Gn 10:32

*These are the clans of Noah's sons, according to their lines of descent, within their nations. From these the nations spread out over the earth after the Flood.* Mention of *Noah's sons* repeats 10:1 and signals the conclusion of the Table. The verb *spread out* prepares the way for the account of the dispersion to follow.

## IMPORTANCE OF GENESIS 10

The Table of Nations is important in six ways. First, the Table is important ethnologically. This Table is without parallel in ancient literature. It is a modified genealogy. The term *son* in Gn 10 may mean "descendant, successor, or nation;" the term *father* may mean "ancestor, predecessor, or founder."[528]

Second, the Table is theologically important. It stresses the natural non-magical explanation of the rapid increase of mankind after the Flood. This natural proliferation was in accord with divine will. Ethnic diversity is a natural product of multiplication of people; therefore ethnological divisions of the human race must be part of God's grand design for the world. Linguistic diversity and dispersion of mankind, however, have another explanation.

Third, the Table is important thematically. The Table logically belongs after the Babel episode of ch 11 for it describes the *spreading* (r. *prd*) in 10:5, 23 or *scattering* (r. *pûš*) in 10:18 of nations *each with its own language* (10:5). Ch 11 also speaks of the *scattering* (r. *pûts*) *over the face of all the earth*. The Table is placed here as a fulfillment of the *be fruitful and multiply and fill the*

---

[528]Youngblood, *BGIC*, 128.

*earth* command. Cf. 1:28 and 9:1. Thus men fulfill the command of God to fill the earth, but only after they are forced to do so by divine judgment.

Fourth, the Table is practically important. It is a bulwark against racial prejudice. The text insists "there is a network of interrelatedness among all people."[529]

Fifth, the Table is symbolically important. Throughout the Table there is a preference for the number seven. While there is symmetry in the structuring of most of the genealogies in this ch, the Canaanite genealogy is asymmetrical—there are no sevens. In all seventy names are listed—fourteen from Japheth, thirty from Ham, twenty-six from Shem. Seventy is a multiple of two numbers (seven and ten) both of which connote completeness, so seventy is a large and complete number. The symbolism of seventy may be intended to represent all nations.[530] This Table anticipates the number of the members of Jacob's family who migrated to Egypt (Gn 46:27; Ex 1:5). Moses himself made the connection between these seventy nations and the number of Jacob's sons (Dt 32:8).

Sixth, the Table is messianically important. It may have influenced the selection of the seventy witnesses in Lk 10:1 (Kidner).

Seventh, the Table is geographically important. It is "a verbal map of the world."[531] It displays the end results of the scattering of mankind caused by the debacle at Babel.[532]

---

[529]Brueggemann, *Genesis*, 93.
[530]Other examples of seventy as complete number: Gn 46:27; Ex 1:5; Dt 10:22; Judg 8:30; 9:2, 5; 2 Kgs 10:1, 6, 7.
[531]Brueggemann, *Genesis*, 91.
[532]Youngblood, *BGIC*, 128.

## OBSERVATIONS

There are many uncertainties about the Table of Nations. In concluding the discussion of this important ch a few observations are in order.

### A. Problem of the Names
*1. Individuals, tribes or places?* Are the names that appear in the Table personal names, or tribal names? One cannot always be sure. For certain some of the names in the Table are those of individuals (e.g., *Japheth, Nimrod*). The Table, however, also contains the names of well-known nations (e.g., *Egypt, Medes, Elam*) and prominent cities (e.g., *Elishah; Sidon*). Some of the names are formulated in a way that cannot possibly refer to individuals. For example, the Table frequent uses plurals (e.g., *Ludites; Caphtorites*). Yet even behind some of the obvious tribal names may be tribal ancestors. Frequently the text indicates that the reference is to a nation or tribe rather than an individual.

*2. Duplicate names.* Why are there duplicate names in the Table? *Sheba, Ophir,* and *Havilah* appear both in the Shemitic and Hamitic lines. Are these to be interpreted as an intermingling of tribes; or is the Table reporting two different ethnic groups that just happen to have the same name?

### B. Antiquity of the Table
There are various indications in the text that the Babel episode (11:1-9) is chronologically prior to the Table of Nations (cf. 10:25). Unfortunately the date for the Babel incident cannot be precisely determined. The mention of Sodom and Gomorrah (10:19) in the Table fixes a lower limit date for this material. The Table must have been compiled prior to about 2000 BC when those two cities were destroyed by God. So the Table repre-

sents the situation as it existed sometime between the Babel episode and the destruction of Sodom and Gomorrah. The Table appears to represent the state of the nations in the days of Abraham.

### C. Classification Problem

Modern scholars classify peoples according to language whereas the Table of Nations classifies according to ethnicity. So a people descended from Ham according to Gn 10 may speak a Shemitic language, and vice versa. For example, the Canaanites were descendants of Ham, but they spoke a Shemitic language. It is not a matter of one system of classification being superior to the other; they are just different. Gn 10 is not a treatise on linguistic relationships; it a factual, historical record of the migrations of men from a common center in Shinar.

### D. Restrictive Nature

Why are so many nations omitted from the Table? The Table is restricted to the sons of Noah and their descendants. Were there others? Some hold that there were peoples in remote regions that survived the Flood.[533] Ramm takes the position that the sons of Noah were Caucasian and so were all of their descendants. Non-Caucasian peoples survived the Flood.[534] If the Flood, however, was anthropologically universal there would have been no survivors except Noah's family. This is what the Bible clearly teaches.

The Table is restricted geographically to those descendants of Noah's sons who founded nations relatively close to Israel. The Table is limited to what could be gathered from travelers and merchants. Places where data

---

[533] J.N. Dawson, *The Meeting Place of Geology and History* (1894; New York: Revell, 1904), 186ff.
[534] Ramm, *CVSS*, 234.

data were readily available receive more attention than those where travel was difficult or occasional.

The Table refers to the primary distribution of men from Shinar over certain districts. It does not attempt to trace subsequent migrations. Peoples could have moved around, mixed, separated, and even adopted new languages etc. The Table is a snapshot rather than a motion picture.

The Table of Nations says nothing about race or racial characteristics except what may be inferred from heredity.

# CONCLUSION

By omitting any reference to Israel, Gn 10 stresses that Elohim is the God of the Gentiles. The ch uses the term *gôy* ("nation, Gentile") 5x, not the word *'am* ("people"). Only in the following ch does the role of Israel among the nations begin to be revealed. So God is interested in all people, in their own right.[535] Their locations and movements were all governed by divine will (Dt 32:8; Acts 17:26). Even those future powers that do such harm to God's people are under his sovereign power.

Ch 10 is transitional. It moves from general history to election history. It was out of concern for the salvation of the nations, that God called Abraham and his posterity.[536] The prediction that all families of the earth will be blessed in Abraham (Gn 12:3) supports this conclusion. God selected the seventy sons of Jacob (Gn 46:27) as the vehicle by which to bless the seventy (symbolic of all) nations of the world.

---

[535] D.E. Gowan, *Genesis 1-11: From Eden to Babel* (ITC; Grand Rapids: Eerdmans, 1988), 114.
[536] Mathews, *NAC*, 430.

# 25
# DISPERSION AT BABEL
# Gn 11:1-9

The division of the world during the time of Peleg (10:25) is now explained in a flashback. This places the event about a hundred years after the Flood (Leupold). Within that time the population might have grown to as many as 30,000 (if each family had about eight children). Kidner is more cautious. He dates the Babel episode either soon after the Flood, or else he limits it to a particular people.

The Babel incident is significant in at least two ways. First, the event has theological implications. The multiplicity of languages in the world does not witness to human ingenuity, but to mankind's defiance of the Creator.

Second, the episode is thematically important. A close relationship exists between this ch and the previous one. Gn 11 is not an attempt to repeat what already has been covered in ch 10. Ch 11 cites the *reason* for the dispersion of peoples previously depicted; ch 10 gives the *results* of the dispersion narrated in ch 11.

## SETTING
## Gn 11:1-3

### A. Postdiluvian Unity (11:1)

*Now the whole earth used the same language and the same words.* As in 9:19 and 10:25 the word *earth* refers to the population of the earth. The writer stresses the unity of the human race with the phrase, *all the world/earth* (5x). The episode cannot be restricted to Japhethites, Hamites or Shemites. The focus of world unity was in the language of mankind (also mentioned 5x).

The human family spoke the same language immediately after the Deluge. Presumably that was also true before the Deluge. *Used the same language* is lit., "were of one speech." They had one way of pronouncing words. *The same words* is lit. "one (kind of) words." This may be simple parallelism. If there is any different nuance in the second expression, it may refer to subject matter. Unified language is an indication of deeper spiritual and cultural unity.

### B. Original Language

From time to time efforts have been made to discover the original language. A sixth century Egyptian king identified the first word spoken by two infants raised by a dumb goatherd as Phrygian—akin to Greek. He concluded that Phrygian was the original language of mankind. James IV of Scotland (13th century) tried the same experiment and discovered the first word to be what he thought was Hebrew. The rabbis also believed the original language was Hebrew. Others have argued that it was a proto-semitic language behind Aramaic, Hebrew and Arabic.

Until the second half of the twentieth century only a few authorities gave support to the concept of one original language. Today the concept of an original language of mankind has received a more favorable reception in the scientific community. Russian scientists have done extensive research on the question. They have even tried to reconstruct some of the basic vocabulary of the original tongue, which they call "proto-World."[537]

---

[537]William Allman "The Mother Tongue," *U.S. News & World Report* (Nov 5, 1990): 60-70.

Dispersion at Babel

## C. Postdiluvian Migration (11:2)

*1. Traveling (11:2a):* ***And it came about as they journeyed eastward.*** For a time after the Flood the human population lived in the mountainous region of Ararat. *Journeyed* (lit., "pulled up stakes") suggests that the postdiluvian population was initially nomadic. *Eastward* (*miqqedem*) is lit., "from the east." In Hebrew this phrase can mean to move in an easterly direction (cf. Gn 12:8).[538] In Gn the east is the direction of separation (Gn 3:24; 4:16; 13:10-12; 25:6; 29:1). The journey is spiritual as well as geographical.[539]

*2. Settling (11:2b):* ***that they found a plain in the land of Shinar and settled there.*** The *plain* is the alluvial Euphrates-Tigris river valleys. *Shinar* (Babylonia) was known for its fertility. *Shinar* is actually southeast of Ararat; but the Hebrews rarely give directions with modern western precision. On *Shinar*, see on 10:10. The human family *settled there* in Shinar. Their action was the opposite of God's command to fill the earth.

## D. Postdiluvian Technology (11:3)

*1. Exhortation (11:3a):* ***And they said to one another, Come, let us make bricks and burn them thoroughly.*** One advantage of living in the plain was the abundance of clay. This led to making bricks for building material. The text does not say that the postdiluvians invented bricks. Both biblical and Mesopotamian traditions speak of cities before the Deluge. Bricks must have been used in some of these cities. The Flood, however, had destroyed all antediluvian cities and structures. For a time after the Flood men were tent-dwellers (cf. 9:21, 27).

---

[538] Others think the meaning is that they moved about in the lands to the east of Israel.
[539] Mathews, *NAC*, 478.

## Biblical Protology

The narrator permits the people to condemn themselves by the proposal he attributes to them. *Said to one another* is lit., "each to his neighbor." There is mutual agreement to change lifestyles. The sin of defying God's postdiluvian directive becomes a matter of public policy. *Come* (r. *yhb*) is an emphatic imperative.

*Burn them thoroughly* is lit., "burn to a burning." The phrase evidences their pride in this newly discovered (or re-discovered) technology of brick-making. The Hebrew phrases in this sentence have slogan-like assonance and cadence.

Early-on men had learned the art of making sun-baked bricks. Burnt bricks, which are stronger, were a later development. The core of a Babylonian Ziqqurat (temple tower) was made of crude sun-dried bricks encased in an outer coating of kiln-fired brick. Generally the Babylonians used only sun-dried bricks in their homes.

2. *Explanation (11:3b):* **And they used brick for stone, and they used tar for mortar.** The clause *they used brick for stone* perhaps serves two purposes. First, the original readers of this text were familiar with the stone monuments of Egypt. Using bricks for a public works project was a novel concept for them. Second, the narrator may have written these words contemptuously. He is emphasizing the impermanence of their edifice. No matter how well-built, brick crumbles into dust over time. The builders did not say *instead of stone*, as though they knew they were using an inadequate substitute. They were arrogant enough to think that their bricks were equivalent to stone!

*They used tar for mortar* indicates that the narrator had "an astonishingly intimate knowledge of Babylonian building techniques."[540] Bitumen boils up from under-

---

[540] Ibid, 64.

ground near Babylon. Numerous Mesopotamian inscriptions speak of *bitumen and brick*. Herodotus was struck by use of bitumen in the area (*His.* 1:179). Structures so bonded have been found in that region. Lack of fuel for ovens resulted in low temperature and poor quality, porous and fragile bricks. Bituminous mastic not only served as a bonding agent, it also added strength to the bricks as well.

# TRANSGRESSION
# Gn 11:4

**A. Proposal** (11:4a, b)

*1. A city (11:4a): **And they said, Come, let us build for ourselves a city.*** The emphatic imperative *come* (r. *yhb*) is repeated from the previous v. This is a somewhat rare exclamation indicating willful resolve. They were encouraged by their previous success in making bricks. This need not mean that the decision was made as soon as the successful making of bricks was discovered. Perhaps this idea occurred to them only when population growth appeared to make scattering a real possibility. Agricultural lifestyle was putting pressure on the space available in the plain of Shinar.

In any case, the words seem to indicate that arrogance and ambition are escalating. They now aspire to move beyond their humble brick dwellings to construction that is large-scale and magnificent. The city they contemplated building is identified in v 9 as Babylon.

In Mesopotamian literature priests consulted gods through omens at every stage of construction. Cylinder seals pictorially represent the gods participating in the construction chores. The Bible presents this building project as human in origin, in fact, as an act of defiance against the stated will of God.

**2. A tower (11:4b): *even a tower with its top in the heavens.*** This united effort was quite ambitious. It involved *a city, even a tower.* There is no special emphasis on the building of the tower. A defensive wall was the hallmark of a city (see 4:17). In the earliest periods cities were not so much designed for habitation as for protection and cultic purposes.

*Its top in the heavens* points to a tower of great height. Popular interpretation sees here the attempt of earth-bound men to become like God who dwells in the heavens.[541] This is clearly not the right interpretation. There is no biblical analogy for the notion that it is possible for men to physically storm heaven. Mesopotamian religion would have found such an idea whimsical. This kind of expression is used elsewhere in the Bible; it means nothing more than great height (cf. Dt 1:28; 9:1). Mesopotamian literature is full of allusions to construction projects that are described in language similar to what is used here.

### B. A Zikkurat?

A zikkurat was a massive and lofty staircase structure constructed for religious purposes. It resembled a man-made mountain. A zikkurat was considered a kind of half-way house where gods might descend to meet men and vice versa. The zikkurat was topped by a small shrine, often painted blue to symbolize the heavens, covered with signs of the Zodiac and other drawings of the heavens.

Nearly every city in Mesopotamia had a ziqqurrat temple-tower. Thirty have been unearthed in twenty-five sites. They varied in size and shape (square; rectangu-

---

[541]Blocher (*In the Beginning*, 203). R.A. Oden, Jr. thinks that assaulting the sky is "a perfect and natural metaphor for the human assault upon the divinely ordained cosmos." "Divine Aspirations in Atrahasis and in Genesis 1-11," *ZAW* 93(1981): 211.

lar), but they usually had a succession of levels (seven the highest known) approached by an external ramp or staircase. The worshiper climbed the outside staircase all the way to the top in the hope that his god would condescend to meet with him in the little chapel there.

Was the tower of Babel a zikkurat? The language used here is actually a stereotype in Mesopotamian literature for zikkurats and especially for the temple of Marduk. Nothing in Gn, however, indicates that the tower was in fact a zikkurat. The zikkurats may have been constructed in imitation of the tower of Babel, not vice versa.

Have archaeologists found the ruins of the Gn 11 tower? Leupold thinks Birs Nimrud—temple of Nebo—at Borsippa fifteen miles southwest of Babylon is it. Others think Esagil—the temple of Marduk in Babylon is the tower of Babel.

**C. Motives** (11:4c, d)

*1. Human pride (11:4b):* **And let us make for ourselves a name.** This language is used elsewhere only of God (Isa 63:12; Jer 32:20; Neh 9:10) or the king (2 Sam 8:13). One makes a name for himself by outstanding deeds. *Name* refers to reputation. The city with its tower is "a monument to egotistical mankind" (Youngblood).

In Mesopotamia kings ensured posthumous fame by inscribing their names and titles on bricks and by depositing cylinder seals in foundations. Perhaps something like that transpired here. The Babel project appears to be an attempt to gain immortality and significance through human achievements. The account makes the point that great works of civilization are often motivated by sinful pride.

*2. Societal unity (11:4d):* **lest we be scattered abroad over the face of the whole earth.** The ultimate goal of the builders was to maintain societal unity. The construction project itself promoted unity. The large masses of people suggest that there was a considerable concentration of authority and organization. Perhaps the tower was intended to point the way back to the center of their civilization, no matter how far people might wander from that point.

God had commanded postdiluvian man to be fruitful, multiply and fill the earth. They chose to do otherwise. Abraham looked for a city whose maker and builder was God. The Babelites built a city to assert their autonomy from God.

*3. Other possible motives.* Although there is no support in the text, commentators have also proposed some additional possible motives for building the tower. Some suggest that the builders were aiming for military or flood security. Still others have proposed the tower was designed to have religious significance.

## EVALUATION
## Gn 11:5-6

### A. Condescension (11:5a)

*And Yahweh came down.* What irony! They built up to defy God; but he came down to frustrate their scheme. Their mighty city and high tower are so puny that God must come down to view it. This v does not impinge on divine omniscience, for coming down to see presupposes prior knowledge in heaven of what was transpiring on earth. The theological implication of this v is that God is not among people on earth as in Gn 2-3; 4:6-9. This is the anthropomorphic way of saying God intervened in the natural course of things (Ex 3:8; Nm 11:17). There may also be in this v a rejection of human efforts to close the gap between God and man.

## B. Examination (11:5b)

*To see the city and the tower which the sons Adam had built.* Yahweh undertook a judicial investigation. This language is used again of Yahweh's actions at Sodom (Gn 18:21). Lest his absolute justice be questioned, God will not pour out judgment without first conducting his own judicial inquiry.

*The sons of Adam* were not the Hamites, or Shemites, or wicked men, but all men. The language is heavily charged with temporal significance. The tower builders were nothing more than earthlings.

The tense of the verb is important. The text (11:8) makes it clear that the building had not been completed. For this reason the NIV renders the verb "were building." The Hebrew verb, however, is perfect, pointing to completed action. The idea is that what they had built thus far indicated their intent.

## C. Confirmation (11:6a)

*And Yahweh said, Behold, they are one people, and they all have one language.* Yahweh's investigation confirmed what the narrator already has reported. The one language, like the tower, is a symbol of their unity in opposition to God. It facilitated working together on the grand project of the city and tower.

## D. Concern (11:6b)

*And this is their beginning of doing, and now nothing that they purpose to do will be withheld to them.* If left unchecked, man would be encouraged by success to undertake ever more bold acts of defiance against God.

*Purpose* (r. *zmm*) means "to consider or devise." It is used also of Yahweh's purpose in judgment. Here it refers to the evil purpose of wicked men. *Withheld* (r. *btsr* in Niphal) means "to cut off, to make inaccessible." The two rare verbs are elsewhere used of God in Job 42:2.

The ability to carry out whatever purpose one has is an attribute of the Deity. Essentially this is an OT way of referring to what theologians call the sovereignty of God. The conjunction of these two verbs in the present narrative indicates that wicked men were on the path to overstepping their God-appointed boundaries.[542] In this way the sin of the tower-builders was the same as the sin of the garden-dwellers in Gn 3.

## JUDGMENT
## Gn 11:7-8

### A. Sentence Determined (11:7)

*Come, let us go down and there confuse their language, that they may not understand one another's speech.* Better division than collective apostasy! *Come* is used in mockery of the stated intentions of the tower builders (vv 3, 4). *Let us* points to the unity of the godhead as in Gn 1:26. This is one of thirteen places where the Jewish scribes altered the text to the singular. *Confuse* ($nāb^elāh$) shuffles the consonants of *let us make bricks* ($nilb^enāh$)—another play on words. Confusion of language reverses the one language and common speech of v 1. *Understand* is lit., "hear."

### B. Sentence Executed (11:8a)

*So Yahweh scattered them abroad from there over the face of the whole earth.* Anthropologists say that the chief barrier among peoples is language. By confusing their speech God scattered mankind from their central location in the plain of Shinar. These words reverse *and they settled there* in v 2. *Upon the face of all the earth* indicates that the will of God for the postdiluvian world

---

[542]Westermann, *Genesis 1-11*, 351f.

## Dispersion at Babel

was accomplished in spite of man's efforts to thwart that will.

### C. Judgment Results (11:8b-9)

*1. Work stoppage (11:8b):* **And they stopped building the city.** The partially built city was a monument to the folly of mankind. Tower building is not the main thrust of the passage. The tower was but a part of the city that men sought to build to frustrate God's command to fill the earth.

*2. Naming (11:9a):* **Therefore its name was called Babel, because there Yahweh confused the language of the whole earth.** *Babel* was written in Assyrian *Bab-ilu*, meaning "gate or court of god." It may be that God gives their name another meaning from a similar sounding root (r. *bll*), "to confuse." On the other hand, this v may explain the original meaning of the name *Babel* to which the Babylonians later gave a new interpretation. In either case the name *Babel* was suitable because there Yahweh confused the language of mankind. This is not an etymological explanation of the meaning of the word *Babel*, but a play on words such as is common in Hebrew narrative. The builders sought a name for themselves; their project received a name that to the Hebrews, at least, pointed to their folly.

*3. Scattering (11:9b):* **And from there Yahweh scattered them abroad over the face of the whole earth.** Use of the name *Yahweh* 3x in vv 8-9 suggests that Moses regards the action of God in confusing the languages as a demonstration of his mercy. God defeated man's purpose so as to prevent him from injuring himself further. In this respect the scattering of the tower transgressors parallels the expulsion of the garden-transgressors.

*4. Parallelism.* The punitive actions of God match the presumptive intentions of the transgressors as indicated in Chart 21.

| Chart 21 Parallelism in the Babel Narrative ||
| --- | --- |
| **Presumptive Intentions** **11:1-4** | **Punitive Actions** **11:5-9** |
| One language/common speech | One people/one language |
| Come let us (twice) | Come let us |
| Build a city with a tower | Ceased to build |
| Make a name | Its name was Babel |
| Lest we be scattered | Yahweh scattered them |

# OBSERVATIONS

### A. Mesopotamian Parallels

The Sumerian epic entitled "Enmerkar and the Lord of Aratta" also speaks of a time when "the whole universe in unison spoke to Enlil [one of the Sumerian gods] in one tongue." It was Enki, the Sumerian god of wisdom, who confounded their speech for some unexplained reason.[543] There is, however, no Mesopotamian parallel to the Babel episode for two reasons. First, the people of that region would not regard the building of a tower as displeasing to God; and second, because the interpretation of the name *Babel* (Babylon) here is unflattering.

Pagan literature made the founding of Babylon an act of the gods at creation. The Babel narrative explodes this myth. Actually the city had a beginning in the most sordid circumstances. So there is an anti-pagan polemical thrust to the biblical account. The historian Berosus may be reflecting the present account when he names Babylon as the first city rebuilt after the Flood.

---

[543]S.N. Kramer, "The 'Babel of Tongues': A Sumerian Version," *ISIBF*, 278-282.

## B. Biblical Theology

The Dispersion account is strongly monotheistic. A general air of "satirical hostility to pagan nations pervades the story."[544] The narrative underscores the absolute supremacy of God. Men did not wish to be scattered; but twice the text states that God scattered them. God responded to man's designs in the same language (*come let us*) that man employed to launch the project.

The Babel episode is never again mentioned in the Bible. This stands in contrast to the judgment on Sodom and Gomorrah mentioned several places in both testaments. Prophecy, however, seems to anticipate the reversal of the Babel curse. "For then I will turn unto peoples a pure language to call, all of them, on the name of Yahweh, to serve him with one shoulder" (Zeph 3:9). Multiple languages divide people; the language of Zion unites people. The day of Pentecost was the harbinger of that new age when the nations in Christ speak the common language of Zion. Those present heard the apostles all praising God each in his own language (Acts 2).

## C. Errors in Interpretation

By answering some basic questions some common errors in the interpretation of the Babel passage can be exposed. First, how was the miracle performed? Was the organ of hearing affected or the speech of mankind? The text seems to endorse the latter position.

Second, when was the miracle performed? Were the effects of the miracle immediate or gradual? Some believers have yielded to the argument of evolutionists that new languages can only emerge over long periods of time. They postulate a huge gap between vv 7 and 8 during which the descendants of Noah spread out from the Plain of Shinar in different groups. Over time each

---

[544]Sarna, *Understanding Genesis*, 64.

group developed its own language. This approach clearly reverses the sequence revealed in Gn 11. The text plainly portrays a miracle that resulted in immediate separation of the various language groups.

Third, did all modern languages come into being at Babel? The short answer is no. The passage does not teach that all present-day languages originated at Babel. The separation caused by the original confusion, however, led eventually to the formation of other languages. When people are separated for any length of time their languages change and eventually become mutually unintelligible. New languages develop in a comparatively short period of time especially among illiterate peoples living in isolation. At Babel the basic language families come into existence. An implication of the account is that no one language is superior to another.

Fourth, did the incident affect the entire human family? Some hold that the confusion of tongues refers only to the Shemitic people. Others limit the passage to the proliferation of Hamitic tongues (Custance) or to Caucasian languages (Ramm). These are the same individuals who hold that the Flood did not in fact destroy all mankind from the earth as the Bible contends. The Bible, however, portrays as clearly as human words can portray that only eight souls survived the Flood. Of necessity then *the whole world* after the Deluge must refer to all humanity that developed from the descendants of Noah.

### D. Thematic Significance

In some respects the judgment on the Babel builders was worse than the Flood. The Flood left no permanent mark on humanity; but the scattering of mankind certainly did. No longer are they one *people* (*'am* in 11:6), but *nations* (*gôyim* in 10:32). Eight souls survived the Flood; no one escaped the judgment at Babel.[545]

The Hebrews marked off literary units by using similar language at the beginning and end. The Babel episode reflects several similarities with Gn 1. For example, as in ch 1 no human principal is mentioned by name in the Babel episode. In both accounts *'ādām* refers to mankind. Both stories refer to the *sky/heaven* (*šāmayim*). The plural cohortative *let us* appears in both chs. The command to *fill the earth* (1:28) is forced upon mankind by the Babel judgment. Kikawada and Quinn observe that thematically the Babel narrative "might be a conclusion, but rhetorically it was a transition to the main subject of his work" viz., Gn 12-50.[546]

One can make a case that the tower builders are the postdiluvian "Cainites." Like Cain they migrated eastward (4:16; 11:2); they built a city to preserve a name (4:17; 11:4); they were skilled in technology (4:19-24; 11:3-4); they experienced judgment in the form of migration (4:12-13; 11:8); but they continued to propagate by God's grace (4:17-24; ch 10).[547]

### E. Literary Quality

Cassuto devotes two full pages to enumerating all the examples of word play in the Babel story— alliterations, paronomasia, etc. Kikawada and Quinn comment:

> The story ... is written in a style that is brilliantly untranslatable. Even a reader without Hebrew can appreciate the intricate architecture of the story, an architecture that even a Babylonian ziggurat builder would have to admire.[548]

---

[545] W.M. Clark disputes the view that the Babel incident is the culmination of sin/judgment in these chs. "The Flood and the Structure of Prepatriarchal History," *ZAW* 81(1971):206.
[546] Kikawada and Quinn, *Before Abraham*, 72.
[547] Waltke, *GAC* 177-78.
[548] Kikawada and Quinn, *Before Abraham*, 72.

The brilliant simplicity of the structure is displayed below:

A. Human unity (11:1-2).
   B. Man speaks and acts (11:3-4).
      **C. Pivot: God comes down to see (11:5).**
   B. God speaks and acts (11:6-7).
A. Human disunity (11:8-9).

## TABLET COLOPHON
## GN 11:10a

*These are the generations of Shem.* This subscription marks the end of the fifth tablet employed by Moses. See introductory notes. The genealogy that follows probably belonged to another tablet, one written or preserved by Terah (11:27).

## CONCLUSION

Degeneration has reached a climax; it is time for Yahweh to set in motion his long-range program for the regeneration of the human race.

# 26
# SHEMITE GENEALOGY
# Gn 11:10b-27a

The primeval history concludes with a genealogy that transitions to the redemptive history that begins with the call of Abram. The opening v of the passage (11:10) looks back to the Flood; the passage then repeats the genealogy from Shem to Peleg (10:22-25; 11:10-16). It concludes by looking forward to the next unit by mentioning Terah and his family (11:26).

## PRELIMINARY OBSERVATIONS

### A. Similarity to Gn 5

The postdiluvian genealogy of legitimate rulers resembles the corresponding antediluvian genealogy in at least six ways. First, both genealogies consist of ten names. Just as Noah was the tenth generation removed from Adam, so Terah, Abram's father, was the tenth generation removed from Noah. Second, both genealogies are linear, aiming to show legitimate succession of rulers. Third, both genealogies display a similar literary pattern. They use similar vocabulary. They announce the age of the patriarch at the birth of his successor son, his number of years after the birth, his fathering of sons and daughters. Both segment into three sons at the conclusion, naming the elect descendant first. Fourth, both genealogies begin and end with a famous name: (Adam/Noah in Gn 5; Shem/Abram in Gn 11. Fifth, both genealogies are conveniently summarized in 1 Chr 1:1-3; 24-27. Sixth, the same kind of textual differences between the Hebrew, Samaritan and Greek texts exist in this genealogy as in ch 5.

## Chart 22
### Textual Variations in Gn 11 Genealogy

| Names | Age at Son's Birth ||| Remaining Years of Life |||
|---|---|---|---|---|---|---|
|  | Heb. | Sam. | Greek | Heb. | Sam. | Greek |
| Shem | 100 | 100 | 100 | 500 | 500 | 500 |
| Arphax. | 35 | 135 | 135 | 403 | 303 | 430 |
| Cainan |  |  | 130 |  |  | 330 |
| Shelah | 30 | 130 | 130 | 403 | 303 | 330 |
| Eber | 34 | 134 | 134 | 430 | 270 | 370 |
| Peleg | 30 | 130 | 130 | 209 | 109 | 209 |
| Reu | 32 | 132 | 132 | 207 | 107 | 207 |
| Serug | 30 | 130 | 130 | 200 | 100 | 200 |
| Nahor | 29 | 79 | 79 | 119 | 69 | 129 |
| Terah | 70 | 70 | 70 | 135 | 75 | 135 |
| Totals | 390 | 1040 | 1470 | 2633 | 1840 | 2840 |

### B. Dissimilarity to Gn 5

There are at least two differences between the Gn 5 genealogy and that in Gn 11. First, the earlier genealogy gives total figures for the ages of the men at death, the latter does not. Second, Gn 5 concludes nearly every paragraph with the refrain *and he died*. That note is missing in Gn 11, giving this genealogy a more optimistic flavor.

The dissimilarity between antediluvian and postdiluvian genealogies perhaps was intended to indicate a discontinuity between these two eras. On the other hand, it may be that the writer simply "invites us to take delight in his ability to create variety for its own sake."[549]

### C. Observations

Half of the names in the Gn 11 genealogy appear in the same order in 10:21-25 where additional details about them are given. This fact supports the conclusion

---

[549] Kikawada and Quinn, *Before Abraham*, 62.

that the list is not artificial; it contains the names of real people who were closely connected with events after the Deluge.

It is probably not the writer's intent to give a complete list of persons in consecutive genealogical succession from Shem to Abram. The main purpose of the Gen 11 genealogy seems to be to provide the briefest possible transition between these two key figures.

### D. Uniqueness

Babylonian genealogies are usually concerned with succession of kings, priests, or scribes. The twenty names appearing in Gn 5 and 11 may have been rulers, but in a different sense. They were the heirs of the earth, the custodians of the messianic promise, and the designated spiritual leaders of mankind. They were links in a chain between Adam, the son of God (Lk 3:38), and Christ, the Son of God.

The primary functions of the biblical genealogies are significantly different from those found in the Ancient Near Eastern examples (Hess). For example, ancient genealogies were designed to enhance the status of some leader. In the Bible, however, the genealogies end with figures that do despicable acts. There is no effort to whitewash the characters of those named. They were flawed men. Nonetheless, they were used of God to accomplish his ultimate purpose.

# POSTDILUVIAN GENERATIONS
# Gn 11:10b-26

The first six individuals in the postdiluvian generations were previously named in ch 10 in the Table of Nations. The last four are names not previously encountered.

A. **Previously Named** (11:10b-19)

*1. Shem (11:10b-11):* ***Shem was 100 years old and he fathered Arphaxad two years after the Deluge. And Shem lived after he became the father of Arphaxad 500 years, and he fathered sons and daughters.*** The opening v of the record clarifies the otherwise ambiguous 10:21, which could be interpreted to mean that Shem was the oldest of Noah's three sons. Two pieces of information in 11:10 cannot be squared with the priority of Shem over Japheth. First, Shem's son was born two years *after* the Flood. Second, he was born when Shem was 100. According to 5:32 Noah was 500 when he fathered his three sons and 600 at the time of the Flood (7:6). If Shem were the firstborn, his son Arphaxad would have been born the year of the Flood, not two years later. The solution must be that Shem was not the firstborn. The ambiguous 10:21 should be read as announcing Japheth as the older brother. If this reasoning is correct, then Noah must have been about 502 or 503 when Shem was born. NIV solves the problem by translating 5:32 "after Noah was 500 years old."

In all Shem lived 600 years, the age of his father at the time of the Flood.

*2. Arphaxad (11:12-13):* ***Now as for Arphaxad he lived 35 years and fathered Shalah. And Arphaxad lived after he fathered Shalah 403 years, and he fathered sons and daughter.*** A major issue faces the interpreter of the Gn 11 genealogy. According to the Hebrew text of 11:12 Arphaxad fathered Shelah at age 35. According to the Greek text, Arphaxad fathered Cainan at 35 and then lived 430 more years. When Cainan had lived 34 years he fathered Shelah, then lived another 330 years. The fact that Cainan's name appears in the genealogy of Christ (Lk 3:35-36) suggests that the Greek

# Shemite Genealogy

version is correct. For some reason a generation has dropped out of the Hebrew text of 11:12.[550]

Another observation about Arphaxad sheds light on this genealogy. In 10:22 Arphaxad is mentioned as the third of Shem's four sons. Here he appears alone, suggesting that priority in lineage is not based on being the firstborn but on God's election. See notes on 10:22.

*3. Shelah (11:14-15):* **Now as for Shelah, he lived 30 years and fathered Eber. And Shelah lived after he fathered Eber 403 years, and he fathered sons and daughters.** See notes on 10:24.

*4. Eber (11:16-17):* **And Eber lived 34 years and fathered Peleg. And Eber lived after he fathered Peleg 430 years, and he fathered sons and daughters.** See notes on 10:21, 24.

*5. Peleg (11:18-19):* **And Peleg lived 30 years and fathered Reu. And Peleg lived after he fathered Reu 209 years, and he fathered sons and daughters.** See notes on 10:25.

## B. Newly Named (11:20-26)

*1. Reu (11:20-21):* **And Reu lived 32 years and fathered Serug. And Reu lived after he fathered Serug 207 years, and he fathered sons and daughters.** The name *Reu* means "friend, companion." This is the only person in the Bible so named, although the name compounded with *el* (God) forms does appear.[551]

*2. Serug (11:22-23):* **And Serug lived 30 years and fathered Nahor. And Serug lived after he fathered Nahor 200 years, and he fathered sons and daughters.** The name Serug means something like "offshoot, de-

---

[550]Some defend the standard Hebrew text by pointing out that Abraham is the tenth generation, which would parallel the tenth generation before the Flood. To get this, however, they have to count the segmented genealogy as part of the linear unlike in Gn 5.

[551]E.g., *Reuel* ("friend of God"), the father-in-law of Moses.

scendant." This is the only person in the Bible to have this name. There is, however, a city by this name twenty miles northwest of Haran mentioned in Assyrian texts.

3. *Nahor (11:24-25):* ***And Nahor lived 29 years and fathered Terah. And Nahor lived after he fathered Terah 119 years, and he fathered sons and daughters.*** The name Nahor means something like "snore, snort" or possibly "nostril." Nahor's grandson is a more prominent Nahor—the brother of Abraham (11:26).

| Chart 23 |||||||||
|---|---|---|---|---|---|---|---|---|
| Gn 11 Interpreted as Consecutive Family Genealogy (Hebrew Text) |||||||||
| YAC | Shem | Arph | She | Eber | Pele | Reu | Ser | Nah | Ter |
| 1659 | **100** | 0 | | | | | | | |
| 1694 | 135 | **35** | 0 | | | | | | |
| 1724 | 165 | 65 | **30** | 0 | | | | | |
| 1758 | 199 | 99 | 64 | **34** | 0 | | | | |
| 1788 | 229 | 129 | 94 | 64 | **30** | 0 | | | |
| 1820 | 261 | 161 | 126 | 96 | 62 | **32** | 0 | | |
| 1850 | 291 | 191 | 156 | 126 | 92 | 62 | **30** | 0 | |
| 1879 | 320 | 220 | 185 | 155 | 121 | 91 | 59 | **29** | 0 |
| 1949 | 390 | 290 | 255 | 225 | 191 | 161 | 129 | 99 | **70** |
| 1997 | 438 | 338 | 303 | 273 | **239** | 209 | 177 | 147 | 118 |
| 1998 | 439 | 339 | 304 | 274 | | 210 | 178 | **148** | 119 |
| 2009 | 450 | 350 | 315 | 285 | | 221 | 189 | | **130** |
| 2027 | 468 | 368 | 333 | 303 | | **239** | 207 | | 148 |
| 2050 | 491 | 391 | 356 | 326 | | | **230** | | 171 |
| 2084 | 525 | 425 | 390 | 360 | | | | | **205** |
| 2097 | 538 | **438** | 403 | 373 | | | | | |
| 2109 | 550 | | 415 | 385 | | | | | |
| 2127 | 568 | | **433** | 403 | | | | | |
| 2159 | **600** | | | 435 | | | | | |
| 2184 | | | | 460 | | | | | |
| 2188 | | | | **464** | | | | | |

Chart 23 assumes a family genealogy without any omissions—probably a faulty assumption. Notes on reading the chart: YAC = Years After Creation. From Chart 18 it is ascertained that the Flood began in 1656 YAC. The Flood lasted a year. Shem's son was born two years after the Flood (1659 YAC). Highlighted numbers are those stated in the text; the rest are computations based on those numbers. The chart reveals that at the time Abram was called out of Ur of Chaldees (Terah 205 = Abram 75) Shem, Arphaxad, Shelah and Eber were still living. Isaac was born when Abraham was 100. At the time of Isaac's birth Shem, Shelah and Eber were still living. Eber outlived Abraham by four years.

4. *Terah (11:26): **And Terah lived 70 years and fathered Abram, Nahor and Haran**.* The name *Terah* means "ibex," a small goat-like wild animal that can still be found in certain regions of Israel today. The rapid decline in the lifespan after the Flood is clearly indicated in the tenth generation following the judgment.

The three sons are not triplets, as later vv will make clear. *Abram* is not named first because he was the firstborn. *Nahor* was given the name of his grandfather. This is the so-called papponymic system of naming children.

## TABLET COLOPHON
## Gn 11:27a

*Now these are the generations of Terah.* The writer and/or preserver of the sixth tablet used by Moses in compiling this history was Terah.

## ORIGIN OF THE RACES[552]

Whether or not there is a scientific basis for dividing mankind into racial groups is debatable. Some believe it is impossible to make racial distinctions among humans; others make two main divisions. Most accept (with modifications) the triadic division: Negroid, Mongoloid, and Caucasoid.

How did these racial differences arise? Some radical evolutionists postulate descent from different non-

---

[552] Based on discussion of B. Ramm, *CVSS*, 235f.

human progenitors. Most anthropologists, however, think that racial features among human beings developed like varieties among animals. Over a period of time people who migrated from a common center developed their own individualities. The laws of heredity and principles of separation and selection operating over a period of time produced the various races of the world. This can be reduced to a simple formula: Race = Heredity + Environment x Time.

The Bible teaches nothing about the origin of the different races except that the original division of the human race was by language, not race. Creationists and anthropologists may not agree on much; but regarding the origin of the races they are in lockstep.

## CONCLUSION

For the writer of Gn genealogical lists were not an end, but a means to an end. The lists in Gn 5 and 11 testify that the promises of the Serpent Crusher (3:15) and the Tent Dweller (9:27) were not canceled due to the failings of the human race. That promise was not thwarted by the Flood or Babel judgments. Ten great patriarchs connect Noah with Abraham and the promise of the coming of one through whom all nations of the earth will be blessed.

# BIBLIOGRAPHY

Aalders, G. Ch. *Genesis* in *Bible Student's Commentary*. Grand Rapids: Zondervan, 1981.

Allis, O.T. *The Five Books of Moses*. Philadelphia: Presbyterian and Reformed, 1949.

Armstrong, K. *In the Beginning: A New Interpretation of Genesis*. New York: Ballantine, 1996.

Archer, Gleason, Jr. *A Survey of Old Testament Introduction*. Chicago: Moody, 1964.

Baxter, J.S. *Explore the Book*. Grand Rapids: Zondervan, 1966.

Blocher, H. *In the Beginning. The Opening Chapters of Genesis*. Downers Grove, Ill.: InterVarsity, 1984.

Boice, James M. *Genesis: Creation and Fall*. Grand Rapids: Baker, 1998.

Bonhoeffer, D. *Creation and Fall*. London: SCM, 1959.

Brueggemann, W. *Genesis* in "Interpretation: A Bible Commentary for Preaching and Teaching." Atlanta: John Knox, 1982.

Brunner, Emil. *Christian Doctrine of Creation and Redemption*. Philadelphia: Westminster, 1952.

Cassuto, U. *A Commentary on the Book of Genesis*. 2 vols. Tran. I. Abrahams. Jerusalem: Magnes, 1961, 1964.

Clines, D.J.A. *The Theme of the Pentateuch*. JSOTSup 10. Sheffeld: JSOT Press, 1978.

Coder, S. Maxwell and G. Howe, *The Bible, Science, and Creation*. Chicago: Moody, 1966.

Daniélou, J. *In the Beginning*. Baltimore-Dublin: Helicon, 1965.

Delitzsch, Franz. *A New Commentary on Genesis*. Trans. by Sophia Taylor. Edinburgh: T. & T. Clark, 1888.

Dillmann, A. *Genesis Critically and Exegetically Expounded.* Trans. by Wm. B. Stevenson. Edinburgh: T. & T. Clark, 1897.

Dorsey, D.A. *The Literary Structure of the OT: A Commentary on Genesis-Malachi.* Grand Rapids: Baker, 1999.

Driver, S.R. *The Book of Genesis.* London: Methuen, 1916.

Eason, J.L. *The New Bible Survey.* Grand Rapids: Zondervan, 1963.

Elliott, R. *The Message of Genesis.* Nashville: Broadman, 1961.

England, Donald. *A Christian View of Origins.* Grand Rapids: Baker, 1972.

Filby, Floyd. *The Flood Reconsidered: A Review of the Evidences of Geology, Archaeology, Ancient Literature and the Bible.* London: Pickering, 1970.

_____. *Creation Revealed.* Westwood, NJ: Revell, 1965.

Gage, W. *The Gospel of Genesis: Studies in Protology and Eschatology.* Winona Lake, Ind.: Carpenter, 1984.

Gowan, D.F. *Genesis 1-11: From Eden to Babel* in "International Theological Commentary." Grand Rapids: Eerdmans, 1988.

Graves, R. and R. Patai, *Hebrew Myths; the Book of Genesis.* Garden City, NY: Doubleday, 1964.

Green, W.H. *The Unity of the Book of Genesis* (1895). Grand Rapids: Baker, 1979.

Griffith-Thomas, W.H. *Through the Pentateuch Chapter by Chapter.* Grand Rapids: Eerdmans, 1957.

Gunkel, Hermann. *The Legends of Genesis.* Schocken Books, 1964.

Hamilton, V.P. *The Book of Genesis: Chapters 1-17* in "New International Commentary on the OT." Grand Rapids: Eerdmans, 1990.

Harrison, R.K. *Introduction to the Old Testament.* London: Tyndale, 1970.
Hauret, Charles. *Beginnings: Genesis and Modern Science.* Dubuque, IA: Priory, 1955.
Heidel, A. *The Babylonian Genesis: The Story of the Creation.* 2nd Ed. Chicago: Univ. of Chicago Press, 1963.
_____. *The Gilgamesh Epic and Old Testament Parallels.* Chicago: Univ. of Chicago Press, 1949.
Hess, R. and D.T. Tsumura, eds. *"I Studied Inscriptions from before the Flood,"* Winona Lake, IN: Eisenbrauns, 1994.
Jacob, B. *The First Book of the Bible.* Ed. and trans. E.I. Jacob and N. Jacob. New York: Ktav, 1974.
Jaki, Stanley. *Genesis 1 Through the Ages* (London: Thomas More, 1992).
Kautzsch, E. ed. *Gesenius' Hebrew Grammar.* Trans. A.E. Cowley. 2nd English ed. Oxford: Clarendon, 1910.
Keil, C.F. *Biblical Commentary on the Old Testament.* KD. Reprint edition. Grand Rapids: Eerdmans, 1971.
Kidner, Derek. *Genesis: An Introduction and Commentary.* Tyndale OT Commentaries. London: Tyndale, 1967.
Kikawada, I.M. and A. Quinn, *Before Abraham Was: The Unity of Genesis 1-11.* Nashville: Abingdon, 1985.
Leupold, H.C. *Exposition of Genesis.* Columbus: Wartburg Press, 1942.
Mathews, K.A. *Genesis 1-11:26*, New American Commentary. Broadman & Holman, 1996.
Miller, P.D., Jr. *Genesis 1-11: Studies in Structure and Theme.* Sheffield: Univ. of Sheffield, 1978.
Morgenstern, Julian. *The Book of Genesis.* New York: Schocken, 1965.

Morris, H.M. *The Genesis Record.* Grand Rapids: Baker, 1976.

_____. *Evolution and the Modern Christian.* Grand Rapids: Baker, 1967.

Morris, H.M. and J.C. Whitcomb, *The Genesis Flood: The Biblical Record and its Scientific Implications.* Philadelphia: Presbyterian & Reformed, 1961.

Nelson, Byron. *The Deluge Story in Stone.* Minneapolis: Bethany Fellowship, 1968.

O'Connell, Patrick. *Science of Today and the Problems of Genesis* (2nd ed; Hawthorne, CA: Christian Book Club of America, 1969.

Patten, D. *The Biblical Flood and the Ice Epoch.* Seattle: Pacific Meridian, 1996.

Pember, G.H. *Earth's Earliest Ages.* 1942. Reprint Grand Rapids: Kragel, 1982.

Pipa, Joseph and David Hall eds. *Did God Create in Six Days?* Taylors, SC: Southern Presbyterian Press, 1999.

Plaut, Gunther. *The Torah; A Modern Commentary.* New York: Union of American Hebrew Congregations, 1974.

Pritchard, James, ed. *Ancient Near Eastern Texts Relating to the OT.* 3rd ed. Princeton, NJ: Princeton University Press, 1969.

Rad, Gerhard von. *Genesis: A Commentary.* Old Testament Library. Philadelphia: Westminster, 1961.

Ramm, B. *The Christian View of Science and Scripture.* 1954; pb. Grand Rapids: Eerdmans, 1976.

Renckens, H. *Israel's Concept of the Beginning: The Theology of Genesis 1-3.* New York: Herder and Herder, 1964.

Richardson, A. *Genesis I-XI.* Torch Bible Commentaries. London: SCM, 1953.

Roop, Eugene. *Genesis.* Believers Church Bible Commentary. Scottsdale, PN: Herald Press, 1987.

Ross, A.P. *Creation and Blessing: A Guide to the Study and Exposition of the Book of Genesis.* Grand Rapids: Baker, 1988.
Ryle, H.E. *The Book of Genesis.* Cambridge: Cambridge University, 1914.
Sailhamer, J.H. *Genesis Unbound.* Sisters, OR: Multnomah, 1996.
———. "Genesis" in *Expositor's Bible Commentary.* Grand Rapids: Zondervan, 1990.
Sarna, N. *Genesis.* JPS Torah Commentary. Philadelphia: Jewish Publication Society, 1989.
———. *Understanding Genesis.* New York: Jewish Theological Seminary, 1966.
Skinner, J.A. *A Critical and Exegetical Commentary on Genesis.* Rev. ed. in International Critical Commentary. Edinburgh: T. & T. Clark, 1930.
Speiser, E.A. *Genesis: Introduction, Translation, and Notes.* Anchor Bible. Garden City, N.Y.: Doubleday, 1964.
Tsumura, D.T. *The Earth and the Waters in Genesis 1 and 2: A Linguistic Investigation.* JSOT-Sup 83; Sheffield: JSOT Press, 1989.
Vawter, B. *A Path through Genesis.* New York: Sheed and Ward, 1956.
Vos, Howard. *Genesis.* Everyman's Bible Commentary. Chicago: Moody, 1982.
Waltke, Bruce and Cathi Fredericks. *Genesis: A Commentary.* Grand Rapids: Zondervan, 2001.
Wenham, Gordon. *Genesis 1-15.* Word Biblical Commentary. Waco: Word, 1987.
Westermann, C. *Genesis 1-11: A Commentary.* Trans. J.J. Scullion. Minneapolis: Augsburg, 1985.
———. *A Thousand Years and a Day.* Muhlenberg Press, 1962.
Whitcomb, John. *The Early Earth.* Grand Rapids: Baker, 1986.

Whitelaw, Thomas. "Genesis," in *Pulpit Commentary*.
Willis, John T. *Genesis*. Abilene, TX: ACU Press, 1984.
Wilmington, H.L. *Wilmington's Guide to the Bible*. Wheaton, IL: Tyndale, 1981.
Wiseman, P.J. *Ancient Records and the Structure of Genesis*. Nashville: Nelson, 1985.
Wright, G.F. *The Origin and Antiquity of Man*, Oberlin, OH: Bibliotheca Sacra, 1912.
Young, D.A. *Creation and the Flood: An Alternative to Creation and Theistic* Evolution. Grand Rapids: Baker, 1977.
Young, E.J. *Studies in Genesis 1*. Philadelphia: Presbyterian & Reformed, 1973.
_____. *An Introduction to the Old Testament*. Grand Rapids: Eerdmans, 1964.
Youngblood, R. *The Book of Genesis: An Introductory Commentary*. Grand Rapids: Baker, 1992.
_____, ed. *The Genesis Debate*. Grand Rapids: Baker, 1990.

## OTHER BOOKS BY THE AUTHOR

Available from College Press, Joplin, Mo.

*The Pentateuch*, 1993, 534 pp.
*The Books of History*, 1995, 747 pp.
*The Wisdom Literature and Psalms*, 1996, 873 pp.
*The Major Prophets*, 1992, 637 pp.
*The Minor Prophets*, 1994, 653 pp.
*1 & 2 Samuel* in "The College Press NIV Commentary," 2000. 541 pp.

Available from Restoration Press, Florida Christian College 1011 Bill Beck Blvd. Kissimmee, Fl 34744. 407-847-8966

*What the Bible Says about the Promised Messiah* 1991, 522 pp.

Available from Amazon.com

*Bible History Made Simple*, 2007, 180 pp.

For articles and commentaries and other materials, check the author's web site: *bibleprofessor.com*